SAT® Strategies for Super Busy Students

2008 Edition

Related Titles for College-Bound Students

SAT Comprehensive Program 2008
SAT Premier Program 2008
12 Practice Tests for the SAT
Inside the SAT: 10 Strategies to Help You Score Higher
SAT 2400, 2008 Edition
SAT Critical Reading Workbook
SAT Math Workbook
SAT Writing Workbook
SAT Vocabulary Flashcards Flip-O-Matic, Third Edition
Extreme SAT Vocabulary Flashcards Flip-O-Matic, Third Edition
The Ring of McAllister: A Score-Raising Mystery Featuring 1,046 Must-Know SAT Vocabulary Words, Third Edition
Frankenstein: A Kaplan SAT Score-Raising Classic, Second Edition
The Tales of Edgar Allan Poe: A Kaplan SAT Score-Raising Classic, Second Edition
Dr. Jekyll and Mr. Hyde: A Kaplan SAT Score-Raising Classic, Second Edition
The Scarlet Letter: A Kaplan SAT Score-Raising Classic, Second Edition
The War of the Worlds: A Kaplan SAT Score-Raising Classic
Wuthering Heights: A Kaplan SAT Score-Raising Classic, Second Edition
Domina El SAT: Prepárate para Tomar el Examen para Ingresar a la Universidad

AP Biology
AP Calculus AB/BC
AP Chemistry
AP English Language & Composition
AP English Literature & Composition
AP Environmental Science
AP European History
AP Human Geography
AP Macroeconomics/Microeconomics
AP Physics B & C
AP Psychology
AP Statistics
AP U.S. Government & Politics
AP U.S. History
AP World History

SAT Subject Test: Biology E/M
SAT Subject Test: Chemistry
SAT Subject Test: Literature
SAT Subject Test: Mathematics Level 1
SAT Subject Test: Mathematics Level 2
SAT Subject Test: Physics
SAT Subject Test: Psychology
SAT Subject Test: Spanish
SAT Subject Test: U.S. History
SAT Subject Test: World History

SAT Strategies for Super Busy Students

10 Simple Steps

(For Students Who Don't Want to Spend Their Whole Lives Preparing for the Test)

2008 Edition

Chris Kensler

KAPLAN PUBLISHING
New York

Vice President and Publisher: Maureen McMahon
Editorial Director: Jennifer Farthing
Contributing Editor: Mark Ward, Brandon Jones, Katie Dewey
Development Editor: Eric Titner
Production Editor: Fred Urfer
Production Designer: Ivelisse Robles Marrero
Typesetter: ITC
Cover Designer: Carly Schnur
Illustrator: Aaron Meshon

Published by Kaplan Publishing, a division of Kaplan, Inc.
1 Liberty Plaza, 24th Floor
New York, NY 10006

Printed in the United States of America

December 2007
10 9 8 7 6 5 4 3 2 1

ISBN-13: 978-1-4195-5161-1

Kaplan Publishing books are available at special quantity discounts to use for sales promotions, employee premiums, or educational purposes. Please email our Special Sales Department to order or for more information at kaplanpublishing@kaplan.com, or write to Kaplan Publishing, 1 Liberty Plaza, 24th Floor, New York, NY 10006.

Table of Contents

Part 4: Understanding the Math Section

Part 5: Final Preparations

Part 6: Take the Practice Test

Part 7: Super Busy Resources

About the Author

Chris Kensler majored in English at Indiana University. He has written over a dozen books, covered a presidential campaign for a national news organization, and edited an arts and culture magazine. He is co-founder of the book packager Paper Airplane Projects with his wife and partner, Heather Kern.

Available Online

FOR ANY TEST CHANGES OR LATE-BREAKING DEVELOPMENTS

kaptest.com/publishing

The material in this book is up-to-date at the time of publication. However, the College Board may have instituted changes in the test after this book was published. Be sure to carefully read the materials you receive when you register for the test. If there are any important late-breaking developments—or any changes or corrections to the Kaplan test preparation materials in this book—we will post that information online at **kaptest.com/publishing.**

FEEDBACK AND COMMENTS

kaplansurveys.com/books

We'd love to hear your comments and suggestions about this book. We invite you to fill out our online survey form at **kaplansurveys.com/books**. Your feedback is extremely helpful as we continue to develop high-quality resources to meet your needs.

Preface

This is the perfect SAT prep book for the overextended high-schooler with a hyperactive lifestyle. *SAT Strategies for Super Busy Students 2008 Edition*, crunches Kaplan's years of test-prep know-how into a book that's fast, easy to read, and effective.

Here's how. Studying for the SAT is pretty straightforward:

- You learn overall test-taking skills and strategies
- You learn Critical Reading section skills and strategies
- You learn Writing section skills and strategies
- You learn Math section skills and strategies
- You practice on a simulated SAT

SAT Strategies for Super Busy Students 2008 Edition, teaches the MOST IMPORTANT skills and strategies in 10 super-organized steps. Each Super Busy step can be completed in one or two evenings or a few study halls. Each step helps you:

- Know the details of an SAT section (Critical Reading, for example)
- Learn the specific skills that help you with that section or subject
- Master Kaplan's proven strategies for answering SAT questions on that section
- Practice what you've learned before you forget it

SAT Strategies for Super Busy Students 2008 Edition, covers general SAT information and strategies (Step 1), the Critical Reading section (Steps 2–3), the Writing section (Steps 4–6), the Math section (Steps 7–9), and stress-relieving and Test Day strategies (Step 10). Each step covers its subject in detail. As you progress through the step you are asked multiple-choice questions about what you just read. Each step ends with sample questions that reinforce what you just learned, quickly and effectively. At the end of the book is a timed, full-length practice SAT. Take it, score it, and you're ready for the real deal.

We recommend giving yourself two to four weeks to finish the 10 *Super Busy* steps and take the practice SAT. If the SAT is next week, go through steps 1 and 10 and take the practice exam. If you have any time after that, learn the strategies for the subjects you had the most trouble with.

OK, you're busy, so let's start.

Part 1

Understanding The SAT

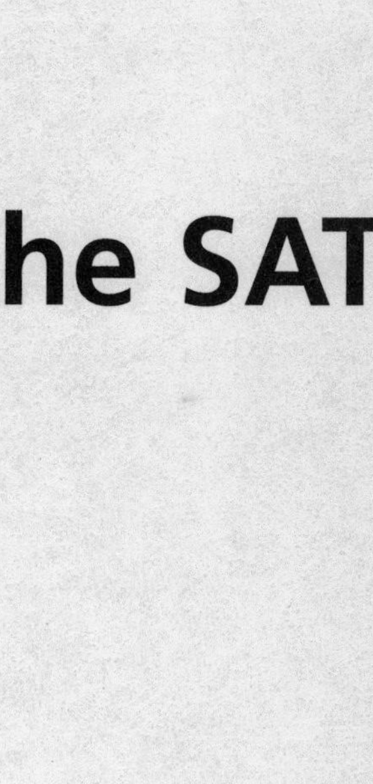

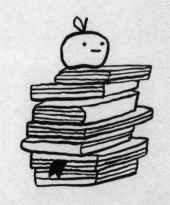

HI
SAT

Step One

Get to Know the SAT

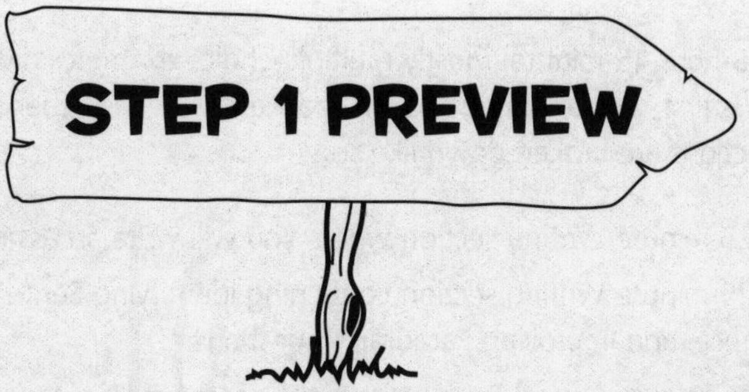

Format

Scoring

The Three Sections

- Critical Reading Section
- How to Approach the SAT Critical Reading Section
- Math Section
- How to Approach the SAT Math Section
- Writing Section
- How to Approach the SAT Writing Section

General Test-Taking Strategies

- Know the SAT's Format
- Know the Directions
- Have a Plan and Stick with it

Summary

The SAT is a 3-hour 45-minute test that measures reading, writing, and math skills. That's the bad part. The good part is that you can improve your score on the SAT without necessarily memorizing a dictionary or becoming a walking calculator. Of course, in this book we'll help you improve your math, writing, and reading skills, but you can also improve your score just by knowing how the SAT is set up and learning how to deal with it. That's what we cover in Step 1.

FORMAT

The SAT is a 3-hour 45-minute, mostly multiple-choice exam. It's divided into ten sections. The Essay is always first, and a writing section is always last. The other sections can appear in any order. The sections are broken down like so:

- One 25-minute Writing section where you will write an essay
- One 25-minute Writing section containing Identifying Sentence Error, Improving Sentence, and Improving Paragraph questions
- Two 25-minute Critical Reading sections containing Sentence Completion questions and long and short Reading Comprehension questions
- One 20-minute Critical Reading section made up of Sentence Completion and Reading Comprehension questions
- One 10-minute Writing section containing Improving Sentence questions
- One 25-minute Math section with multiple-choice questions
- One 25-minute Math section with multiple-choice questions and Grid-in questions
- One 20-minute Math section with multiple-choice questions
- One 25-minute Experimental section (Critical Reading, Writing, or Math)

Experimental Section

The Experimental section is used by the test makers to try out new questions, but it does not affect your score. It can show up anywhere on the exam and will look like any Critical Reading, Writing (except the Essay), or Math section. Do not try to figure out which SAT section is experimental. You won't be able to tell the difference, and you cannot work on any other section anyway, so treat all the sections as if they count.

SCORING

You gain one point for each correct answer on the SAT and lose a FRACTION of a point for each wrong answer (except with Grid-ins, where you lose nothing for a wrong answer). You do not gain or lose any points for questions you leave blank.

The totals for the three sections are added up to produce three raw scores. These raw scores are then converted into scaled scores, with 200 as the lowest score and 800 the highest. Each raw point is worth approximately 10 scaled points. Those scores combine to equal your final score, which ranges from 600–2400.

Registering Online

- Check www.collegeboard.com for complete information about registering for the SAT.
- Register online at www.collegeboard.com/sat/html/satform.html. Not all students are eligible to register online; read the instructions and requirements carefully.
- Register early to secure the time you want at the test center you want.
- The basic fee at press time is $43 in the United States. This price includes reports for you, your high school, and up to four colleges and scholarship programs.

THE THREE SECTIONS

Critical Reading Section

There are two kinds of questions on the Critical Reading section: Sentence Completion and Reading Comprehension questions.

Sentence Completion questions test your ability to see how the parts of a sentence relate. About half will have one word missing from a sentence; the rest will have two words missing. Both types test vocabulary and reasoning skills.

Reading Comprehension questions test your ability to understand a piece of writing. The passages are either short (100-–150) or long (400–850 words), and at least one part contains two related readings, or paired passages. Most Reading Comprehension questions test how well you understand the passage, some make you draw conclusions from what you've read, and some test your vocabulary knowledge.

The Sentence Completion questions are arranged in order of difficulty. The first few questions in a set are meant to be fairly easy. The middle few questions will be a little harder, and the last few are the most difficult. Keep this in mind as you work through these questions. On the contrary, Reading Comprehension questions are not arranged by difficulty. Whenever you find yourself spending too much time on a Reading Comprehension question, you should skip it and return later.

How to Approach the SAT Critical Reading Section

To do well on SAT Critical Reading, you need to be systematic in your approach to each question type. Sentence Completion questions are designed to be done relatively quickly. That means you can earn points fast, so you should do these first. Reading Comprehension takes a lot longer, so don't leave yourself just five minutes to do a passage. We will cover each question type and how to approach it in detail in the upcoming steps.

Important

Remember, you earn just as many points for an easy question as you do for a hard one.

Math Section

There are two kinds of questions on the Math section, broken down like so:

Multiple-choice questions detailing basic and advanced math concepts with five answer choices make up the bulk of this section.

Grid-in questions are not multiple-choice. Instead of picking an answer choice, you write your response in a little grid like this:

These questions test the same math concepts as the multiple-choice math questions.

Test Tools

Besides the basics—No. 2 pencils, erasers, a photo ID, and your admission ticket— you should bring the following items to the test center:

- Watch or stopwatch that you know how to use
- Calculator that you know how to use
- Snacks for the breaks

How to Approach the SAT Math Section

All sets of SAT Math questions start off with the easiest questions and gradually increase in difficulty. Always be aware of the difficulty level as you go through a Math question set. The further along you are in a set, the more difficult the questions will be, and the more traps the question will have. (We go into math traps in detail in Step 8.)

To maximize your Math score, you need to:

- Work systematically
- Use your time efficiently

The key to working systematically is to THINK ABOUT THE QUESTION before you look for the answer. A few seconds spent up front looking for traps, thinking about your approach, and deciding whether to tackle the problem now or come back to it later will pay off in points. On basic problems, you may know what to do right away. But on hard problems, the few extra seconds are time well spent.

Writing Section

There are three question types and an essay on the Writing section, broken down like so:

The **Essay** is a student-produced writing sample based on a specific assignment prompt. There are either one or two quotations before the prompt that serve to shape the topic of the Essay. You will be given two pages to write your persuasive essay.

Multiple-choice questions comprise the second part of the Writing section. The three question types are as follows:

Identifying Sentence Error questions ask you to choose the appropriate error from a sentence. There is also the option of *no error*.

Improving Sentence questions ask you to fix or re-word a part of a given sentence. There is also the option of *no error*.

Improving Paragraph questions give you a sampling of an essay with each sentence numbered. The questions will ask you to correct one of these sentences or to combine two or more sentences to make a more cohesive paragraph.

All of these question types test grammar, reasoning, and vocabulary skills.

How to Approach the SAT Writing Section

None of the question types in the Writing section are ordered by difficulty. Easy and hard questions are mixed up, so it is important to decide which questions can be done quickly and which will take more time. Strong knowledge of grammar and sentence structure will go a long way in helping you make that decision. We will discuss helpful strategies and approaches for honing these skills in the coming chapters.

GENERAL TEST-TAKING STRATEGIES

We will go into more section-specific strategies in later steps, but for now, let's go over some basic test tips.

Know the SAT's Format

The first time you see an SAT should NOT be on Test Day. On the day of the test, you should recognize Sentence Completion questions, Improving Paragraph questions, Grid-ins, and the setup of any other question type or section on the test. If you are reading this book in the recommended amount of time (two to four weeks), we will introduce you to the format of each section and question type as you go along. If you are cramming, take 10 minutes now to familiarize yourself with the practice SAT at the back of the book.

Know the Directions

One of the easiest things you can do to help your performance on the SAT is to understand the directions before taking the test. Knowing the instructions beforehand will save you precious time reading them on Test Day. The directions NEVER change, so learn them now.

If you are completing this book in the recommended amount of time, you will learn each set of directions as you read each chapter. If you are cramming, go to the first page of each chapter, and read the directions for each question type.

Have a Plan and Stick with it

Now that you know some basics about how the test is set up, you can approach each section with a plan. Kaplan has come up with a seven-step plan that organizes the way you approach the SAT:

1. Think about the question before you look at the answers
2. Pace yourself
3. Know when a question is supposed to be easy or hard
4. Move around within a section
5. Be a good guesser
6. Be a good gridder
7. Two-minute warning: locate quick points

1. Think About the Question Before you Look at the Answers

The people who write the SAT put distractors among the answer choices. *Distractors* are answer choices that look right, but aren't. If you jump into the answer choices without thinking about what you're looking for, you're much more likely to fall into a test writer's trap. So, always think for a second or two about the question before you look at the answers.

2. Pace Yourself

The SAT gives you a lot of questions to answer in a short period of time. One of the biggest complaints students had about the updated SAT is that they ran out of time. To get through a whole section, you can't spend too much time on any one question. Keep moving through the test at a good speed; if you run into a hard question, circle it in your test booklet, skip it, and come back to it later if you have time. Remember, you get the same amount of points for easy questions as you do for hard ones.

3. Know When a Question is Supposed to be Easy or Hard

Some SAT questions are more difficult than others. Except for the Writing section and Reading Comprehension questions, the questions are generally designed to get tougher as you work through a set, and the pattern starts over for each question type. So if a section begins with a set of regular math questions, those questions will begin with an easy one and then gradually become more difficult. If the section proceeds to a set of Grid-in questions, this set will also progress from easy to difficult.

		Arranged Easiest to Hardest?
Math	Regular math	Yes
	Grid-ins	Yes
Critical Reading	Sentence Completion	Yes
	Short Reading Comprehension	No
	Long Reading Comprehension	No
Writing	Essay	NA
	Identifying Sentence Errors	No
	Improving Sentences	No
	Improving Paragraphs	No

As you work, always be aware of where you are in a set. When working on the easy problems, you can generally trust your first impulse—the obvious answer is likely to be right. As you get to the end of the problem set, you need to be more suspicious of obvious answers because the answer should not come easily. If it does, look at the problem again. Your chosen answer may be a distractor—a wrong answer choice meant to trick you.

Hard SAT questions are usually tough for two reasons:

1. Their answers are not immediately obvious.
2. The question stems do not ask for information in a straightforward way.

Here's an easy Sentence Completion question.

> Known for their devotion, dogs were often used as symbols of ---- in Medieval and Renaissance painting.
>
> (A) breakfast
> (B) tidal waves
> (C) fidelity
> (D) campfires
> (E) toothpaste

The correct answer, *fidelity* (C), probably leapt right out at you. This question would likely be at the beginning of a problem set. Easy questions are purposely designed to be easy, and their answer choices are purposely obvious.

Now here is virtually the same question made hard.

> Known for their ----, dogs were often used as symbols of ---- in Medieval and Renaissance painting.
>
> (A) dispassion . . bawdiness
> (B) fidelity . . aloofness
> (C) monogamy . . parsimony
> (D) parity . . diplomacy
> (E) loyalty . . faithfulness

This question would likely be at the end of a problem set. This time the answer is harder to find. For one thing, the answer choices are far more difficult. In addition, the sentence contains two blanks.

The correct answer is (E). Did you fall for (B) because the first word is *fidelity*? (B) is a good example of a distractor.

4. Move Around Within a Section

On a test at school, you probably spend more time on the hard questions than you do on the easy ones because hard questions are usually worth more points. On the SAT, this strategy will not help and will actually hurt your total score.

As we said before, pace yourself. But don't be careless. Don't rush through the easy problems just to get to the hard ones. When you run into questions that look tough, circle them in your test booklet, and skip them for the time being. (Make sure you skip them on your answer grid, too.) Then, if you have time, go back to them AFTER you have answered the easier ones. Sometimes, after you have answered some easier questions, troublesome questions can get easier.

Important

You CANNOT skip from section to section. You can only skip around within a section.

Don't spend so much time answering one tough question that you use up three or four questions' worth of time. That costs you points, especially if you don't get the hard question right.

Remember, the name of the game is to get as many points as possible, so you need to score points as quickly as possible.

5. Be a Good Guesser

On the SAT, you will be faced with questions that you don't know how to answer and need to guess. We highly encourage guessing on the SAT, as long as you are making educated guesses. Simply guessing randomly will most likely cost you points, but if you can eliminate one or more answers that are definitely wrong, you'll turn the odds in your favor and come out ahead by guessing.

Here's why. If you get an answer wrong on any multiple-choice question on the SAT, you lose one-fourth of a point. The fractional points you lose are supposed to offset the points you might get "accidentally" by guessing the correct answer. By learning Kaplan's techniques, you can eliminate a few answer choices on most questions, even if you have no idea what the right answer is. By learning how to eliminate wrong answer choices, you can actually turn the guessing "penalty" to your advantage.

Let's take a close look at this to make sure you are confident with this strategy. By eliminating one wrong answer in five, you are down to four answer choices, so you have a 1 in 4 chance of guessing correctly. Thus, for every four questions you answer, you should get 1 right and 3 wrong. 1 right = 1 point. 3 wrong = 3/4 points. 1 – 3/4 = 1/4 point

By eliminating just one answer choice and guessing on four questions, you have gained one-fourth of a point! This may not seem like a lot, but over the course of a long test, these fractions really add up and can increase your score significantly. And, of course, if you can eliminate two or three wrong answers, your chances—and score—improve even more.

Take a look at this question again:

Known for their devotion, dogs were often used as symbols of ---- in Medieval and Renaissance painting.

(A) ~~breakfast~~
(B) ~~tidal waves~~
(C) fidelity
(D) ~~campfires~~
(E) ~~toothpaste~~

Chances are, you recognized that choice (A), *breakfast*, was wrong. You then looked at the next answer choice, and then the next one, and so on, eliminating wrong answers to find the correct answer. This process is usually the best way to work through multiple-choice SAT questions. If you still don't know the right answer but can eliminate one or more wrong answers, YOU SHOULD GUESS.

6. Be a Good Gridder

Don't make mistakes filling out your answer grid. When time is short, it's easy to get confused skipping around a section and going back and forth between your test book and your grid. If you misgrid just one question, you can misgrid several others before realizing your error—if you realize it at all. You can lose a TON of points this way.

To avoid mistakes on the answer grid:

- Always circle the answers you choose. Circling your answers in the test book makes it easier to check your grid against your book.
- Grid five or more answers at once. Don't transfer your answers to the grid after every question. Transfer your answers after every five questions, or, in the Reading Comprehension section, at the end of each reading passage. That way, you won't keep breaking your concentration to mark the grid. You'll save time and improve accuracy.

Important Exception

When time is running out at the end of a section, start gridding one by one so you don't get caught at the end with ungridded answers.

- Put a big circle in your test book around the number of any questions you skip; they'll be easy to locate when you return to them. Also, if you realize later that you accidentally skipped a box on the grid, you can more easily check your grid against your book to see where you went wrong.
- Write in your booklet. Take notes, circle hard questions, underline things, etc. Proctors collect booklets at the end of each testing session, but the booklets are not examined or reused.

7. Two-Minute Warning: Locate Quick Points

When you start to run out of time, locate and answer any of the quick points that remain. For example, some Reading Comprehension questions will ask you to identify the meaning of a particular word in the passage. Those can be done at the last minute, even if you haven't read the passage.

These SAT facts and strategies apply to the upcoming Critical Reading, Math, and Writing strategies. Use what you've learned here on the practice questions that follow. By the time you finish this book and are ready to take the practice test, these strategies will come naturally.

SUMMARY

- **Format:**
  - — The SAT is a 3-hour 45-minute exam
  - — The SAT exam has 10 sections that test skills in writing, critical reading, and math. There is always an experimental section that does not affect your score
- **Scoring:**
  - — You gain 1 point for each correct answer and lose a fraction of a point for each wrong answer
  - — You do not gain or lose anything for questions that are left blank
  - — The totals for the three exam sections are converted into three raw scores, which are then converted into scaled scores, ranging from 200–800. The scaled scores are combined to form your final score, which ranges from 600–2400.
- **The Three SAT Exam Sections:**
  - — Critical Reading section
    - Sentence completion questions that test your ability to see how the parts of a sentence relate
    - Reading comprehension questions that test your ability to understand a piece of writing
    - You should be systematic in your approach to each type of question. Sentence completion questions are designed to be answered quickly, so you should consider completing these first
  - — Math section
    - Multiple-choice questions that cover basic, intermediate, and advanced math concepts
    - Each multiple choice question has five answer choices
    - For grid-in questions you write your response onto a provided grid
    - The difficulty of the math questions increases as the test progresses, so work systematically and use your time efficiently
  - — Writing section
    - The Essay portion of the exam requires a written response to a specific prompt
    - Identifying Sentence error questions ask you to choose the appropriate error from a given sentence
    - Improving Sentence questions ask you to fix or re-word a part of a given sentence
    - Improving Paragraph questions give you a part of an essay, with each sentence numbered, and you are asked to correct one of these sentences or combine various sentences to make a coherent paragraph.
    - The questions in the Writing section are not ordered by difficulty

- **General Test-Taking Strategies:**
  - — Know the format of the SAT exam
  - — Know the test directions
  - — Have a plan and stick with It: Kaplan's 7-step plan organizes the way you approach the SAT:
    - Step One: Think about the question before you look at the answers
    - Step Two: Pace yourself
    - Step Three: Know when a question is supposed to be easy or hard
    - Step Four: Move around within a section (but you cannot move around between different sections)
    - Step Five: Be a good guesser. Guessing is highly encouraged on the SAT's, but only if it is an educated guess because randomly guessing will make you lose points
    - Step Six: Be a good gridder
    - Step Seven: Two-minute warning: locate quick points

Part 2

Understanding the Critical Reading Section

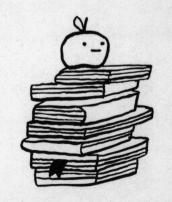

ENGLISH

Step Two

Sentence Completion Questions

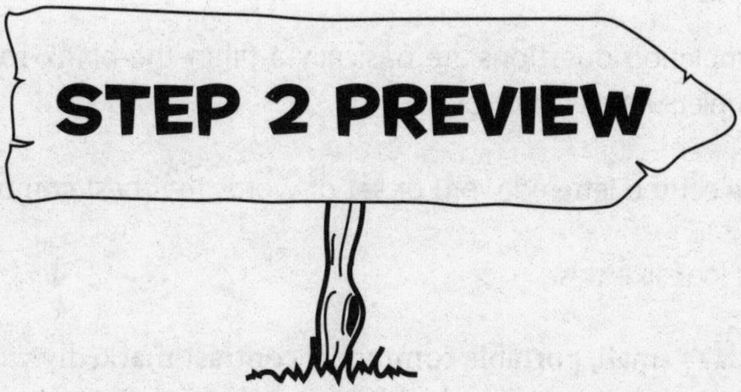

The Gist of it

How to Get a High Score

- Kaplan's Four-Step Method for Sentence Completion Questions
- Clue Words
- The Tough Questions
- If all Else Fails—Guess!

Summary

Practice

Answers and Explanations

Sentence Completion questions are probably the most student-friendly question type on the Critical Reading section. This is because they give you some context in which to think about vocabulary words, and unlike Reading Comprehension questions, they require you to pay attention to just one sentence at a time. Here's the outline for how to approach Sentence Completion questions:

THE GIST OF IT

Sentence Completion questions are basically a fill-in-the-blank format. The instructions for Sentence Completions are as follows.

Directions: Select the lettered word or set of words that best completes the sentence.

The questions look like this:

To show difference
↑ Compare two diff things.

Today's small, portable computers contrast markedly with the earliest electronic computers, which were - - - - -.

(A) effective → influential
(B) invented → making smt for the first time
(C) useful → helpful
(D) destructive → destroy
(E) enormous → extremly larg / To emphasize smt

In this example, the new, small, portable computers are contrasted with old computers. You can infer that old computers must be the opposite of small and portable, so (E), *enormous*, is the answer.

As you can see, you need to determine the relationship between the parts of the sentence to figure out which word gives the sentence its intended meaning. We'll show you how to do this.

HOW TO GET A HIGH SCORE

Master these strategies, and you're on your way to acing Sentence Completion questions.

Kaplan's Four-Step Method for Sentence Completion Questions

This is Kaplan's most powerful method for tackling Sentence Completion questions. If you can master these strategies, you will be on your way to a higher score.

Step 1: Read the sentence for clue words
Step 2: Predict the answer

Step 3: Select the best match

Step 4: Plug your answer choice into the sentence

Step 1. Read the Sentence for Clue Words

Think about the sentence for a second or two. Figure out what the sentence means, taking special note of the clue words. A word like but tells you to expect a CONTRAST coming up; a word like moreover tells you that what follows is a CONTINUATION of the same idea Clue words such as *and*, *but*, *such as*, and *although* tell you how the parts of the sentence will relate to each other.

Step 2. Predict the Answer

Decide what sort of word should fill the blank or blanks. Do this before looking at the answer choices. You don't have to make an exact prediction; a rough idea of the kind of word needed will do. It's often enough simply to predict whether the missing word is positive or negative.

Step 3. Select the Best Match

Compare your prediction to each answer choice. Read every answer choice before deciding.

Step 4. Plug Your Answer Choice into the Sentence

Put your answer choice in the blank or blanks. You should be able to come up with your final answer. Only one choice should really make sense. If you've gone through the four steps and more than one choice seems possible, eliminate the choices you can, guess, and move on. If all of the choices look great or all of the choices look terrible, circle the question and come back when you're done with the section.

Let's unleash the powers of Kaplan's Four-Step Method on a sample question.

> The king's - - - - decisions as a diplomat and administrator led to his legendary reputation as a just and - - - - ruler.
>
> (A) quick . . capricious
> (B) equitable . . wise
> (C) immoral . . perceptive
> (D) generous . . witty
> (E) clever . . uneducated

Step 1. Read the Sentence for Clue Words

The clue here is the phrase *led to*. You know that the kind of decisions the king made gave him a *reputation as a just and - - - - ruler*. So, whatever goes in both blanks must be consistent with *just*.

Step 2. Predict the Answer

Both blanks must contain words that are similar in meaning. Because of his - - - - decisions, the king is viewed as a just and - - - - ruler. Thus, if the king's decisions were good, he'd be remembered as a good ruler, and if his decisions were bad, he'd be remembered as a bad ruler. *Just*, which means fair, is a positive-sounding word; you can predict that both blanks will be similar in meaning and that both will be positive words. You can write a "+" in the blanks or over the columns of answer choices to remind you.

Step 3. Select the Best Match

One way to do this is to determine which answers are both positive and similar. In (A), *quick* and *capricious* are not both positive and similar. (*Capricious* means erratic or fickle.) In (B), *equitable* means fair. *Equitable* and *wise* are similar, and they are both positive. When you plug them in, they make sense, so (B) looks right. But check out the others to be sure. In (C), *immoral* and *perceptive* aren't similar at all. *Perceptive* is positive, but *immoral* is not. In (D), *generous* and *witty* are both positive adjectives, but they are not really similar and don't make sense in the sentence. *Generous* decisions would not give one a reputation as a *witty* ruler. In (E), *clever* and *uneducated* are not similar. *Clever* is positive, but *uneducated* is not.

Step 4. Plug Your Answer Choice into the Sentence

"The king's *equitable* decisions as a diplomat and administrator led to his legendary reputation as a just and *wise* ruler." (B) makes sense in the sentence. So, (B) is your answer.

Clue Words

To do well on Sentence Completion questions, you need to understand how a sentence fits together. Clue words help you do this. The more clues you get, the clearer the sentence becomes and the better you can predict what goes in the blanks. So, let's delve further into the fascinating subject of clue words. Take a look at this example.

> Though some have derided it as - - - - , the search for extraterrestrial intelligence has actually become a respectable scientific endeavor.

Here, the word *though* is an important clue. *Though* contrasts the way some have derided, belittled, or ridiculed the search for extraterrestrial intelligence, with the fact that that search has become respectable. Another clue is *actually*. *Actually* completes the contrast: *Though* some see the search in one way, it has *actually* become respectable.

You know that whatever goes in the blank must complete the contrast implied by the word *though*. So, to fill in the blank, you need a word that would be used to describe the opposite of a respectable scientific endeavor. *Useless* or *trivial* would be good predictions for the blank.

Let's put your deeper understanding of clue words to the test. Use clue words to predict the answers to the two questions below. First, look at the sentences without the answer choices and:

- Circle clue words.
- Think of a word or phrase that might go in each blank.
- Write your prediction below each sentence.

1. One striking aspect of Caribbean music is its - - - - of many African musical - - - - , such as call-and-response singing and polyrhythms.

   Predictions: Style ____________________

2. Although Cézanne was inspired by the Impressionists, he - - - -their emphasis on the effects of light and - - - - an independent approach to painting that emphasized form.

   Predictions: ____________________ ____________________

Here are the questions with their answer choices (and with their clue words italicized). Find the right answer to each question, referring to the predictions you just made.

1. One striking aspect of Caribbean music is its - - - - of many African musical - - - - , *such as* call-and-response singing and polyrhythms.

   (A) recruitment . . groups
   (B) proficiency . . events
   (C) expectation . . ideas
   (D) absorption . . forms
   (E) condescension . . priorities

2. *Although* Cézanne was inspired by the Impressionists, he - - - - their emphasis on the effects of light and - - - - an independent approach to painting that emphasized form.

   (A) accepted . . developed
   (B) rejected . . evolved
   (C) encouraged . . submerged
   (D) dismissed . . aborted
   (E) nurtured . . founded

The answers to the questions are (D) and (B), respectively. In question 1, *such as* tells you that the second blank must be something (genres, practices, or forms) of which call-and-response singing and polyrhythms are examples. *Although in* question 2 tells you that the first blank must contrast with Cézanne's being *inspired* by the Impressionists.

The Tough Questions

Sentence Completion questions go from easiest to hardest—the higher the question number, the harder the question, so the last few questions in a set are usually pretty difficult. If you're getting stuck, we have a few special techniques to pull you through:

- Avoid tricky wrong answers.
- Take apart tough sentences.
- Work around tough vocabulary.

Avoid Tricky Wrong Answers

Toward the end of a set, watch out for tricky answer choices. Avoid:

- Words that sound right because they're hard
- Two-blankers in which one word fits but the other doesn't

The following example would be the seventh question of a 10-problem set.

> Granted that Janyce is extremely - - - -, it is still difficult to imagine her as a professional comedian.
>
> (A) dull
> (B) garrulous
> (C) effusive
> (D) conservative
> (E) witty

Read this sentence carefully or you may get tricked. If you read too quickly, you might think, "If Janyce is hard to imagine as a comedian, she's probably extremely dull or conservative. So I'll pick either (A) or (D)." But the sentence is saying something else.

Remember to pick up the clues. The key here is the clue word *granted*. It's another way of saying *although*. So the sentence means, "Sure Janyce is funny, but she's no professional comedian." Therefore, the word in the blank must resemble *funny*. That means (E), *witty*, is correct.

Now don't pick an answer just because it sounds hard. *Garrulous* means talkative, and *effusive* means overly expressive. You might be tempted to pick one of these simply because they sound impressive. But they're put there to trick you. Don't choose them without good reason.

Now let's look at a two-blank sentence. The following example is another seventh question of a 10-problem set.

When the state government discovered that thermal pollution was killing valuable fish, legislation was passed to - - - - the dumping of hot liquid wastes into rivers and to - - - - the fish population.

(A) discourage . . decimate
(B) regulate . . quantify
(C) facilitate . . appease
(D) discontinue . . devastate
(E) prohibit . . protect

Look at all the choices. Check out the first blank first. Legislation was not passed to *facilitate* dumping, so that eliminates choice (C). The other four are all possible.

Now check the second blanks. The legislature wouldn't pass a law to *decimate*, *quantify*, or *devastate* the fish population, so (A), (B), and (D) are wrong. Only choice (E), *prohibit . . protect*, fits for both blanks. The legislature might well pass a law to prohibit dumping hot liquids and to protect fish.

Take Apart Tough Sentences

Look at the following example, the sixth question of a nine-problem set.

Although this small and selective publishing house is famous for its - - - - standards, several of its recent novels have a mainly popular appeal.

(A) proletarian
(B) naturalistic
(C) discriminating
(D) imitative
(E) precarious

What if you were stumped and had no idea which word to pick? Try this strategy. The process might go like this:

(A) Proletarian standards? Hmmm . . . sounds weird.
(B) Naturalistic standards? Not great.
(C) Discriminating standards? Sounds familiar.
(D) Imitative standards? Weird.
(E) Precarious standards? Nope.

(C) sounds best and, as it turns out, is correct. Although the small publishing house has discriminating, or picky, standards, several of its recent novels appeal to a general audience.

Now try a complex sentence with two blanks. Remember our rules:

- Try the easier blank first.
- Save time by eliminating all choices that won't work for one blank.

The following example is the fifth question of a nine-problem set.

> These latest employment statistics from the present administration are so loosely documented, carelessly explained, and potentially misleading that even the most loyal senators will - - - - the - - - - of the presidential appointees who produced them.
>
> (A) perceive . . intelligence
> (B) understand . . tenacity
> (C) recognize . . incompetence
> (D) praise . . rigor
> (E) denounce . . loyalty

It's not so easy to see what goes in the first blank, so try the second blank. You need a word to describe presidential appointees who produced the *loosely documented*, *carelessly explained*, and *misleading* statistics. It is definitely going to be negative. The only second-word answer choice that is definitely negative is (C), *incompetence*, or inability to perform a task. Now try recognize in the first blank. It fits, too. (C) must be correct.

Work Around Tough Vocabulary

The following example is the second question of a nine-problem set.

> Despite her - - - - of public speaking experience, the student council member was surprisingly cogent and expressed the concerns of her classmates persuasively.
>
> (A) hope
> (B) depth
> (C) method
> (D) lack
> (E) union

If you don't know what *cogent* means, work around it. From the sentence, especially the clue word *and*, you know that cogent goes with "expressed the concerns of her classmates persuasively." So you don't have to worry about what cogent means. All you need to know is that the student council member was persuasive despite a - - - - of speaking experience. Only (D), *lack*, fits. "Despite her *lack* of public speaking experience, the student council member expressed the concerns of her classmates persuasively." (By the way, *cogent* means convincing, or believable, roughly the same as expressing concern persuasively.)

Let's look at another Sentence Completion problem. This time the tough vocabulary is in the answer choices. This example is the sixth question of a nine-question set.

> Advances in technology occur at such a fast pace that dictionaries have difficulty incorporating the - - - - that emerge as names for new inventions.
>
> (A) colloquialisms
> (B) euphemisms
> (C) compensations
> (D) neologisms
> (E) ~~clichés~~

Whatever goes in the blank has to describe *names for new inventions*. If you don't know what the words *colloquialisms* or *euphemisms* mean, don't give up. Exclude as many choices as you can, and guess among the remaining ones.

You can eliminate (C) and (E) right off the bat. They don't describe names for new inventions. Now you can make an educated guess. Again, educated guessing will help your score more than guessing blindly or skipping the question.

By studying word roots (see Appendix B, Building Your Vocabulary), you might know that *neo-* means new, so the word *neologisms* might be the best choice for names of new inventions. In fact, it's the right answer. *Neologisms* are newly coined words.

If All Else Fails—Guess!

If you're really stumped, don't be afraid to guess. Eliminate all answer choices that seem wrong and guess from the remaining choices.

Now get ready to practice the strategies you've learned on this Sentence Completions practice set.

SUMMARY

- **The Gist of Sentence Completion Questions:**
  - Sentence Completion questions are often in a fill-in-the-blank format
  - You need to determine the relationship between the parts of the sentence to figure out which word gives the sentence its meaning
- **Kaplan's Four-Step Method for Sentence Completion Questions:**
  - Step 1: Read the sentence for clue words and look for words of contrast (*but*) and continuity (*and*, *but*, *such* as, *although*)

- — Step 2: Try to predict the answer by deciding what kind of word should fill the blank before looking at the answer choices
- — Step 3: Compare your prediction to the answer choices and select the best match
- — Step 4: Put your answer choice into the blank and make sure it makes sense

- **Clue Words:**
  - — Circle clue words
  - — Think of a word or phrase that might go in each blank
  - — Write your prediction below each sentence
- **The Tough Questions:**
  - — Sentence Completion questions go from easiest to hardest
    - Avoid tricky wrong answers: words that sound right because they're hard or two-blankers in which one word fits but the other doesn't
    - Take apart tough sentences
    - Work around tough vocabulary: you don't necessarily have to know what every word of the sentence means
  - — If all else fails, make an educated guess!

PRACTICE

Select the lettered word or set of words that best completes the sentence.

1. The stranger was actually smaller than he looked; looming up suddenly in the dark alley, he was - - - - in the eyes of the beholder by the alarm he inspired.

(A) worsened
(B) magnified
(C) disparaged
(D) disfigured
(E) admonished

2. Although the risk of a nuclear accident remained - - - - , the public's concern about such an accident gradually - - - - .

(A) steady . . waned
(B) acute . . persisted
(C) unclear . . shifted
(D) obvious . . endured
(E) pressing . . remained

3. Prior to the American entrance into World War I, President Woodrow Wilson strove to maintain the - - - - of the United States, warning both sides against encroachments on American interests.

(A) involvement
(B) belligerence
(C) versatility
(D) magnanimity
(E) neutrality

4. The graceful curves of the colonial-era buildings that dominated the old part of the city contrasted sharply with the modern, - - - - subway stations and made the latter appear glaringly out of place.

(A) festive
(B) grimy
(C) angular
(D) gigantic
(E) efficient

5. The discovery of the Dead Sea Scrolls in the 1940s quickly - - - - the popular imagination, but the precise significance of the scrolls is still - - - - by scholars.

(A) impressed . . understood
(B) alarmed . . obscured
(C) troubled . . perceived
(D) sparked . . disputed
(E) eluded . . debated

6. In Kafka's characteristically surreal story "The Hunger Artist," the main character "entertains" the public by starving himself until he is too - - - - to survive.

(A) glutted
(B) lachrymose
(C) emaciated
(D) superfluous
(E) satiated

7. Recent editions of the Chinese classic *Tao Te Ching*, based on manuscripts more authoritative than those hitherto available, have rendered previous editions - - - - .

(A) incomprehensible
(B) interminable
(C) inaccessible
(D) obsolete
(E) illegible

8. Despite their outward resemblance, the brothers could not be more - - - - temperamentally; while one is quiet and circumspect, the other is brash and - - - - .

(A) inimical . . timid
(B) passionate . . superficial
(C) dissimilar . . audacious
(D) different . . forgiving
(E) alike . . respectful

9. Her scholarly rigor and capacity for - - - - enabled her to undertake research projects that less - - - - people would have found too difficult and tedious.

(A) fanaticism . . slothful
(B) comprehension . . indolent
(C) analysis . . careless
(D) negligence . . dedicated
(E) concentration . . disciplined

ANSWERS AND EXPLANATIONS

1. B

The clue here is the phrase was *actually smaller than he looked*. The missing word has to mean made larger or made to seem larger. Choice (B), *magnified*, is the answer. Disparaged (C) means belittled. *Admonished* (E) means scolded.

2. A

The word *although* indicates contrast. The contrast is between the *risk* and the *public's concern*. Choice (A) is the only one that presents a clear contrast: the risk didn't decrease, but the public's concern did.

3. E

The phrase *warning both sides against encroachments on American interests* indicates that Wilson was attempting to prevent each side from taking an action that would force the United States to get involved in the war. Choice (E), *neutrality*, gets this point across. *Involvement* (A) suggests the opposite of the correct answer. *Belligerence* (B) is the quality of being warlike; *versatility* (C) means being able to handle a variety of different situations; *magnanimity* (D) is generosity.

4. C

You're specifically told that there's a contrast between the buildings and the subway stations. Checking the answer choices for a word that contrasts in meaning with *graceful curves*, you find that the answer is (C), *angular*, which means jagged or angled.

5. D

The word *but* indicates contrast. If you plug in the answer choices, (D) makes the most sense: the public became quickly excited about the issue, but agreement among experts as to the significance of the scrolls has been slower in coming. None of the other choices provides a clear contrast of ideas.

6. C

The missing word describes people who *starve themselves* and become malnourished. Choice (C), *emaciated*, which means extremely thin, is the only choice that really fits. (A) and (E) are the exact opposites of what's needed, and *lachrymose* (B) means tearful.

7. D

If new editions of this book are based on *more authoritative*, or more accurate, manuscripts, previous editions would be rendered out-of-date, or *obsolete* (D)—scholars wouldn't use the old editions because the new ones are markedly superior. However, the new edition wouldn't render the old edition *incomprehensible* (A), *interminable* (B), *inaccessible* (C), or *illegible* (E).

8. C

The clue word *despite* indicates that the brothers must have different temperaments, making *dissimilar* (C) and *different* (D) both possibilities. The second word has to contrast with *quiet and circumspect* and be similar in tone to *brash; audacious*, or bold, is the only choice that makes sense, so (C) is correct.

9. E

It's easier to start with the second blank. You need a word that goes with *rigor* and contrasts with finding things *difficult and tedious. Slothful* (A) and *indolent* (B) both mean lazy, so they're the opposite of what you need. Only *dedicated* (D) and *disciplined* (E) fit. Eliminate the other choices and try (D) and (E) in the first blank. The correct choice will be a quality held by a dedicated, rigorous scholar, so *concentration* (E) is the answer. *Negligence* (D) is the opposite of what you're looking for.

Step Three

Reading Comprehension Questions

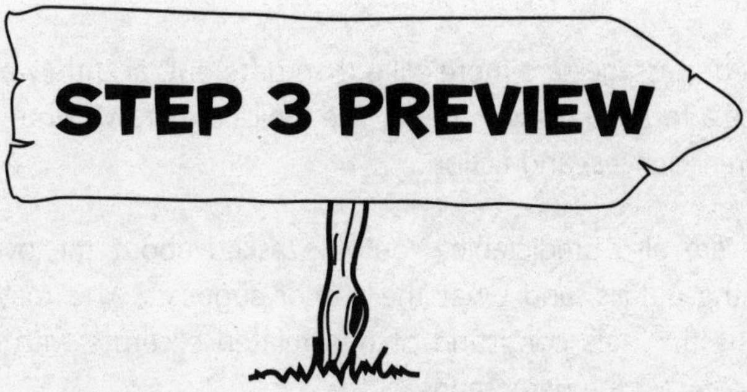

Here's your outline for how to approach Reading Comprehension questions:

THE GIST OF IT

The instructions for the Reading Comprehension section are simple:

Directions: Answer the questions based on the information in the accompanying passage or passages.

The two types of passages are more alike than different, and they are predictable because the test makers use a formula to write them. The topics are drawn from the arts, humanities, social sciences, natural sciences, and fiction.

The questions are also predictable. You'll be asked about the overall tone and content of a paragraph, the details, and what the author suggests. You may also have a few "paired paragraph" question sets consisting of two related excerpts with questions that ask you to compare and contrast the paragraphs.

Reading Comprehension questions ARE NOT ordered by difficulty. Don't get bogged down on a hard, early question because the next one could be easier. You should also answer all of the questions for short passages before attacking the longer passages. Every question is worth the same number of points, and working through the shorter passages is faster than working through the longer ones.

HOW TO GET A HIGH SCORE

Types of Reading Comprehension Questions

When you read passages on the SAT, you're reading for a specific purpose: to be able to correctly answer as many questions as possible. Fortunately, the SAT tends to use the same kinds of Reading Comprehension questions over and over again, so whatever the passage is about and however long it may be, you can expect the same four basic question types:

- Big Picture
- Little Picture
- Inference
- Vocabulary-in-Context

You can expect slightly more than half of the questions to be Little Picture and Inference questions; fewer (approximately 30 percent to 40 percent) will be about Big Picture issues and Vocabulary.

Big Picture Questions

Big Picture questions test how well you understand the passage as a whole. They ask about:

- The main point or purpose of a passage or individual paragraphs
- The author's overall attitude or tone
- The logic underlying the author's argument
- How ideas relate to each other in the passage

If you're stumped on a Big Picture question, even after reading the passage, do the Little Picture questions first. They can help you fill in the big picture. Big Picture questions will usually be at the end of the question set anyway, so you can often use the question order to help you get a deeper understanding of the whole passage.

Here are two sample Big Picture questions.

Based on the passage, the author believes that extraterrestrial life

(A) exists only in science fiction
(B) is abundant throughout the universe
(C) will not be discovered in our lifetime
(D) is physically impossible
(E) may never be discovered because life may take vastly different forms in other galaxies

The author describes his experience as a grocery store clerk and waiter in order to

(A) show that you should always treat others as you want to be treated
(B) explain why he became a writer
(C) suggest that believing in yourself is the key to success
(D) demonstrate the value of hard work
(E) emphasize the importance of a good education

Little Picture Questions

About a third of Reading Comprehension questions are Little Picture questions that ask about localized bits of information—usually specific facts or details from the passage. These questions usually give you a line reference—a clue to where in the passage you'll find your answer. Beware of answer choices that seem to reasonably answer the question in the stem but that don't make sense in the context of the passage or that are true but refer to a different section of the text.

Little Picture questions test:

- Whether you understand significant information that's stated in the passage
- Your ability to locate information within a text
- Your ability to differentiate between main ideas and specific details

Sometimes the answer to a Little Picture question will be directly in the line or lines that are referenced. Other times, you might need to read a few sentences before or after the referenced line(s) to find the correct answer. When in doubt, use the context (surrounding sentences) to confirm the right choice.

Here are some sample Little Picture questions.

The inspiration for Mary Shelley's "monstrous creation" (line 17) came from

(A) a ghost story popular at the time
(B) a tale she remembered from her early childhood
(C) a nightmare she had
(D) a conversation with Lord Byron
(E) a story in the local newspaper

In the phrase "hideous progeny" (line 18), Shelley is referring to

(A) her daughter
(B) her novel
(C) her editor
(D) herself
(E) the reader

Inference Questions

If you've taken any practice SAT exams, you probably noticed that many Reading Comprehension questions begin as follows: "It can be inferred that the author. . . ." To *infer* is to draw a conclusion based on reasoning or evidence. For example, if you wake up in the morning and there's three feet of fresh snow on the ground, you can safely infer that school will be cancelled.

Often, writers will use suggestion or inference rather than state ideas directly. But they will also leave you plenty of clues so you can figure out just what they are trying to convey. Inference clues include word choice (diction), tone, and specific details. Say a passage states that a particular idea *was perceived as revolutionary*. You might infer from the use of the word *perceived* that the author believes the idea was not truly revolutionary but only *perceived* that way.

Thus, Inference questions test your ability to use the information in the passage to come to a logical conclusion. The key to Inference questions is to stick to the evidence in the text.

Most Inference questions have pretty strong clues, so avoid any answer choices that seem far-fetched. If you can't find any evidence in the passage, then it probably isn't the right answer.

Here are two sample Inference questions.

> The author suggests that Henry Ford's experience working on his father's farm
>
> (A) was traumatic
> (B) inspired Ford to become an engineer
> (C) turned Ford away from his desire to be a farmer
> (D) was uneventful
> (E) gave him the courage to try out some of his inventions

> It can be inferred from the passage that the author
>
> (A) agrees with Ford that the present is the only thing that matters
> (B) believes that Ford placed too much emphasis on success
> (C) thinks Ford's industrial revolution undermined basic human values
> (D) believes we should be less dependent upon automobiles
> (E) believes Americans are too materialistic

Make sure you read Inference questions carefully. Some answer choices may be true, but if they can't be inferred from the passage and don't correspond to the passage as a whole or the specific part of the passage cited in the question, then they can't be the correct answer.

Vocabulary-in-Context Questions

Vocabulary-in-Context questions ask about the usage of a single word. These questions do not test your ability to define hard words like *archipelago* and *garrulous*. Instead, they test your ability to infer the meaning of a word from context. Words tested in SAT questions are usually fairly common words with more than one definition. But that's the trick!

Many of the answer choices will be different definitions of the tested word, but only one will work in context. Vocabulary-in-Context questions almost always have a line reference, and you should always use it! Sometimes one of the answer choices will jump out at you. It will be the most common meaning of the word in question—but it's RARELY right. You can think of this as the *obvious* choice. Say *curious* is the word being tested. The obvious choice is *inquisitive*. But curious also means *odd*, and that's more likely to be the answer.

Using context to find the answer will help keep you from falling for this kind of trap. But you can also use these obvious choices to your advantage. If you get stuck on a Vocabulary-in-Context question, you can eliminate the obvious choice and guess from the remaining answers.

Here's our strategy for Vocabulary-in-Context questions: Once you find the tested word in the passage, treat the question like a Sentence Completion question. Pretend the word is a blank in the sentence. Read a line or two around the imaginary blank if you need to. Then predict a word for that blank. Check the answer choices for a word that comes close to your prediction. .

Here's a sample Vocabulary-in-Context question.

The word *abandon* as used in line 32 most nearly means

(A) without restraint or control
(B) to leave alone
(C) to surrender
(D) to move on
(E) unusual or abnormal

Paired Passages

Most versions of the SAT have at least one paired passage. A paired passage is two separate, shorter passages that each relate to the same topic. Questions following paired passages are generally ordered in this way: The first few questions relate to the first passage, the next few to the second passage, and the final questions ask about the passages as a pair.

Don't let the paired passages intimidate you—they're not twice as hard as the single reading selections. In fact, students often find the paired passages the most interesting selections on the test.

To tackle paired passages:

1. Skim Passage 1, looking for the drift (as you would with a single passage).
2. Do the question or questions that relate to the first passage.
3. Skim the second passage, looking for the drift and thinking about how the second passage relates to the first.
4. Do the question or questions that relate to the second passage.
5. Next do the questions that ask about the relationship between the two passages.

Because you have to keep track of two different viewpoints with paired passages, it's especially important to read actively. Remember to ask yourself, "What are these passages about? What is each author's point? What is similar about the two passages? What is different?"

Some Thoughts on Skimming

You are reading Reading Comprehension passages for one reason: to score points on the SAT. The best way to read for points is to skim (read quickly and lightly). You skim when you look up information in a phone book or when you read a newspaper article only long enough to get an idea of the story.

Kaplan's Keys to Skimming

Quick Like a Bunny

The way your eyes move across each line of type and return to the beginning of the next line is your tracking style. You want your tracking style to be light and quick like a bunny, rather than heavy and deliberate like a . . . that's right, a turtle. Move your eyes lightly over the page, grouping words. Don't read each word separately. You want to increase your reading rate, but don't go too fast, or you won't remember anything.

Don't Talk to Yourself

Subvocalizing means sounding out words as you read. Even if you don't move your lips, you're probably subvocalizing if you read one word at a time. Subvocalizing costs you time because you can't read faster than you speak. If you group words, you won't subvocalize.

Keep Asking Yourself Where the Writer is Going

Each SAT passage takes you on a fascinating journey, and every passage contains phrases or paragraph breaks that signal the next phase of the magical trip. As you skim the passage, notice especially where the writer changes course.

Some Thoughts on Paraphrasing

Paraphrasing means condensing a long passage into a few sentences that highlight the most important parts of the long passage. Reading Comprehension questions often ask you to paraphrase when they ask a Big Picture question: what a passage, or part of it, means. The right answer choice correctly paraphrases the meaning of the passage or excerpt. That means it restates the meaning without losing any important points.

Kaplan's Keys to Paraphrasing

We have a good way to answer a paraphrasing question:

1. Read the question stem. That's the partial sentence leading to the answer choices.
2. Read the lines the question refers you to, searching for the relevant phrases. (If a question gives you a line reference, be sure to read a line or two before and after it, too.)
3. Think of your own paraphrase for what's being asked.
4. Find a similar answer choice.

KAPLAN'S FIVE-STEP METHOD FOR READING COMPREHENSION QUESTIONS

Kaplan's method for improving your Reading Comprehension score uses the skills we just covered, so if you were pressed for time and skipped right to this page, take five minutes to skim the skills first, then go to the method.

Step 1: Read the question stem.

Step 2: Locate the material you need.

Step 3: Think up YOUR idea of the right answer.

Step 4: Scan the answer choices.

Step 5: Select your answer.

Let's go through these carefully, in the order you should do them.

Step 1. Read the Question Stem

Read the question very carefully. Make sure you understand what the question is asking before you go back to the passage.

Step 2. Locate the Material You Need

If the question gives you a line reference, also read the material in the passage that surrounds the line. The surrounding material clarifies what the question is asking. If you're not given a line reference, scan the passage to find the place in the passage the question is asking about. Read those few sentences.

Step 3. Think Up YOUR Idea of the Right Answer

Don't come up with a precise answer. You don't have time. You need only a general sense of what you're after, so you can recognize the correct answer quickly when you read the choices.

Step 4. Scan the Answer Choices

Find the one that fits YOUR idea of the right answer. If you don't find one, eliminate wrong choices by checking back to the passage. Rule out choices that are (A) too extreme, (B) go against common sense, and (C) sound reasonable but don't make sense in the context of the passage.

Step 5. Select Your Answer

You've eliminated the obvious wrong answers. One of the remaining should match YOUR right answer. If you're left with more than one contender, consider the passage's main idea, then make your best guess.

Extra Strategies for Long Passages

You use the same skills and strategies to tackle long passages as short passages. The subject matter and questions are also about the same for both passage types. The difference? With longer passages, you need to work harder to stay focused and organized. Here's how.

Know the Question Order

Reading Comprehension questions have a specific order on longer passages: the first few questions ask about the beginning of the passage, and the last few ask about the end.

Read the Introduction

Each passage begins with a brief introduction. *Don't skip this part.* The introduction helps you focus your reading.

Map it

Longer passages cover many different aspects of a topic. The first paragraph might introduce the subject, the second paragraph might present one viewpoint, and the third paragraph might argue for a different viewpoint. Within each of these paragraphs, there are several details that help the author convey a message. Because there is a lot to keep track of, you need to mark up the passage as follows:

- Write simple notes in the margin as you read.
- Write down the purpose of each paragraph.
- Underline key points.
- Concentrate especially on places where the author expresses an opinion. Most Reading Comprehension questions hinge on opinions and viewpoints, not facts.

These notes are your Passage Map. The Passage Map helps you find the part of the passage that contains the information you need. The process of creating your Passage Map also forces you to read actively. This is especially helpful in the SAT's second and third hour, when your energy is flagging. Because you are constantly trying to identify the author's viewpoint and the purpose of each sentence and paragraph, you will be working hard to understand what's happening in the passage. This translates into points on the test.

WHEN TIME IS RUNNING OUT

We told you to save long passages for last, so you may find yourself up against the clock. It's always best to skim the passage before you hit the questions. But if you only have a few minutes left, here's how to score fast points.

You can answer Vocabulary-in-Context questions and many Little Picture questions without reading the passage. If the question has a line reference, locate the material you need to find your answer and follow the Five-Step Method as usual. You won't have the overall picture to guide you, but you might be able to reach the correct answer just by focusing on the little picture and using the context around a particular word or line.

Also, remember to skip around within the section if you need to. You can tackle the passages in any order you like within the same section. So, if you can see from the introductions that one passage will be much more interesting to you than the others, work through that one first—you're likely to read it faster and more actively than the rest. But don't skip around after you've read most or all of a passage. You've already invested your time reading, so try all the questions that go with it before you move to another text.

SUMMARY

- **The Gist of It:**
  - — Topics of reading passages are drawn from the arts, humanities, social sciences, natural sciences, and fiction
  - — You will be asked about the overall tone and content of a paragraph, the details, and what the author is suggesting in a passage
- **Types of Reading Comprehension Questions:**
  - — Big Picture Questions
    - Tests how well you understand the passage as a whole
    - Tests how well you understand the main point or purpose of a passage or individual paragraphs, the author's overall attitude or tone, the logic underlying the author's argument, and how ideas relate to each other in the passage
  - — Little Picture Questions
    - Ask about localized bits of information—generally specific facts or details from the passage
    - Tests whether you understand key information stated in the passage, your ability to locate information within a text, and your ability to differentiate between main ideas and specific details
  - — Inference Questions
    - Ask you to draw a conclusion based on reasoning or evidence
  - — Vocabulary-in-Context Questions
    - Ask about the usage of a single word and your ability to infer the meaning of a word based on how it's used
- **Paired Passages:**
  - — Two separate, shorter passages that each relate to the same topic
  - — Tips for answering paired passages questions
    - Skim passage 1 and look for the main drift
    - Answer the question or questions that relate to the first passage

  - Skim passage 2 and look for the drift while thinking about how the 2nd passage relates to the 1st
  - Answer the questions that relate to the 2nd passage
  - Finally, answer the questions that ask about the relationship between both passages

- **Kaplan's Keys to Skimming:**
  - Grouping words together helps you skim more quickly and prevents subvocalization, which means sounding out words as you read, slowing your reading rate
  - Keep asking yourself where the writer is going and notice where the writer changes course in a passage
- **Kaplan's Keys to Paraphrasing:**
  - Read the question stem
  - Read the lines that the question refers to, searching for relevant phrases
  - Try to paraphrase what is being asked in a question
  - Try to predict your answers and locate a similar answer choice
- **Kaplan's Five-Step Method for Reading Comprehension Questions:**
  - Step 1: Read the question then the stem
  - Step 2: Locate the material you need
  - Step 3: Think up your idea of the right answer
  - Step 4: Scan the answer choices
  - Step 5: Select the answer that best matches your guess
- **Extra Strategies for Long Passages:**
  - Know the question order: the first few questions ask about the beginning of the passage and the last few ask about the end
  - Read the introduction
  - Map it
    - Write simple notes in the margin
    - Write down the purpose of each paragraph
    - Underline key points
    - Focus especially on places where the author expresses an opinion
- When Time is Running Out
  - Answer Vocabulary-in-Context questions and Little Picture questions without reading the passage

PRACTICE

Answer the questions based on the information in the accompanying passage or passages.

Questions 1–9 are based on the following passages.

The following passages present two views of the genius of Leonardo da Vinci. Passage 1 emphasizes Leonardo's fundamentally artistic sensibility. Passage 2 offers a defense of his technological achievements.

Passage 1

What a marvelous and celestial creature was Leonardo da Vinci. As a scientist and engineer, his gifts were unparalleled. But his accomplishment in these capacities was hindered by the fact that he was, before all else, an artist. As one conversant with the perfection of art, and knowing the futility of trying to bring such perfection to the realm of practical application, Leonardo tended toward variability and inconstancy in his endeavors. His practice of moving compulsively from one project to the next, never bringing any of them to completion, stood in the way of his making any truly useful technical advances.

When Leonardo was asked to create a memorial for one of his patrons, he designed a bronze horse of such vast proportions that it proved utterly impractical—even impossible—to produce. Some historians maintain that Leonardo never had any intention of finishing this work in the first place. But it is more likely that he simply became so intoxicated by his grand artistic conception that he lost sight of the fact that the monument actually had to be cast. Similarly, when Leonardo was commissioned to paint the *Last Supper*, he left the head of Christ unfinished, feeling incapable of investing it with a sufficiently divine demeanor. Yet, as a work of art rather than science or engineering, it is still worthy of our greatest veneration, for Leonardo succeeded brilliantly in capturing the acute anxiety of the Apostles at the most dramatic moment of the Passion narrative.

Such mental restlessness, however, proved more problematic when applied to scientific matters. When he turned his mind to the natural world, Leonardo would begin by inquiring into the properties of herbs and end up observing the motions of the heavens. In his technical studies and scientific experiments, he would generate an endless stream of models and drawings, designing complex and unbuildable machines to raise great weights, bore through mountains, or even empty harbors.

It is this enormous intellectual fertility that has suggested to many that Leonardo can and should be regarded as one of the originators of modern science. But Leonardo was not himself a true scientist. "Science" is not the hundred-odd principles or *pensieri** that have been pulled out of his *Codici*. Science is comprehensive and methodical thought. Granted, Leonardo always became fascinated by the intricacies of specific technical challenges. He possessed the artist's interest in detail, which explains his compulsion with observation and problem solving. But such things alone do not constitute science, which requires the working out of a systematic body of knowledge—something Leonardo displayed little interest in doing.

**pensieri*: thoughts (Italian)

Passage 2

As varied as Leonardo's interests were, analysis of his writings points to technology as his main concern. There is hardly a field of applied mechanics that Leonardo's searching mind did not touch upon in his notebooks. Yet some of his biographers have actually expressed regret that such a man, endowed with divine artistic genius, would "waste" precious years of his life on such a "lowly" pursuit as engineering.

To appreciate Leonardo's contribution to technology, one need only examine his analysis of the main problem of technology—the harnessing of energy to perform useful work. In Leonardo's time, the main burden of human industry still rested on the muscles of humans and animals. But little attention was given to analyzing this primitive muscle power so that it could be brought to bear most effectively on the required tasks. Against this background, Leonardo's approach to work was revolutionary. When he searched for the most efficient ways of using human muscle power, the force of every limb was analyzed and measured.

Consider Leonardo's painstaking building approach to the construction of canals. After extensive analysis of the requirements for a particular canal by hand, he concluded that the only reasonable solution was to mechanize the whole operation. Then he considered and ultimately discarded numerous schemes to clear excavated material by wheeled vehicles. It was not that Leonardo underestimated wheeled vehicles. But he realized that a cart is useful only on level ground; on steep terrain the material's weight would nullify the effort of the animal. Having systematically rejected several solutions in this way, Leonardo began to examine the feasibility of excavation techniques incorporating a system of cranes. Power was again his main concern. To activate a crane, the only transportable motor available at the time would have been a treadmill, a machine that converts muscle power into rotary motion. This is not to suggest that Leonardo invented the external treadmill. However, it was Leonardo who first used the principle of the treadmill rationally and in accordance with sound engineering principles.

Because Leonardo's insights were sometimes so far beyond the standards of his time, their importance to the development of modern engineering is often underestimated. Many scholars, in fact, still regard his work merely as the isolated accomplishments of a remarkably prophetic dreamer, refusing to concede that Leonardo was one of our earliest and most significant engineers.

1. The author of Passage 1 seems to regard the *perfection of art* (line 7) as

(A) a more valuable goal than scientific accomplishment

(B) achievable only with diligence and constant effort

(C) applicable to the solving of technical problems

(D) a model to which scientists should aspire

(E) unattainable in the fields of science and engineering

2. The author of Passage 1 considers the Last Supper ultimately successful as a work of art because it

(A) is much sought-after by collectors
(B) emphasizes the role of the Apostles in comforting Christ before his crucifixion
(C) captures the divinity of Christ on the eve of his death
(D) depicts a well-known moment in the history of Christianity
(E) conveys the anxiety felt by Christ's Apostles

3. The word *variability* in line 10 most nearly means

(A) comprehensiveness
(B) changeability
(C) uncertainty
(D) confusion
(E) disorder

4. In lines 39–40, the author most likely describes the way Leonardo *turned his mind to the natural world* in order to show that

(A) Leonardo's mind was constantly leaping from one topic to another
(B) elements of the natural world are all interconnected
(C) Leonardo's mind was preoccupied with scientific experiments
(D) Leonardo preferred artistic pursuits to scientific inquiry
(E) Leonardo tended to become distracted by his artistic projects

5. The author of Passage 1 is critical of Leonardo's pensieri (line 54) primarily because they

(A) are factually incorrect
(B) do not constitute a systematic body of thought
(C) contradict widely accepted scientific principles
(D) were never thoroughly tested
(E) are based on intuition rather than observation

6. In the last paragraph of Passage 1, the author's attitude towards modern scientific investigation can best be characterized as

(A) sentimental
(B) disparaging
(C) respectful
(D) detached
(E) superficial

7. In lines 97–104, the discussion of *wheeled vehicles* is presented in order to support the author's point about Leonardo's

(A) thoroughness in examining all possible solutions to a problem
(B) tendency to let his artistic genius interfere with his effectiveness as an engineer
(C) ability to arrive immediately at the best way of approaching a technical task
(D) harmful practice of moving from one idea to the next
(E) underestimation of traditional technology

8. The author of Passage 1 would probably regard the painstaking analysis of canal-building described in Passage 2 as an example of Leonardo's

(A) revolutionary approach to work
(B) ability to complete ambitious engineering projects
(C) artistic fascination with details
(D) predisposition to lose interest in specific problems
(E) penchant for designing unbuildable machines

9. How would the author of Passage 2 respond to the implication in Passage 1 that Leonardo's insights did not result in *truly useful technical advances* (lines 14–15)?

(A) Usefulness is not an appropriate criterion for judging solutions to technical problems.
(B) Leonardo would have accomplished more had he not been distracted by his artistic endeavors.
(C) Leonardo's invention of the external treadmill is one of countless useful advances he instigated.
(D) Leonardo's ideas were so advanced that they often could not be put into practice in his time.
(E) Leonardo's contributions to modern engineering have been deliberately ignored by many scholars.

Questions 10–11 refer to the following passage.

What will be "cool" next year? Though it's impossible to predict with certainty, profit-minded fashion designers, music industry executives, and television producers would very much like to have a leg up on their competition. In fact, this ever-accelerating quest to spot trends and trendsetters has spawned a new industry. Trend-analysis experts specialize in predicting what will be in and what will be out. Some firms hire legions of young people to track the interests and fads of their contemporaries. One especially innovative trend-spotting firm uses the Internet to compile massive amounts of data from its informants, known as "field correspondents."

10. As used in the passage, *spawned* (line 8) most nearly means

(A) paved the way for
(B) illustrated the wisdom of
(C) questioned the necessity of
(D) given rise to
(E) shown the need for

11. Based on the passage, the author would most likely agree that

(A) those who pursue information about future trends will likely be frustrated in this attempt
(B) the predictions of trend-analysis experts should be regarded with at least some skepticism
(C) young people are a vital resource for those who would predict future trends
(D) the increasing pressure to predict trends has had a negative effect on the fashion, music, and television industries
(E) the Internet is a valuable tool in the process of analyzing data about future trends

Questions 12–13 refer to the following passage.

There are three good reasons that schools should restore the study of Latin. First, because Latin is a logically structured language, and knowledge of it helps students to better understand the structure of English. Second, a familiarity with Latin is an incalculable aid in enlarging one's vocabulary in English, since so many words in that language derive from Latin roots. Finally, Latin serves as a gateway to the remarkable civilization of Ancient Rome, whose literature and culture have had a permanent influence on our society. As evidence of this assertion, we need only consider the influence of Republican Rome on the Founding Fathers of the United States.

12. The author's primary purpose in writing the passage was most likely to

(A) narrate
(B) describe
(C) entertain
(D) analyze
(E) persuade

13. The author mentions the influence of Republican Rome on the Founding Fathers primarily in order to

(A) show the lasting influence of Roman culture on our society
(B) illustrate the benefits of enlarging one's vocabulary
(C) persuade the reader to re-examine the U.S. Constitution
(D) provide a link between Latin classes and history and government classes in school
(E) refute the argument that learning Latin is irrelevant and impractical

Questions 14–17 refer to the following passages.

Paragraph 1

More than 40 years ago, Newton Minow, then head of the Federal Communications Commission, described television as a "vast wasteland." If he were evaluating TV today, his opinion would be little changed. The amount of violence in television drama series seems to increase every year, while competition for ratings has driven news programs to effectively enter the entertainment business. It is even arguable that sports coverage, one of the strengths of television in the 1970s and 1980s, has declined in quality. And public-affairs program producers trot out the same gallery of talking heads—self-proclaimed "experts" who reduce complex arguments to sound bites. In an industry where programmers search in vain for fresh ideas, it is no wonder that attention spans are short and cliché is king.

Paragraph 2

Critics of television often focus on the prevalence of violence in today's programming. However, even after years of study, researchers cannot prove the existence of a link between TV violence and antisocial behavior in real life. One study, for example, studied youngsters in both Michigan and Ontario, Canada who watched the same programs. No connection between viewing habits and behavior could be established convincingly.

Beguiled perhaps by the violence issue, critics of TV regularly fail to acknowledge the medium's educational value. With the advent of cable, many new channels have flourished by focusing on such fields as public affairs, medicine, travel, history, and science.

14. The author of Passage 1 criticizes all the following types of television programming EXCEPT

(A) news programs
(B) sports coverage
(C) dramatic series
(D) soap operas
(E) public affairs shows

15. The phrase *cliché is king* in lines 19–20 of Passage 1 implies that the author regards television programming as

(A) stimulating and thought-provoking
(B) violent and demeaning
(C) exciting and suspenseful
(D) unoriginal and stale
(E) difficult to understand

16. In Passage 2, which of the following does the author mention in order to defend television programming?

(A) studies that established links between viewing habits and behavior
(B) the quality of sports coverage during the 1970s and 1980s
(C) the educational potential of the medium
(D) public affairs experts who help viewers to understand complex arguments
(E) the superiority of American television programming compared to that of Canada

17. Both passages address

(A) news coverage on television
(B) violence on television
(C) the variety of cable television channels
(D) differences between Canadian and American television
(E) regulation by the Federal Communications Commission

ANSWERS AND EXPLANATIONS

The italicized intro reveals the basic contrast between the two passages: Author #1 stresses Leonardo's "artistic sensibility," while Author #2 stresses his "technological achievements." Author #1 argues that Leonardo's artistic mentality interfered with his real accomplishments. He "tended toward variability and inconstancy in his endeavors," he was impractical and restless, and despite his extraordinary inventiveness, he was more of an artist than a true scientist. Author #2 has a diametrically opposite view, arguing that Leonardo was an engineering genius, that his approach to scientific problems was thoroughly systematic. With that basic difference in mind, let's rack up some points.

1. E

The overall point of paragraph 1 is that Leonardo's accomplishments as a scientist and engineer were limited by the fact that he approached everything as an artist—he moved compulsively from one engineering project to the next because he realized that "the perfection of art" was not attainable in those fields.

2. E

The author's opinion of the Last Supper is expressed pretty clearly at the end of paragraph 2—despite its shortcomings, it is "worthy of our greatest veneration" because it "succeeded brilliantly in capturing the acute anxiety of the Apostles."

3. B

The author expands on Leonardo's "variability and inconstancy" at the end of the paragraph—we're told that Leonardo made a habit of "moving compulsively from one project to the next." So variability means "changeability" in this context.

4. A

Leonardo's approach to natural science is scatter-brained; he begins by "inquiring into the properties of herbs," and ends up "observing the motions of the heavens." So the author is describing it as an example of his "mental restlessness . . . when applied to scientific matters."

5. B

The author's criticism of the pensieri is that while they reflect Leonardo's "compulsion with observation and problem-solving . . . such things alone do not constitute science, which requires the working out of a systematic body of knowledge."

6. C

The author presents modern scientific investigation as "the working out of a systematic body of knowledge," implying throughout that Leonardo wasn't sufficiently disciplined in his work to pursue this. Essentially, the author's attitude towards science is respectful.

7. A

The underlying point of paragraphs 2 and 3 is that Leonardo was exhaustive in his approach to engineering problems. Wheeled vehicles are discussed to show that Leonardo was farsighted enough to realize that they weren't the solution to the problem of mechanizing canals.

8. C

The overall point of passage 1 is that Leonardo's artistic temperament adversely affected his approach to science and engineering. We're told in the last paragraph that "he possessed an artist's interest in detail, which explains his compulsion with observation and problem-solving." Consequently, the author of passage 1 would probably see Leonardo's painstaking work on canals in this light.

9. D

The last paragraph of passage 2 explains why Leonardo's accomplishments as an engineer are so often overlooked. We're told that Leonardo's insights were often "far beyond the standards of his time." And so choice (D)—Leonardo was too advanced—would be the most appropriate response to the first author's criticism.

10. D

The passage suggests that an entire industry has been *created* by the drive to predict trends. The specific sentence says, "In fact, this ever-accelerating quest to spot trends and trendsetters has spawned a new industry." In other words, a new industry has been *triggered*. (A) is wrong because the quest didn't just *pave the way* for an industry, it actually helped create an industry. As for (B), it isn't complete enough: It doesn't convey the full idea that an industry was actually created. (C) is totally wrong—it didn't question the need at all. And (E) means much the same thing as (B).

11. B

Compare each choice against what you know from the passage. (A) is extreme. Though the text says it's impossible to predict trends with certainty, it doesn't suggest that everyone who pursues knowledge about trends will be frustrated. (C) is a misused detail. We know that "some" companies hire young people, not that most companies do—or even that this is vital or particularly effective. (D) is out-of-scope. These industries are interested in trends, but we don't know what kind of effect this is having. (E) is an overstatement, as only one firm is described as using the Internet, and there's no indication as to its value. (B) is correct: The author says that it is impossible to predict what will be cool next year, so it makes sense to regard the predictions about trends with skepticism.

12. E

The key word is *should* in the first sentence. The passage opens with an assertion, which the author then argues in favor of. (A) is out since there is no story here. So is (B) because the study of Latin is described only to make an argument. (C) is completely incorrect, and (D) is incomplete: The passage is somewhat analytical, but this is done in order to present an argument.

13. A

The key phrase in the mention of Republican Rome and the description of the Founding Fathers is "as evidence of this assertion." This "assertion" is the assertion that Roman culture has had a permanent influence on modern society. With (B), enlarging one's vocabulary is identified as a benefit of learning Latin, but it has nothing to do with the Founding Fathers. (C) is out of scope. (D) is close, but not entirely correct. Latin is discussed, but not other classes. And with (E), while the author plainly considers Latin relevant and practical, the influence of Republican Rome on the Founding Fathers does not specifically relate to this view.

14. D

Keep in mind that you're not asked for a program the author *might* criticize, you're asked for a program she hasn't *explicitly* criticized. Also, since this is an elimination question, your answer needs to be the one that is *not* mentioned in the passage. The only answer choice that isn't criticized in the text is (D) This is a little tricky: Though soap operas are a type of program we'd expect the author to criticize, soap operas are not actually mentioned, so this is the correct answer.

15. D

Locate the phrase in paragraph 1 and examine the context for clues. A *cliché* is a trite expression or idea; look for an answer choice that captures this sense. With (A), the author doesn't think television programming is thought-provoking, she thinks it lacks originality. As for (B), it is consistent with the author's point-of-view, but it doesn't address the question. The author does believe that TV is excessively violent, but this isn't implied by the phrase *cliché is king*. (E) isn't the point. (D) makes sense, since the "programmers search in vain for fresh ideas."

16. C

Examine the structure of Passage 2. How does the author support the argument? The final two sentences in the paragraph are great clues. (A) is the opposite case: No links were established. (B) is a detail that appears in Passage 1, not in Passage 2. (D) is out of scope. As for (E), while there is mention of a study of Michigan and Canadian children, there is no description of either area as producing superior programming.

17. B

Compare the passages for common ground. Eliminate answer choices that appear in just one passage (or in neither passage). (A) and (E) are mentioned only in Passage 1. (C) and (D) are mentioned only in Passage 2.

Part B

Understanding the Writing Section

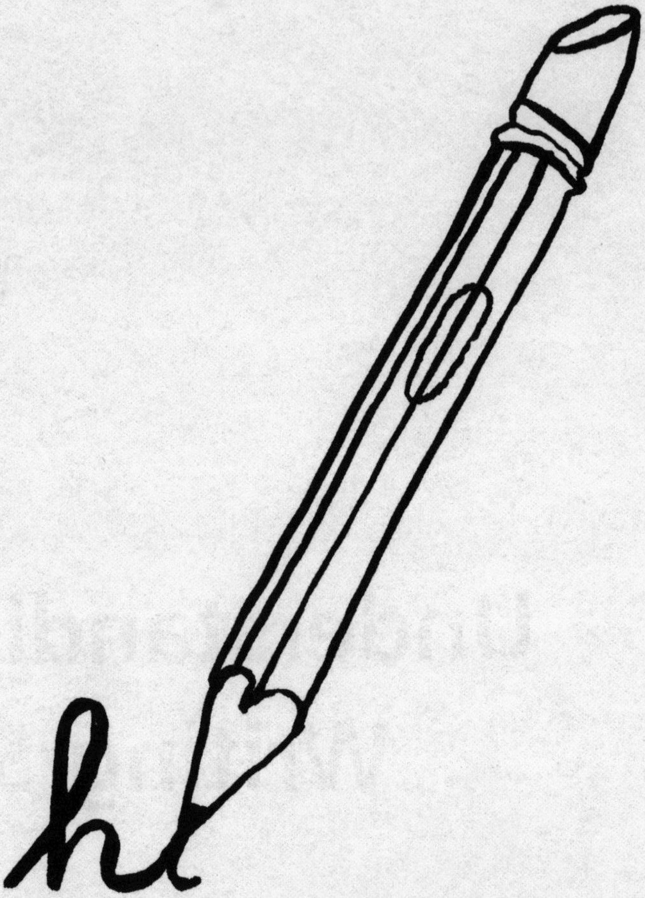
hi

Step Four
The Essay

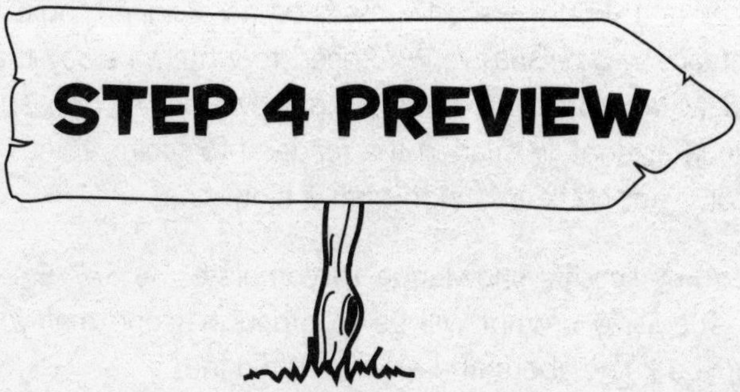

The Gist of it

- The Directions
- Scoring
- Essay Writing FAQs

How to Get a High Score

- Kaplan's Four-Step Method for Essay Writing
- Step 1. Think: Minutes 1–2
- Step 2. Organize: Minutes 3–7
- Step 3. Write: Minutes 8–22
- Step 4. Fix: Minutes 23–25

Summary

Practice

Sample Essays

- Grade 6 Essay
- Grade 4 Essay
- Grade 2 Essay

The Essay component of the Writing section is worth 30 percent of your total section score, which is why it may seem frightening and be a source of major stress. But that is only because you might be unfamiliar with what graders are looking for. Understanding the Essay component and having a plan of attack will help you relax and get a higher score.

THE GIST OF IT

Your task is to write a short, persuasive essay on an assigned topic. The most important word in that last sentence was *persuasive*. You need to write an essay that convinces the reader of your point of view. You can write the best essay ever on the pros and cons of achieving world peace, but if you have not persuaded the reader into seeing things from a particular point of view (pro OR con—not both), you won't get a high score.

You don't need any specific knowledge to complete the SAT Essay. There's no real way to "study" for it. The Essay prompt will be so broad in scope that you'll be able to apply it to something that you know about and are interested in.

Colleges will be able, at no charge, to view and print essays written by individual students who request that a college receive their scores. We suspect that college admissions officials, being short on time, will probably not, as a rule, read an extra essay. But they may use it for comparison's sake with a student's application essay or if a student's score indicates a major discrepancy with the rest of his application package. The Essay may also be used to supplement or replace a college's current application essay or for college placement purposes, and the scores may be used as an extra measure of a student's ability.

The Directions

The directions for the essay are simple:

Directions: Think carefully about the issue presented in the following excerpt and the assignment below.

> "If there were in the world today any large number of people who desired the happiness of others more than they desired their own happiness, we could have paradise in a few years."
>
> — Bertrand Faberge

Assignment: Is the "paradise" the writer mentions something that you think is possible, considering your own views on human nature? In an essay, support your position by discussing an example (or examples) from literature, science and technology, the arts, current events, or your own experience or observation.

The quotes or excerpt serve primarily as springboards, or food for thought. They are there to help jumpstart your creative juices and to give you some ideas about how to build your essay. That's helpful, especially when you're asked to write on demand. Whereas you are free to refer directly to the quote(s) or excerpt in your essay, the assignment will not require you to do so.

The main goal is to address the topic raised in the assignment. The "side" you take in your essay is irrelevant; there are no right and wrong answers when it comes to the position you choose. So choose whichever position you feel more comfortable with, and that will enable you to develop your ideas and write the stronger essay.

Scoring

The SAT Essay is scored holistically by two readers. *Holistically* means your essay gets a single score—a number—that indicates its overall quality. This number takes into account a bunch of essay characteristics (keep reading).

The number assigned to your essay will range from a high of 6 to a low of 0. Your essay is read and scored by two people, so the scores they each assign to your essay will be added together to get a total score. This total score will range from a high of 12 to a low of 0.

Here is a look at what the criteria for each score is like:

6: Outstanding Essay

Convincingly and insightfully fulfills the writing assignment; ideas are well developed, clearly presented, and logically organized; superior command of vocabulary, grammar, style, and accepted conventions of writing; a few minor flaws may occur.

5: Solid Essay

Convincingly fulfills the writing assignment; ideas are adequately developed, clearly presented, and logically organized; strong command of vocabulary, grammar, style, and accepted conventions of writing; some minor flaws may occur.

4: Adequate Essay

Fulfills the writing assignment; ideas are adequately developed, presented, and organized; satisfactory command of vocabulary, grammar, style, and accepted conventions of writing; some flaws may occur.

3: Limited Essay

Doesn't adequately fulfill the writing assignment; ideas aren't adequately developed, clearly presented, or logically organized; unsatisfactory command of vocabulary, grammar, style, and accepted conventions of writing; contains many flaws.

2: Flawed Essay

Doesn't fulfill the writing assignment; ideas are vague; poorly presented, and not logically organized; poor command of vocabulary, grammar, style, and accepted conventions of writing; contains numerous serious flaws.

1: Deficient Essay

Doesn't fulfill the writing assignment; ideas are extremely vague, very poorly presented, and not logically organized; extremely poor command of vocabulary, grammar, style, and accepted conventions of writing; is so seriously flawed that basic meaning is obscured.

0: Incorrect Essay

Essay was not written on the given topic.

Essay Writing FAQs

So you now know what the directions look like and what your task will be, and you also know what you need to receive a good score on your essay. Before we show you how to write a great essay, we want to address some of the basics about the SAT Essay (and to offer you some additional tips and tricks!). Here are our answers to some frequently asked questions.

How Long Should the Essay Be?

The length of an essay is no assurance of its quality. However, it's hard to develop an argument in depth, something the graders look for, in 200 words, but don't ramble, digress, or write off topic just to make your essay longer. Practice writing organized essays with developed examples, and you'll find yourself writing more naturally. Aim for 300–450 words as you practice.

Can I Get Extra Paper?

No. The test booklet has 46 lines, or two pages, for the Essay. If your handwriting is large, it may be a challenge to fit in all your ideas. You won't get any additional sheets, so practice printing, writing smaller, or whatever else works.

How Many Examples Should I Use?

A good essay can have a single well-developed example; two or more examples can also make for a strong essay, but they in themselves won't guarantee a 5 or 6. However, many undeveloped examples make for weak—and low-scoring—essays.

What If I'm Not a "Writer"?

Writing essays may not be your favorite pastime, but you can still succeed on the SAT Essay. If the essay is essentially well written, just staying on topic can earn you a good score. If your writing is weak, focus on building a well-supported argument; if you have that, other weaknesses and writing errors will be less important.

What's the Best Subject to Write About?

Examples based on literary or historical topics won't necessarily receive a higher score than those based on personal experience. Choose examples that you can write about with confidence; don't try to impress the readers. If you do choose personal experience, try to choose examples that focus on self-improvement, positive acts, or creative work. Remember that colleges may use these essays as additional personal statements.

What's the Best Way to Practice?

There is simply no substitute for writing essays under test-like conditions. Practice writing as many essays as possible between now and Test Day. And it's also a good idea to practice at the same time of day that you will be writing on Test Day.

Be hard on yourself. Don't allow yourself any extra minutes to complete an essay, and don't look at essay topics in advance. Practice writing on *no more* than a total of 46 lines on two pages. After each practice essay, score yourself based on the guidelines provided in this book. As part of your self-evaluation, determine which types of examples are most useful to you and what types of errors you make most often.

Then analyze how well you followed Kaplan's methods in constructing your essay and what you might focus on for improvement. Do you have a tendency to rush your plan, or do you find that you haven't left time to proofread? Practice to make your pacing reliable.

Finally, get a second opinion. Ask someone else to read and critique your practice essays. If you know someone else who's taking the SAT, you might agree to assist each other in this way. Knowing whether another person can follow your reasoning is the single most important learning aid you can have for the essay.

What If English Isn't My Native Language?

The SAT Essay section can be a special challenge for the international student or English-as-a-Second Language student here in the United States. The SAT Essay is different from the TOEFL Essay because the prompt can be more complex and may use language that is harder to understand.

But you don't need complex sentences. Keep your usage as simple as you need to ensure control; this isn't the time for experimental writing. On the SAT, you will be taking a position on the prompt, something that sometimes, but not always, happens on the TOEFL. However, you will still be planning your essay using all the same tools covered in this book.

Practice deciphering the prompts and writing essays. Make a special point of leaving time to proofread your essays after you've finished them, and revise anything that makes your writing unclear. There's a strong connection between your English reading skills and your writing skills, so keep reading as well.

HOW TO GET A HIGH SCORE

So now you know what kind of essay prompt you can expect to see on the SAT. Kaplan has a great attack strategy for writing the essay.

Kaplan's Four-Step Method for Essay Writing

After you read the essay prompt, you:

Step 1: **T**HINK about the topic (2 minutes)

Step 2: **O**RGANIZE your paragraphs (5 minutes)

Step 3: **W**RITE your essay (15 minutes)

Step 4: **F**IX any mistakes (3 minutes)

We know what you're thinking: Wait, I don't start writing for seven minutes? This test is long and hard! Every minute counts! You are right. Every minute does count, so you need to use your minutes the *right* way. Here's our minute-by-minute rundown of the "TOWF" method.

Step 1. Think: Minutes 1–2

This step takes two minutes. That leaves you 23 minutes to organize, write, and fix your essay. Do NOT write anything during these two minutes. There's plenty of time for that later. Use these precious 120 seconds for thinking and nothing else.

Read the topic statement and assignment carefully. The topic statement is going to be very broad. To narrow it down, you need to come up with an argument that specifically addresses the topic. Let's say that you get the prompt from our sample essay question: *Is the "paradise" the writer mentions something that you think is possible, considering your own views of human nature?*

You need to take a specific example or examples from your personal experience, current events, history, literature, or any other discipline, and use these examples to compose an essay that answers this statement persuasively, one way or the other.

Pick a Side

Decide either to agree or disagree with the topic statement. For example, you might agree with the statement by saying that this paradise is something that's possible, or you might disagree by saying you do not think it is possible. You do not want to say that you can kind of see things from both sides, even if that is, in fact, the case. If you're not sure what you think, pick the side you think you can best back up with examples.

Choose Your Examples

Once you have picked your side, you must choose examples that back up your argument. Think of 2–3 examples that you can write about intelligently and passionately. Let's agree that this paradise is possible. Here are some possible examples to back up your opinion:

Is the "paradise" the writer mentions something that you think is possible, considering your own views of human nature?

YES—human nature is good and generous

1. Regular people volunteer to help the less fortunate all the time.
2. Bono is always helping to fight hunger and makes a big difference, and he's just one guy.
3. The United States sends aid to poor countries.

Once you have your examples, organize them in a way you think would flow best from paragraph to paragraph. You can do this by numbering your examples, as we did.

Use Specific Evidence

You've got to cite evidence to support your examples. When you are thinking of your examples, also be thinking about one piece of evidence for each of your examples. Like so:

1. Regular people volunteer to help the less fortunate all the time.

   EXAMPLE: My sister spends every Sunday morning at the soup kitchen downtown.
2. Bono is always helping to fight hunger and makes a big difference, and he's just one guy.

   EXAMPLE: U2's lead singer went on a tour with the former U.S. Secretary of the Treasury to Africa and got him to admit there's a huge problem with starvation there, and the United States needs to do something about it.
3. The United States sends aid to poor countries.

   EXAMPLE: Congress just passed over $100 million in aid to drill for potable water in famine-struck African villages.

Step 2. Organize: Minutes 3–7

This step takes up to five minutes. That may seem like a lot of time to spend before you write a single essay sentence. But taking a few minutes to organize your essay is definitely worth the time. If you take a few minutes to outline what you want to write, the essay will be a lot easier to write once you start it. The time you take organizing will reduce the time it takes to write your essay.

So you have your argument, your examples, and your evidence in your head. It's time to plan your essay. Use the margins on your test booklet to outline your ideas. Here is how your essay paragraphs should be organized:

Paragraph 1:

- Clearly state your argument.
- Briefly mention the evidence that you're going to cite in support of that argument.

Middle Paragraphs (2–3 paragraphs):

- Explore and explain your evidence in detail. These paragraphs explain how the evidence supports the argument.

Last Paragraph:

- Briefly summarize your argument.

So, sticking with "people are good/paradise is possible," an outline might look like this:

P1. I think paradise is possible, because there are a bunch of people who are kind and generous. For example, my sister, Bono, and the aid the United States gives to poor countries.

P2. My sister is a freshman in high school. She is on the soccer team, has a part-time job, and helps out with chores at home. She is very busy. But she still finds time every Sunday to help at the YMCA soup kitchen downtown.

P3. My sister is young but that doesn't mean one person can't do a lot. Bono went on a tour of Africa with Paul O'Neil in 2002. O'Neil was skeptical, but Bono proved to him that we could help.

P4. U.S. Congress approved over $100 million for drilling extra deep wells in villages in Africa. Where does that money come from? From all of us. We're all helping.

P5. In conclusion, my sister, Bono, and this country's elected officials and taxpayers prove that human nature is good and that we can all work to get closer to the paradise the writer talks about.

Step 3. Write: Minutes 8–22

So what's left? Writing your high-scoring essay. The writing step of your essay should take about 15 minutes. That's plenty of time to write three to five solid paragraphs if you work from a prepared outline. To write your strongest essay, *follow your outline*. You spent five minutes thinking about and organizing your essay, so stick to it. Don't freak out and write from the opposing point-of-view. Trust your outline and yourself.

Remember to write clearly, write concisely, write complete sentences, and use proper grammar. But you only have a few minutes, so write quickly, too. Here is a quickly written essay from our outline.

The writer hopes that there are enough people in the world who think about others before they think about themselves. While I'm not sure actual "paradise" can be attained, I do think human nature is good enough for us to at least get closer to it. I only have to look as far as my sister for an example of a kind and generous person. But I can also easily cite a celebrity singer, as well as the Congress and the people of the United States, to illustrate the basic goodness of people, and our ability to make the world a better place.

My little sister is 14 years old and a freshman in high school. Some people think that kids this age only think about themselves, their clothes, and MTV. This is not true. My sister is on the soccer team and has a parttime job helping my dad with his cleaning business. She also has her fair share of chores at home. But my little sister still finds time to volunteer every Sunday morning at the soup kitchen at the downtown YMCA. No body told her to do this, she does it because she wants to help others. She is intersted in making the world a better place, and she's only 14!

My sister is young, so she can only do so much. But that doesn't mean one person can't make a huge difference on the lives of others. The lead singer of the band U2, Bono, is an example of this. Bono spends a lot of time when his band isn't touring doing good deeds. In 2002 Bono decided he was going to help the peopl in Africa get wate they could drink. Africa is in a drought and all of the wells have dried up. Bono knows they need to dig deeper wells, but it's expensive to do that and they don't have any money. So Bono convinced then U.S. Secretary of the Treasury Paul O'Neil to come to Africa with him. O'Neil did, he saw how much they needed wells, and he came back and told the president.

Once the president was involved, Congress passed a spend bill that will gives over $100 million to Africa to dig these deep wells. These wells are not only going to make life better for Africans, it is going to save lives. But this $100 million doesn't just come out of thin air. Our tax dollars pays for this. That means we, as Americans, are spending money to help people we don't even know. Sure bono makes a big difference, and our elected officials have to get involved, but when it comes right down to it, we are the ones doing the good deed.

In conclusion, I think it is obvious from these examples that people are basic kind and generous. My sister, Bono, former Treasury Secretary O'Neil, and the American people are all examples of people who are putting the happiness of others before their own. We may not get to paradise in a few years, as the author says we might, but we will definitely live in a kinder, friendlier, and safer world.

Step 4. Fix: Minutes 23–25

This step takes two minutes. It involves proofreading and fixing your essay. All you'll need to do is fix minor grammatical and/or spelling errors, change a few words here and there, and, maybe, add a sentence or two for clarity's sake.

If you spend the bulk of the 25 minutes thinking about, outlining, and writing the essay, the repair step should entail nothing more than putting the finishing touches on an already strong essay.

Here is our fixed essay:

The writer Bertrand Faberge hopes that there are enough people in the world who think about others before they think about themselves. While I'm not sure the "paradise" he mentions can be attained, I do think human nature is good enough for us to at least get closer to paradise. I only have to look as far as my sister for an example of a kind and generous person. But I can also easily cite a celebrity singer, as well as the Congress and the people of the United States, to illustrate the basic goodness of people, and our ability to make the world a better place.

My little sister is 14 years old and a freshman in high school. Some people think that kids this age only think about themselves, their clothes, and MTV. This is not true. My sister is on the soccer team and has a parttime job helping my dad with his cleaning business. She also has her fair share of chores at home. But my little sister still finds time to volunteer every Sunday morning at the soup kitchen at the downtown YMCA. Nobody told her to do this. She does it because she wants to help others. She is interested in making the world a better place, and she's only 14!

My sister is young, so she can only do so much. But that doesn't mean one person can't make a huge difference in the lives of others. The lead singer of the band U2, Bono, is an example of this. Bono spends a lot of time when his band isn't touring doing good deeds. In 2002 Bono decided he was going to help the people in Africa get water they could drink. Africa is in a drought and all of the shallow wells have dried up. Bono knows they need to dig deeper wells, but it's expensive to do that and they don't have any money. So Bono convinced the US Secretary of the Treasury Paul O'Neil to come to Africa with him. O'Neil did, he saw how much they needed wells, and he came back and told the president.

Once the president was involved, Congress passed a spending bill that will give over $100 million to Africa to dig these deep wells. These wells are not only going to improve the lives of Africans, they will also save lives. But this $100 million doesn't just come out of thin air. Our tax dollars pays for this. That means we, as Americans, are spending money to help people we don't even know. Sure, Bono makes a big difference, and our elected officials have to get involved, but when it comes right down to it, we are the ones doing the good deed.

In conclusion, I think it is obvious from these examples that people are basically kind and generous. My sister, Bono, former Treasury Secretary O'Neil, and the American people are all examples of people who are putting the happiness of others before their own. We may not get to paradise in a few years, as the author hopes, but we will definitely live in a kinder, friendlier, and safer world.

Did you see how we proofread and fixed the essay. Small corrections can score you big points. That's why it is so important to proofread.

Now that you know Kaplan's Four-Step Method, you are ready to write your best essay on the SAT. Here are just a couple of other suggestions to think about when you get ready to write.

Don't Write Just About Personal History, If Possible

Essay topics are so broad that you can always steer your essay toward a subject that you are familiar with. Just make sure you:

- Address the topic that you are given.
- Write persuasively.

The object is to convince your reader to see something from your point of view. Don't worry about what the reader thinks—write about what *you* think. You are NOT fair and balanced! (Well, you should be fair, but definitely not balanced.)

Then, if the topic allows, it's a good idea to include references to current events, history, and literature in your essay. Now, you don't *have* to use these things as examples. You could also just use your personal experience. But if the essay topic allows it, and you have a good example from history, famous books, or the nightly news, please include it.

Why? Your essay is being graded by high school teachers and college professors. You know teachers—they want to know that the things they have taught you are sinking in. They'll be impressed by an essay that goes beyond your personal experience. But if you don't have any such supporting evdience from the outside world, don't force it. Go with what you know.

Be Neat

Your essay must be readable. If you edit what you've written, do it neatly. If you add a word, change a phrase, or cross out a sentence, do it carefully. It may sound silly, but neatness matters. It matters a lot. Why? The graders have tons of essays to read and grade. That means they don't spend much time reading your essay (about a minute, on average). They aren't going to read an essay three or four times in order to decipher hard-to-read words or sentences. They are going to read it once, score it, and move on. Make life easier for them by writing neatly, and they'll be more inclined to make life easier for you.

To sum up: You're not expected to produce a perfect piece of writing. The graders know that you have only 25 minutes to think about, write, and proofread your work. What they expect is an organized and readable piece of writing that makes an argument supported by real examples.

SUMMARY

- **The Gist of It:**
  - — You are asked to write a short, persuasive essay on an assigned topic
- **Scoring:**
  - — Your essay is graded holistically by two readers. The highest score each reader can give an essay is 6 and the lowest is 0. Both scores are combined for a total score out of 12.
  - — 6: Outstanding Essay
    - Convincingly and insightfully fulfills the writing assignment; ideas are very well developed, presented and organized; superior use of vocabulary, grammar and style
  - — 5: Solid Essay
    - Convincingly fulfills the writing assignment; ideas are adequately developed, logically organized, and has a strong use of vocabulary, style and grammar
  - — 4: Adequate Essay
    - Fulfills the writing assignment; ideas are adequately represented and has a satisfactory use of grammar and style
  - — 3: Limited Essay
    - Does not adequately fulfill the writing assignment; ideas are not logically organized
  - — 2: Flawed Essay
    - Doesn't fulfill the writing assignment; ideas are vague
  - — 1: Deficient Essay
    - Doesn't fulfill the writing assignment: poor organization, use of vocabulary, grammar and style
  - — 0: Incorrect Essay
    - Essay was not written on the presented topic
- **Essay Writing FAQs:**
  - — How long should the essay be?
    - Aim for 300–450 words but remember that the length of an essay is no assurance of quality
  - — Can I get extra paper?
    - NO
  - — How many examples should I use?
    - Sometimes a single well-developed example can make for a good essay and sometimes it takes two or more. Just make sure not to have underdeveloped examples
  - — What if I'm not a "writer"?
    - Try your best to stay on topic and focus on building a well-supported argument
  - — What's the best subject to write about?
    - Choose examples that you can write about with confidence
    - Do not choose a topic to write about just because it sounds smart

- What's the best way to practice?
  - Write as many practice essays as you can under test-like conditions
- What if English is not my native language?
  - You don't need to write complex sentences
  - Practice reading and understanding the prompts and writing essays
  - Try to leave enough time to proofread your essays

- **Kaplan's Four-Step Method for Essay Writing:**
  - Step 1: Think about the topic (2 minutes)
    - Pick a side
    - Choose your examples
    - Use specific evidence
  - Step 2: Organize your paragraphs (5 minutes)
  - Step 3: Write your essay (15 minutes)
    - Don't write about personal history, if possible
    - Be neat
  - Step 4: Fix any mistakes (3 minutes)

PRACTICE

This is your chance to put TOWF to work. Give yourself 25 minutes to:

THINK about the topic (2 minutes)
ORGANIZE the paragraphs (5 minutes)
WRITE your essay (15 minutes)
FIX any mistakes (3 minutes)

After you finish, read the three sample essays—a strong essay, a mediocre essay, and a weak essay—and the sample grader comments. Use these essays and comments to judge the quality of your own essays.

You will have 25 minutes to write your essay in your test booklet (two pages).

Directions: Think carefully about the issue presented in the following excerpt and the assignment below.

> "Don't flatter yourself that friendship authorizes you to say disagreeable things to your intimates. The nearer you come into relation with a person, the more necessary do tact and courtesy become. Except in cases of necessity, which are rare, leave your friend to learn unpleasant things from his enemies; they are ready enough to tell them."
>
> — Oliver Wendell Holmes, *The Autocrat of the Breakfast-Table*

> "A good friend can tell you what is the matter with you in a minute. He may not seem such a good friend after telling."
>
> — Arthur Brisbane, *The Book of Today*.

Assignment: Should friends be honest with each other, even if a truthful comment could be hurtful? In an essay, support your position by discussing an example (or examples) from literature, science and technology, the arts, current events, or your own experience or observation.

Organize your paragraphs here.

Write your essay here.

SAMPLE ESSAYS

Grade 6 Essay

One of the defining qualities of a good friendship is that both friends can be completely honest with each other. This does not mean that the two friends don't consider each others feelings or blurt out comments without thinking, but it does mean that each person can rely on the other to tell the truth, even if the truth can sometimes be awkward or hurtful.

My sister and I have always been close friends, even when we were younger. When my sister was in junior high school and I was in elementary school, she decided to get her hair permed because all of her friends were doing the same thing. Unfortunately, the treatment didn't work well on her hair and she ended up with a big, frizzy clump of curls that stuck out on the sides. Most of her friends didn't have the courage to tell her that it didn't look good. Instead, they just made fun of her behind her back. So it was up to me to tell her the truth. I was a bit scared to confront my older sister, because I knew that she would be upset. But I also knew that she would be more upset if no one dared to be honest with her. A few years earlier, we were in the opposite roles, and she had gently but firmly advised me against a choice that I later realized would have been embarrassing for me when I started school.

Although my sister was hurt when I told her that the perm didn't look good, she was more hurt to learn that some of her other friends had thought the same thing but hadn't said anything to her. She was angry with me at first for making a negative comment, but in the end she was glad I had told her so that she could go back to the hair stylist to fix the problem. Since my sister was very concerned about her appearance and personal style at that time in her life, she appreciated my honesty because it helped her get through a tough situation and our friendship grew stronger as a result of this experience.

In the years since this incident, my sister and I have both continued to be honest and upfront with each other, and we value this aspect of our relationship. After all, friendly honesty is far better than hostile honesty, so being a good friend involves telling the truth, no matter what the circumstances. Honesty truly is an essential component of a good friendship.

(388 words)

Grader's Comments: The author begins this essay with a clear statement based on the prompt, showing that she has clearly understood the topic. The remainder of the essay presents and develops an example to support her opinion. The example provided is relevant to multiple aspects of the prompt—the importance of honesty in friendship as well as the possibility that being honest can be difficult in certain situations.

The essay is well organized, with a clear narrative flow framed by a cohesive introduction and conclusion. The structure of the essay reflects that the author took time to plan before writing and carefully followed her plan as she composed her essay. Although the vocabulary used in the essay is not very sophisticated, the author's ideas are communicated effectively. Finally, there are few grammatical or spelling errors: *others* instead of *other's* in the first paragraph; a couple of sentences lacking commas in the second and third paragraphs.

This author clearly managed her time effectively so that she could proofread her essay.

Grade 4 Essay

Being honest is part of being a good friend. However, their are times when you shouldn't be completely honest because what you say might hurt your friend's feelings. For example, imagine that your best friend tells you his parents are getting divorced. He is obviously upset by this even though you know his parents haven't been getting along well because he constantly complained about their fights and even joked about hoping they'd get a divorce so he wouldn't have to listen to them anymore.

In this situation, reminding your friend of his earlier comments or pointing out that his parents will be happier apart isn't the right thing to do because at a time like this you're friend doesn't need you to tell him the harsh truth, he needs you to by sympathetic and supportive. It's pretty likely that he'll hear all about the negative things from other people or even from his parents, so your job as his best friend is to try not to say or do anything unpleasant.

Another example could be if you're friend has bought something that she's really excited about. You might not agree that she's made a good choice or you might not like what she bought, but you don't need to spoil her enthusiasm by making a negative comment. Again, this is a time when you should keep quiet about your own opinion so that your friend can be happy.

There are certain situations when it's okay not to tell the complete truth to your friends. You should never lie to your friends, but an important part of being a good friend is knowing when to be totally honest and when to keep silent because a truthful comment could do more harm than good.

(292 words)

Grader's Comments: The author introduces his essay with a clear statement of his opinion, showing that he has understood the prompt. His two examples provide decent support for the topic, but the second example is vague and not well developed. The author would have a stronger essay if he expanded upon the prompt and provided additional details for the first example rather than trying to include a weak second example. Having a clear plan could help to accomplish this change in structure.

The essay is fairly well organized, with several keywords (*However, For example, Another example, Again*) that add structure to the author's argument. The weakest parts of this essay are some simplistic language and awkward sentences: in the second paragraph, the second sentence is long and wordy, and the third sentence is a run-on sentence and is very difficult to follow, so the author's meaning almost gets obscured by the effort it takes to decipher his thoughts. There are also a few usage/spelling errors: *their* instead of *they're* in the first paragraph; *you're* instead of *your* in the second and third paragraphs.

The author needs to be more deliberate when writing the essay and needs to proofread to catch these spelling errors and prevent run-on sentences or awkward sentence structure.

Grade 2 Essay

No matter what, friends should tell each other the truth. That's the whole point of having friends, so you have some people around you that you can trust and talk to and that you know will tell you everything. Friends can tell you negative things in a kind way so you can here the truth even if its not so good. Enemies tell you the same negative things in a mean way because their trying to hurt you. But friends can accomplish this in a nicer way.

Its important to know and learn the truth even if its about yourself or its something you don't want to face. You need honest friends to tell you the truth, because they do it out of love not hate like enemies.

(128 words)

Grader's Comments: This author starts strongly with a clear statement of her opinion, which is directly related to the topic of the prompt. However, the author continues with a series of generalizations, none of which are specific examples to support her opinion. She needs to spend more time planning her essay to make sure that she's got at least one strong example to include to support her argument.

This essay does not follow an organized structure, and it lacks good transitions and keywords. To improve this part of her writing, the author should make an outline during her planning stage and should focus on using several keywords while she writes, which will give her essay a stronger and clearer structure.

The author's language is simplistic and repetitive. The essay contains several grammatical and spelling errors: *that* twice instead of *whom/who* when referring to *people* in the first paragraph; *here* and *their* are misused for *hear* and *they're* in the second paragraph; *its* is misused numerous times for *it's* in the second and third paragraphs. The author should study the SAT grammar materials to improve this aspect of her writing and should also be sure to proofread to avoid careless errors.

Step Five

Multiple-Choice Questions

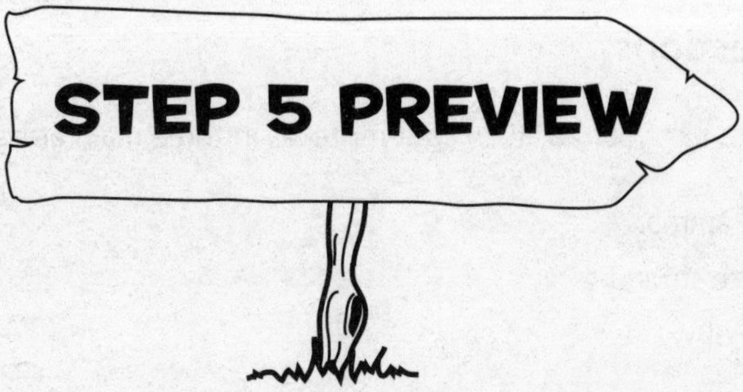

The Gist of it

- Usage Questions
- Sentence Correction Questions
- Paragraph Correction Questions

How to Get a High Score

- Kaplan's Four-Step Method for Usage Questions
- Kaplan's Four-Step Method for Sentence Correction Questions
- Kaplan's Five-Step Method for Paragraph Correction Questions

Summary

Practice

Answers and Explanations

Each of the SAT Writing multiple-choice question types is based on your catching mistakes and fixing errors (or not) in sentences and short paragraphs. In this chapter, we'll show you how you can catch and, if necessary, fix them.

Let's deal with each question type one by one.

THE GIST OF IT

Usage Questions

Usage questions test your ability to spot mistakes in three main areas of written English:

- Basic grammar
- Sentence structure
- Choice of words

Remember, the Writing section measures your ability to recognize acceptable and unacceptable uses of *written* English. Standard *written* English is a bit more formal than the average person's spoken English. Things that you're used to saying in everyday conversation may well be considered wrong when you write them down.

Standard written English is the kind of English that you find in textbooks and the kind of English your professors will expect you to use on college papers. That's why they test it on the SAT.

Directions

The directions for Usage questions will look pretty much like this:

> **Directions:** The following sentences contain problems in grammar, usage, diction (choice of words), and idiom.
>
> Some of the sentences are correct.
> No sentence contains more than one error.
>
> You will find that the error, if there is one, is underlined and lettered. Elements of the sentence that are not underlined will not be changed. In choosing answers, follow the requirements of standard written English.
>
> If there is an error, select the one underlined part that must be changed to make the sentence correct and fill in the corresponding oval on your answer sheet.
> If there is no error, fill in answer oval (E).

Example:

Although the number of firms declaring
A
bankruptcy keep growing, the mayor claims that the
B C
city is thriving. No error
D E

Spot the Mistake!

All Usage questions are "Spot-the-Mistake" type questions. You're given a sentence with four words or phrases underlined. The underlined parts are labeled (A) through (D). One of the underlined pieces may contain a grammar mistake. You're supposed to spot it and fill in the corresponding oval on your grid. If the sentence is mistake-free, the correct answer is (E), *No error*.

You need to decide which, if any, underlined word or phrase needs to be changed to make the sentence grammatically correct. You should assume that the parts of the sentence that are not underlined are correct because they cannot be changed.

Sentence Correction Questions

Whereas the errors in the Usage questions consist of single words or short phrases, the errors in the Sentence Correction questions generally involve the structure of the whole sentence. Thus, they can be a little harder than Usage questions. No need to worry though, because we have strategies to help you beat these tough questions. However, knowing the format is half the battle.

Directions

The directions for Sentence Correction questions will look pretty much like the directions that follow. Read them now so that you don't have to waste time trying to figure out what to do with Sentence Correction questions on test day.

> **Directions:** The following sentences test correctness and effectiveness of expression. In choosing answers, follow the requirements of standard written English; that is, pay attention to grammar, choice of words, sentence construction, and punctuation.
>
> In each of the following sentences, part of the sentence or the entire sentence is underlined. Beneath each sentence you will find five ways of phrasing the underlined part. Choice A repeats the original; the other four are different.
>
> Choose the answer that best expresses the meaning of the original sentence. If you think the original is better than any of the alternatives, choose it; otherwise, choose one of the others. Your choice should produce the most effective sentence—clear and precise, without awkwardness or ambiguity.

Example:

> The Emancipation Edict freed the Russian serfs in 1861; that being four years before the Thirteenth Amendment abolished slavery in the United States.
>
> (A) in 1861; that being four years
> (B) in 1861 and is four years
> (C) in 1861 and this amounts to four years
> (D) in 1861, being four years
> (E) in 1861, four years

Fix the Mistake!

Remember our "Spot-the-Mistake" strategy from the Usage section? We've got a similar strategy for Sentence Corrections. We call Sentence Correction questions "Fix-the-Mistake" questions because, in addition to finding the mistake in each sentence, you have to pick the answer choice that best corrects it. Like we said, a little harder.

In each of these questions, you're given a sentence, part or all of which is underlined. There are five answer choices: the first one reproduces the underlined part of the sentence exactly, and the other four rephrase the underlined portion in various ways.

You have to pick the best choice to replace the underlined portion of the sentence. The correct answer must produce a sentence that's not only grammatically correct, but also effective: it must be clear, precise, and free of awkward verbiage. (Don't know what awkward verbiage is? Anything that sounds like the phrase "awkward verbiage.")

Paragraph Correction Questions

Paragraph Correction questions follow short essays that are three to five paragraphs long. The short essays can be about any topic. You do not have to know anything about the topic. Most Paragraph Correction questions ask you to clean up awkward and ambiguous sentences. The most important thing with these questions is their *context*. You can't determine the best way to repair bad sentences without knowing what comes before and after them.

A few Paragraph Correction questions will also ask you about the overall organization of the essay. Again, context is critical. You can't, for example, decide which of five sentences best concludes an essay without knowing what the essay is all about.

Directions

Here they are. You know the drill.

Directions: The passage below is an early draft of an essay. Parts of the passage need to be rewritten.

Read the passage and answer the questions that follow. Some questions are about individual sentences or parts of sentences; in these questions, you are asked to select the choice that will improve sentence structure and word choice. Other questions refer to parts of the essay or the entire essay and ask you to consider the organization and development of the essay. You should follow the conventions of standard written English in answering the questions. After you have chosen your answer, fill in the corresponding oval on your answer sheet.

There are three basic types of Paragraph Correction questions:

- General organization questions
- Revising sentences questions
- Combining sentences questions

General Organization Questions

If you've got a firm grasp of the essay after your first read through it, you should jump right to the general organization questions. Do these questions while the essay is fresh in your mind. On the other hand, if your grasp of the essay is a bit shaky, work on general organization questions last. Start with questions that ask you to revise or combine sentences. Doing so should improve your grasp of the overall essay, making it easier for you to tackle the general organization questions later.

Revising Sentences Questions

Take a look at the following paragraph and question. The question focuses on a single word in one sentence, but to answer this typical example of a revision question, you'll need to reread the entire paragraph.

> **(1)** The Spanish-American War was one of the shortest and most decisive wars ever fought. **(2)** The postwar settlement, the Treaty of Paris, reflected the results of the fighting. **(3)** Under its terms, Spain was compelled to cede large territories in North America and the Pacific. **(4)** The United States gained control over some of these territories, including Puerto Rico and Guam. **(5)** It was reduced in status from a major to a minor power. **(6)** The United States, in contrast, emerged from the war as a world power, and would soon go on to become a major participant in Asian and European affairs.

In context, which is the best version of the underlined part of sentence 5?
It was reduced in status from a major to a minor power.

(A) (As it is now)
(B) Spain was reduced
(C) The war caused Spain to be reduced
(D) As a result of the war, it had been reduced
(E) It had now been reduced [Answer: B]

Sentence 5 refers to Spain's status. That much should have been clear to you by reading sentences 2, 3, 4, and 6. The pronoun *it*, however, makes sentence 5 ambiguous. What does *it* refer to? To make this sentence less ambiguous, *it* should be changed to the noun *Spain*. That leaves (B) and (C) as possible correct answers. Because (B) is a more concise and less awkward construction than (C), (B) is correct.

Combining Sentences

Take a look at the following paragraph and question.

> **(6)** Albert Einstein was a great physicist. **(7)** He won a Nobel Prize in Physics. **(8)** He got the prize for his research into the photoelectric effect. **(9)** Later physicists demonstrated the validity of Einstein's ideas.

Which of the following is the best way to combine sentences 7 and 8?
He won a Nobel Prize in Physics. He got the prize for his research into the photoelectric effect.

(A) The Nobel Prize in Physics that he won was for his research into the photoelectric effect.
(B) Having researched the photoelectric effect, he won a Nobel Prize in Physics.
(C) He won a Nobel Prize in Physics for his research into the photoelectric effect.
(D) He got the prize in physics, the Noble Prize in Physics, for his research into the photoelectric effect.
(E) Because of his research into the photoelectric effect he got the Nobel Prize in Physics. [Answer: C]

Did you choose (C)? It's the best written and most economical of the choices. Whether you're asked to revise or combine sentences, the correct answer will often (but not always) be the shortest answer. Good writing is concise.

HOW TO GET A HIGH SCORE

Kaplan's Four-Step Method for Usage Questions

To tackle Usage questions, Kaplan's test experts have devised a four-step method that will guide you in answering these types of questions. The four steps are as follows:

Step 1. Read the whole sentence, *listening* for the mistake.

Step 2. If you clearly hear the mistake, choose it and move on.

Step 3. If not, read each underlined choice, and eliminate choices that contain no errors.

Step 4. Choose from the remaining choices (don't be afraid to choose E).

Try this out on our earlier example. Start by reading it to yourself.

Although (A) the number of firms declaring bankruptcy keep (B) growing, the mayor claims that (C) the city is thriving. (D) No error (E)

Did you hear the mistake? If so, your work is done, fill in the appropriate oval, and move on. If you didn't hear the mistake on the first reading, go back, read each underlined part, and start eliminating underlined parts that are right.

The word *although* seems fine in this context. The word *keep* is a plural verb, but its subject is *number*, which is singular. That seems to be a mistake. The phrase *claims that* sounds all right; it has a singular verb for a singular subject, *mayor*. Similarly, *is thriving* sounds all right, and it too provides a singular verb for the singular subject *city*. Choice (B) contains the mistake, so (B) is the correct answer.

This is a classic example of subject–verb agreement, which is a common question type in the Writing section. It's so much easier to spot errors when you know what to look for, so it would benefit you to go over some common grammar rules.

Keep in mind that not all the Usage questions on the Writing section contain errors. When you're reading a sentence just to spot mistakes, don't insist that they're there. Don't fall into the trap of spotting mistakes where there are none. Remember, choice (E), No error, is the correct answer to Usage questions about ONE in FIVE times. If you find that you have chosen (E) only once or twice, chances are you're spotting mistakes that aren't there.

Kaplan's Four-Step Method for Sentence Correction Questions

Step 1. Read the sentence carefully and listen for a mistake.

Step 2. Identify the error or errors.

Step 3. Predict a correction.

Step 4. Check the choices for a match that doesn't introduce a new error.

Let's use the method on the example on page 73.

Step 1. Read the Sentence Carefully, and Listen for a Mistake

The stem sentence (sentence in question) in the example just doesn't sound right.

Step 2. Identify the Error or Errors

The semicolon and phrase *that being* sound like the wrong way of joining the two parts of the sentence.

Step 3. Predict a Correction

The semicolon and *that being* seem unnecessary. Joining the two sentence fragments with a simple comma would probably work. Plug in your choice to be sure it sounds best.

Step 4. Check the Choices for a Match that Doesn't Introduce a New Error

Choice (E) has just a comma. Is that enough? All the answer choices begin with *in 1861* and end with *four years*, so you have to look at what comes in between to see what forms the best link. Scan the choices, and you'll find that *and is* in (B), *this amounts to* in (C), and *being*, preceded by a comma, in (D) are no better than (A) because they are wordy and awkward phrases. Choice (E) is the best way to rewrite the underlined portion of the sentence, so (E) is the correct answer.

Remember, not every sentence contains an error. Choice (A) is correct about ONE in FIVE times. In any event, because you should begin by reading the original sentence carefully, you should never waste time reading choice (A).

Kaplan's Five-Step Method for Paragraph Correction Questions

Kaplan's method works for all three kinds of Paragraph Correction questions.

Step 1. Read the passage quickly for the overall idea and tone.

Step 2. Read the question.

Step 3. Reread relevant portion and its context.

Step 4. Predict the correction.

Step 5. Check for a match that doesn't introduce a new error.

Step 1. Read the Passage Quickly for the Overall Idea and Tone

Read the entire passage quickly. Get a sense of the passage's overall main idea, as well as the main idea of each paragraph. This will come in handy when you're asked to answer questions about the passage as a whole.

Step 2. Read the Question

Now read the question closely. Make sure that you understand exactly what you're asked to do. Questions that require you to revise or combine sentences will supply you with the sentences or sentence numbers. Questions that ask about the entire essay generally won't refer to specific sentences.

Step 3. Reread the Relevant Portion and its Context

Go back and reread that sentence or two that the question is about. But don't stop there. This next part is very important! Also *reread the sentences before and after the target sentence(s).* This will provide you with the context (the surrounding ideas or information) for the sentence(s). Context helps you to choose the best answer from the answer choices.

For those questions about the essay as a whole, skim quickly over the entire essay to re-familiarize yourself with its contents.

Step 4. Predict the Correction

Say in your head what you think the correct sentence or answer should be.

Step 5. Check for a Match that Doesn't Introduce a New Error

Go to the answer choices and pick the choice that best matches the sentence or idea in your head. Make sure the one you pick doesn't introduce a new mistake if you are correcting a sentence.

To summarize: read the essay quickly; read the question; reread the target sentences and the sentences that surround them; make up a sentence that would eliminate the mistake; and choose the answer choice that best matches your sentence. The following practice set will help you get a handle on this approach and the methods for the other two question types.

SUMMARY

- **The Gist of It:**
  - — Usage Questions
    - Tests your ability in basic grammar, sentence structure, and choice of words
    - All usage questions are "spot the mistake" type questions—you need to decide if any of the underlined words or phrases need to be changed to make the sentence grammatically correct
  - — Sentence Correction Questions
    - Involve the structure of the whole sentence
    - All sentence correction questions are "fix-the-mistake" type questions—in addition to spotting the mistake in each sentence, you have to pick the answer choice that best corrects it
  - — Paragraph Correction Questions
    - Ask you to fix awkward and ambiguous sentences
    - The most important thing about these questions is their context
    - Includes general organization questions, revising sentences questions, and combining sentences questions
- **Kaplan's Four-Step Method for Usage Questions:**
  - — Step 1: Read the whole sentence, listening for the mistake
  - — Step 2: If you clearly hear the mistake, choose it and move on
  - — Step 3: If not, read each underlined choice and eliminate choices that contain no errors
  - — Step 4: Choose from the remaining choices
- **Kaplan's Four-Step Method for Sentence Correction Questions:**
  - — Step 1: Read the sentence carefully and listen for a mistake
  - — Step 2: Identify the error or errors
  - — Step 3: Predict a correction
  - — Step 4: Check the choices for a match that doesn't introduce a new error
- **Kaplan's Five-Step Method for Paragraph Correction Questions:**
  - — Step1: Read the passage quickly for the overall idea and tone
  - — Step 2: Read the question
  - — Step 3: Reread the relevant portion and its context
    - For the questions that ask about the essay as a hole, quickly skim over the entire passage again
  - — Step 4: Predict the correction
  - — Step 5: Check for a match that doesn't introduce a new error

PRACTICE

1. Raoul gave Frederick very little warning before striking (A) a match and setting fire to his (B) entire collection of documents, which (C) had been painstakingly (D) compiled over the course of several decades. No error (E)

2. Diabetes can strike anyone, irregardless (A) of age; nevertheless, (B) many people still make (C) the mistake of considering (D) it a geriatric disease. No error (E)

3. At (A) the counseling center, a person (B) should feel free to (C) express their true emotions without fear of (D) ridicule or reprisal. No error (E)

4. We expect (A) this election to be hotly contested, (B) since already (C) both the incumbent and her challenger have complained (D) of negative campaigning. No error (E)

5. The first public school in North America, Boston Latin School, begun teaching (A) its (B) classical curriculum in 1635, one year before (C) Harvard University was founded. (D) No error (E)

6. The point at issue was whether (A) the dock workers, which (B) were an extremely vocal group, (C) would decide to return (D) to work. No error (E)

7. Lost in the forest (A) on a cold night, the hunters built (B) a fire to keep themselves (C) warm and to frighten away (D) the wolves. No error (E)

8. Drinking carbonated beverages (A) and eating food that (B) contain (C) chemical preservatives can be unhealthy when indulged in to excess. (D) No error (E)

9. In the United States, an increasing number of commuters that believe their families to be immune from the perils of city life.

(A) that believe their families to be
(B) that believe their families are
(C) believes their families are
(D) who believe their families to be
(E) believe their families to be

10. The ancient Chinese were convinced that air was composed of two kinds of particles, one inactive and one active, the latter of which they called yin and we today call oxygen.

(A) one inactive and one active, the latter of which they called yin and we today call oxygen
(B) an inactive and an active one called yin, now known as oxygen
(C) an inactive type and the active type they called yin we now know to be oxygen
(D) inactive and active; while they called the active type yin, today we call it oxygen
(E) contrasting the inactive type with the active ones they named yin and we call oxygen

11. Even after becoming blind, the poet John Milton's daughters took dictation of his epic poem Paradise Lost.

(A) the poet John Milton's daughters took dictation of his epic poem *Paradise Lost*
(B) the poet John Milton's daughters taking dictation, his epic poem *Paradise Lost* was written
(C) the epic poem *Paradise Lost* was dictated by the poet John Milton to his daughters
(D) the epic poem *Paradise Lost* was dictated to his daughters by the poet John Milton
(E) the poet John Milton dictated his epic poem *Paradise Lost* to his daughters

12. Historians of literacy encounter a fundamental obstacle, no one can know for certain how many people could read in earlier centuries.

(A) obstacle, no one can know for certain
(B) obstacle; no one can know for certain
(C) obstacle; no one being able to know for certain
(D) obstacle; none of whom can know with certainty
(E) obstacle and no one can know for certain

13. Once an enclave of privileged white males, the Wodehouse Club's directors have now decided to adopt a more inclusive membership policy.

(A) Once an enclave of privileged white males, the Wodehouse Club's directors have
(B) The directors of the Wodehouse Club, which was once an enclave of privileged white males, have
(C) Though once an enclave of privileged white males, the Wodehouse Club's directors
(D) Once an enclave of privileged white males, the Wodehouse Club's directors having
(E) The directors of the enclave of privileged white males, the Wodehouse Club, has

14. Finland's national epic, the *Kalevala*, based on an oral tradition that the Balto-Finnish people preserved for some 2,500 years despite the upheavals of history and the pressures of foreign domination.

(A) based on an oral tradition that
(B) being based on an oral tradition that
(C) is based on an oral tradition; this
(D) basing itself on an oral tradition which
(E) is based on an oral tradition that

15. Had Churchill sent planes to defend Coventry from the German air raid, the Nazis would have realized that their secret code had been broken by the Allies.

    (A) Had Churchill sent planes to defend Coventry
    (B) If Churchill would have sent planes to defend Coventry
    (C) Churchill having sent planes to defend Coventry
    (D) If Churchill sent planes to defend Coventry
    (E) Churchill, by sending planes to Coventry to defend it

16. After depositing and burying her eggs, the female sea turtle returns to the water, never to view or nurture the offspring that she is leaving behind.

    (A) never to view or nurture the offspring that she is leaving behind
    (B) never to view or nurture the offspring which she had left behind
    (C) never to view nor nurture the offspring that are being left behind
    (D) never to view or nurture the offspring she has left behind
    (E) never to view or nurture the offspring who she has left behind

Questions 17–20 are based on the following essay, which is a response to an assignment to write about the foreign policy of the United States.

(**1**) Recent events in the Middle East have once again led to calls for the United States to resolve an international conflict. (**2**) The last great superpower, the nations of the world expect the U.S. to use its military force to restore peace wherever war breaks out. (**3**) Like some hero in a Clint Eastwood film, the U.S. is in a unique position to dictate global justice and play peacemaker to the world. (**4**) But should the U.S. continue to play this role?

(**5**) The arguments for playing the peacemaker role are inextricably linked to our democratic beliefs. (**6**) Throughout history, the people of the U.S. have struggled against oppression for more fair and democratic society. (**7**) In the War of Independence, for example, Americans overthrew the tyranny of a British government. (**8**) In the Civil Rights movement of the 1960s, Black people fought for equal status in American society. (**9**) We have fought hard for our democratic rights consequently we believe that every country in the world deserves the same. (**10**) But our beliefs in democracy and equality does not mean we should get involved in every situation. (**11**) The War of Vietnam showed that even for a country so powerful as the United States, not every battle can be won. (**12**) After Vietnam, the U.S. has clearly been trying to minimize its use of force to solve international crises. (**13**) In addition, where military intervention is inevitable, other countries have been involved in diplomatic and military initiatives. (**14**) In the Gulf War and the War in the former Yugoslavia, the U.S led a group of major countries in the attempt to restore order. (**15**) This was beneficial because many European countries have been content to take a back seat in such conflicts—even when the bloodshed is occurring very close to them. (**16**) Rather than playing the lone peacemaker, the U.S. should be a team leader in world affairs—working with other powers in the search for freedom.

17. Which of the following versions of sentence 4 (reproduced below) provides the most effective transition between the first and second paragraphs?

    But should the U.S. continue to play this role?

    (A) (As it is now.)
    (B) This is just as it should be, for who else would do it?
    (C) I believe that it is time for the U.S. to relinquish this role.
    (D) The arguments for the U.S. taking this role are irrefutable.
    (E) And the U.S is also expected to send aid to less fortunate countries.

18. Which of the following is the best revision of sentence 9 (reproduced below)?

    We have fought hard for our democratic rights consequently we believe that every country in the world deserves the same.

    (A) (As it is now)
    (B) Having fought hard for our democratic rights, we consequently believed that every country in the world deserves the same.
    (C) We have fought hard for our democratic rights, and we believe that every country in the world also deserves those rights.
    (D) We have fought hard for our democratic rights, therefore we believe that every country in the world deserves the same.
    (E) Not only have we fought hard for our democratic rights, but we also have the belief that every country in the world deserves to fight for their rights, too.

19. Which of the following would be the most logical place to introduce a paragraph break (ending one paragraph and beginning a new one)?

    (A) Between sentences 6 and 7
    (B) Between sentences 8 and 9
    (C) Between sentences 9 and 10
    (D) Between sentences 10 and 11
    (E) Between sentences 11 and 12

20. All of the following strategies are used by the author of the passage EXCEPT

    (A) making an analogy
    (B) using a rhetorical question
    (C) referring to historical examples
    (D) analyzing both sides of an issue
    (E) quoting the views of politicians

Questions 21–24 are based on the following essay, which was written in response to an assignment to write a letter to the editor of a local newspaper.

(1) I agree with the school board's recent decision to require high school students to complete a community service requirement before graduating. **(2)** As a student who has both worked and volunteered, my volunteer experience has truly enriched me as a person. **(3)** When I worked at a hamburger joint all I was caring about was the money. **(4)** Tutoring disadvantaged children taught me to appreciate how much I have.

(5) Volunteering teaches you different lessons than working for pay does. **(6)** Your paycheck is not your motivation but something higher. **(7)** In today's consumer-oriented society, it is especially important that students learn to value something other than material things. **(8)** Taking care of elderly patients at a hospital can teach them respect for age. **(9)** Getting together with a nonprofit group to clean up abandoned neighborhoods can teach them the importance of teamwork and of doing good for others. **(10)** There is simply no way they can get so many good lessons out of the types of paying jobs available to them. **(11)** This is why I support the school board's decision. **(12)** Furthermore, it is feasible for low-income students, despite what critics have said.

21. Which of the following is the best way to revise the underlined portion of sentence 2 (reproduced below)?

As a student who has both worked and volunteered, my volunteer experience has truly enriched me as a person.

(A) my experience as a volunteer has been the thing that has truly enriched me as a person

(B) I have truly been enriched by my volunteer experience

(C) it is by volunteering that I have truly become an enriched person

(D) I will have truly been enriched by my volunteer experience

(E) that which has truly enriched me as a person is my volunteer experience

22. In context, which is the best way to revise and combine the underlined portions of sentences 3 and 4 (reproduced below)?

When I worked at a hamburger joint all I was caring about was the money. Tutoring disadvantaged children taught me to appreciate how much I have.

(A) Working at a hamburger joint, it was only the money that mattered to me, and tutoring disadvantaged children

(B) While working at a hamburger joint all I was caring about was the money, until tutoring disadvantaged children

(C) Although the money was the only thing that mattered to me while working at a hamburger joint, when I tutored disadvantaged children

(D) Despite working at the hamburger joint, where all I was caring about was the money, by contrast when I was tutoring disadvantaged children

(E) When I worked at a hamburger joint all I cared about was the money, but tutoring disadvantaged children

23. In context, which version of sentence 6 (reproduced below) is the clearest?

Your paycheck is not your motivation but some-thing higher.

(A) (As it is now)

(B) Your paycheck is not what motivates you but it is something higher.

(C) You are motivated not by your paycheck but by something higher.

(D) Your paycheck is not what you are being motivated by but something higher.

(E) Not your paycheck, something higher, is your motivation.

24. The author could best improve sentence 12 by

(A) explaining how the requirement is feasible for low-income students

(B) including a definition of "low income"

(C) outlining other criticisms of the proposal

(D) providing examples of volunteer opportunities

(E) acknowledging the opinions of high school students

ANSWERS AND EXPLANATIONS

1. B

Whose collection of documents was it? It is not clear from the sentence whether *his* refers to Raoul or to Frederick; hence, this is a case of vague pronoun reference.

2. A

There is no such word as *irregardless*. People who make this mistake are probably conflating *irrespective* and *regardless*, either of which would be correct here.

3. B

The subject should be the plural noun *people* in order to agree in number with the pronoun *their*.

4. E

This sentence contains no error.

5. A

Even if you didn't know that a past participle can't stand alone, *begun* should still have sounded wrong to you.

6. B

The pronoun *which* should never be used to refer to people. *Which* should be changed to *who*.

7. E

This sentence contains no error.

8. C

The subject of contain is *food*, which is singular. So, the sentence should say *contains*.

9. E

In the original form of the sentence, the word *that* forms a dependent clause and leaves the sentence without a main verb. The main verb should be *believe*, which is plural because its subject is *commuters*.

10. D

This sentence contains a great deal of information. Choice (D) is the most successful in conveying that information clearly and logically.

11. B

John Milton has to be the subject of the sentence. The introductory phrase in this sentence can't modify anything else.

12. E

A semicolon separates two complete, but related, sentences.

13. B

The sentence contains a misplaced modifier: *Once an enclave of privileged white males* refers to the *Wodehouse Club*, not to its *directors*. Choice (B) correctly places the modifying phrase right next to the thing it's describing. (C) and (D) do not correct the misplaced modifier, and (D) is a fragment. (E) is poorly worded, and the verb *has* does not agree with the subject, *directors*.

14. E

To correct this sentence fragment, all you need to do is insert the helping verb *is* before the participle *based*. *Based*, *being based*, and *basing* are all verb forms that cannot stand on their own as a sentence's main verb.

15. A

The first clause of the sentence correctly sets up a condition that was not fulfilled: Churchill did not send planes to defend Coventry, and hence, the Nazis did not realize the Allies had broken their code. Choice (A) is another way of saying *If Churchill had sent planes to defend Coventry*. (B) is grammatically unsound: *if he would have* is a very common error. Watch out for it! (C) and (E) are fragments, and (D) uses a wrong verb tense (*sent* for the past perfect *had sent*).

16. D

The present perfect *has left* makes the sequence of events clearer than the present progressive *is leaving*. Note that *nor* in (C) is wrong.

17. A

The question is an effective rhetorical device here. In effect, the rest of the essay is spent trying to answer it. The author goes on to examine both sides of the issue, presenting the pros and cons of designating the United States as the world's peacekeeper, and finally decides on a qualified "no" answer. (B) is inconsi-stent with the author's logic in the second half of the essay. (C) does not provide an effective transition; it's too much of a jarring contrast to the next few sentences, in which the author enumerates the reasons for America's traditional role as peacekeeper. (D) is inconsistent with the author's logic (the author does, in fact, refute these arguments). (E) strays far from the topic of the essay, in extraneous and irrele-vant information.

18. C

The sentence as it stands is a run-on, and if you look closely, you'll notice that it's also slightly illogical. It's saying that because we fought for our rights, we believe that every country deserves the same—to fight for its rights! The two ideas are closely related, but the second is not a direct result of the first. Rather, both things (one, that we fought for our democratic rights, and two, that we think other people deserve democratic rights) are a consequence of our general belief that equality is a good thing. Therefore, *and* is a better connecting word here—choice (C). (D) merely reproduces the original error (run-on), (B) retains the ambiguity of the original sentence, and (E) is illogical, wordy, and awkward.

19. C

In the first half of paragraph 2, the author presents the arguments for America's playing a peacemaker role. With sentence 10, the author shifts gears and begins presenting the counter-argument. The rest of the passage builds a case *against* America's playing the sole peacekeeper and intervening in every situation. Therefore, this would be the most logical place for a paragraph break: whenever you introduce a new idea, topic, or line of reasoning, you should begin a new paragraph. You might have been tempted to pick (D), placing the transition sentence at the end of paragraph 2 rather than at the beginning of paragraph 3. However, this choice would leave the final paragraph without a topic sentence, and readers would think that sentence 10 was introducing a paragraph about Vietnam.

20. E

Though the passage is about foreign policy, the author doesn't quote the views of specific politicians anywhere in the passage—so (E)'s the answer here. Let's check off the remaining choices. The author uses (A), an analogy, (comparing the United States to the hero in a Clint Eastwood movie) as well as a rhetorical question, (B), in sentence 4. The entire essay consists of an analysis of two sides of an issue (C), and there are plenty of examples drawn from U.S. history.

21. B

The sentence contains a dangling modifier: my volunteer experience cannot be modified by a clause beginning, "*As a student*...." (B) fixes this problem by recasting the sentence so that *I* is the subject. Of the wrong choices, only (D) correctly uses *I* as the subject, but (D)'s use of the future tense is inconsistent with the rest of the sentence.

22. E

(E) corrects the inconsistency in tense and skillfully conveys the sense of contrast between the two clauses with the conjunction *but*. Choice (A) contains a misplaced modifier. The clause, *Working at a hamburger joint*, which describes the author, must be followed by *I*, not *it*, and does not convey an idea of contrast. (B), too, contains a misplaced modifier, and its use of *until* changes the original meaning of the sentence. (C) is incorrect in context because of its use of *when*. (D) is also incorrect in context because of its use of *when*; moreover, its use of *Despite* is inappropriate.

23. C

Although it is clear from the context that the author means one is motivated by something higher than a mere paycheck, in the sentence as written it sounds as though it is the paycheck—not the motivation—that is something higher. (C) is the only choice that clearly conveys the correct meaning. (B), (D), and (E) have the same problem in meaning as the original sentience; moreover, (D) is unnecessarily wordy and (E) is awkward and grammatically incorrect.

24. A

Sentence 12 brings up an entirely new idea at the end of the essay and would therefore be best improved if it expanded on this idea, as (A) suggests. As for (B), there is no need for a definition of low income, because this is a commonly used term. Including other criticisms would only introduce more new ideas at the last minute, so (C) is no good. (D) fails because the author gives examples of volunteer opportunities elsewhere in the essay. Finally, (E) is out because student opinion is irrelevant.

Step Six

The 21 Most Common Grammar Errors

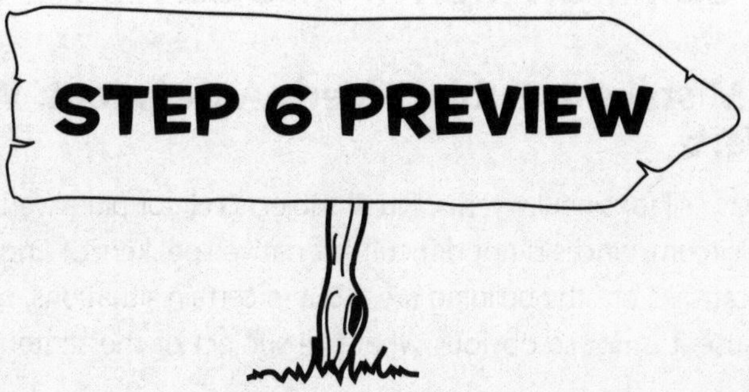

16 Most Common Identifying Sentence Error Mistakes

- Common Mistake 1: Subject–Verb Agreement: When Subject Follows Verb
- Common Mistake 2: Subject–Verb Agreement: When Subject and Verb are Separated
- Common Mistake 3: Subject–Verb Agreement: When the Subject Seems Plural
- Common Mistake 4: Confusion of Simple Past and Past Participle
- Common Mistake 5: Confusion of Infinitive and Gerund
- Common Mistake 6: Nonidiomatic Preposition After Verb
- Common Mistake 7: Wrong Word
- Common Mistake 8: Wrong Tense
- Common Mistake 9: Number Agreement Problems
- Common Mistake 10: Pronoun in the Wrong Number
- Common Mistake 11: Pronoun in the Wrong Case in Compound Noun Phrases
- Common Mistake 12: Pronoun Shift
- Common Mistake 13: Pronoun With Ambiguous Reference
- Common Mistake 14: Faulty Comparison
- Common Mistake 15: Misuse of Adjective or Adverb
- Common Mistake 16: Double Negative

5 Most Common Improving Sentence Errors

- Common Mistake 1: Run-on Sentences
- Common Mistake 2: Sentence Fragments
- Common Mistake 3: Misplaced Modifiers
- Common Mistake 4: Faulty Parallelism
- Common Mistake 5: Faulty Coordination/Subordination

Wordiness: How to Avoid it

Summary

Although the SAT Writing questions will test your knowledge of grammar and usage, you won't have to recite any rules on the exam. In fact, you don't have to know all the rules perse; you just have to be able to recognize when something is not correct. So instead of trying to review all of the rules, we'll show you the top errors you need to watch out for on the SAT. Once you are used to seeing these mistakes, you'll have an easier time spotting them on Test Day.

16 MOST COMMON IDENTIFYING SENTENCE ERROR MISTAKES

Common Mistake 1: Subject–Verb Agreement: When Subject Follows Verb

Singular subjects call for singular verbs. Plural subjects call for plural verbs. Subject–verb agreement under normal circumstances is not difficult for native speakers of English. You know better than to say "Americans is" or "the building are." But in certain situations, subject–verb agreement can be tricky because it is not so obvious what the subject of the sentence is.

For example, it's tricky when the subject comes after the verb, as it does in a clause beginning with the word "there." Take a look at the following:

> Despite an intensive campaign to encourage conservation, there is many Americans who have not accepted recycling as a way of life.

This sentence demonstrates one of *the most common* of all subject–verb agreement errors found on the Writing section. It generally occurs once or twice on the test. The subject of the sentence is not "there." The subject is "Americans," which is plural. Therefore, the singular verb is incorrect; "is" should be replaced by the plural verb "are."

Here's another example in which the subject follows the verb.

> High above the Hudson River rises the gleaming skyscrapers of Manhattan.

This sentence is tricky because there is a singular noun, "the Hudson River," before the verb "rises." But the later noun "skyscrapers" is actually the subject. Think about it. What's doing the rising? Not the river, the skyscrapers. The subject is plural, and so the verb should be "rise."

Common Mistake 2: Subject–Verb Agreement: When Subject and Verb are Separated

The SAT has another way to complicate a simple thing like subject–verb agreement. They insert some additional information about the subject before the verb appears.

Expect to see *at least* one question like this on the Writing section.

The local congressman, a reliable representative of both community and statewide interests, are among the most respected persons in the public sector.

The way to determine whether the verb agrees with the subject is to identify the subject of the sentence. You see the plural "community and statewide interests" right in front of the verb "are," but that's not the subject. It's part of the modifying phrase that's inserted between the subject "congressman," which is singular, and the verb, which should also be singular, "is."

Don't let intervening phrases fool you! In the example above, the commas were a tip-off that the verb was separated from the subject. Another tip-off is a preposition such as "of":

The collection of paintings entitled "Clammy Clam Clams" are one of the most widely traveled exhibits in recent years.

Again, you should first find the subject of the sentence. The subject is "collection." The phrases that follow the subject, e.g., "of paintings" and "entitled 'Clammy Clam Clams,'" merely modify (or describe) the subject. The true subject is singular, and so the verb should be "is."

The SAT writers like this type of question because the intervening modifying phrases or clauses can cause you to lose track of the subject. These phrases simply modify the subject they follow, without changing its number. Don't be fooled by the placement of these intervening phrases.

Common Mistake 3: Subject–Verb Agreement: When the Subject Seems Plural

Sometimes the sentence includes what seems to be, but in fact is not, a plural subject. Tricky, eh? Here's an example.

Neither ambient techno nor trance were a part of mainstream listening habits in the United States 10 years ago.

This sentence is tough because it has two subjects, but these two singular subjects do not add up to a plural subject. When the subject of a sentence is in the form "neither _____ nor ____" or in the form "either _____ or ____" and the nouns in the blanks are singular, the verb should be singular. In the sentence above, it's as if "ambient techno" and "trance" act as subjects one at a time. Thus, the verb should be the singular "was." If the nouns in a neither–nor or either–or construction are plural, then a plural verb is correct.

Here are some other constructions that seem to make plural (compound) subjects but actually don't.

- _____ along with _____
- _____ as well as _____
- _____ in addition to _____

In these constructions, the noun in the first blank is the true subject and what follows is, grammatically speaking, just an intervening modifying phrase. If the first noun is singular, the verb should be singular. Look at this sentence, for example.

> Poor pitching, along with injuries and defensive lapses, are among the problems that plagued last year's championship team.

The phrase "along with injuries and defensive lapses" is a modifying phrase that separates the subject "poor pitching" from the verb "are." This sentence is tricky because there seem to be three problems that plagued the baseball team. But, in fact, phrases like "along with" or in "addition to" do not work in the same way as the conjunction "and" does. If the above sentence had begun "Poor pitching, injuries, *and* defensive lapses," the plural verb "are" would have been correct. However, as written, the sentence has only one subject, "poor pitching," and its verb should be "is."

So beware of fake compound subjects. Check for compound subject constructions and intervening phrases.

Common Mistake 4: Confusion of Simple Past and Past Participle

A typical error tested on the Writing section is confusion between the simple past and the past participle forms of a verb. A past participle form may be sneakily substituted for the simple past form, as in this sneaky sentence.

> Several passersby seen the bank robber leaving the scene of his crime.

The verb form "seen" is the past participle and should be used only with a helping verb, such as "have" or "be." This sentence requires the simple past form "saw."

The Writing section will almost always have a Identifying Sentence Error question in which the simple past is used with a helping verb or in which the past participle is used without a helping verb. Therefore, these are good mistakes to be able to spot.

For regular verbs, the simple past and past participle are identical, ending in -ed. But irregular verbs like "see" usually have two different forms for simple past and past participle. The following is a list of irregular verbs that have appeared on the SAT. These are the simple past and past participle forms that are most often confused. Instead of listing them alphabetically, we have grouped them by pattern.

Irregular Verbs

Infinitive	Simple Past	Past Participle
break	broke	broken
speak	spoke	spoken
freeze	froze	frozen
forget	forgot	forgotten
get	got	gotten
ride	rode	ridden
rise	rose	risen
arise	arose	arisen
drive	drove	driven
write	wrote	written
eat	ate	eaten
fall	fell	fallen
give	gave	given
take	took	taken
shake	shook	shaken
see	saw	seen
ring	rang	rung
sing	sang	sung
sink	sank	sunk
shrink	shrank	shrunk
drink	drank	drunk
begin	began	begun
swim	swam	swum
run	ran	run
come	came	come
become	became	become
do	did	done
go	went	gone
blow	blew	blown
grow	grew	grown
know	knew	known
throw	threw	thrown
fly	flew	flown
draw	drew	drawn

Note the patterns. Verb forms that end in -oke, -oze, -ot, -ode, -ose, -ove, -ote, -ang, -ank, -an, -an, -am, -ame, -ew, or -ook are simple past. Verb forms that end in -en, -wn, -ung, -unk, -un, -um, -ome, and -one, are past participles. Train your ear for irregular verb forms that aren't already second nature to you.

Common Mistake 5: Confusion of Infinitive and Gerund

Some questions test your sense of idiomatic use of English. Please note: we said *idiomatic*, not *idiotic*. "Idiomatic use" means combinations of words that *sound* right or words that *sound* right in particular contexts.

For example, there is generally at least one Identifying Sentence Error question in which the infinitive is used where a gerund would be appropriate, or vice versa, as in the following example.

> Team officials heralded Cap Day as an attempt at attracting a larger turnout of fans.

This sentence is unidiomatic. There's no grammar rule that explains why it's wrong to say "an attempt at attracting." But if you have a good sense of idiom, your ear tells you it should be "an attempt to attract." This sentence confuses the -ing gerund form with the to + verb infinitive form. Sneaky! Here's another sentence.

> Surveillance cameras are frequently placed in convenience stores to prevent customers to shoplift.

After "prevent" you don't use the infinitive but rather the word "from" plus the gerund. The sentence should end "to prevent customers from shoplifting."

Why? There's no real grammatical reason. That's just the way we say and write it in English. You have to trust yourself on these. Whereas there are some general patterns, there are no hard and fast rules that determine when to use an infinitive or gerund, and there are so many possible combinations that there's no way to list all that could possibly appear on the Writing section. But don't worry. You don't need to see every possible combination in advance. Just remember to prick up your ears whenever an infinitive or gerund is underlined on the test.

Common Mistake 6: Nonidiomatic Preposition After Verb

The Writing section also tests your recognition of prepositions that idiomatically combine with certain verbs. Here's a sentence that uses the wrong preposition.

> City Council members frequently meet until the early morning hours in order to work in their stalemates.

It's not always wrong to write "work in." You might use it to speak about the field one *works in* or the place one *works in*. But this combination does not correspond to the meaning of this sentence. The writer means to say "work through" or "work out"—that is, overcome—the stalemates.

Here's another sentence with the wrong preposition.

The rapper's new CD was frowned at by many parents because of its violent lyrics.

That's just not the way we say it in English. The preferred verb–preposition combination is "frowned upon." That's the idiomatic expression. Once again, this is an area where you'll have to trust your ear. Just remember to pay attention and think for a moment when you see an underlined preposition after a verb.

Here are some more verb–preposition idioms.

Commonly Tested Verb–Preposition Combinations

abide by	consist of	object to
abide in	contribute to	participate in
accuse of	count (up)on	pray for
agree to	cover with	prevent from
agree with	decide (up)on	prohibit from
agree on	depend (up)on	protect from
apologize for	differ from	provide with/for
apply to	differ with	recover from
apply for	differ over	rely (up)on
approve of	differ about	rescue from
argue with	discriminate against	respond to
argue about	distinguish from	stare at
arrive at	dream of	stop from
believe in	dream about	subscribe to
blame for	escape from	substitute for
care about	excel in	succeed in
care for	excuse for	thank for
charge for	forget about	vote for
charge with	forgive for	wait for
compare to	hide from	wait on
compare with	hope for	work with
complain about	insist (up)on	worry about

Common Mistake 7: Wrong Word

The English language contains many pairs of words that sound alike but are spelled differently and have different meanings. Expect to encounter ONE OR TWO Identifying Sentence Error questions that test your ability to distinguish between problematic word pairs. Here are some examples.

Accept/Except

To *accept* is to take or receive something that is offered. "Dad said he would accept my apology for putting a dent in his new car, but then he grounded me for two weeks."

To *except* is to leave out or exclude. "The soldier was excepted from combat duty because he had poor field vision." *Except* is usually used as a preposition meaning, "with the exception of, excluding." "When the receptionist found out that everyone except him had received a raise, he demanded a salary increase as well."

Adapt/Adopt

To *adapt* is to change (oneself or something) to become suitable for a particular condition or use. "Fred tried to adapt his Volkswagen for use as a submarine by gluing the windows shut and attaching a periscope to the roof."

To *adopt* is to make something one's own. "My neighbors decided to adopt a child."

Affect/Effect

To *affect* (verb) is to have an influence on something. "Al refused to let the rain affect his plans for a picnic, so he sat under an umbrella and ate potato salad." Affect as a noun is only used as a psychology term meaning an emotion or a desire.

To *effect* is to bring something about or cause something to happen. "The young activist received an award for effecting a change in her community." An *effect* (noun) is an influence or a result "The newspaper article about homeless animals had such an effect on Richard that he brought home three kittens from the shelter."

Afflict/Inflict

To *afflict* is to torment or distress someone or something. It usually appears as a passive verb. "Jeff is afflicted with severe migraine headaches."

To *inflict* is to impose punishment or suffering on someone or something. "No one dared displease the king, for he was known to inflict severe punishments on those who upset him."

Allusion/Illusion

An *allusion* is an indirect reference to something, a hint. "I remarked that Sally's boyfriend was unusual looking; this allusion to his prominent tattoos did not please Sally."

An *illusion* is a false, misleading, or deceptive appearance. "A magician creates the illusion that something has disappeared by hiding it faster than the eye can follow it."

Emigrate/Immigrate

To *emigrate* is to leave one country for another country and is usually used with the preposition from. "Many people emigrated from Europe in search of better living conditions."

To *immigrate* is to enter a country to take up permanent residence there and is usually used with the preposition *to*. "They immigrated to North America because land was plentiful."

Eminent/Imminent

Someone who is *eminent* is prominent or outstanding. "The eminent archeologist Dr. Wong has identified the artifact as prehistoric in origin."

Something that is *imminent* is likely to happen soon or is impending. "After being warned that the hurricane's arrival was imminent, beachfront residents left their homes immediately."

Lay/Lie

To *lay* is to place or put something, and this verb usually does have a "something," a direct object, following it. One form, *laid*, serves as the simple past and the past participle of *lay*. "Before she begins her pictures, Emily lays all of her pencils, brushes, and paints on her worktable to avoid interruptions while she draws and paints," and "He can never remember where he laid his keys."

To *lie* is to recline, to be in a lying position, or to be at rest. This verb never takes a direct object: you do not lie anything down. The simple past form of *lie* is *lay*; the past participle is *lain*. Notice that the past form of *lie* is identical with the present form of lay. This coincidence complicates the task of distinguishing the related meaning of lay and lies. "Having laid the picnic cloth under the sycamore, they lay in the shady grass all afternoon."

Okay fine. Let's let this one lie for now.

Leave/Let

To *leave* is to depart, to allow something to remain behind after departing, or to allow something to remain as it is. The irregular verb form *left* serves as both the simple past and the past participle. "I boarded my plane and it left, leaving my baggage behind in Chicago." When *leave* is used in the third sense—to allow something to remain as it is—and followed by alone, this verb does overlap with *let*. "If parents leave (or let) a baby with a new toy alone, she will understand it as quickly as if they demonstrated how the toy works."

To *let* is to allow or to rent out. These are the verb's core meanings, but it also combines with several different prepositions to produce various specific senses. *Let* is irregular. One form (*let*) serves as present, past, and past participle. "The French border police would not let the Dutch tourist pass without a passport."

Raise/Rise

To *raise* is to lift up or to cause to rise or grow, and it usually has a direct object: You raise dumbbells, roof beams, tomato plants, and children. *Raise* is a completely regular verb. "The trade tariff on imported leather goods raised the prices of Italian shoes."

To *rise* is to get up, to go up, and to be built up. This verb never takes a direct object: You do not rise something; rather, something rises. The past and past participle forms are irregular; rose is the simple past, risen the past participle. "Long-distance commuters must rise early, often before the sun has risen."

Set/Sit

The difference between *set* and *sit* is very similar to the difference between lay and lie and the difference between raise and rise. To *set* is to put or place something, to settle it, or to arrange it. But *set* takes on other specific meanings when it combines with several different prepositions. *Set* is an irregular verb in that one form (*set*) serves as present, past, and past participle. Set usually takes a direct object: You set a ladder against the fence, a value on family heirlooms, or a date for the family reunion. "The professor set the students' chairs in a semicircle to promote open discussion."

To *sit* is to take a seat or to be in a seated position, to rest somewhere, or to occupy a place. This verb does not usually take a direct object, although you can say, "The usher sat us in the center seats of the third row from the stage." The irregular form *sat* serves as past and past participle. Usually, no direct object follows this verb. "The beach house sits on a hill at some distance from the shoreline."

Common Mistake 8: Wrong Tense

Here's a sentence with a verb in the wrong tense.

> Over the last half-century, the building of passenger airliners had grown into a multibillion-dollar industry.

In a one-verb sentence like this one, time-descriptive phrases help you determine what the time frame of a sentence is. The action being described is a process that began during the last half-century and that is continuing to the present day. Any action starting in the past and continuing today is expressed by a verb in the present perfect tense. The present perfect form of this verb is "has grown." Using the verb "had" makes it seem that passenger airliners aren't being made anymore. That can't be! The key is to pay attention to the time cues in the sentence. With practice, you'll be able to spot mistakes like this with confidence.

Another type of sentence might have two verbs and an unnecessary or confusing shift in tense. Here's an example.

> Many superb tennis players turn professional at an alarmingly early age, but because of their lack of physical stamina, suffered early in their careers.

When there are two verbs in a sentence, first study the time relation between the verbs, and determine whether it is logical as presented. In this sentence, the verb in the first clause of this sentence is "turn," a present tense verb. The action is not occurring at any specified occasion but in the general present. The verb "suffered" is in the simple past, but it should remain in the general present, even though the phrase early in their careers may suggest a past time. Be sure that there is a logical relation between the verbs when two are presented in the same sentence.

Common Mistake 9: Number Agreement Problems

The Writing section also tests number agreement between the singular or plural noun and the phrase or word describing it. For instance, a noun may be plural while a phrase describing the noun belongs with a singular noun. That sounds complicated, but fortunately, you don't need to be able to explain the grammar involved; you just need to be able to spot this type of mistake. Here's an example.

> The advertisement in the newspaper requested that only persons with a high school diploma apply for the position.

Nouns in a sentence must have logical number relations. The noun in question, the subject of the second clause of this sentence, is "persons," a plural noun. However, the noun "diploma" is singular. Because the phrase "with a high school diploma" is singular, it seems to say that "persons" share one diploma, when in fact each person has his own diploma. The underlined phrase should read "with high school diplomas."

Here's an example of number disagreement in which a singular noun is coupled with a plural subject.

> Mary's rose gardens are considered by many to be the symbol of beauty in the neighborhood.

Again, identify the subject of the sentence, "gardens." The noun that corresponds to the subject is "symbol," a singular noun. There is no agreement in number between gardens and symbol. Each individual garden is a symbol; many gardens would not be a single symbol. The plural form, "symbols," would make this sentence grammatically correct. Make sure that the nouns in a sentence logically agree in number.

Common Mistake 10: Pronoun in the Wrong Number

You'll be tested on your ability to tell whether or not a noun and the pronoun that refers to that noun agree in number. A singular pronoun should be used to refer to a singular noun; a plural pronoun should be used with a plural noun. In the following examples, the pronoun does not match the noun it refers to in number.

> The typical college student has difficulty adjusting to academic standards much higher than those of their school.

The pronoun "their" should refer to a plural noun, but in this sentence, it refers back to the student, a singular noun. Therefore, the pronoun should be the singular form "his" or "hers" and not the plural form "their." Look for the same kind of mistake in the next sentence.

> Most infants, even unusually quiet ones, will cry with greater intensity when it begins teething.

The error in this sentence is just the opposite from that in the first example. The subject is "infants," a plural noun. But the pronoun that refers back to this plural noun is "it," a singular form. The correct form of the pronoun is "they," referring back to the plural subject. Be sure that a pronoun agrees with its antecedent in number.

Common Mistake 11: Pronoun in the Wrong Case in Compound Noun Phrases

An incorrect pronoun case is an error of the "between you and I" variety. Pronouns can either be *subjects* performing actions (I went, you saw, he ate, they sang, etc.) or *objects* receiving actions or objects (with me, give you, see her, stop them, etc.). Usually the choice of pronoun is obvious, but when pronouns are in a compound noun phrase, it's easier to make a mistake. Can you identify the compound phrase in the sentence below and the error in the choice of pronoun?

> Him and the rest of the team stopped by the malt shop for milkshakes after the game.

In this sentence, the compound subject is "Him and the rest of the team." To identify the error, isolate the pronoun from the compound. Take away the second part of the compound subject (and the rest of the team), and you are left with "him." As you can see, *him* is incorrect because *him* wouldn't stop by the malt shop; *he* would. The correct pronoun case for this sentence is "he," the subject form.

Can you identify and isolate the incorrect pronoun in the following sentence?

> Uncle John and Aunt Rosie join my parents and I for dinner every Thursday.

In this sentence, the compound noun phrase in question is "my parents and I," the object of the verb. Ignoring the phrase "my parents," you can now read the sentence: Uncle John and Aunt Rosie join *I* for dinner every Thursday. Naturally, the pronoun "I" is the incorrect form of the personal pronoun; the correct form is "me," the object form.

Common Mistake 12: Pronoun Shift

"Pronoun shift" is a switch in pronoun person or number within a given sentence. Here's an example.

> One cannot sleep soundly if you exercise vigorously before retiring to bed.

The subject in the first clause is "one," and the subject in the second clause is "you." These two pronouns refer to the same performer of two actions, so they should be consistent in person and number. The sentence should not shift to the second person "you" form.

Look for another kind of pronoun shift in the next sentence.

> If someone loses his way in the airport, they can ask any employee for directions.

The subject is "someone" in the first clause, but "they" in the second clause. Clearly, both pronouns refer to the same agent; the performer(s) of both actions, losing and asking, is the same. This switch in number from singular to plural is not grammatical. In creating such a sentence, sneaky SAT writers play on a common logical confusion. In English, singular words like "one," "someone," and "a person" can represent people in general. So can plural words like "people" or "they." Be on the lookout when general statements use pronouns because this is one of the most common mistakes made in the English language, and consider whether these pronouns are consistent.

Common Mistake 13: Pronoun with Ambiguous Reference

There are two ways the Writing section might test your ability to recognize an ambiguous pronoun reference. First, you may be given a sentence in which it is impossible to determine what noun the pronoun refers. Take a look at this example.

> The United States entered into warmer relations with China after its compliance with recent weapons agreements.

To which country does the pronoun "its" refer? Grammatically and logically, either country could be the antecedent of the pronoun. With the limited information provided by this sentence alone, you simply can't determine which country the pronoun stands in for. Its reference is ambiguous.

Pronoun reference can also be ambiguous if the pronoun's antecedent is not explicitly stated in the sentence.

> After the derailment last month, they are inspecting trains for safety more often than ever before.

Who is "they"? There is no group of people identified in this sentence to whom the pronoun could refer. You can logically infer that *they* refers to agents of a railroad safety commission, but because these inspectors are not explicitly mentioned in the sentence, the personal pronoun cannot be clear. Be sure to locate the antecedent of any pronoun in Identifying Sentence Error sentences.

Common Mistake 14: Faulty Comparison

Most faulty comparisons happen when two things that logically cannot be compared are compared. A comparison can be faulty either logically or grammatically. Look for the faulty comparison in the sentence below.

> A Nobel Peace Prize winner and the author of several respected novels, Elie Wiesel's name is still less well known than last year's Heisman Trophy winner.

In every sentence, you should first identify what things or actions are being compared. In this sentence, Elie Wiesel's *name* is compared to last year's Heisman Trophy winner. This comparison is faulty because a person's name is compared to another person. If the first item were Elie Wiesel, then the comparison would be valid.

Try to identify the faulty comparison in the next sentence.

> To lash back at one's adversaries is a less courageous course than attempting to bring about reconciliation with them.

The comparison in this sentence is logically correct in that two actions are compared. But the problem lies in the grammatical form of the words compared. An infinitive verb, "to lash," expresses the first action, but a gerund, "attempting," expresses the second action. These verb forms should match to make the comparison parallel. If "lashing" replaced "to lash," the comparison would be grammatically parallel and logically valid. Check all comparisons for logic and grammatical consistency.

Common Mistake 15: Misuse of Adjective or Adverb

These questions test your ability to recognize misuses of one-word modifiers. Keep in mind that adjectives modify nouns and adverbs modify verbs, adjectives, and other adverbs. Now ask yourself what the underlined word is intended to modify as you look at the sentence below.

The applicants for low-interest loans hoped to buy decent built houses for their families.

The word "decent" is an adjective. However, this modifier describes an adjective, explaining how the houses were built. Thus, the modifier needs to be the adverb *decently*, not the adjective *decent*. A word that modifies an adjective like "built" is an adverb. So the word needed in this sentence is the adverb decently. Notice also that this adverb ends in -ly, *the most common adverbial ending.*

Now take a look at the second sentence.

The critics who reviewed both of David Eggers's novels like the second one best.

The word "best" is a superlative modifier. Superlative adverbs and adjectives (adverbs and adjectives ending in –est (biggest, loudest, fastest, etc.) and should express comparisons between three or more things or actions. *Comparative* adverbs and adjectives end in -er (bigger, louder, faster, etc.) and express comparisons between two things or actions. This sentence compares critics' responses to only two novels by David Eggers. Thus, instead of the superlative "best," this sentence needs the comparative modifier "better."

Remember that some adjectives and adverbs, usually those of two or more syllables, form the comparative with "more" instead of the -er ending, and "most" instead of the -est ending converts some modifiers to superlatives.

Trust your ear to distinguish adjectives from adverbs in Writing section Identifying Sentence Error questions, but do *listen* carefully. Pay close attention when you decide whether a sentence needs a comparative or superlative modifier.

Common Mistake 16: Double Negative

Don't use no double negatives on the Writing section. Get it? In standard written English, it is incorrect to use two negatives together unless one is intended to cancel out the other. Notice the two negative words in this sentence.

James easily passed the biology exam without hardly studying his lab notes.

"Without" is a negative, as is any word that indicates absence or lack. "Hardly" is a less familiar negative; it also denotes a scarcity of something but perhaps not a total absence. With these two negatives, the sentence is incorrect.

Now look at the next sentence.

> In the history of the major leagues, barely no one has maintained higher than a .400 batting average for an entire season.

Clearly, "no one" is a negative, but so is "barely." Just like "hardly" does, this word indicates a scarcity of something or an almost total absence. In Identifying Sentence Error questions, be on the lookout for negatives that are not obviously negative, such as *hardly*, *barely*, and *scarcely*.

5 MOST COMMON IMPROVING SENTENCE ERRORS

Common Mistake 1: Run-On Sentences

The Improving Sentence questions on the Writing section usually include one or two run-on sentences. In a typical run-on sentence, two independent clauses—each of which could stand alone as a complete sentence—are erroneously joined together, either without punctuation or, most often, with just a comma. Here's an example.

> The decrease in crime can be attributed to a rise in the number of police officers, more than 500 joined the force in the last year alone.

Both clauses in this sentence are independent; each could stand alone as a sentence. So it's incorrect to join them with a comma.

There are several ways to correct run-on sentences. One way is simply to change the comma into a period, producing two separate sentences:

> The decrease in crime can be attributed to a rise in the number of police officers. More than 500 joined the force in the last year alone.

A second way is to change the comma into a semicolon. A semicolon can be described as a "weak period." It's used to indicate that two clauses are grammatically independent but that the ideas expressed are not so independent as to warrant separate sentences. Substituting a semicolon for the comma would make this sentence correct and show that the two ideas are equally important and closely related.

> The decrease in crime can be attributed to a rise in the number of police officers; more than five hundred joined the force in the last year alone.

This is a popular correction choice for test makers to use, so be on the lookout for semicolons in place of commas.

But there are other ways to join two independent clauses. In the next example, the two clauses are independent, but one is logically subordinate to (of lesser importance than) the other. To make the correction, you can convert the independent clause expressing the subordinate idea into a grammatically subordinate, or dependent, clause.

> Litigation against chicken farms continues to increase year after year, farmers are now introducing organic and free-range chickens.

Although the clauses in this sentence are grammatically independent, they are not unrelated. Logically, the second clause depends on the first one; it seems to express a response to what is described in the first clause. You can logically infer that the farmers are introducing these chickens because the number of litigations against them is great. So, a good way to correct the error in this sentence would be to make the second clause grammatically dependent on the first clause, as follows.

> Because litigation against chicken farms continues to increase year after year, farmers are now introducing organic and free-range chickens.

A fourth way to correct a run-on sentence is simply to compress the two independent clauses to one. This can be done in sentences in which the independent clauses have the same subject, as in the sentence below.

> The Humber Bridge in Britain was completed in 1981, it is the longest single-span suspension bridge in the world.

In this sentence, the subject of the second clause is the pronoun "it," which refers to the subject of the first clause, the Humber Bridge. Thus, both clauses share the same subject. To correct this run-on sentence, remove both the comma and the pronoun "it," and insert the coordinating conjunction "and." The sentence now reads as:

> The Humber Bridge in Britain was completed in 1981 and is the longest single-span suspension bridge in the world.

Now the sentence consists of one independent clause with a compound predicate and only one subject.

Common Mistake 2: Sentence Fragments

The Improving Sentence section usually includes one or two sentence fragments. Sentence fragments come in many forms, but they all share the same problem: they cannot stand alone because they are not independent clauses. A sentence must contain a subject and verb (a clause) *and* express a complete thought (be independent). What looks like a sentence on the Writing section may actually be merely a fragment. Take a look at the following example.

> Whereas many office managers are growing more and more dependent on facsimile machines, others resisting this latest technological breakthrough.

This just sounds wrong, doesn't it? Here's why. This is a sentence fragment because it has no independent clause. The first clause begins with the subordinating conjunction "whereas," and the phrase following the comma contains the incomplete verb form "resisting." Plus, a sentence should always have at least one clause that could stand alone, and here neither of the clauses can do that. The easiest way to repair this sentence is to insert the helping verb "are."

> Whereas many office managers are growing more and more dependent on facsimile machines, others are resisting this latest technological breakthrough.

Here's another sentence fragment.

> In the summertime, the kindergarten class that plays on the rope swing beneath the crooked oak tree.

Once again, the sentence clause cannot stand alone. Here we have a fragment not because something is missing, but because something is included that makes the clause dependent. The word "that" makes everything after the comma a dependent clause. Simply remove the word "that," and look at what you get.

> In the summertime, the kindergarten class plays on the rope swing beneath the crooked oak tree.

Now you have a grammatically complete sentence that is shorter than the fragment.

Common Mistake 3: Misplaced Modifiers

A modifier is a word or group of words that gives the reader more information about a noun or verb in the sentence. To be grammatically correct, the modifier must be positioned so that it is unambiguous which word is being modified. In order to achieve that, the modifier should be placed *as close as possible* to the word it modifies. Here is an example of a misplaced modifier:

> Flying for the first time, the roar of the jet engines intimidated the small child, and he grew frightened as the plane roared down the runway.

The modifying phrase above is found at the beginning of the sentence: "Flying for the first time." A modifying phrase that begins a sentence should relate to the sentence's subject. Usually, a comma sets off this kind of introductory modifier, and then the subject immediately follows the comma.

Logically, in this example, you know that it is the child who is flying for the first time. But because of the grammatical structure of the sentence (the placement of the modifier), the sentence actually states that it is the *roar* that is flying for the first time. Of course, this doesn't make sense: roars don't fly for the first time (or the second time or the third time). The sentence needs to be revised so that the modifier is as close as possible to the noun it modifies.

> Flying for the first time, the small child was intimidated by the roar of the jet engines and grew frightened as the plane roared down the runway.

Here's another example of a sentence with a misplaced modifier.

> An advertisement was withdrawn by the producer of the local news program that was considered offensive by the city's minority communities.

Grammatically, the phrase "that was considered offensive by the city's minority communities" refers to "the local news program," because this is the nearest noun. Is that what the writer means? Is it the local news program or the advertisement that was offensive to the minority communities? If the writer means to say that the advertisement was deemed offensive, she should rewrite the sentence as follows to make her idea clear.

> The producer of the local news program withdrew an advertisement that was considered offensive by the city's minority communities.

The same goes with this next sentence.

> The despondent little girl found her missing doll playing in the backyard under the swing.

The position of the modifying phrase "playing in the backyard under the swing" suggests that the girl's *missing doll* was playing in the yard, not the despondent little girl. Once again, the modifier is misplaced; it is not near enough to the noun it is intended to modify (girl) to prevent confusion. Here's how the sentence should be revised.

> Playing in the backyard under the swing, the despondent little girl found her missing-doll.

Common Mistake 4: Faulty Parallelism

Certain sets of words in a sentence, or the general design of a sentence, often require a parallel construction—that is, the words or phrases must share the same grammatical structure. If they don't, the sentence will be off-balance. For example, compare these two sentences.

> My hobbies include swimming, gardening, and to read science fiction.

> My hobbies include swimming, gardening, and reading science fiction.

In the first sentence, two of the hobbies use the –ing gerund form, but the third uses a different structure—the infinitive. The sentence is not parallel. In the second version, all three hobbies correctly use the same –ing form, creating a balanced sentence.

Two kinds of parallel construction errors are used over and over again on the Writing section. The first occurs in sentences with pairs of connective words that require parallelism. These connective words include those in the following list.

neither . . . nor

either . . . or

both . . . and

the better . . . the better

the more . . . the more (or less)

not only . . . but also

In the sentence below, look at that first pair of words, neither . . . nor, and the phrases that follow both words.

> Nineteenth-century nihilists were concerned with neither the origins of philosophical-thought <u>nor how societal laws developed</u>.

The phrases following the words "neither" and "nor" must be parallel in grammatical structure. That is, if a noun phrase ("the origins of philosophical thought") follows *neither*, then a noun phrase must follow *nor*, too. But here, nor is followed by "how societal laws developed"—a dependent clause. The two parts of the sentence are not grammatically parallel.

In this example, because the dependent clause is the underlined part of the sentence, it must be rewritten as a noun phrase ("nor the development of societal laws") to make the sentence parallel. Now both connective words are followed by a noun and a prepositional phrase. The sentence now has a proper parallel construction.

Another situation that demands parallel grammatical structure occurs when a sentence contains a list of two or more items. That list can comprise two or more nouns or noun phrases, verbs or verb phrases, or dependent clauses. Any kind of list calls for grammatically parallel items. Look for the faulty parallelism in the sentence below:

> To run for a seat in the United States Senate, a candidate must be an adult at least 30 years of age, a citizen of the United States, and is to reside in the state to be represented.

This sentence lists three requirements of running for United States Senate. The first two phrases in the list, "an adult at least 30 years of age" and "a citizen of the United States," are both nouns modified by prepositional phrases. The third phrase in the list, "is to reside in the state" is a verbal phrase (the present tense form "is" plus the infinitive form "to reside").

Two noun phrases + One verbal phrase = Bad parallelism!

To correct this error, transform the verbal phrase into a noun phrase so it matches the structure of the other two items on the list. Thus, if a person is to live in a state to be elected to the Senate, he or she must be a resident of the state.

Use parallel structure with connective phrases such as neither … nor and lists.

Common Mistake 5: Faulty Coordination/Subordination

These two kinds of errors occur when sentence clauses are joined incorrectly. Faulty coordination and faulty subordination are closely related, but they require separate explanations.

Coordination between two clauses is faulty if it doesn't express the logical relation between the clauses. Often, this error involves a misused conjunction. A conjunction is a connective word joining two clauses or phrases in one sentence. The most common conjunctions are as follows:

and

but

because

however

for

or

Identify the conjunction in the following sentence. Why does it fail to connect the clauses logically?

> Ben Franklin was a respected and talented statesman, and he was most famous for his discovery of electricity.

To identify and correct the faulty coordination, determine how the two clauses are related. Does the conjunction "and" best express the relationship between the two facts the writer states about Ben Franklin? "And" normally expresses a consistency between two equally emphasized facts. However, the fact that Franklin is best known for his discovery of electricity is presented *in contrast to* the fact that he was a talented statesman. Thus, the use of *and* is an error in coordination.

A better way to connect these two contrasting ideas would be to use the conjunction *but*, which indicates some contrast. In this sentence, *but* points to a common expectation. An individual usually distinguishes herself or himself in one field of accomplishment: in politics or in science, but not in both. So Franklin's distinction in two diverse fields seems to contradict common expectations and calls for a *but*.

Faulty subordination is most often found on the Writing section in a group of words that contains two or more subordinate, or dependent, clauses but no independent clause. There are several connective words that, when introducing a sentence or clause, always indicate that the phrase that follows is dependent, or subordinate. They are as follows:

since
because
so that
if

Whenever a dependent clause begins a sentence, an independent clause must follow somewhere in the sentence. Look at the group of words below and identify the faulty subordination.

> Since the small electronics industry is one of the world's fastest growing sectors, because demand for the computer chip continues to be high.

"Since" indicates that the first clause in the group of words is subordinate and needs to be followed by an independent clause. But "because" in the second clause indicates that the second clause is also subordinate. The sentence is faulty because there is no independent clause to make the group of words grammatically complete. Result: two sentence fragments. The second connective word "because" should be eliminated to make the group of words a complete and logical sentence. With this revision, the *since* clause expresses a cause, and the independent clause expresses an effect or result.

WORDINESS: HOW TO AVOID IT

Before moving on to the practice questions, we thought it was important to mention one more key to performing successfully on the Writing section. A common flaw in many sentences and paragraphs is wordiness.

Wordy phrases are like junk food: they add only calories and no nutrition. Many people make the mistake of writing *at the present time* or *at this point in time* instead of the simpler *now* or *take into consideration* instead of simply *consider* in an attempt to make their prose seem more scholarly or more formal. It doesn't work. Instead, their prose ends up seeming inflated and pretentious. Don't waste your words or your time.

Wordy:

I am of the opinion that the aforementioned managers should be advised that they will be evaluated with regard to the utilization of responsive organizational software for the purpose of devising a responsive network of customers.

Concise:

We should tell the managers that we will evaluate their use of flexible computerized databases to develop a customer's network.

SUMMARY

- **16 Most Common Identifying Sentence Error Mistakes:**
  - — Common Mistake 1: subject-verb agreement
    - When subject follows verb
      - Singular subjects = singular verbs
      - Plural subjects = plural verbs
  - — Common Mistake 2: subject-verb agreement
    - When subject and verb are separated
      - Identify the subject of the sentence
      - Don't let intervening phrases fool you
  - — Common Mistake 3: subject-verb agreement
    - When the subject seems plural
      - When the subject of a sentence is in the form "neither ______ nor ______ " or in the form "either ______ or ______"and the nouns in the blanks are singular, the verb should be singular
      - If the nouns in a neither-nor or either-or construction are plural, then a plural verb is correct
  - — Common Mistake 4: Confusion of simple past and past participle
    - For regular verbs, the simple past and the past participle are identical and end in *-ed*
    - For irregular verbs like *see*, there are usually two different forms for simple past and past participle.
    - Patterns
      - Verbs that end in –oke, -oze, -ot, -ode, -ose, -ang, -ank, -an, -am, -ame, -ew, or –ook are simple past.
      - Verbs that end in *–en, -wn, -ung, -unk, -un, -um, -ome*, and *–one* are past participles
  - — Common Mistake 5: Confusion of infinitive and gerund
    - Some questions on the SAT test your idiomatic use of English
    - Often questions use the infinitive where a gerund would be appropriate, or vise versa

- Common Mistake 6: Nonidiomatic preposition after verb
  - Some questions test your ability to recognize common verb-preposition idioms
- Common Mistake 7: Wrong word
  - There are many words in English that sound alike but are spelled differently and have different meanings:
    - Accept/Except
    - Adapt/Adopt
    - Affect/Effect
    - Afflict/Inflict
    - Allusion/Illusion
    - Emigrate/Immigrate
    - Eminent/Imminent
    - Lay/Lie
    - Leave/Let
    - Raise/Rise
    - Set/Sit
- Common Mistake 8: Wrong tense
  - In a one-verb sentence, time descriptive phrases help you figure out what time frame the sentence is
  - In a two-verb sentence, first study the time relation between the verbs and determine whether it is logically presented
- Common Mistake 9: Number agreement problems
  - Some questions test number agreement between the singular or plural noun and the phrase or word describing it
  - Nouns in a sentence must have logical relations
- Common Mistake 10: Pronoun in the wrong number
  - A singular pronoun should be used to refer to a singular noun
  - A plural pronoun should be used with a plural noun
- Common Mistake 11: Pronoun in the wrong case in compound noun phrases
  - An incorrect pronoun case is an error of the "between you and I" variety
  - Pronouns can either be subjects performing actions or objects receiving actions or objects.
- Common Mistake 12: Pronoun shift
  - A pronoun shift refers to a switch in pronoun person or number within a given sentence
  - Make sure pronouns are consistent in person and number
- Common Mistake 13: Pronoun with ambiguous reference
  - It is often impossible to determine what noun the pronoun refers
  - Sometimes the pronoun's antecedent is not explicitly stated in the sentence
- Common Mistake 14: Faulty comparison

    - Most faulty comparisons happen when two things that logically cannot be compared are compared
    - Comparisons can be faulty either logically or grammatically
  - Common Mistake 15: Misuse of adjective or verb
    - Remember that adjectives modify nouns and adverbs modify verbs, adjectives, and other adverbs
  - Common Mistake 16: Double negative
    - In standard written English, it is incorrect to use two negatives together unless one is intended to cancel out the other.
    - Watch out for negatives that are obviously negative such as *hardly*, *barely*, and *scarcely*.
- **5 Most Common Improving Sentence Errors:**
  - Common Mistake 1: run-on sentences
    - A typical run-on sentence usually has two independent clauses that could stand alone as a complete sentence
    - It is incorrect to join independent clauses together with a comma
    - You could join the clauses together by using a semi-colon, by converting the independent clause expressing the subordinate idea into a grammatically subordinate or dependent clause, or by compressing the two independent clauses into one
  - Common Mistake 2: Sentence fragments
    - Sentence fragments can not stand alone because they are not independent clauses
    - A sentence must have a subject and verb and express a complete thought
  - Common Mistake 3: Misplaced modifiers
    - Modifiers must be positioned so that it is unambiguous which word is being modified
    - The modifier should be placed as close as possible to the word it modifies
  - Common Mistake 4: Faulty parallelism
    - The general design of a sentence sometimes requires parallel construction, or the same grammatical structure.
    - Use parallel structure with connective phrases such as *neither…nor*, and with lists
  - Common Mistake 5: Faulty coordination/subordination
    - Faulty coordination is when a sentence does not express the logical relation between the clauses, often as a result of a misused conjunction
    - Faulty subordination is most often found in a group of words that contains two or more subordinate, or dependent clauses but no independent clause
- **Wordiness: How to Avoid it:**
  - Use *now* instead of *at the present time*
  - Use *consider* instead of *take into consideration*

Part 4

Understanding the Math Section

Step Seven

Comprehensive Math Review

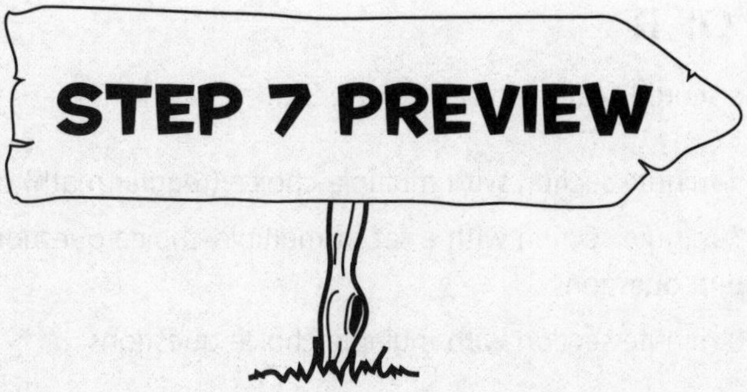

The Gist of it

- The Directions
- Scoring

Tested Math Concepts

- Basic Math Concepts
- Advanced Math Concepts

Summary

You should approach the SAT Math section with a definite plan of action. You need to know what to expect beforehand so you are ready with the right strategies. Steps 7–9 show you what you will find on the SAT Math section and how you can tackle it quickly and correctly.

These steps are a little longer than the rest, and they're very important, so take twice as much time as you have been spending on the previous chapters.

THE GIST OF IT

There are three scored Math sections on the SAT:

- One 25-minute section with multiple-choice (regular math) questions
- One 25-minute section with a set of multiple-choice questions and a set of 10 Grid-in questions
- One 20-minute section with multiple-choice questions

The SAT Math question sets start off easy and gradually increase in difficulty. ALWAYS be aware of the difficulty level as you go through a question set. The harder the question, the more traps you have to avoid.

The Directions

You'll save time by knowing the directions. The directions are the same for every test, so with a little practice, you can skip the directions and go straight to the first question.

Multiple-Choice Questions

The multiple-choice questions count for over one half of your total math score. We have a lot of techniques you can use to attack these questions, which we'll get to soon.

Time—25 Minutes
20 Questions

Directions: For this section, solve each problem and decide which is the best of the choices given. Fill in the corresponding oval on the answer sheet. You may use any available space for scratchwork.

Notes

1. Calculator use is permitted.
2. All numbers used are real numbers.
3. Figures are provided for some problems. All figures are drawn to scale and lie in a plane UNLESS otherwise indicated.
4. Unless otherwise specified, the domain of any function f is assumed to be the set of all real numbers x for which $f(x)$ is a real number.

Reference Information

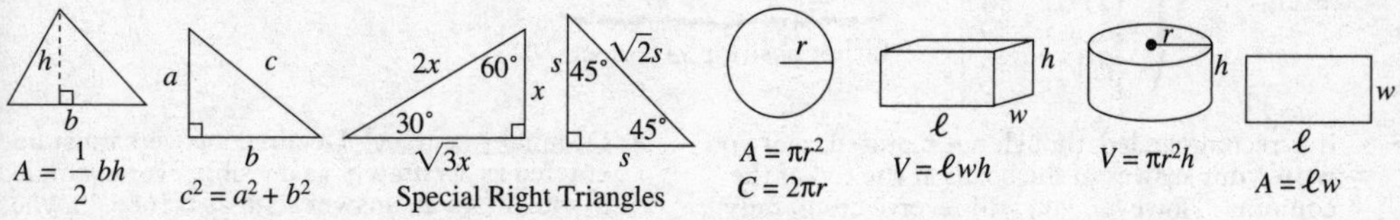

The sum of the measures in degrees of the angles of a triangle is 180.
The number of degrees of arc in a circle is 360.
A straight angle has a degree measure of 180.

Note (2) means you won't have to deal with imaginary numbers, such as i (the square root of −1).

Note (3) tells you diagrams are drawn to scale, which means you can use these diagrams to estimate measurements. However, if the diagrams are labeled "Figure not drawn to scale," you can't do this.

Saying the figures "lie in a plane" simply means you are dealing with flat figures, like rectangles or circles, unless the question says otherwise.

Read these directions carefully at least five times. By the day of the test you should know these formulas by heart. If you forget, you'll know where to find them.

Grid-in Questions

You get 10 Grid-ins in one of the Math sections. The Grid-in section on the SAT is more like math tests at school—you figure out your own answer and fill it in on a special grid. Some Grid-ins have only one correct answer, whereas others have several possible correct answers. There is no penalty for wrong answers on the Grid-in section. Here are the directions:

DIRECTIONS FOR STUDENT-PRODUCED RESPONSE QUESTIONS

For each of the questions below (9–18), solve the problem and indicate your answer by darkening the ovals in the special grid. For example:

Answer: 1.25 or $\frac{5}{4}$ or 5/4

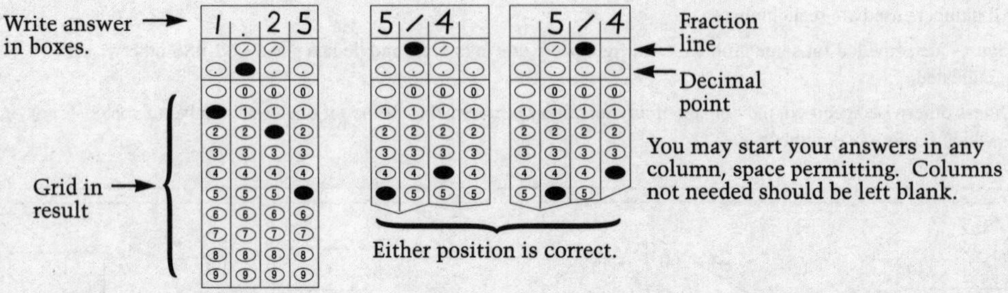

- It is recommended, though not required, that you write your answer in the boxes at the top of the columns. However, you will receive credit only for darkening the ovals correctly.
- Grid only one answer to a question, even though some problems have more than one correct answer.
- Darken no more than one oval in a column.
- No answers are negative.
- Mixed numbers cannot be gridded. For example: the number $1\frac{1}{4}$ must be gridded as 1.25 or 5/4.

(If  is gridded, it will be interpreted as $\frac{11}{4}$ not $1\frac{1}{4}$.)

- Decimal Accuracy: Decimal answers must be entered as accurately as possible. For example, if you obtain an answer such as 0.1666. . ., you should record the result as .166 or .167. **Less accurate values such as .16 or .17 are not acceptable.**

Acceptable ways to grid $\frac{1}{6}$ =.1666. . .

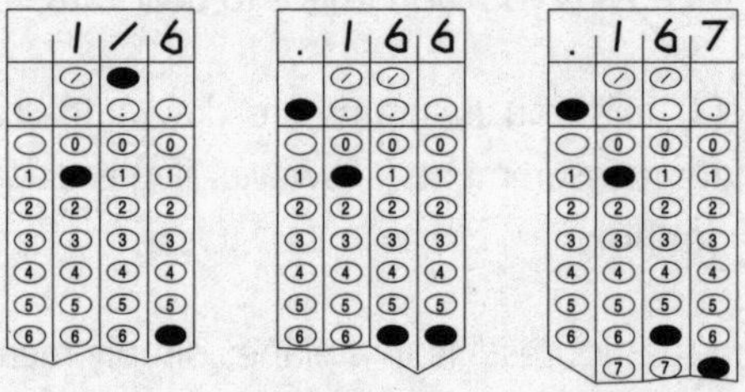

Each Grid-in question provides four boxes and a column of ovals—or bubbles—to write your answer in. You write your numerical answer in the boxes first—one digit, decimal point, or fraction sign per box. Then you fill in the appropriate bubbles. The numbers you fill in are really just an aid; they're to help you grid in the bubbles properly and are not read by the scoring computer.

You CANNOT grid:

- Negative answers
- Answers with variables (*x, y, w*, etc.)
- Answers greater than 9,999
- Answers with commas (write 1000, not 1,000)
- Mixed numbers (such as $2\frac{1}{2}$, which must be gridded as $\frac{5}{2}$ or 2.5)

If you come up with any of these answers to a question, you are wrong or need to convert.

Scoring

On the multiple-choice questions, you gain one point for each correct answer and lose a FRACTION of a point for each wrong answer. You do not gain or lose any points for questions you leave blank.

However, on Grid-in questions, you lose *nothing* for a wrong answer. That's why you must always fill in an answer on the Grid-ins—you have absolutely, positively *nothing* to lose.

The total points are added up to produce a raw Math score. This raw score is then converted into a scaled score, with 200 as the lowest score and 800 the highest.

TESTED MATH CONCEPTS

There are a handful of math skills tested OVER AND OVER AGAIN on the SAT. When you are confident that you understand these math concepts, the SAT Math section gets a whole lot easier. Our techniques for solving these problems work with both types of SAT Math questions.

Of course there are many other math concepts that the SAT also covers. After you finish Step 7, turn to Resource A: SAT Math in a Nutshell. Go through the 100 concepts listed there, and circle the ones you are unsure of. Learn four of those concepts a day, and you should know them all well within a month.

Basic Math Concepts

Remainders

Remainder questions can be easier than they look. Lots of people think you have to solve for a certain value in a remainder question, but that's usually not the case. Take this example:

> When n is divided by 7, the remainder is 4. What is the remainder when $2n$ is divided by 7?
>
> (A) 0
> (B) 1
> (C) 2
> (D) 3
> (E) 4

This question doesn't depend on knowing the value of n. In fact, n has an infinite number of possible values. The easy way to solve this kind of problem is to pick a number for n. Since the remainder when n is divided by 7 is 4, pick any multiple of 7 and add 4. The easiest multiple to work with is 7. So, 7 + 4 = 11. Plug 11 in for n and see what happens:

What is the remainder when $2n$ is divided by 7?

. . . the remainder when 2(11) is divided by 7?

. . . the remainder when 22 is divided by 7?

. . . $\frac{22}{7}$ = 3 remainder 1

The remainder is 1 when $n = 11$. So the answer is (B). The remainder will also be 1 when $n = 18$, 25, or 46.

Averages

Instead of giving you a list of values to plug into the average formula $\left(\frac{\text{Sum of Terms}}{\text{Number of Terms}}\right)$, SAT average questions often put a spin on the problem, like so:

The average weight of five amplifiers in a guitar shop is 32 pounds. If four of the amplifiers weigh 25, 27, 19, and 35 pounds, what is the weight of the fifth amplifier?

(A) 28 pounds
(B) 32 pounds
(C) 49 pounds
(D) 54 pounds
(E) 69 pounds

This problem tells you the average of a group of terms and asks you to find the value of a missing term. To get the answer, you need to work with the sum. Let x = the weight of the fifth amplifier. Plug this into the formula for average:

$$\text{Average} = \frac{\text{Sum of Terms}}{\text{Number of Terms}}$$

$$32 = \frac{25 + 27 + 19 + 35 + x}{5}$$

$$32 \times 5 = 25 + 27 + 19 + 35 + x$$

The average weight of the amplifiers times the number of amplifiers equals the total weight of the amplifiers. The new formula is:

Average × Number of Terms = Sum of Terms

Remember this version of the average formula so you can find the total sum whenever you know the average of a group of terms and the number of terms. Now you can solve for the weight of the fifth amplifier:

$$32 \times 5 = 25 + 27 + 19 + 35 + x$$
$$160 = 106 + x$$
$$54 = x$$

So the weight of the fifth amplifier is 54 pounds, choice (D). Rock on.

Ratios

SAT test writers often try to get you to set up the wrong ratio in ratio questions. Don't be angry with them. Understand that they can't help themselves, and calmly work around their tricks.

> Out of every 50 CDs produced in a certain factory, 20 are scratched. What is the ratio of nondefective CDs produced to scratched CDs produced?
>
> (A) 2:5
> (B) 3:5
> (C) 2:3
> (D) 3:2
> (E) 5:2

You need to find the parts and the whole in the problem. In this case, the total number of CDs is the whole, and the number of nondefective CDs and the number of scratched CDs are the parts that make up this whole. You're given a part-to-whole ratio (the ratio of scratched CDs to all CDs) and asked to find a part-to-part ratio (the ratio of nondefective CDs to scratched CDs).

If 20 CDs out of every 50 are scratched, the remaining 30 CDs must be OK. So the part-to-part ratio of good to scratched CDs is $\frac{30}{20}$, or $\frac{3}{2}$, which is equivalent to 3:2, choice (D). If you hadn't identified the part and the whole first, it would be easy to get confused and compare a part to the whole, like the ratios in answer choices (A), (B), and (E).

This approach also works for ratio questions where you need to find actual quantities.

> Out of every 5 CDs produced in a certain factory, 2 are scratched. If 2,200 CDs were produced, how many were scratched?

Here you need to find a quantity: the number of defective CDs. If you're looking for the actual quantities in a ratio, set up and solve a proportion. You're given a part-to-whole ratio (the ratio of scratched CDs to all CDs) and total CDs produced. You can find the answer by setting up and solving a proportion:

$$\frac{\text{Number-of-scratched-CDs}}{\text{Total-number-of-CDs}} = \frac{2}{5} = \frac{x}{2{,}200}$$

$$x = \text{number of scratched CDs}$$

$$5x = 4{,}400\left(\text{by cross-multiplying } \frac{2}{5} = \frac{x}{2{,}200}\right)$$

$$x = 880 \text{ (by dividing both sides by 5)}$$

Remember that ratios compare only relative size; they don't tell you the actual quantities involved. Distinguish clearly between the parts and the whole in ratio problems.

Rates

A rate is a ratio that compares quantities measured in different units. In the following problem, the units are dollars and headphones.

> If 8 headphones cost a dollars, b headphones would cost how many dollars?
>
> (A) $8ab$
>
> (B) $\frac{8a}{b}$
>
> (C) $\frac{8}{ab}$
>
> (D) $\frac{a}{8b}$
>
> (E) $\frac{ab}{8}$

What makes this rate problem difficult is the variables. It's hard to get a clear picture of the relationship between the units. You need to pick numbers for the variables to make the relationship between the units clearer.

Pick numbers for a and b that will be easy for you to work with. Let $a = 16$. Then 8 headphones cost \$16. So the cost at this rate $= \frac{\$16}{8 \text{ headphones}} = \$2$ per headphone.

Let $b = 5$. So the cost of 5 headphones at this rate is 5 headphones × \$2 per headphone = \$10. Now plug in $a = 16$ and $b = 5$ into the answer choices to see which one gives you a value of 10.

Choice (A): $8 \times 16 \times 5 = 640$. Eliminate.

Choice (B): $\frac{8 \times 16}{5} = \frac{128}{5}$. Eliminate.

Choice (C): $\frac{8}{16 \times 5} = \frac{1}{10}$. Eliminate.

Choice (D): $\frac{16}{8 \times 5} = \frac{2}{5}$. Eliminate.

Choice (E): $\frac{16 \times 5}{8} = 10$.

Since (E) is the only one that gives the correct value, it is correct. Those are some cheap headphones.

Percents

In percent problems, you're usually given two pieces of information and asked to find the third, like so:

> Last year Aunt Edna's annual salary was $20,000. This year's raise brings her to an annual salary of $25,000. If she gets a raise of the same percentage every year, what will her salary be next year?
>
> (A) $27,500
> (B) $30,000
> (C) $31,250
> (D) $32,500
> (E) $35,000

When you see a percent problem, remember the following formulas.

If you are solving for a percent: $\frac{\text{Part}}{\text{Whole}} = \text{Percent}$

If you need to solve for a part: Percent × Whole = Part

This problem asks for Aunt Edna's projected salary for next year—that is, her current salary plus her next raise. You know last year's salary ($20,000) and you know this year's salary ($25,000), so you can find the difference between the two salaries:

$\$25{,}000 - \$20{,}000 = \$5{,}000 = \text{her raise}$

Now find the percent this raise represents by using the formula: Percent = $\frac{\text{Part}}{\text{Whole}}$. Since Aunt Edna's raise was calculated on last year's salary, divide by $20,000. Be sure you know which whole to plug in. Here you're looking for a percentage of $20,000, not of $25,000.

$$\text{Percent} = \frac{\$5{,}000}{\$20{,}000} = \frac{1}{4} = 25\%$$

You know Aunt Edna will get the same percent raise next year, so solve for the part. Use the formula: Percent × Whole = Part. Make sure you change the percent to either a fraction or a decimal before beginning calculations.

Her raise next year will be 25% × \$25,000 = $\frac{1}{4}$ × 25,000 = \$6,250. Add that amount to this year's salary and you have her projected salary:

> \$25,000 + \$6,250 = \$31,250, or answer choice (C).

Aunt Edna must be doing something right.

Simultaneous Equations

To get a numerical value for each variable in a simultaneous equation, you need as many different equations as there are variables to solve for. So, if you have two variables, you need two distinct equations.

> If $p + 2q = 14$ and $3p + q = 12$, then $p =$
> (Note: This is a Grid-in, so there are no answer choices.)

You could tackle this problem by solving for one variable in terms of the other and then plugging this expression into the other equation. But the simultaneous equations that appear on the SAT can usually be handled in an easier way.

Combine the equations by adding or subtracting them, to cancel out all but one of the variables. You can't eliminate p or q by adding or subtracting the equations in their present forms. But if you multiply the second equation by 2:

$$2(3p + q) = 2(12)$$
$$6p + 2q = 24$$

Now when you subtract the first equation from the second, the q's will cancel out so you can solve for p:

$$\begin{array}{r} 6p + 2q = 24 \\ -[p + 2q = 14] \\ \hline 5p + 0 = 10 \end{array}$$

If $5p = 10$, $p = 2$. On the answer sheet, you would grid in the answer 2.

Symbolism

You should be quite familiar with the arithmetic symbols +, –, ×, ÷, and %. Finding the value of 10 + 2, 18 – 4, 4 × 9, or 96 ÷ 16 is easy.

However, on the SAT, you may also come across bizarre symbols. You may even be asked to find the value of 10 ★ 2, 5 ❄ 7, 10 ✸ 6, or 65 ❤ 2.

The SAT test makers put strange symbols in questions to confuse or unnerve you. Don't let them. The question stem always tells you what the strange symbol means. Although this type of question may look difficult, it is really an exercise in plugging in. Look at the example on the next page:

> If $a \star b = \overline{a + b}$ for all non-negative numbers, what is the value of $10 \star 6$?
>
> (A) 0
> (B) 2
> (C) 4
> (D) 8
> (E) 16

To solve, just plug in 10 for *a* and 6 for *b* into the expression $\overline{a + b}$. That equals $\overline{10 + 6}$ or $\overline{16}$ or 4, choice (C).

Special Triangles

Look for the special triangles in geometry problems. Special triangles contain a lot of information. For instance, if you know the length of one side of a 30-60-90 triangle, you can easily work out the lengths of the others. Special triangles allow you to transfer one piece of information around the whole figure.

The following are the special triangles you should look for on the SAT. You don't have to memorize the ratios (they'll be listed in the instructions), but you should be able to recognize them.

Equilateral Triangles

All interior angles are 60°, and all sides have equal length.

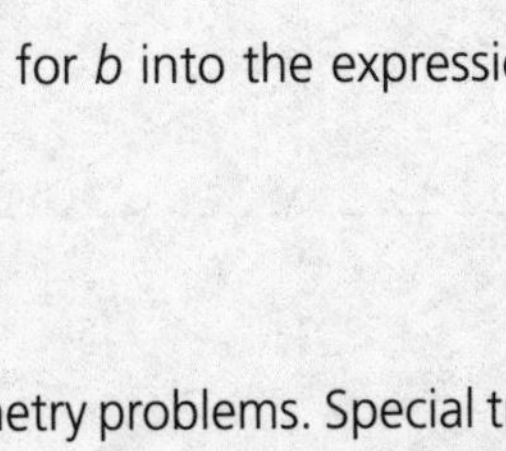

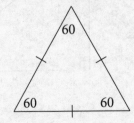

Isosceles Triangles

Two sides have equal length, and the angles facing these sides are equal.

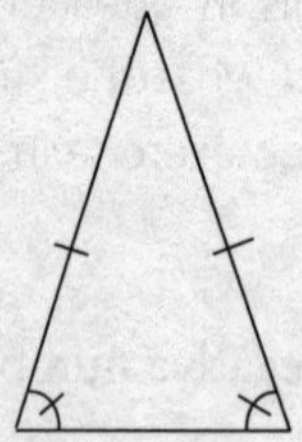

Right Triangles

These contain a 90° angle. The sides are related by the Pythagorean theorem: $a^2 + b^2 = c^2$, where a and b are the legs and c is the hypotenuse.

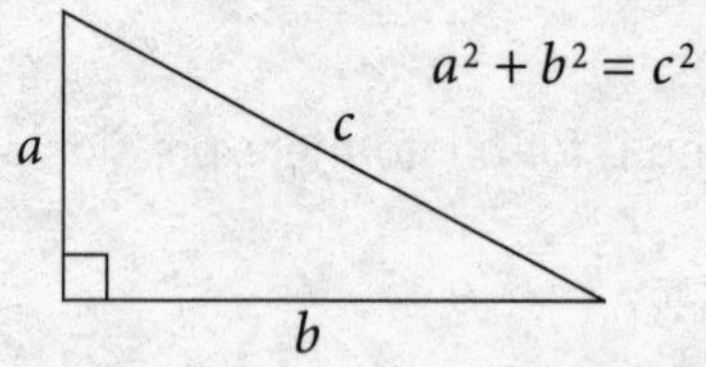

The "Special" Right Triangles

Many triangle problems contain "special" right triangles, whose side lengths always come in predefined ratios. If you recognize them, you won't have to use the Pythagorean theorem to find the value of a missing side length.

The 3-4-5 Right Triangle

(Be on the lookout for multiples of 3-4-5 as well.)

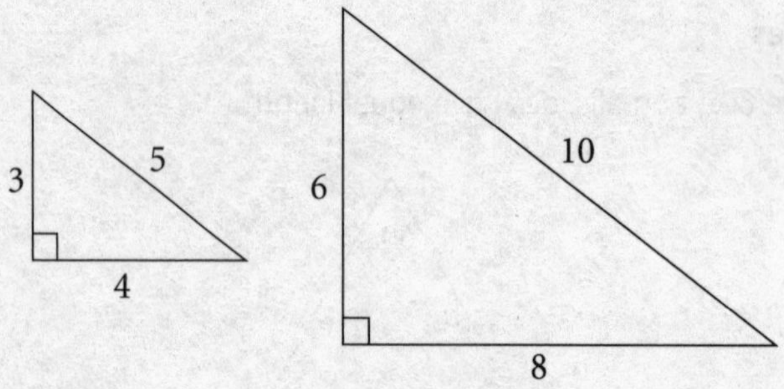

The Isosceles Right Triangle

(Note the side ratio: 1 to 1 to $\sqrt{2}$.)

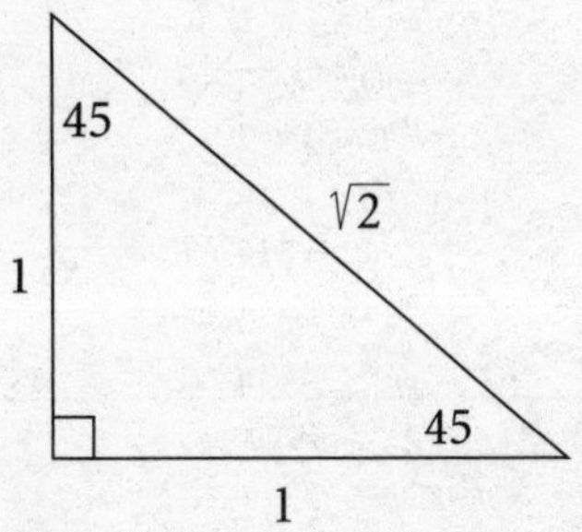

The 30-60-90 Right Triangle

(Note the side ratio: 1 to $\sqrt{3}$ to 2, and which side is opposite which angle.)

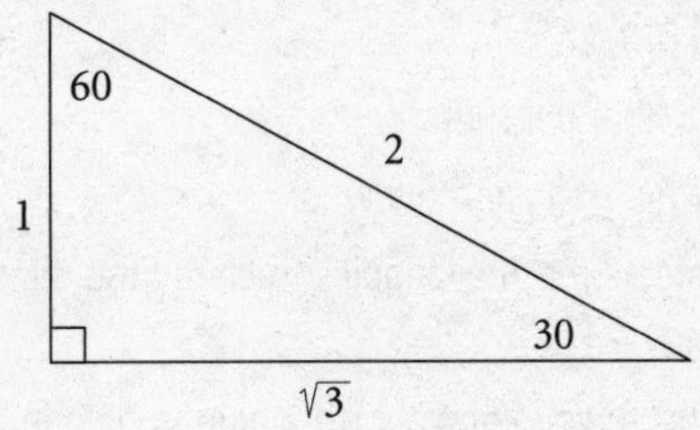

Now that we've gone through all the special triangles, try this problem.

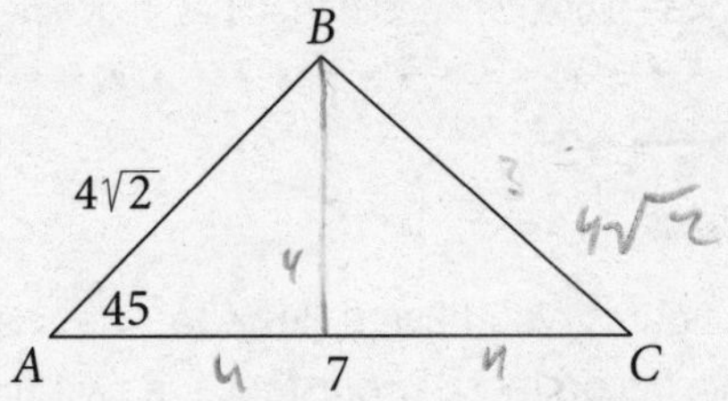

Note: Figure not drawn to scale.

In the triangle above, what is the length of side BC ?

(A) 4
(B) 5
(C) $4\sqrt{2}$
(D) 6
(E) $5\sqrt{2}$

You can drop a vertical line from B to line AC. This divides the triangle into two right triangles. Now you know two of the angles in the triangle on the left: 90° and 45°. The third angle must also be 45°, so this is an isosceles right triangle, with sides in the ratio of 1 to 1 to $\sqrt{2}$. The hypotenuse is $4\sqrt{2}$, so both legs have length 4.

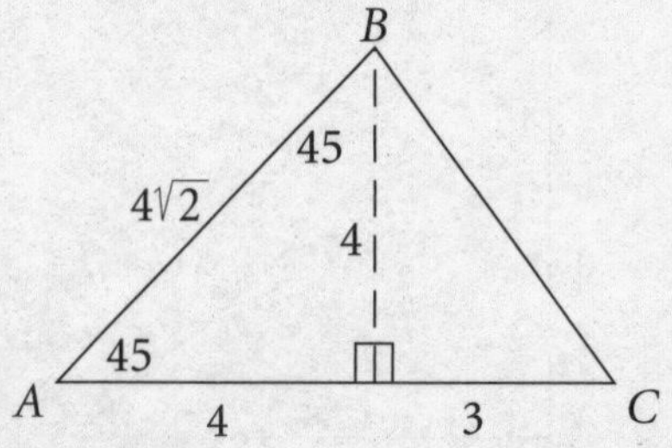

Now you can see that the legs of the smaller triangle on the right must be 4 and 3, making this a 3-4-5 right triangle, and the length of hypotenuse BC is 5. Choice (B) is correct.

Basic Math Tips

Averages—Work with the sum.

Ratios—Identify the parts and the whole.

Rates—Pick numbers for the variables to clarify the relationship between units.

Percents—Make sure you know which whole to plug in.

Simultaneous Equations—Combine equations by adding or subtracting them to cancel out all but one variable.

Special Triangles—Look for special triangles in geometry problems.

Multiple and Strange Figures

In a problem that combines figures, you have to look for the relationship between the figures. Look for pieces that they have in common. For instance, if two figures share a side, information about that side will probably be the key.

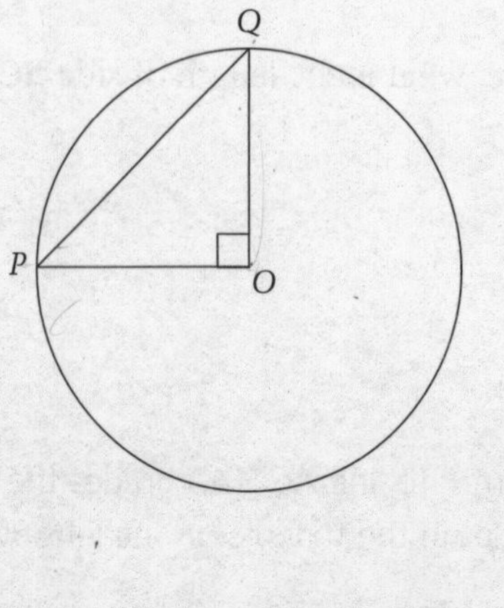

In the figure above, if the area of the circle with center O is 9π, what is the area of triangle POQ π

(A) 4.5
(B) 6
(C) 9
(D) 3.5π
(E) 4.5π

In this case, the figures don't share a side, but the triangle's legs are important features of the circle—they are radii. You can see that $PO = OQ =$ the radius of circle O. The area of the circle is 9?. The area of a circle is πr^2, where $r =$ the radius. So $9\pi = \pi r^2$, $9 = r^2$, and the radius = 3.

The area of a triangle is $\frac{1}{2}$ base × height. Therefore, the area of ΔPOQ is $\frac{1}{2}(\text{leg}_1 \times \text{leg}_2) =$

$$\frac{1}{2}(3 \times 3) = \frac{9}{2} = 4.5\text{, choice (A).}$$

But what if, instead of a number of familiar shapes, you are given something like this?

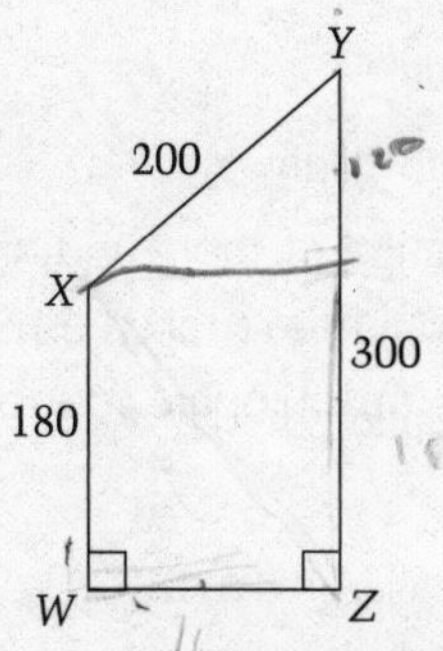

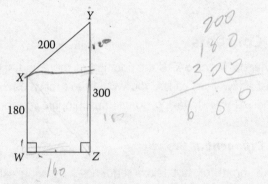

What is the perimeter of quadrilateral *WXYZ*?

(A) 680
(B) 760
(C) 840
(D) 920
(E) 1,000

Try breaking the unfamiliar shape into familiar ones. Once this is done, you can use the same techniques that you would for multiple figures. Perimeter is the sum of the lengths of the sides of a figure, so you need to find the length of *WZ*. Drawing a perpendicular line from point *X* to side *YZ* will divide the figure into a right triangle and a rectangle. Call the point of intersection *A*.

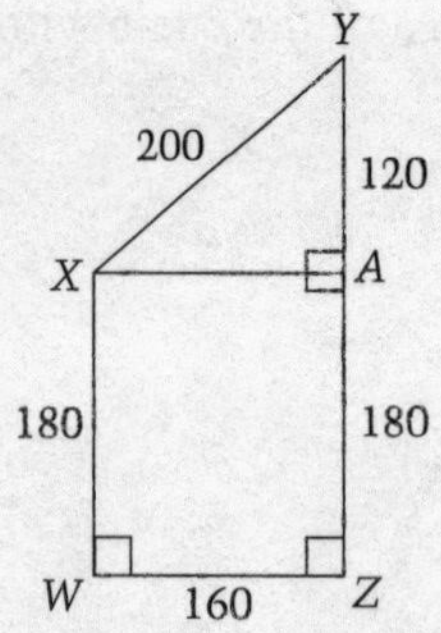

Opposite sides of a rectangle have equal length, so $WZ = XA$ and $WX = ZA$. WX is labeled as 180, so $ZA = 180$. Because YZ measures 300, AY is $300 - 180 = 120$. In right triangle XYA, hypotenuse $XY = 200$, and leg $AY = 120$; you should recognize this as a multiple of a 3-4-5 right triangle. The hypotenuse is 5×40, one leg is 3×40, so XA must be 4×40 or 160. (If you didn't recognize this special right triangle, you could have used the Pythagorean theorem to find the length of XA.) Because $WZ = XA = 160$, the perimeter of the figure is $180 + 200 + 300 + 160 = 840$, answer choice (C).

Advanced Math Concepts

One of the big recent changes in the SAT is the addition of more and harder math like algebra-II. If you had been born just a few years earlier, you would have taken an SAT that tested only basic math. But, alas, this is the SAT you are taking, so we must prepare you for the more difficult math.

Sequences Involving Exponential Growth

The name sounds like a mouthful, but relax: sequences involving exponential growth—also known as geometric sequences—are a tough but manageable area of SAT math.

What is a geometric sequence, and what does it take to ace questions about them on the SAT? A geometric sequence of numbers is simply one in which a constant ratio exists between consecutive terms. Questions about geometric sequences are likely to hinge on this formula:

> If r is the ratio between consecutive terms, a_1 is the first term, and a_n is the nth term, then $a_n = a_1 r^{n-1}$

This is how the SAT might ask a question about geometric sequences.

If the first term in a geometric sequence is 4 and the fifth term is 64, what is the eighth term?

(A) 512
(B) 864
(C) 1,245
(D) 13,404
(E) 22,682

First, use the formula to solve for r:

$64 = 4r^4$
$16 = r^4$
$r = 2$

Now, using $r = 2$, solve for a_8:

$a_8 = 4(2)^7$
$a_8 = 512$

If r is the ratio between consecutive terms, a_1 is the first term, and a_n is the nth term, then $a_n = a_1 r^{n-1}$

Sets

The things in a set are called *elements* or *members*. The union of sets, sometimes expressed with the symbol ∪, is the set of elements that are in either or both of the different sets you start with. Think of the union set as what you get when you merge sets. For example, if Set $A = \{1, 2\}$ and Set $B = \{3, 4\}$, then $A \cup B$ {1, 2, 3 ,4}.

The intersection of sets, sometimes expressed with the symbol ∩, is the set of elements common to the respective sets you start with. For example, if Set $A = \{1, 2, 3\}$ and Set $B = \{3, 4, 5\}$, then $A \cap B = \{3\}$.

Try to work through the following example.

If Set *R* contains 6 distinct numbers and Set *S* contains 5 distinct letters, how many elements are in the union of the two sets?

(A) 1
(B) 5
(C) 6
(D) 8
(E) 11

Because Set R and Set S contain different kinds of elements, no element is in both sets. So the union set of S and R—$S \cup R$—contains everything in each: 6 + 5 = 11.

Sets

Think of the union of sets as what you get when you merge the sets. Think of the intersection of sets as the overlap of the sets.

Absolute Value

The absolute value of a number is the distance between that number and zero on the number line. Because absolute value is a distance, it is always positive. The absolute value of 7 is 7; this is expressed as $|7| = 7$. Similarly, the absolute value of –7 is 7: $|-7| = 7$. Every positive number is the absolute value of two numbers: itself and its negative counterpart. As you'll see in the next example, the SAT sometimes connects the concept of absolute value to the concept of inequalities.

If $|r + 7| < 2$, which of the following statements are true?

I. $r < -9$
II. $r < -5$
III. $r > -9$

(A) I only
(B) II only
(C) III only
(D) I and II only
(E) II and III only

You can solve this problem algebraically, as shown below, or you can think about what the inequality would look like on a number line. You can express $|r + 7| < 2$ *as the difference between r and –7 is less than* 2 and determine that r must be between –5 and –9:

$r + 7 < 2$ and $-r - 7 < 2$
$r < -5$ and $-r < 9$
$r < -5$ and $r > -9$

Absolute value

The distance of a number from zero on the number line.

Rational Equations and Inequalities

A rational equation or inequality is one that contains at least one fraction in which the numerator and denominator are polynomials.

For all values of x not equal to –2 or 3,

$\dfrac{x^4 - 5x^3 - 2x^2 + 24x}{x^2 - x - 6}$ is equal to

(A) $x2 - 4x$
(B) $x2 - 5x - 2$
(C) $x + 24$
(D) x
(E) $x - 4$

Picking Numbers is the easiest way to solve this problem. Say $x = 2$:

$$\frac{2^4 - 5(2^3) - 2(2^2) + 24(2)}{2^2 - 2 - 6} = \frac{16 - 5(8) - 2(4) + 24(2)}{4 - 2 - 6} = \frac{16 - 40 - 8 + 48}{-4} = \frac{16}{-4} = -4$$

Now find the choice with a value of –4 when $x = 2$. Only (A) works: $2^2 - 4(2) = 4 - 8 = -4$. So, (A) is the correct answer.

Radical Equations

Like rational equations, radical equations—ones with at least one variable under a radical sign—follow the same rules as other kinds of algebraic equations, so solve them accordingly. What makes radical equations special is that the last step in isolating the variable is often to square both sides of the equation. Look at the following example.

If $4 - \sqrt{n} = -1$, what is the value of n?

(A) 3
(B) 5
(C) 9
(D) 25
(E) 81

Apply the same algebraic steps here as you would in any other question involving an equation, isolating the variable step by step. Just remember to square both sides of the equation as your last step. (Notice that (B) is a trap set for test takers who forget to do so. We will cover math traps in more detail in Step 9.)

$4 - \sqrt{n} = -1$

$5 = \sqrt{n}$

$(5)^2 = (\sqrt{n})^2$

$25 = n$

Manipulation with Integer and Rational Exponents

Not every exponent on the SAT is a positive integer. Numbers can be raised to a fractional or negative exponent. Although such numbers follow their own special rules, they adhere to the same general rules of exponents that you've probably worked with before.

If $x = \frac{1}{4}$, $x^{-4} =$

(A) $\frac{-1}{256}$

(B) $\frac{-1}{16}$

(C) 4

(D) 16

(E) 256

To find the value of a number raised to a negative power, rewrite the number without the negative sign in front of the exponent as the bottom of a fraction. Then, place 1 as the numerator of the fraction: $3^{-2} = \frac{1}{3^2} = \frac{1}{9}$. In this case:

$$x^{-4} = \frac{1}{x^4} = \frac{1}{\left(\frac{1}{4}\right)^4} = \frac{1}{\left(\frac{1}{256}\right)} = 256$$

Direct and Inverse Variation

In direct variation, $y = kx$, where k is a nonzero constant. In direct variation, the variable y changes directly as x does. If a unit of Currency A is worth 2 units of Currency B, then $A = 2B$. If the number of units of B were to double, the number of units of A would double, and so on for halving, tripling, etc.

In inverse variation, $xy = k$, where x and y are variables and k is a constant. A famous inverse relationship is *rate* × *time* = *distance*. Imagine having to cover a distance of 24 miles. If you were to travel at 12 miles per hour, you'd need 2 hours. But if you were to cut your rate in half, you would have to double your time. This is just another way of saying that rate and time vary inversely. The following is an example of direct and indirect variation.

If the length of a sea turtle is directly proportional to its age, and a 2-year-old sea turtle is 3 inches long, how many feet long is an 80-year-old sea turtle?

(A) 10
(B) 12
(C) 100
(D) 120
(E) 144

Relate the length of the turtle to its age. Use the equation to find the length of an 80-year-old sea turtle in inches; then convert from inches to feet. Because length is directly proportional to age, you can represent their relationship as $l = ka$, where l is length, a is age, and k is a constant:

$3 = k(2)$

$1.5 = k$

$l = 1.5(80) = 120$ inches $= 10$ feet

(A) is the correct answer.

Function Notation and Evaluation

A few questions on Test Day will probably focus on functions and use standard function notation such as $f(x)$. Evaluating a function sounds fancy, but it mostly involves substitution of numbers for variables—a skill you should already be familiar with.

For example, to evaluate the function $f(x) = 5x + 1$ for $f(3)$, replace x with 3 and simplify: $f(3) = 5(3) + 1 = 15 + 1 = 16$

The example below presents a slightly more complex variation: a composition of functions. $h[g(a)]$ requires you to first evaluate $g(a)$, and then apply h to the result.

If $g(a) = (a + 4)^2$ and $h(b) = 2b - 7$, then what is the value of $h[g(2)]$?

(A) 1
(B) 36
(C) 45
(D) 65
(E) 79

Follow the order of operations:

$g(2) = (2 + 4)^2 = 6^2 = 36$

$h(36) = 2(36) - 7 = 72 - 7 = 65$

Concepts of Domain and Range

The domain of a function is the set of values for which the function is defined. The domain of $f(x) = \frac{1}{1-x^2}$ is all values of x except 1 and –1, because for those values, the denominator has a value of 0 and is therefore undefined. The range of a function is the set of outputs or results of the function. The range of $f(x) = x^2$ is all numbers greater than or equal to zero because x^2 cannot be negative.

If $f(a) = a^2 + 7$ for all real values of a, which of the following is a possible value of $f(a)$?

(A) –2
(B) 0
(C) $\sqrt{5}$
(D) $\sqrt{7}$
(E) $100\sqrt{3}$

If a is a real number, then a^2 must be positive or equal to zero. Think about how this limits the range of $f(a)$: If $a = 0$, then $f(a) = 7$. All other values of a result in a higher value of $f(a)$. Only (E) is greater than 7.

Functions

The domain of a function is the set of values for which the function is defined. The range of a function is the set of possible values of the function.

Functions as Models

The SAT might challenge your ability to relate functional relationships to real-life situations. For example, you may be asked to interpret data about the relationship between the selling price of a car and the number of cars that sell at that price.

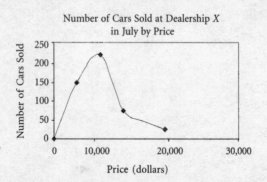

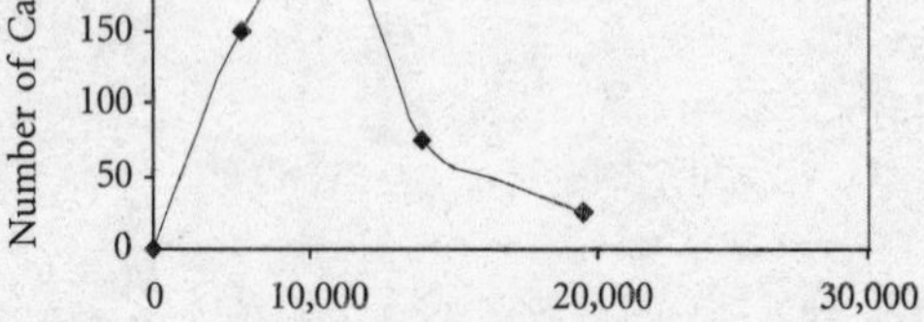

The graph on the previous page represents the number of cars sold at Dealership X in July. If the dealer wants to sell the maximum number of cars possible in August, at what price should he set the cars, based on his sales in July?

(A) 5,000
(B) 10,000
(C) 15,000
(D) 20,000
(E) 22,500

Make sure to read your graphs carefully, knowing what each axis represents. If you are not careful, you may choose the incorrect answer that is meant as a trap.

Use the graph of July to figure out which price point sold the most cars. The peak value is \$10,000, which sold 225 cars. Based on this information, the dealer should price cars at \$10,000 (B) in August and hope to sell the maximum number of cars that he can in that month.

Linear Functions—Equations and Graphs

You'll most likely see a question or two on the SAT involving equations and graphs of linear functions. A linear function is simply an equation whose graph is a straight line. For example:

Which of the following equations describes a line perpendicular to the line $y = 7x + 49$?

(A) $y = -7x - 49$
(B) $y = -\frac{1}{7}x + 10$
(C) $y = \frac{1}{7}x + 7$
(D) $y = 7x - 49$
(E) $y = 7x + 14$

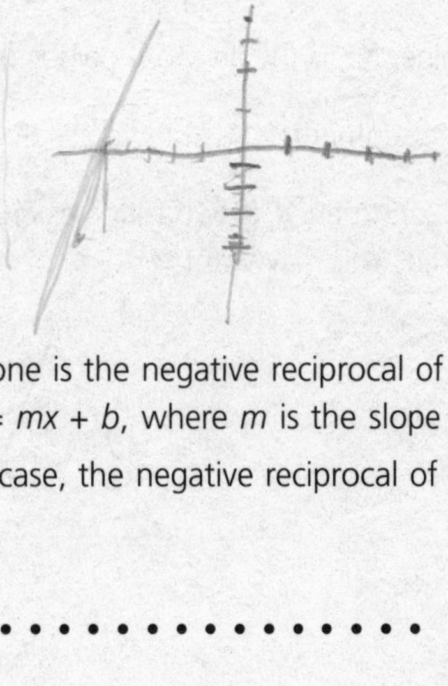

If two lines are perpendicular, then the slope of one is the negative reciprocal of the slope of the other. These lines are written in the form $y = mx + b$, where m is the slope and b is the y-intercept, or the value of y when $x = 0$. In this case, the negative reciprocal of 7 is $-\frac{1}{7}$. The only equation with this slope is (B).

Slopes

Parallel lines have equal slopes. Perpendicular lines have negative reciprocal slopes.

Quadratic Functions–Equations and Graphs

A quadratic function is one that takes the form $f(x) = ax^2 + bx + c$. Rather than take the form of a straight line as, you'll recall, a linear function does, the graph of a quadratic function is a parabola. As the question next illustrates, a quadratic function question could be similar to a quadratic equations question.

If $x^2 - 7x + 12 = 0$, what is the sum of the two possible values of x?

(A) –4
(B) –1
(C) 3
(D) 4
(E) 7

Factor:

$x^2 - 7x + 12 = 0$

$(x - 4)(x - 3) = 0$

$x = 4$ or $x = 3$

$4 + 3 = 7$

Geometric Notation for Length, Segments, Lines, Rays, and Congruence

You should expect SAT geometry questions to use the symbols $\leftrightarrow$, —, and $\cong$.

$\leftrightarrow$ signifies a line. $\overleftrightarrow{XY}$ is the line that passes through points X and Y.

— signifies line segment: $\overline{XY}$ is the line segment whose endpoints are X and Y.

$\cong$ symbolizes congruence. If two triangles are congruent, they coincide exactly when superimposed. You may want to think of two congruent figures as identical twins.

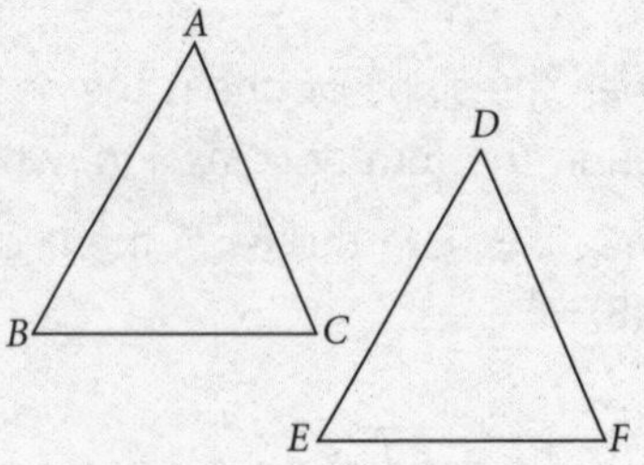

Note: Figures not drawn to scale.

$\angle CAB \cong \angle FDE$ and $\angle ABC \cong \angle DEF$. Which of the following must be true?

I. $\Delta ABC \cong \Delta DEF$

II. Triangles *ABC* and *DEF* are similar.

III. $\overline{AB} = \overline{DE}$

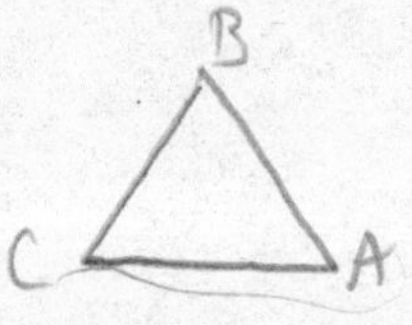

(A) II only

(B) III only

(C) I and III

(D) II and III

(E) I, II, and III

When a figure is not drawn to scale, it is most likely drawn in a misleading way. This figure certainly looks as though *ABC* and *DEF* are identical and that all their parts are congruent, but you can't assume that based on the information in the problem. You may want to draw your own diagrams to think about some of the different possibilities. All we know about these triangles is that they share two angles. Therefore, the third angle of each triangle must also be congruent. This tells us that the triangles are similar because their angles are the same. However, we know nothing about the lengths of the sides—one triangle could be much smaller than the other; thus, choice (A) is the correct answer.

Trigonometry as an Alternative Method of Solution

Now more than ever, the SAT will reward test takers who recall the special relationships in 45-45-90 and 30-60-90 right triangles:

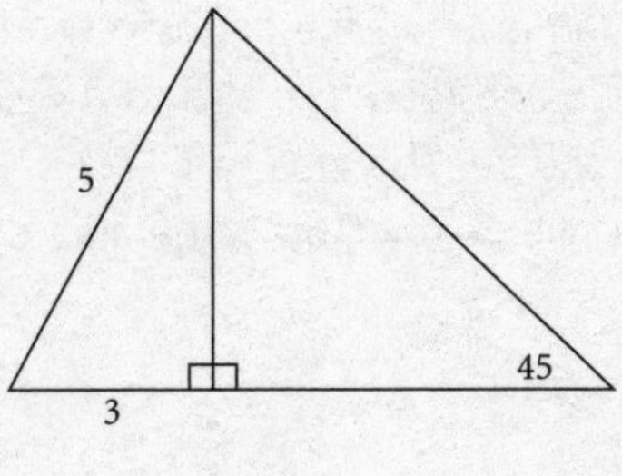

What is the total area of the figure above?

To find the area of a triangle, you need its height and the length of its base. Think about the information presented in the figure. What other data can you derive from it? The triangle on the left is a special triangle with side lengths of 3, 4, and 5. (You could also find the missing side using the Pythagorean theorem.) The triangle on the right is a 45-45-90 triangle, so its base must also equal 4. The total area of the figure is $\frac{1}{2}(3 + 4)(4) = 14$.

Properties of Tangent Lines

When a line is tangent to a circle, the radius of the circle is perpendicular to the line at the point of contact. Look at the following example.

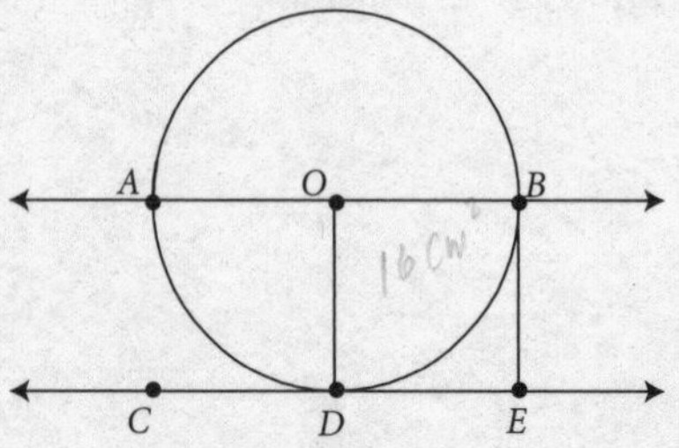

In the figure above, *AB* is the diameter of the circle, and *CE* is tangent to the circle at point *D*. *AB* is parallel to *CE*. If the area of quadrilateral *OBED* is 16 cm^2, what is the area of the circle whose center is at *O*?

(A) 4 cm^2
(B) 4π cm^2
(C) 8π cm^2
(D) 16π cm^2
(E) 256 cm^2

Because there's a circle in this problem, you can be sure you'll need the radius at some point. To figure out how to get that from the area of quadrilateral *OBED*, you'll need to use the rest of the information in the question stem. It may be helpful to add a few angles to the figure—for instance, because *CE* is tangent to the circle at point *D*, it is perpendicular to the radius of the circle at that point. The information given in the first two sentences of the question stem tells you that *OD* is perpendicular to *CE* and therefore also to *AB*. *OB* and *OD* are both radii of the circle, so quadrilateral *OBED* is a square. The area of *OBED* is 16, so each side has a length of 4. This is also the radius of the circle. $4^2\pi = 16\pi$ is the area of the circle, so you should have chosen answer (*D*).

Coordinate Geometry

Coordinate geometry questions on the SAT tend to focus on the properties of straight lines. The equation of a straight line is $y = mx + b$, where *y* and *x* are the infinite number of coordinated (*x*, *y*) pairs that fall on the line. *b* is the *y*-intercept, or the value of *y* when $x = 0$. *m* is the slope of the line and is expressed $\frac{3Y}{3X}$, or $\frac{y_2 - y_1}{x_2 - x_1}$. What this means, exactly, is that the slope or steepness of a line is the change in y-values in relation to the change in corresponding *x*-values. Positive slopes tilt upward to the right. Negative slopes tilt downward to the right. A horizontal line has a slope of zero. A vertical line has an undefined slope. Parallel lines have equal slopes. Perpendicular lines have negative reciprocal slopes.

As this question illustrates, the SAT may also ask you to identify the midpoint of a line segment or the distance between two points.

If point P is at (8, 10) and point Q is at (0, 4), what is the midpoint of PQ?

(A) (0, 10)
(B) (4, 2)
(C) (4, 5)
(D) (4, 7)
(E) (9, 2)

The midpoint of a line segment whose ends are at the points (x_1, y_1) and (x_2, y_2) is the point $\left(\frac{x_1 + x_2}{2}, \frac{y_1 + y_2}{2}\right)$. Now plug in the numbers from the question.

$x = \frac{8 + 0}{2} = \frac{8}{2} = 4$

$y = \frac{10 + 4}{2} = \frac{14}{2} = 7$

The midpoint is (4, 7).

Distance Formula

The distance between the points (x_1, y_1) and (x_2, y_2) is given by the distance formula: $(x_1, y_1)^2 + (x_2, y_2)^2$.

Qualitative Behavior of Graphs and Functions

The SAT will likely ask you to show an understanding of a general or particular property of a complex graph, such as the one in this example:

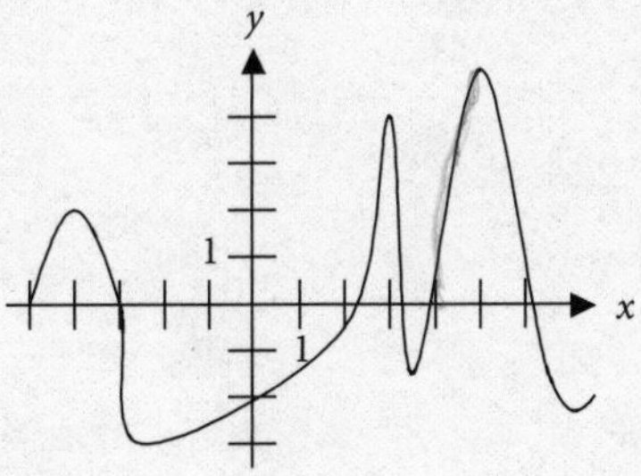

The figure above shows the graph of $f(x)$. At how many values of x does $f(x)$ equal 4?

(A) 0
(B) 1
(C) 2
(D) 3
(E) 4

The value of $f(x)$ is measured on the y-axis. Find 4 on the y-axis, and then see how many points on the graph have a y-value of 4. The points are approximately (3, 4), (4.7, 4), and (5.4, 4). So your answer here is 3, choice *(D)*.

Transformations and Their Effect on Graphs of Functions

A transformation is an alteration in a function. An SAT question might present a graph and ask you to identify a specific transformation, such as in the following question.

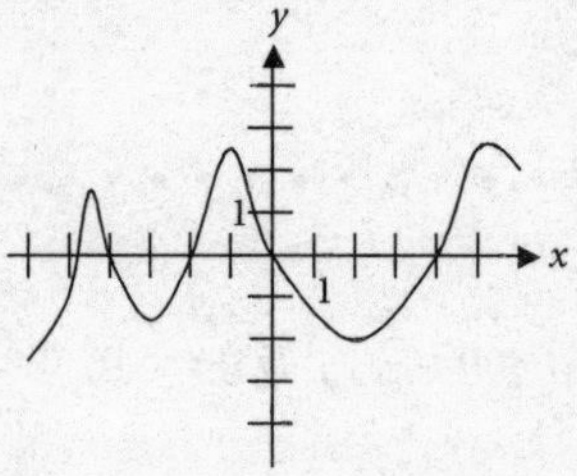

The figure above shows the graph of the function $r(x)$. Which of the following figures shows the graph of the function $r(x - 2)$?

(A) 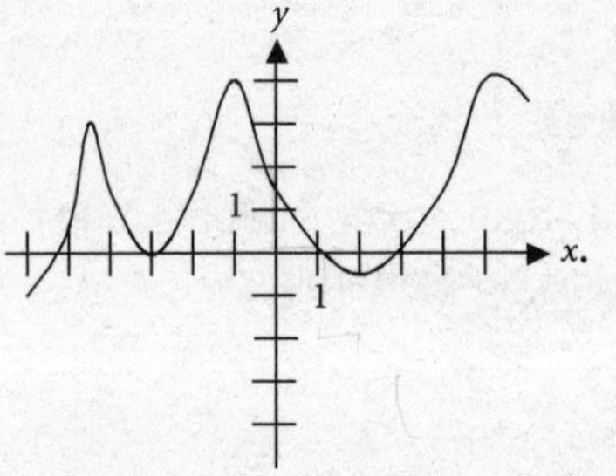

(B) 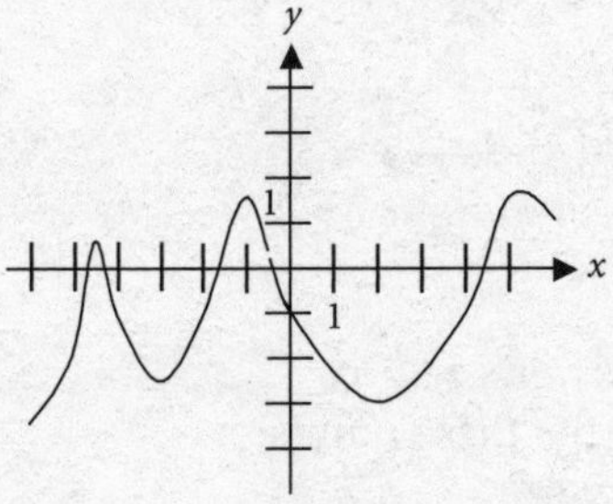

(C) 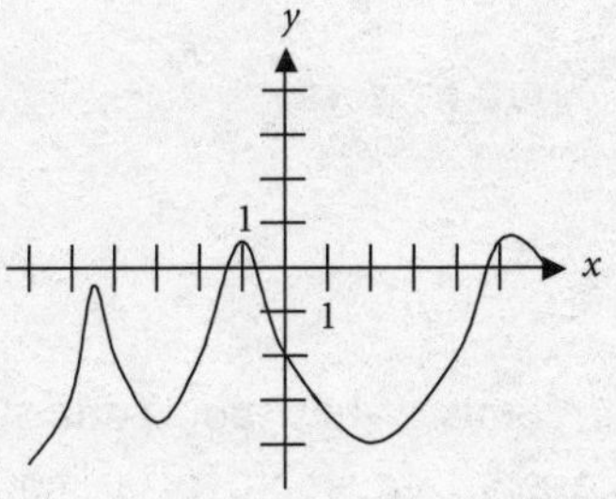

(D) 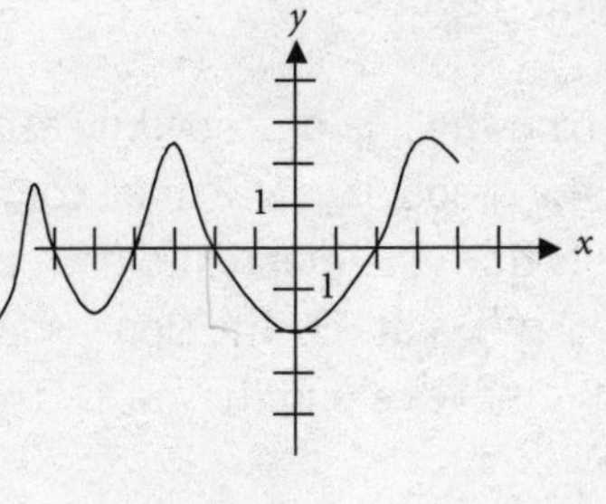

(E) 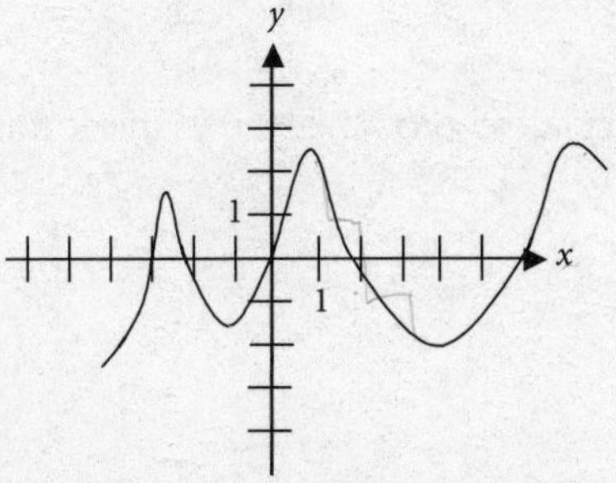

The graph of $r(x-2)$ will look like the graph of $r(x)$ shifted two units to the right. You can check this by plugging in a few points. For example, $r(-1) = 2.5$, so $r(1-2)$ should equal 2.5. This is only true of answer (E).

Data Interpretation, Scatterplots, and Matrices

Some SAT questions focus on the test taker's ability to interpret, evaluate, and draw conclusions from data presented in matrices or, like those below, in scatterplots.

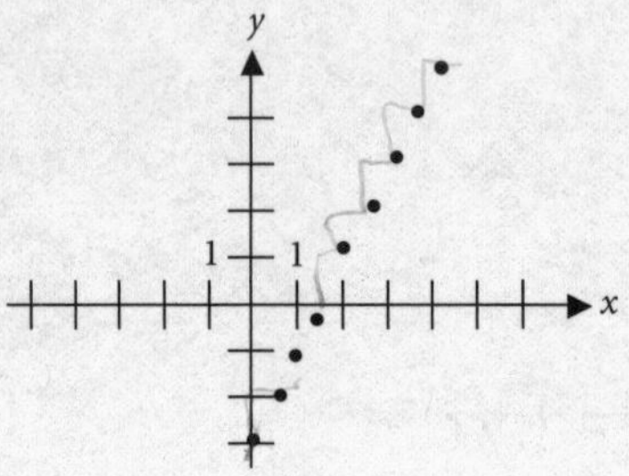

Which of the following equations best fits these points?

(A) $y = 3x + 2$
(B) $y = 3x - 2$
(C) $y = 2x + 3$
(D) $y = 2x - 3$
(E) $y = x - 3$

Try to figure out what sort of line would fit these points. What should the slope be? What should the y-intercept be? Remember that the standard equation for a line is in the form $y = mx + b$, where m is the slope and b is the y-intercept.

If you think visually, you might want to try sketching the line described by each answer choice to see which one fits the closest to the points on the graph. If you're more comfortable working with numbers, you could try plugging a few points from the graph into each possible equation to see which one works. The y-intercept of this graph is at –3. The slope is around 2 because the graph is raised about 2 units for every 1 unit it moves along the x-axis. The answer is (D).

Geometric Probability

Geometric probability questions ask you to calculate a probability. Use the formula:

$$\text{Probability} = \frac{\text{Desired outcome}}{\text{Possible outcome}}.$$

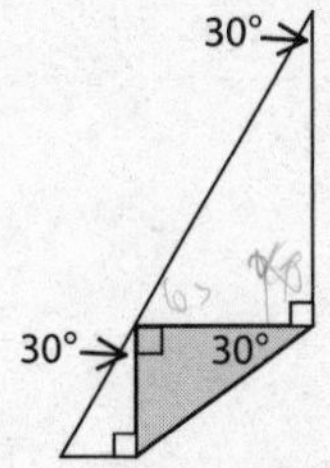

What is the probability that a point selected at random from the interior of the figure above will fall within the shaded region?

(A) $\frac{\sqrt{3}}{13}$

(B) $\frac{3}{13}$

(C) $\frac{6}{13}$

(D) $\frac{1}{3}$

(E) $\frac{1}{2}$

The probability that a randomly selected point will fall into the shaded region is equal to the area of the shaded region divided by the area of the entire figure. The figure is made up of three 30-60-90 triangles, so you can calculate the ratio of the lengths of the bases and heights of the various triangles and then find their areas.

This will be easier though if you pick a number to be the length of the base of the smallest triangle. The lengths of the sides of a 30-60-90 triangle are in the ratio $x:x\sqrt{3}:2x$. If the length of the smallest triangle is 1, its height is $\sqrt{3}$. This is also the length of the base of the middle triangle. The height of the middle triangle is $\sqrt{3} \times \sqrt{3} = 3$, which is also the length of the base of the largest triangle. The height of the largest triangle is $3\sqrt{3}$.

Area of smallest triangle: $\frac{1}{2}(1)\left(\sqrt{3}\right) = \frac{\sqrt{3}}{2}$

Area of middle triangle: $\frac{1}{2}\left(\sqrt{3}\right)(3) = \frac{3\sqrt{3}}{2}$

Area of largest triangle: $\frac{1}{2}(3)\left(3\sqrt{3}\right) = \frac{9\sqrt{3}}{2}$

Probability $= \frac{\text{Desired outcome}}{\text{Possible outcome}}$

Probability that a point will lie in the shaded region:

$$\frac{\frac{3\sqrt{3}}{2}}{\frac{3\sqrt{3}}{2}+\frac{3\sqrt{3}}{2}+\frac{9\sqrt{3}}{2}}=\frac{\frac{3\sqrt{3}}{2}}{\frac{13\sqrt{3}}{2}}=\frac{3}{13}$$

Now that you know what will be tested on the Math section, you need to know how to effectively work through the Math section. Step 8 will show you our best strategies for scoring high in Math, and a practice test using the concepts you just learned will follow. If you are struggling with any of the practice questions, be sure to come back to this step for review.

SUMMARY

- **The Gist of It:**
  - 3 scored Math sections
    - 25 minute multiple-choice section
    - 25 minute multiple-choice and grid-in questions section
    - 20 minute multiple-choice section
  - Questions get progressively harder as the test progresses
- **Directions:**
  - You won't have to deal with imaginary numbers
  - Diagrams are always drawn to scale, unless otherwise noted
  - You cannot grid negative answers, variables, answers greater than 9,999, answers with commas, or mixed numbers
- **Scoring:**
  - On multiple-choice questions you gain one point for each correct answer and lose a fraction of a point for each wrong answer
  - You do not gain or lose anything for answers left blank
  - On the grid-in questions you lose nothing for an incorrect answer
- **Basic Math Concepts Tested:**
  - Remainders
  - Averages: Working with the sum
  - Ratios: Identifying the parts and the whole
  - Rates: Picking numbers for the variables to clarify the relationships between units
  - Percents: Making sure you know which whole to plug in
  - Simultaneous Equations: Combining equations by adding or subtracting them to cancel out all but one variable
  - Symbolism

- — Triangles: Understanding special triangles, isosceles triangles, right triangles, special right triangles
- — Multiple and strange figures: looking for the relationship between the figures

- **Advanced Math Concepts Tested:**
  - — Sequences Involving Exponential Growth
  - — Sets
  - — Absolute Value
  - — Rational Equations and Inequalities
  - — Radical Equations
  - — Manipulation with Integer and Rational Exponents
  - — Direct and Inverse Variation
  - — Function Notation and Evaluation
  - — Concepts of Domain and Range
  - — Functions as Models
  - — Linear Functions- Equations and Graphs
  - — Quadratic Functions
  - — Geometric Notation for Length, Segments, Lines, Rays and Congruence
  - — Trigonometry as an Alternative Method of Solution
  - — Properties of Tangent Lines
  - — Coordinate Geometry
  - — Qualitative Behavior of Graphs and Functions
  - — Transformations and Their Effect on Graphs of Functions
  - — Data Interpretation, Scatterplots, and Matrices
  - — Geometric Probability

Step Eight

Strategies for Acing the Math Section

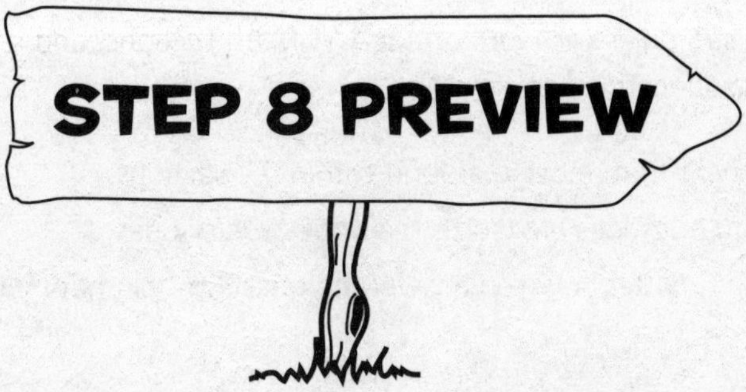

How to Get a High Score

- Kaplan's Five-Step Method for Math Question
- Alternative Techniques
- Grid-in Strategies
- Strategies for Educated Guessing
- Using your Calculator (or Not)

Summary

Practice

Answers and Explanations

When you take a math test at school, you probably approach it something like this:

- You work through the problems in order.
- You spend more time on the hard questions than the easier ones because they are worth more points.
- You often show how you worked through every step of a solution because many teachers give credit for doing the appropriate steps, even with the wrong answer.

None of these strategies will work on the SAT Math sections, and if you approach it that way, your score will suffer. Thus, on the SAT:

- You benefit from moving around within the sections.
- The hard questions are worth the same as easy ones.
- It doesn't matter how you answer the question—all that matters is picking the right answer.

The strategies in this chapter are designed with the above ideas in mind. Study the strategies, and practice using them on the practice set at the end of this chapter. Mastering these strategies will help improve your score.

HOW TO GET A HIGH SCORE

Kaplan's Five-Step Method for Math Questions

Now you know the two kinds of questions you'll see on the SAT Math sections and the concepts that will be tested. To maximize your score on these questions, you need to work systematically. Just like the Critical Reading and Writing questions, the key to working systematically on Math questions is to think about the question before you look for the answer. On basic problems, you may know what to do right away. But on harder problems, a few extra seconds spent looking for traps, thinking about your approach, and deciding whether to work on the problem now or come back to it later is very important.

Kaplan's Five-Step Method is a good system for tackling all SAT Math problems. Here it is:

Step 1: Estimate the question's difficulty.

Step 2: Read the question.

Step 3: Skip or do?

Step 4: Look for fastest approach.

Step 5: Make an educated guess.

Consider the following problem:

12. At a certain diner, Joe orders three strips of bacon and a cup of warm milk and is charged \$2.25. Stella orders two strips of bacon and a cup of warm milk and is charged \$1.70. What is the price of two strips of bacon?

(A) \$0.55
(B) \$0.60
(C) \$1.10
(D) \$1.30
(E) \$1.80

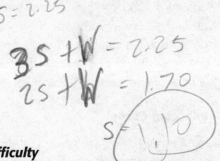

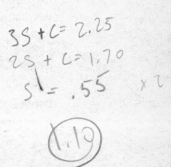

Step 1. Estimate the Question's Difficulty

All SAT Math questions are arranged in order of difficulty. Decide whether the question is basic, medium, or hard. Within a set, the first questions are basic, the middle ones moderately difficult, and the last ones are hard. Question 12 above is a moderately difficult word problem.

On difficult questions, watch out for "Math Traps" (see Step 9). Hard questions are often misleadingly worded to trip you up. Make sure you know what's being asked.

Step 2. Read the Question

If you try to start solving the problem before reading it all the way through, you may end up doing unnecessary work. Question 12 looks straightforward, but read through it carefully, and you'll see a slight twist. You're asked to find the cost of two strips of bacon, not one. Many people will find the price of a single bacon strip and forget to double it. Pity these poor people, but don't be one.

Step 3. Skip or Do

If a problem renders you clueless, circle it in your test booklet and move on. Spend your time on the problems you can solve, then come back to the ones you had trouble on later, if you have time.

Step 4. Look for the Fastest Approach

On an easy question, all the information you need to solve the problem may be given up front in the question stem or in a diagram. Harder questions often hide the information that will help you solve the problem. Because questions are arranged in order of difficulty, you should be a little wary of question 12. If you get the answer too easily, you may have missed something. (In this case, you're asked to find the price of two strips of bacon, not one.)

Look for shortcuts. Sometimes the obvious way of doing a problem is the long way. If the method you choose involves lots of calculating, look for another route. There's usually a shortcut you can use that won't involve tons of arithmetic.

In question 12, the cost of bacon and warm milk could be translated into two distinct equations using the variables *b* and *m*. You could find *m* in terms of *b*, then plug this into the other equation. But if you think carefully, you'll see there's a quicker way. The difference in price between three bacon strips and a cup of warm milk and two bacon strips and a cup of warm milk is the price of one bacon strip. So one bacon strip costs $2.25 – $1.70 = $0.55. (Remember, you have to find the price of two strips of bacon. Twice $0.55 is $1.10.)

Step 5. Make an Educated Guess

If you've tried solving a problem and are stuck, cut your losses. Eliminate any wrong answer choices you can, make an educated guess, and move on. (Guessing strategies are covered in detail later in this chapter.)

Let's say it's taking too long to solve the bacon and milk problem. Can you eliminate any answer choices? The price of two pieces of bacon and a cup of warm milk is $1.70. That means the cost of two bacon strips alone can't be $1.80, which eliminates choice (E). Now you can choose between the remaining choices, and your odds of guessing correctly have improved.

Alternative Techniques

Kaplan's Five-Step Method for Math Questions will help you save time and avoid mistakes on the SAT. But the Five-Step Method is not foolproof. Luckily, there are usually a lot of different ways to get to the right answer to a Math problem. On the SAT, there are two techniques in particular that can be useful when you don't see a way to solve the problem: Picking Numbers and Backsolving. Each takes longer than traditional methods, but they're worth trying if you have enough time.

Picking Numbers

Sometimes you get stuck on a Math question just because it's too general or abstract. A good way to bring an abstract question to its knees and make it beg for sweet mercy is to substitute particular numbers for its variables. This Picking Numbers strategy works especially well with even/odd questions.

If a is an odd integer and b is an even integer, which of the following must be odd?

(A) $2a + b$
(B) $a + 2b$
(C) ab
(D) a^2b
(E) ab^2

Rather than trying to wrap your brain around abstract variables, simply pick numbers for a and b. When it comes to adding, subtracting, and multiplying evens and odds, what happens with one pair of numbers generally happens with all similar pairs. Just say, for the time being, that $a = 3$ and $b = 2$. Plug those values into the answer choices, and there's a good chance that only one choice will be odd:

(A) $2a + b = 2(3) + 2 = 8$
(B) $a + 2b = 3 + 2(2) = 7$
(C) $ab = (3)(2) = 6$
(D) $a^2b = (3^2)(2) = 18$
(E) $ab^2 = (3)(2^2) = 12$

Choice (B) is the only odd one for $a = 3$ and $b = 2$, so it must be the one that's odd no matter what odd number a and even number b actually stand for. The answer is (B).

Another good situation for Picking Numbers is when the answer choices to a percent problem are all percents.

From 1985 to 1990, the population of Pod x increased by 20 percent. From 1990 to 1995, the population increased by 30 percent. What was the percent increase in the population over the entire 10-year period 1985–1995?

(A) 10%
(B) 25%
(C) 50%
(D) 56%
(E) 60%

Instead of trying to solve this problem in the abstract, pick a number for the original 1985 population and see what happens. There's no need to pick a realistic number. You're better off picking a number that's easy to work with. And in percent problems the number that's easiest to work with is almost always 100.

Say the 1985 population was 100. Then what would the 1990 population be? Twenty percent more than 100 is 120. Now, if the 1990 population was 120, what would the 1995 population be? What's 30 percent more than 120? Be careful. Don't just add 30 to 120. You need to find 30 percent of 120 and add that on. Thirty percent of 120 is (.30)(120) = 36. Add 36 to 120 and you get a 1995 population of 156. What percent greater is 156 than 100? That's easy—that's why we picked 100 to start with. It's a 56 percent increase. The answer is (D).

A third good situation for Picking Numbers is when the answer choices to a word problem are algebraic expressions.

If n Velcro tabs cost p dollars, then how many dollars would q Velcro tabs cost?

(A) $\frac{np}{q}$

(B) $\frac{nq}{p}$

(C) $\frac{pq}{n}$

(D) $\frac{n}{pq}$

(E) $\frac{p}{nq}$

The only thing that's hard about this question is that it uses variables instead of numbers. So, make it real. Pick Numbers for the variables. Pick Numbers that are easy to work with. Say $n = 2$, $p = 4$, and $q = 3$. Then the question becomes: "If 2 Velcro tabs cost \$4.00, how many dollars would 3 Velcro tabs cost?" That's easy—\$6.00. When $n = 2$, $p = 4$, and $q = 3$, the correct answer should equal 6. Plug those values into the answer choices and see which one yields 6:

(A) $\frac{np}{q} = \frac{(2)(4)}{3} = \frac{8}{3}$

(B) $\frac{nq}{p} = \frac{(2)(3)}{3} = \frac{6}{3} = 2$

(C) $\frac{pq}{n} = \frac{(4)(3)}{2} = \frac{12}{2} = 6$

(D) $\frac{n}{pq} = \frac{2}{(4)(3)} = \frac{2}{12} = \frac{1}{6}$

(E) $\frac{p}{nq} = \frac{4}{(2)(3)} = \frac{4}{6} = \frac{2}{3}$

Choice (C) is the only one that yields 6, so it must be the correct answer.

When Picking Numbers for an abstract word problem like this one, try all five answer choices. Sometimes more than one choice will yield the correct result. When that happens, pick another set of numbers to weed out the coincidences. Avoid picking 0 and 1—these often give several "possibly correct" answers.

Backsolving

On some Math questions, when you can't figure out the question, you can try working backwards from the answer choices. Plug the choices back into the question until you find the one that works. Backsolving works best:

- When the question is a complex word problem and the answer choices are numbers
- When the alternative is to set up multiple algebraic equations

Don't Backsolve:

- If the answer choices include variables
- On algebra questions or word problems that have ugly answer choices such as radicals and fractions (plugging them in takes too much time)

Complex question, simple answer choices—Sometimes Backsolving is faster than setting up an equation. For example:

A music club draws 27 patrons. If there are 7 more hippies than punks in the club, how many patrons are hippies?

(A) 8
(B) 10
(C) 14
(D) 17
(E) 20

The five answer choices represent the possible number of hippies in the club, so try them in the question stem. The choice that gives a total of 27 patrons, with seven more hippies than punks, will be the correct answer.

Plugging in choice (C) gives you 14 hippies in the club. Because there are 7 more hippies than punks, there are 7 punks in the club. But $14 + 7 < 27$. The sum is too small, so there must be more than 14 hippies. Eliminate answer choices (A), (B), and (C).

Either (D) or (E) will be correct. Plugging in (D) gives you 17 hippies in the club and $17 - 7$, or 10 punks: $17 + 10 = 27$ patrons total. Answer choice (D) is correct.

Algebra problems with multiple equations

If $a + b + c = 110$, $a = 4b$ and $3a = 2c$, then $b =$

(A) 6
(B) 8
(C) 9
(D) 10
(E) 14

You're looking for *b*, so plug in the answer choices for *b* in the question and see what happens. The choice that gives us 110 for the sum $a + b + c$ must be correct.

Start with the midrange number 9, choice (C):

If $b = 9$, then $a = 4 \times 9 = 36$.

$2c = 3a = 3 \times 36 = 108$

$c = 54$

$a + b + c = 36 + 9 + 54 = 99$

Because this is a smaller sum than 110, the correct value for b must be greater. Therefore, eliminate answer choices (A), (B), and (C). Now plug in either (D) or (E), and see if it works. If it doesn't, the remaining choice must be correct.

Short on time? Try guessing between (D) and (E). But guess intelligently. Because (C) wasn't far wrong, you want a number just slightly bigger. That's choice (D).

Grid-in Strategies

The Grid-in section is special. Grid-ins have no multiple-choice answers and there is no penalty for wrong answers. You have to figure out your own answer and fill it in on a special grid. Following are a few extra strategies to keep in mind for grid-in questions.

Write Your Answers in the Number Boxes

This doesn't get you points by itself, but you will make fewer mistakes if you write your answers in the number boxes. You may think that gridding directly will save time, but writing first, then gridding, helps ensure accuracy, which means more points.

Always Start Your Answer in the First Column Box

You can start in any column, it's a free country, but we recommend you submit happily to the totalitarian dictates of this strategy. If you always start with the first column, even if your answer has only one or two figures, your answers will always fit. Because there is no oval for 0 in the first column, grid an answer of 0 in any other column.

Important

If your answer is .7, don't grid 0.7! You can't grid a 0 in the first column.

In a Fractional Answer, Grid (/) in the Correct Column

The sign (/) separates the numerator from the denominator. It appears only in columns two and three. A fractional answer with four digits—like 31/42—won't fit.

Change Mixed Numbers to Decimals or Fractions Before You Grid

If you try to grid a mixed number, it will be read as a fraction and be counted wrong. For example, $4\frac{1}{2}$ will be read as the fraction $\frac{41}{2}$, which is $20\frac{1}{2}$. So, first change mixed numbers to fractions or decimals, and then grid in. In this case:

- Change $4\frac{1}{2}$ to $\frac{9}{2}$ and grid in the fraction; or
- Change $4\frac{1}{2}$ to 4.5 and grid in the decimal.

Watch Where You Put Your Decimal Points

A few pointers:

- For a decimal less than 1, such as .127, enter the decimal point in the first box.
- Only put a zero before the decimal point if it's part of the answer, as in 20.5—don't put one there (if your answer is, say, .5) just to make your answer look more accurate.
- Never grid a decimal point in the last column.

With Long or Repeating Decimals . . .

. . . grid the first three digits only and plug in the decimal point where it belongs. Say three answers are .45454545, 82.452312, and 1.428743. Grid .454, 82.4, and 1.42, respectively.

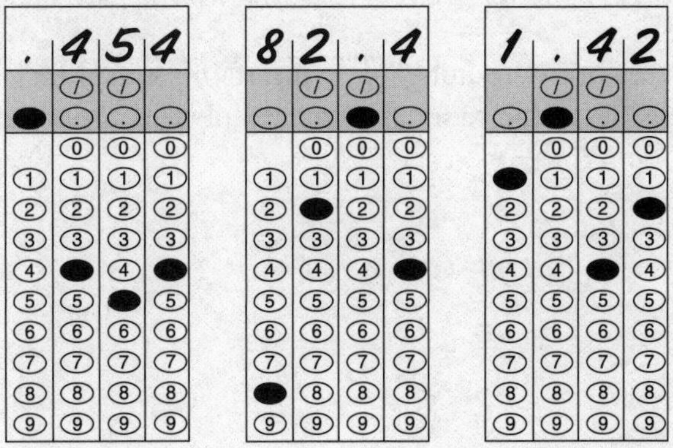

You could round 1.428743 up to the nearest hundredth (1.43). But it's not required, though, so don't bother. You could make a mistake. Note that rounding to an even shorter answer—1.4—would be incorrect.

More than One Right Answer? Choose One and Enter it

Say you're asked for a two-digit integer that is a multiple of 2, 3, and 5. You might answer 30, 60, or 90. Whichever you grid would be right.

Some Grid-ins Have a Range of Possible Answers

Suppose you're asked to grid a value of m where $1 - 2m < m$ and $5m - 2 < m$. Solving for m in the first inequality, you find that $\frac{1}{3} < m$. Solving for m in the second inequality, you find that $m < \frac{1}{2}$. So $\frac{1}{3} < m < \frac{1}{2}$. Grid in any value between $\frac{1}{3}$ and $\frac{1}{2}$. Gridding in $\frac{1}{3}$ or $\frac{1}{2}$ would be wrong. When the answer is a range of values, it's often easier to work with decimals: $.333 < m < .5$. Then you can quickly grid .4 (or .35 or .45, etc.) as your answer.

Strategies for Educated Guessing

To make an educated guess, you need to eliminate answer choices that you know are wrong, and guess from what's left. The more answer choices you can eliminate, the better chance you have of guessing the correct answer from what's left over. You do this by:

- Eliminating unreasonable answer choices
- Eliminating the obvious on hard questions
- Eyeballing lengths, angles, and areas
- Finding the range on Grid-ins

Eliminate Unreasonable Answer Choices

Before you guess, think about the problem, and decide which answers don't make sense.

> The ratio of celebrities to nobodies in a certain room is 13:11. If there are 429 celebrities in the room, how many nobodies are there?
>
> (A) 143
> (B) 363
> (C) 433
> (D) 507
> (E) 792

Solution:

- The ratio of celebrities to nobodies is 13:11, so there are more celebrities than nobodies.
- Because there are 429 celebrities, there must be fewer than 429 nobodies.
- So you can eliminate choices (C), (D), and (E).
- The answer must be either (A) or (B), so guess. The correct answer is (B).

Eliminate the Obvious on Hard Questions

On the hard questions late in a set, obvious answers are usually wrong. So eliminate them when you guess. This DOES NOT hold true for early, easy questions, when the obvious answer could be right. In the following difficult problem, found late in a question set, which obvious answer would you eliminate?

> A number x is increased by 30 percent, and then the result is decreased by 20 percent. What is the final result of these changes?
>
> (A) x is increased by 10 percent
> (B) x is increased by 6 percent
> (C) x is increased by 4 percent
> (D) x is decreased by 5 percent
> (E) x is decreased by 10 percent

If you picked (A) as the obvious choice to eliminate, you'd be right. Most people would combine the decrease of 20 percent with the increase of 30 percent, getting a net increase of 10 percent. That's the easy, obvious answer, but not the correct answer. If you must guess, avoid (A). The correct answer is (C).

Eyeball Lengths, Angles, and Areas on Geometry Problems

Use diagrams that accompany geometry problems to help you eliminate wrong answer choices. First make sure that the diagram is drawn to scale. Diagrams are always drawn to scale UNLESS there's a note like this: "Note: Figure not drawn to scale." If it's not drawn to scale, DO NOT use this strategy. If it is, estimate quantities or eyeball the diagram, then eliminate answer choices that are way too large or too small.

Length—When a geometry question asks for a length, use the given lengths to estimate the unknown length. Measure off the given length by making a nick in your pencil with your thumbnail. Then hold the pencil against the unknown length on the diagram to see how the lengths compare. Try it.

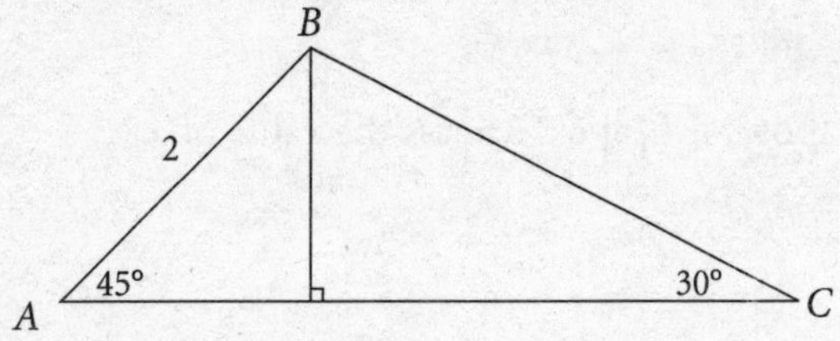

In the figure above, what is the length of *BC* ?

(A) $\sqrt{2}$
(B) 2
(C) $2\sqrt{2}$
(D) 4
(E) $4\sqrt{2}$

Solution:

- *AB* is 2, so measure off this length on your pencil.
- Compare *BC* with this length.
- *BC* appears almost twice as long as *AB*, so *BC* is about 4.
- Because $\sqrt{2}$ is about 1.4 and *BC* is clearly longer than *AB*, choices (A) and (B) are too small.
- Choice (E) is much greater than 4, so eliminate that.
- Now guess between (C) and (D). The correct answer is (C).

Angles—You can also eyeball angles. To eyeball an angle, compare the angle with a familiar angle, such as a straight angle (180°), a right angle (90°), or half a right angle (45°). The corner of a piece of paper is a right angle, so use that to see if an angle is greater or less than 90°.

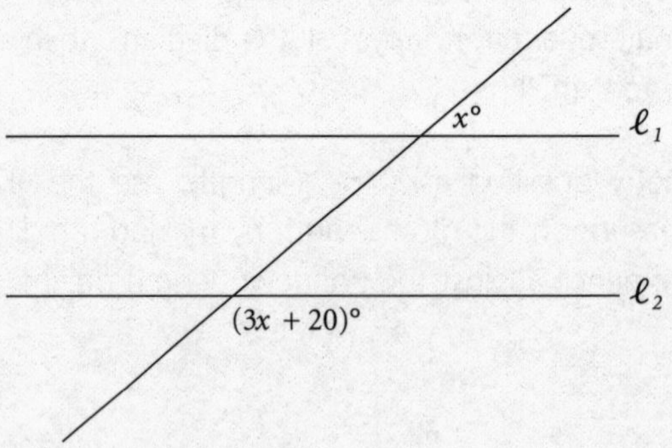

In the figure above, if $\ell_1 \parallel \ell_2$, what is the value of x ?

(A) 130
(B) 100
(C) 80
(D) 50
(E) 40

Solution:

- You see that x is less than 90 degrees, so eliminate choices (A) and (B).
- Because x appears to be much less than 90 degrees, eliminate choice (C).
- Now, pick between (D) and (E). In fact, the correct answer is (E).

Areas—Eyeballing an area is similar to eyeballing a length. You compare an unknown area in a diagram to an area that you do know.

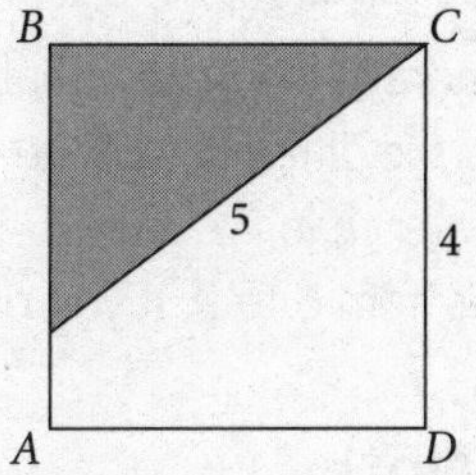

In square *ABCD* above, what is the area of the shaded region?

(A) 10
(B) 9
(C) 8
(D) 6
(E) 4

Solution:

- Because *ABCD* is a square, it has area 4^2, or 16.
- The shaded area is less than one half the size of the square, so its area must be less than 8.
- Eliminate answer choices (A), (B), and (C). The correct answer is (D).

Find the Range on Grid-ins—Then Guess

On Grid-ins, there are no answer choices to eliminate, but you won't lose points for guessing. So if you are stuck, try to estimate the general range of the answer, and guess. Here are examples of hard Grid-in questions.

1. If the three-digit number 11Q is a prime number, what digit is represented by Q?
2. The sum of five consecutive odd integers is 425. What is the greatest of these integers?
3. A triangle has one side of length 3 and another of length 7. If the length of the third side is a solution to the equation $x^2 - 2x = 63$, what is the length of the third side?

Solutions:

1. Because Q is a digit, it must be one of the integers 0 through 9. Eliminate all the even digits because they are divisible by 2. And eliminate 5 because any number ending with 5 is divisible by 5. You can also eliminate 1 and 7 because they are divisible by 3 (the digits add up to a multiple of 3). You are left with 3 and 9 to pick between. The correct answer is 3.
2. Because the integers are consecutive, they are all about the same size. So the number we are looking for is an odd number around $425 \div 5$, which is 85. The right answer is 89.
3. Even if you can't solve that quadratic, you know that one side of a triangle has to be less than the sum and greater than the difference of the other two sides. So the third side is less than $7 + 3$, or 10, and greater than $7 - 3$, or 4. Since solutions to SAT quadratics are usually integers, pick an integer from 5 to 9. If you picked 9, you'd be right.

Using your Calculator (or Not)

Thank you for slogging through all of these SAT Math techniques. Now we've gotten to the question most students really care about:

What about my calculator?

You're allowed to use a calculator on the SAT. But that's not all good. Yes, you can do computations faster. But you may be tempted to waste time using a calculator on questions that shouldn't involve lengthy computation. Remember, you never need a calculator to solve an SAT problem. If you ever find yourself doing extensive calculations—elaborate division or long drawn-out multiplication—stop. You probably missed a shortcut.

Should I Just Leave it at Home?

No. Bring it. By zeroing in on the parts of problems that need calculation, you can increase your score and save yourself time.

What Kind of Calculator Should I Bring?

One that you're comfortable with. If you don't have a calculator now, buy one right away, and practice using it between now and Test Day. You can use just about any small calculator except:

- Calculators that print out your calculations
- Handheld minicomputers or laptop computers
- Any calculators with a typewriter keypad
- Calculators with an angled readout screen
- Calculators that require a wall outlet

When Should I Use My Calculator?

Calculators help the most on Grid-ins. Both Grid-ins and multiple-choice questions will sometimes involve computation—never as the most important part of the question, but often as a final step.

Because Grid-ins don't give you answer choices to choose from, it's especially important to be sure of your work. Calculators can help you check your work and avoid careless errors.

Remember, a calculator can be useful when used selectively and strategically. Not all parts of a problem will necessarily be easier with a calculator. Consider this problem:

> If 4 grams of cadmium yellow pigment can make 3 kilograms of cadmium yellow oil paint, how many kilograms of paint could be produced from 86 grams of pigment?

This word problem has two steps. Step one is to set up the following proportion:

$$\frac{4\text{ g}}{3\text{ kg}} = \frac{86\text{ g}}{x\text{ kg}}$$

A little algebraic engineering tells you that:

$$x\text{ kg} = \frac{3\text{ kg} \times 86\text{ g}}{4\text{ g}}$$

Here's where you whip out that calculator. This problem has now been reduced down to pure calculation: $(3 \times 86) \div 4 = 64.5$.

Common Calculator Mistake #1: Calculating Before You Think

On the Grid-in problem below, how should (and shouldn't) you use your calculator?

> The sum of all the integers from 1 to 44, inclusive, is subtracted from the sum of all the integers from 7 to 50, inclusive. What is the result?

The Wrong Approach

1. Grab calculator.
2. Punch in all the numbers.
3. Put down answer and hope you didn't hit any wrong buttons.

You might be tempted to punch in all the numbers from 1 to 44, find their sum, then do the same for the numbers 7 through 50, and subtract the first sum from the second. But doing that means punching 252 keys. The odds are you'll hit the wrong key somewhere and get the wrong answer. Even if you don't, punching in all those numbers takes too much time.

The Kaplan Approach

1. Think first.
2. Decide on the best way to solve the problem.
3. Only then, use your calculator.

The right approach is to think first. The amount of computation involved in directly solving this tells you that there must be an easier way. You'll see this if you realize that both sums contain the same number of consecutive integers. Each integer in the first sum has a corresponding integer 6 greater than in the second sum:

1	7
+2	+8
+3	+9
.	.
.	.
.	.
+42	+48
+43	+49
+44	+50
=	=

As you'll see in the Math Traps step, the way to find the number of integers in a consecutive series is to subtract the smallest from the largest and add 1 (44 – 1 = 43; 43 + 1 = 44 OR 50 – 7 = 43; 43 + 1 = 44). So there are 44 pairs of integers that are 6 apart.

Therefore, the total difference between the two sums will be the difference between each pair of integers times the number of pairs. Now take out your calculator, punch "6 × 44 =," and get the correct answer of 264, with little or no time wasted.

Important

If you're just punching keys instead of thinking, you're approaching the problem the wrong way.

Common Calculator Mistake #2: Forgetting the Order of Operations

Even when you use your calculator, you can't just enter numbers in the order they appear on the page—you've got to follow the order of operations. This is a very simple error, but it can cost you lots of points. The order of operations is "PEMDAS," which stands for:

- Parentheses first, then deal with
- Exponents, then
- Multiplication and
- Division, and finally
- Addition and
- Subtraction

That means you do whatever is in parentheses first, then deal with exponents, then multiplication and division (from left to right), and finally addition and subtraction (from left to right). For example, say you want to find the value of the expression $\frac{x^2 + 1}{x + 3}$ when $x = 7$.

If you just punched in "7 × 7 + 1 ÷ 7 + 3 =" you would get the wrong answer.

The correct way to work it out is:

$(7^2 + 1) \div (7 + 3) = (7 \times 7 + 1) \div (7 + 3) = (49 + 1) \div 10 = 50 \div 10 = 5$

Combining a calculator with an understanding of when and how to use it can help you boost your score.

On page 173 is a practice set testing all of the concepts dicussed in Step 7. Don't forget the Five-Step Method and the other strategies discussed in this step. Good luck.

SUMMARY

- **Kaplan's Five-Step Method for Math Questions:**
  - — Step 1: Estimate the question's difficulty
  - — Step 2: Read the question
  - — Step 3: Skip or do?
  - — Step 4: Look for fastest approach
  - — Step 5: Make an educated guess
- **Alternative Techniques:**
  - — Picking Numbers: Substitute particular numbers for its variables
  - — Backsolving
- **Grid-In Strategies:**
  - — Write your answers in the number boxes
  - — Always start your answer in the first column
  - — In a fractional answer, grid (/) in the correct column
  - — Change mixed numbers to decimals or fractions before you grid
  - — Watch where you put your decimal points

  - With long or repeating decimals grid the first three digits only and plug in the decimal point where it belongs
  - More than one right answer? Choose one and enter it
  - Some grid-ins have a range of possible answers
- **Strategies for Educated Guesses:**
  - Eliminate unreasonable answer choices
  - Eliminate the obvious for hard questions
  - Eyeball lengths, angles, and areas
  - Find the range on grid-ins
- **Using Your Calculator (or Not):**
  - You are allowed to use your calculator, so bring it
  - Calculators help most on grid-ins

PRACTICE

1. Which of the following lists three fractions in ascending order?

(A) $\frac{9}{26}, \frac{1}{4}, \frac{3}{10}$

(B) $\frac{9}{26}, \frac{3}{10}, \frac{1}{4}$

(C) $\frac{1}{4}, \frac{9}{26}, \frac{3}{10}$

(D) $\frac{1}{4}, \frac{3}{10}, \frac{9}{26}$

(E) $\frac{3}{10}, \frac{9}{26}, \frac{1}{4}$

2. $\frac{7}{5} \times \left(\frac{3}{7} - \frac{2}{5}\right) =$

(A) $\frac{1}{165}$

(B) $\frac{1}{35}$

(C) $\frac{1}{25}$

(D) $\frac{9}{15}$

(E) 1

3. The union of sets A, B, and C is {1, 2, 3, 4, 5, 6, 7}, the intersection of Sets A, B, and C is {0}, (empty set) and Set A = {1, 2, 3, 4}. If Set B contains a greater number of elements than does Set C, what is the largest possible value of the sum of the elements of Set B?

4. Which of the following is the greatest integer less than 630,000 that can be written using all of the digits from 1 to 6?

(A) 629,999

(B) 654,321

(C) 624,531

(D) 621,543

(E) 625,431

5. A certain store stocks 5 different brands of ice cream, and sells a pint of each for \$2.75, \$3.25, \$2.50, \$3.25, and \$3.00, respectively. What is the positive difference between the mode price and the median price?

(A) \$0.05

(B) \$0.25

(C) \$0.30

(D) \$0.50

(E) \$0.75

6. What is the average (arithmetic mean) of n, $n + 1$, $n + 2$, and $n + 3$?

(A) $n + 1$

(B) $n + 1\frac{1}{2}$

(C) $n + 2$

(D) $n + 2\frac{1}{2}$

(E) $n + 6$

7. If the average of $27 - x$, $x - 8$, and $3x + 11$ is y, what is the average of $2y$ and $\frac{2y}{3}$?

(A) $4x + 40$

(B) $x + 10$

(C) $\frac{8x + 80}{3}$

(D) $\frac{4x + 40}{3}$

(E) $\frac{2x + 20}{3}$

8. A baseball player runs from first base to second base at an average speed of f meters per minute and from second base to third base at an average speed of $f + 4$ meters per minute. If the distance d, in meters, from first base to second base is the same as the distance from second base to third base, which of the following represents the average speed at which the player runs from first-to-second-to-third base?

(A) $\frac{f^2 - 4f}{f+4}$

(B) $\frac{2f^2 + 8f}{f+2}$

(C) $\frac{f^2 + 8f}{f+4}$

(D) $\frac{f^2 + 4f}{2(f+2)}$

(E) $\frac{f^2 + 4f}{(f+2)}$

9. If 1 "triminute" is equivalent to 3 minutes, how many triminutes are equivalent to 2.5 hours?

(A) 50
(B) 150
(C) 250
(D) 300
(E) 450

10. A store sells a watch for a profit of 25 percent of the wholesale cost. What percent of the selling price of the watch is the store's profit?

(A) 12.5%
(B) 20%
(C) 25%
(D) 50%
(E) 75%

11. The population of a certain town increases by 50 percent every 50 years. If the population in 1950 was 810, in what year was the population 160?

(A) 1650
(B) 1700
(C) 1750
(D) 1800
(E) 1850

12. $6\sqrt{9} \times 2\sqrt{16} =$

(A) 72
(B) 144
(C) 288
(D) 864
(E) 1,728

13. If $m^{\frac{3}{2}} = 8$, what is the value of m?

(A) 2
(B) 4
(C) 6
(D) 10
(E) $16\sqrt{2}$

14. If $xyz \neq 0$, then $\frac{x^2y^6z^{10}}{xy^3z^5} =$

(A) xy^2z^2
(B) xy^3z^5
(C) $x^2y^2z^2$
(D) $x^2y^3z^5$
(E) $x^3y^9z^{15}$

ANNUAL TOURISM REVENUE IN CITY X
1986–1992

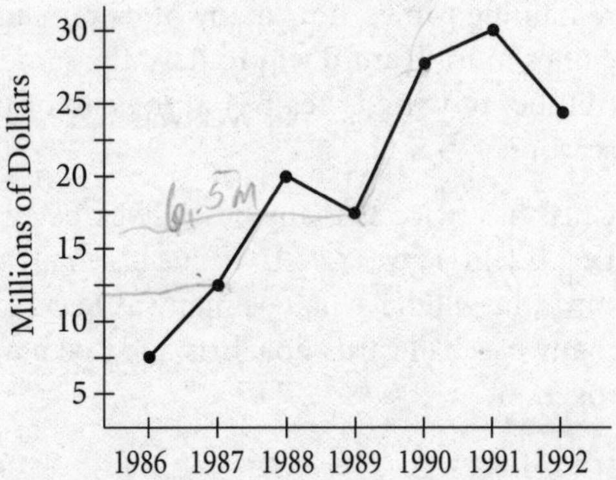

15. The graph above represents the annual revenue from tourism in City X over a 7-year period. During which of the following periods was the change in tourism revenues greatest?

(A) 1986–1987
(B) 1987–1988
(C) 1989–1990
(D) 1990–1991
(E) 1991–1992

Number of Sandwiches Ordered			
Department	Ham and Cheese	Vegetable	Roast Beef
Human Resources	3	1	2
Engineering	2	2	5
Customer Service	4	2	0

Cost of Sandwiches			
Store	Ham and Cheese	Vegetable	Roast Beef
Dave's	\$2.00	\$1.50	\$3.00
Joe's	\$1.50	\$2.00	\$3.50

16. A company decided to order sandwiches for the company picnic. The tables above show how many of each type of sandwich each department in the company ordered, along with the cost of each type of sandwich from two sandwich shops. If the Engineering department ordered its sandwiches from Dave's, how much would it spend?

(A) \$10.00
(B) \$10.50
(C) \$11.00
(D) \$22.00
(E) \$24.50

17. Which of the following is equivalent to $3x^2 + 18x + 27$?

(A) $3(x^2 + 6x + 3)$
(B) $3(x + 3)(x + 6)$
(C) $3(x + 3)(x + 3)$
(D) $3x(x + 6 + 9)$
(E) $3x^2 + x(18 + 27)$

18. If $|2x + 9| = 33$, $x =$

(A) –21
(B) –12
(C) –12 or –21
(D) 12 or –21
(E) 12

19.
```
  BEE
 +SEA
 IDEA
```

In the correctly worked addition problem above, A, B, D, E, I, and S each represent a different digit. What is the smallest possible value of D?

20. If $|a - b| > 0$, which of the following CANNOT be true?

I. $a > b$

II. $a < b$

III. $a = b$

(A) I only
(B) II only
(C) III only
(D) I and III only
(E) II and III only

21. If $n > 4$, which of the following is equivalent to $\frac{n - 4\sqrt{n} + 4}{\sqrt{n} - 2}$?

(A) $\sqrt{n}$
(B) $2\sqrt{n}$
(C) $\sqrt{n} + 2$
(D) $\sqrt{n} - 2$
(E) $n + \sqrt{n}$

22. At a clothing company, each blouse requires 1 yard of material, 4 shirts require 2 yards of material, and 1 blouse and 2 dresses require 4 yards of material. How many yards of material are needed to make 1 blouse, 1 shirt, and 1 dress?

23. In a certain baseball league, each team plays 160 games. After playing half of their games, Team *A* has won 60 games and Team *B* has won 49 games. If Team *A* wins half of its remaining games, how many of its remaining games must Team *B* win to have the same number of wins as Team *A* at the end of the season?

24. Chris has twice as many baseball cards as Lee. If Chris gives Lee 10 of his baseball cards, he will have half as many as Lee. How many baseball cards do Chris and Lee have together?

(A) 10
(B) 20
(C) 30
(D) 40
(E) 60

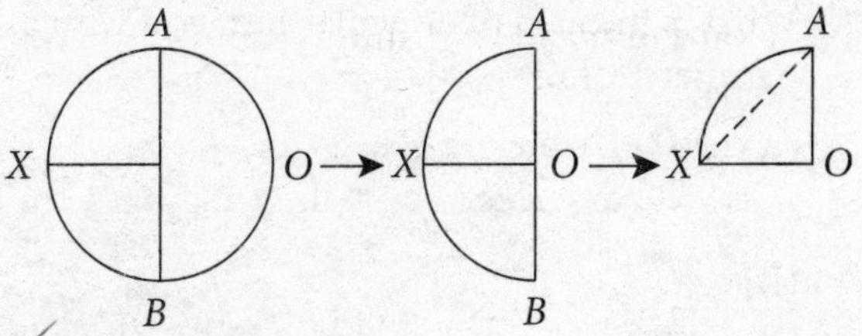

25. In the figure above, a circular sheet of paper is folded along diameter AB, and then along radius OX. If the folded paper is then cut along dotted line AX and unfolded, which of the following could result?

(A) 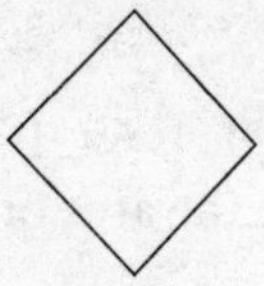
(B) 
(C) 
(D) 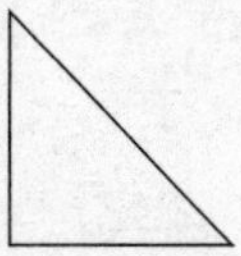
(E) 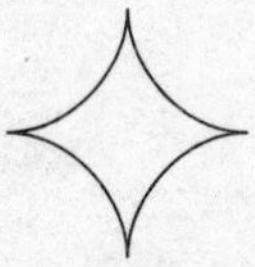

26. If 3 coins are tossed simultaneously, what is the probability of getting exactly 2 tails?

27. In $\overline{PS}$ above, $PQ = 3$, $RS = 4$, and $PS = 10$. What is the distance from S to the midpoint of $\overline{QR}$?

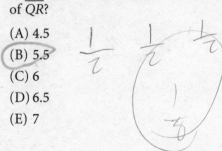

(A) 4.5
(B) 5.5
(C) 6
(D) 6.5
(E) 7

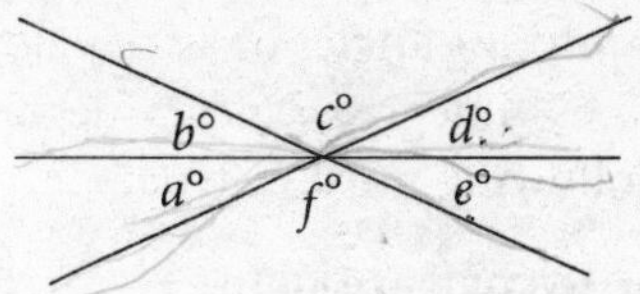

28. Which of the following must be true of the angles marked in the figure above?

I. $a + b = d + e$
II. $b + e = c + f$
III. $a + c + e = b + d + f$

(A) I only
(B) I and II only
(C) I and III only
(D) II and III only
(E) I, II, and III

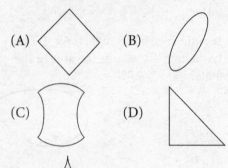

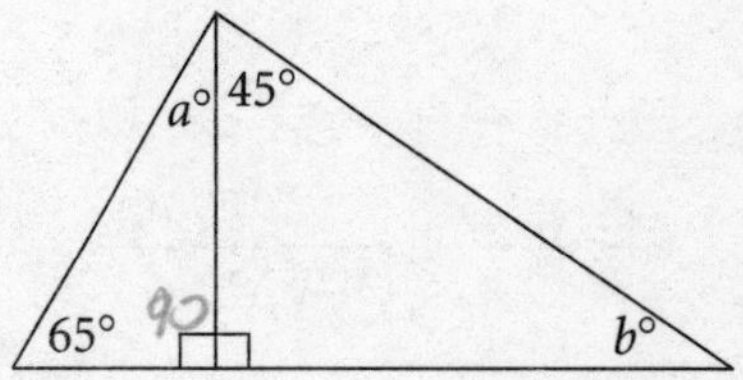

Note: Figure not drawn to scale.

29. In the figure above, what is the value of $a + b$?

(A) 45
(B) 70
(C) 90
(D) 145
(E) 170

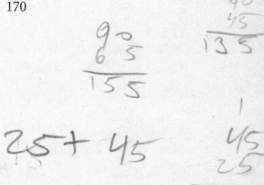

30. If the 3 interior angles of a triangle are x degrees, $x - 4$ degrees, and $2x$ degrees, which of the following must be true:

I. The triangle is right.

II. $3x - 5 = 133$

III. If the measure of the smallest angle is increased by 48 degrees, the resulting angle would be right.

(A) I only

(B) II only

(C) III only

(D) II and III only

(E) None of the above

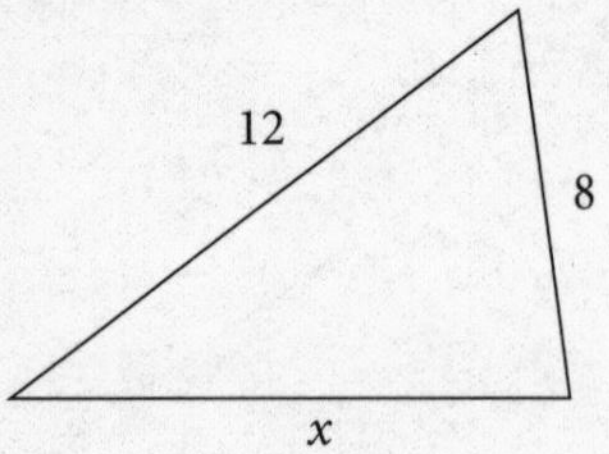

31. Based on the figure above, if x is an integer, what is the probability that x is even?

(A) $\frac{1}{5}$

(B) $\frac{2}{5}$

(C) $\frac{7}{15}$

(D) $\frac{1}{20}$

(E) $\frac{2}{25}$

32. What is the area of a regular hexagon with a perimeter of 6?

(A) $\frac{3\sqrt{3}}{2}$

(B) $\frac{3\sqrt{2}}{2}$

(C) $\frac{2\sqrt{6}}{3}$

(D) $\frac{3\sqrt{3}}{4}$

(E) $\frac{\sqrt{3}}{4}$

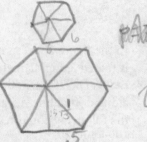

33. The perimeter of a rectangle is $6w$. If one side has length $\frac{w}{2}$, what is the area of the rectangle?

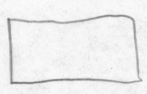

(A) $\frac{w^2}{4}$

(B) $\frac{5w^2}{4}$

(C) $\frac{5w^2}{2}$

(D) $\frac{11w^2}{4}$

(E) $\frac{11w^2}{2}$

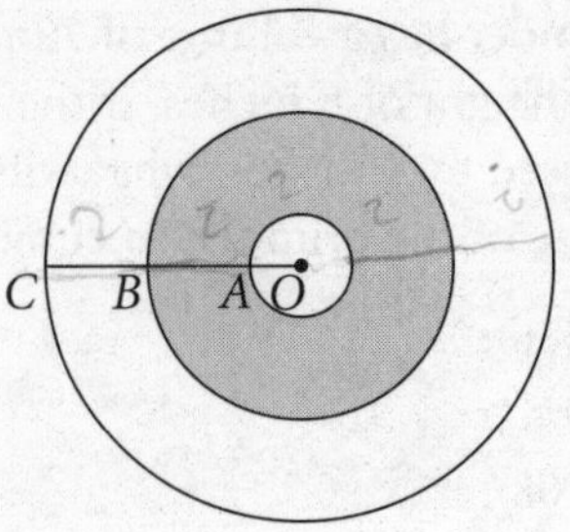

34. The diagram above shows three circles, all of which share a common origin O. If the lengths of $\overline{AB}$ and $\overline{BC}$ are both equal to the diameter of the smallest circle, what is the probability that a randomly selected point within the diagram will fall within the shaded region?

(A) $\frac{8}{25}$

(B) $\frac{9}{25}$

(C) $\frac{1}{9}$

(D) $\frac{5}{8}$

(E) $\frac{8}{9}$

35. If an arc with a length of 12π is $\frac{3}{4}$ of the circumference of a circle, what is the shortest distance between the endpoints of the arc?

(A) 4

(B) $4\sqrt{2}$

(C) 8

(D) $8\sqrt{2}$

(E) 16

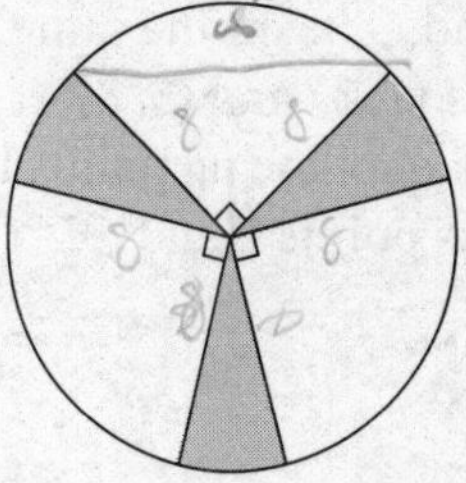

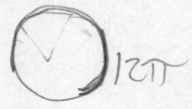

36. In the circle above, 3 right angles have vertices at the center of the circle. If the radius of the circle is 8, what is the combined area of the shaded regions?

(A) 8π

(B) 9π

(C) 12π

(D) 13π

(E) 16π

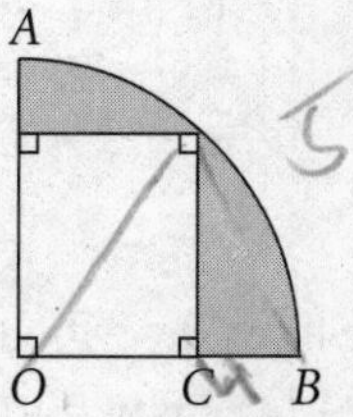

37. In the figure above, AB is an arc of a circle with center O. If the length of arc AB is 5π and the length of CB is 4, what is the sum of the areas of the shaded regions?

(A) $25\pi - 60$

(B) $25\pi - 48$

(C) $25\pi - 36$

(D) $100\pi - 48$

(E) $100\pi - 36$

38. Points P and Q lie on the same line and have coordinates (1, 3) and (5, 8), respectively. Which of the following points lies on the same line as points P and Q?

(A) (–4, –5)
(B) (–3, –2)
(C) (–2, –3)
(D) (–1, –4)
(E) (0, –1)

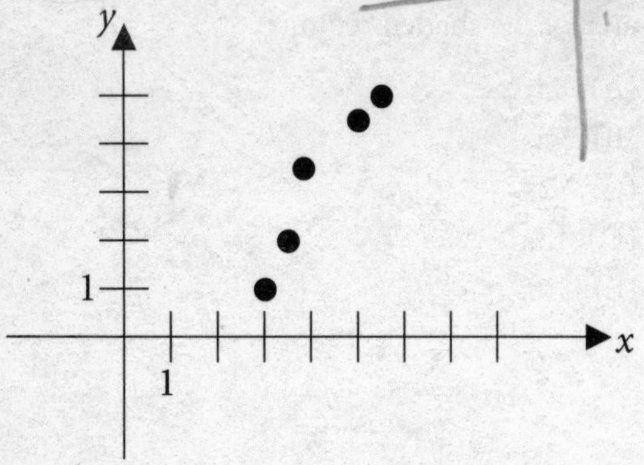

39. Which of the lines described by the following equations best fits these points?

(A) $y = 0.3x - 3$
(B) $y = 0.7x + 2$
(C) $y = 1.3x - 3$
(D) $y = 1.4x + 5$
(E) $y = 4x - 3$

40. A cylinder has a volume of 72π cubic inches and a height of 8 inches. If the height is increased by 4 inches, what will be the new volume of the cylinder, in cubic inches?

(A) 576π
(B) 9π
(C) 108π
(D) 328π
(E) 76π

ANSWERS AND EXPLANATIONS

1. D

The same three fractions appear in each answer choice, and we need to arrange these in ascending order.

Convert fractions to decimals, using your calculator:

$\frac{1}{4} = 0.25$

$\frac{3}{10} = 0.3$. This is a less than $\frac{1}{3}$, but more than $\frac{1}{4}$.

$\frac{9}{26} = 0.346$. This is greater than $\frac{3}{10}$.

The correct ascending order is $\frac{1}{4}, \frac{3}{10}, \frac{9}{26}$.

2. C

We could perform the subtraction within the parentheses and then multiply, but it's simpler to use the distributive law.

$$\frac{7}{5} \times \left(\frac{3}{7} - \frac{2}{5}\right) = \frac{7}{5} \times \frac{3}{7} - \frac{7}{5} \times \frac{2}{5}$$

$$= \frac{3}{5} - \frac{14}{25}$$

$$= \frac{3}{5} \times \frac{5}{5} - \frac{14}{25}$$

$$= \frac{15}{25} - \frac{14}{25} = \frac{1}{25}$$

3. 18

In some combination, B and C together contain {5, 6, 7}. Think about the possibilities, given that B contains more elements than C does and that you're asked to maximize the sum of the elements in B. Make B = {5, 6, 7} and make C the empty set. Then the sum of the elements of $B = 5 + 6 + 7 = 18$.

4. E

To arrange the digits into the largest number, you want to put the biggest digits in the highest-value places. For the number to be less than 630,000, it must start with 62. The next largest digit, 5, must go in the thousands' place, and 4 in the hundreds' place. Three goes in the tens' place, and since 2 is already used, 1 is left for the ones' place. This gives us 625,431, answer choice (E).

5. B

The mode of a group of terms is the value that occurs most frequently. The only price that occurs more than once is \$3.25, so it is the mode price. The median is the middle term in a group arranged in numerical order. If the prices are listed in either ascending or descending order, the third and middle term is \$3.00. So the difference between the mode and median prices is \$3.25 – \$3.00 = \$0.25.

6. B

Don't let the n variables bother you; the arithmetic performed is the same.

Method I:

Add the terms and divide by the number of terms. Since each term contains n, we can ignore the n and add it back at the end. Without the ns, we get $\frac{0 + 1 + 2 + 3}{4} = \frac{6}{4} = 1\frac{1}{2}$.

The average is $n + 1\frac{1}{2}$.

Method II:

These are just evenly spaced numbers (regardless of what n is). Since there are 4 of them, the average is midway between the second and third terms: midway between $n + 1$ and $n + 2$, or $n + 1\frac{1}{2}$.

7. D

In terms of y, the average of $2y$ and $\frac{2y}{3}$ is

$$\frac{2y+\frac{2y}{3}}{2}=\frac{\frac{6y}{3}+\frac{2y}{3}}{2}$$
$$=\frac{8y}{3}\times\frac{1}{2}$$
$$=\frac{8y}{6}$$
$$=\frac{4y}{3}$$

Next, solve for y as the average of $27 - x$, $x - 8$, and $3x + 11$:

$$y=\frac{27-x+x-8+3x+11}{3}$$
$$y=\frac{30+3x}{3}$$
$$y=\frac{3(x+10)}{3}$$
$$y = x + 10$$

Plug this into $\frac{4y}{3}$:

$$=\frac{4(x+10)}{3}$$
$$=\frac{4x+40}{3}$$

8. E

Pick numbers. Say $f = 4$ and $d = 16$. Then the time it took to get from first to second is $\frac{16}{4}$ minutes and the time it took to get from second to third is $\frac{16}{8} = 2$ minutes. Average speed is $\frac{\text{total distance}}{\text{total time}} = \frac{16+16}{4+2} = \frac{32}{6} = \frac{16}{3}$. Which choice has a value of $\frac{16}{3}$ when $f = 4$ and $d = 16$? Only (E).

9. A

First we need to know how many minutes are in two and a half hours. Since there are 60 minutes in an hour, there are $60 \times 2.5 = 150$ minutes in 2.5 hours. Since there are three minutes in every "triminute", we can divide the number of minutes in 2.5 hours by 3 to get the number of triminutes in 2.5 hours. $150 \div 3 = 50$, choice (A). We can write this whole sequence down as one equation:

$$2.5 \text{ hours} \times \frac{60 \text{ minutes}}{1 \text{ hour}} \times \frac{1 \text{ triminute}}{3 \text{ minutes}} =$$
50 triminutes

Notice how all the units neatly cancel out.

This problem could also be answered by Backsolving. Let's start by trying choice (C), 250 triminutes. 250 triminutes times 3 minutes per triminute equals 750 minutes. 750 minutes divided by 60 minutes per hour equals 12.5 hours, not 2.5. Eliminate choice (C) and try something smaller. Choice (B) gives us 7.5 hours, still too many. At this point, we know the answer must be choice (A), and this proves to be correct. 50 triminutes times 3 minutes per triminute equals 150 minutes; 150 minutes divided by 60 minutes per hour equals 2.5 hours, exactly what we're looking for.

10. B

The easiest approach is to pick a sample value for the wholesale cost of the watch, and from that, work out the profit and selling price. As usual with percent problems, it's simplest to pick 100. If the watch cost the store \$100, then the profit will be 25% of \$100, or \$25. The selling price equals the cost to the store plus the profit: \$100 + \$25, or \$125.

The profit represents $\frac{25}{125}$ or $\frac{1}{5}$ of the selling price.

The percent equivalent of $\frac{1}{5}$ is 20%.

11. C

Since the population increases by 50 percent every 50 years, the population in 1950 was 150 percent, or $\frac{3}{2}$, of the 1900 population. This means the 1900 population was $\frac{2}{3}$ of the 1950 population. Similarly, the 1850 population was $\frac{2}{3}$ of the 1900 population, and so on. You can just keep multiplying by $\frac{2}{3}$ until you get to a population of 160.

1950: $810 \times \frac{2}{3} = 540$ in 1900

1900: $540 \times \frac{2}{3} = 360$ in 1850

1850: $360 \times \frac{2}{3} = 240$ in 1800

1800: $240 \times \frac{2}{3} = 160$ in 1750

The population was 160 in 1750.

Another approach is to work forward from the population of 160 until reaching 810; then determine how far back the population of 160 must have been. During each 50-year period, the population increases by 50 percent, or by $\frac{1}{2}$.

160: $160 + \frac{1}{2}(160) = 240$

240: $240 + \frac{1}{2}(240) = 360$

360: $360 + \frac{1}{2}(360) = 540$

540: $540 + \frac{1}{2}(540) = 810$

So, if the population was 810 in 1950, it must have been 540 in 1900, 360 in 1850, 240 in 1800, and 160 in 1750.

12. B

The expression $6\sqrt{9} \times 2\sqrt{16}$ can be simplified by taking the square roots of 9 and 16, respectively:

$6\sqrt{9} \times 2\sqrt{16} =$

$(6 \times 3) \times (2 \times 4) = 18 \times 8 = 144$

So choice (B) is correct.

13. B

$m^{\frac{3}{2}} = 8$

$\sqrt[2]{m^3} = 8$

$m^3 = 64$

$m = 4$

14. B

First break up the expression to separate the variables, transforming the fraction into a product of three simpler fractions:

$$\frac{x^2y^6z^{10}}{xy^3z^5} = \left(\frac{x^2}{x}\right)\left(\frac{y^6}{y^3}\right)\left(\frac{z^{10}}{z^5}\right)$$

Now carry out each division by keeping the base and subtracting the exponents.

$\frac{x^2}{x} = x^{2-1} = x$

$\frac{y^6}{y^3} = y^{6-3} = y^3$

$\frac{z^{10}}{z^5} = z^{10-5} = z^5$

The answer is the product of these three terms, or xy^3z^5.

15. C

The amount of tourism revenue generated in a certain year is represented as the vertical distance from the bottom of the graph to the point above that year. The key along the vertical axis tells you that the income is measured in millions of dollars. Looking at the graph you can see that the greatest change in revenue occurs between 1989 and 1990, when it jumps from \$17.5 million to \$27.5 million, for an increase of \$10 million.

16. D

You only need one line from each table to find the answer to this question. Multiply the cost of each type of sandwich from Dave's by the number of that type of sandwich the engineering department ordered, then add those numbers to get the total cost: 2($2.00) + 2($1.50) + 5($3.00) = $4.00 + $3.00 + $15.00 = $22.00.

17. C

First factor out the number (3) common to all terms: $3x^2 + 18x + 27 = 3(x^2 + 6x + 9)$

This is not an answer choice, so you must factor the polynomial.

$x^2 + 6x + 9$ is of the form $a^2 + 2ab + b2$, with $a = x$ and $b = 3$.

So, $x^2 + 6x + 9 = (x + 3)^2$ or $(x + 3)(x + 3)$.

Therefore, $3x^2 + 18x + 27 = 3(x + 3)(x + 3)$.

An alternative method would be to multiply out the answer choices, and see which matches $3x^2 + 18x + 27$.

Choice (A): $3(x^2 + 6x + 3) = 3x^2 + 18x + 9$. Reject.

Choice (B): $3(x + 3)(x + 6) = 3(x^2 + 6x + 3x + 18)$. Using FOIL:

$= 3(x^2 + 9x + 18)$

$= 3x^2 + 27x + 3(18)$. Reject.

Choice (C): $3(x + 3)(x + 3) = 3(x^2 + 3x + 3x + 9)$. Using FOIL:

$= 3(x^2 + 6x + 9)$

$= 3x^2 + 18x + 27$. Correct.

18. D

If $|2x + 9| = 33$, then $2x + 9 = 33$ or $2x + 9 = -33$, so $2x = 24$ or $2x = -42$, and $x = 12$ or $x = -21$.

19. 2

The first thing to notice about this problem is that $E + A$ equals either A or $10 + A$. Since each letter represents only one digit, $E + A$ must equal A, since E cannot be 10. Therefore, $E = 0$. If we plug this into the problem, we get:

$$\begin{array}{r} \text{B 0 0} \\ +\ \text{S 0 A} \\ \hline \text{I D 0 A} \end{array}$$

so

$$\begin{array}{r} \text{B} \\ +\ \text{S} \\ \hline \text{I D} \end{array}$$

So I must be 1, and B plus S must be 12 or more (since if $B + S$ were 10 or 11, the second letter in the answer would be E or I, not D). Therefore, the smallest possible value of D is 2. Note that there are several different possibilities for A, B, and S, but we don't need to find these to solve the problem.

20. C

That $|a - b| > 0$ doesn't mean $a - b > 0$. It's also possible that $-(a - b) > 0$. If the absolute value of the difference between a and b is greater than 0, that means that either $a > b$ or $a < b$, so both I and II can be true. If $a = b$, then $|a - b|$ is equal to 0, not greater than 0, so III cannot be true.

21. D

We must try to get rid of the denominator by factoring it out of the numerator. $n - 4\sqrt{n} + 4$ is a difficult expression to work with. It may be easier if we let $t = \sqrt{n}$. Keep in mind then that $t^2 = (\sqrt{n})(\sqrt{n}) = n$. Then $n - 4\sqrt{n} + 4 = t^2 - 4t + 4$.
Using FOIL in reverse, $t^2 - 4t + 4 = (t - 2)(t - 2) = (\sqrt{n} - 2)(\sqrt{n} - 2)$.

So $\dfrac{n - 4\sqrt{n} + 4}{\sqrt{n} - 2} = \dfrac{(\sqrt{n} - 2)(\sqrt{n} - 2)}{\sqrt{n} - 2} = \sqrt{n} - 2$.

Or pick a number for n (a perfect square, such as 25, is a good choice) and try each answer choice. Whichever method you use, choice (D) is correct.

22. 3

We need to keep track of the amount of material that it takes to make each of the different items of clothing. Each blouse requires 1 yard of material. Four shirts require 2 yards of material; therefore, each shirt requires $\frac{2}{4}$, or $\frac{1}{2}$ yard. One blouse and 2 dresses require a total of 4 yards. One of these yards goes to the blouse, leaving 3 yards for the 2 dresses, so a single dress requires $\frac{3}{2}$, or $1\frac{1}{2}$, yards of material. Now let's find how much we need for the assortment we want: 1 blouse, 1 shirt, 1 dress. One blouse takes 1 yard. One shirt takes $\frac{1}{2}$ yard. And the dress takes $1\frac{1}{2}$ yards. So the amount of material needed is $1 + \frac{1}{2} + 1\frac{1}{2}$ yards, or 3 yards.

23. 51

Since the teams have played half their games, there are 80 games left. If Team *A* wins half its remaining games, that's another 40 games, for a total of 60 + 40, or 100, games. Team *B* has won 49 games so far, so in order to tie Team *A*, it must win another 100 – 49, or 51, games.

24. C

Let *C* represent the number of baseball cards Chris has, and *L* represent the number of baseball cards Lee has. Since Chris has twice as many baseball cards as Lee, we can write

$C = 2L$.

If Chris gives Lee 10 baseball cards, then he will have 10 fewer, or $C - 10$, and Lee will have 10 more, or $L + 10$. In this case Chris would end up with half as many as Lee, so

$C - 10 = \frac{1}{2}(L + 10)$.

We have 2 equations with 2 variables. Solve for *C* and *L*. Substitute the first expression for *C*—that is, $C = 2L$—into the second equation and solve for *L*.

$$2L - 10 = \frac{1}{2}(L + 10)$$
$$4L - 20 = L + 10$$
$$3L = 30$$
$$L = 10$$

25. A

Label a point *Y* directly across the circle from point *X* to keep track of what's happening to the circle as we fold it.

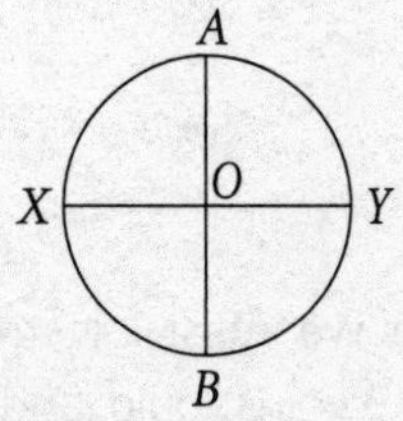

The first fold, along diameter *AB*, brings *Y* right on top of *X*.

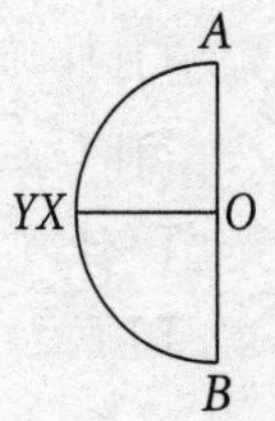

The second fold, along radius *OX*, brings *B* right on top of *A*.

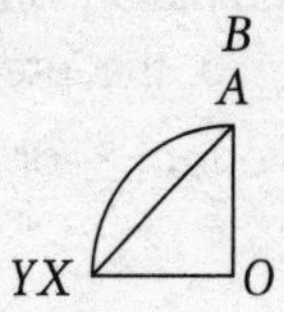

With the first fold, we have two semicircular pieces of paper, one on top of the other, folded along *AB*. If we were to cut the line *AX* after the first fold, we would also cut the top piece from *A* to *Y*. With the second fold, there are 4 quarter-circles. Cutting through the top piece from *A* to *X*, we would also cut through the second piece from *A* to *Y*, the third piece from *B* to *Y*, and the fourth piece from *B* to *X*. This would leave a square with the 4 corners *A*, *X*, *B*, and *Y* and the center *O* after the paper was unfolded:

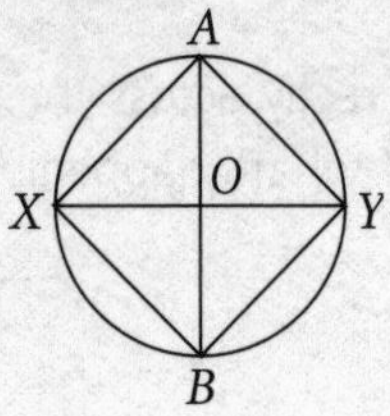

26. $\frac{3}{8}$ or .375

To solve this one we must determine how many different ways the 3 coins could land, and then count the number of possibilities that have exactly 2 coins tails-up. It's easiest to do this systematically on paper, using "H" for "Heads" and "T" for "Tails."

H-H-H	T-H-H
H-H-T	T-H-T
H-T-H	T-T-H
H-T-T	T-T-T

Be sure to find every combination. There are 8 possible outcomes when the 3 coins are thrown. Only 3 of them have exactly 2 tails showing. (Remember: The combination with 3 tails up doesn't fit the description.) So the probability of getting exactly two tails is 3 out of 8, or $\frac{3}{8}$.

27. B

$QR = PS - (PQ + RS)$

$QR = 10 - (3 + 4) = 10 - 7 = 3$

$\frac{QR}{2} = 1.5$

$\frac{QR}{2} + RS = 1.5 + 4 = 5.5$

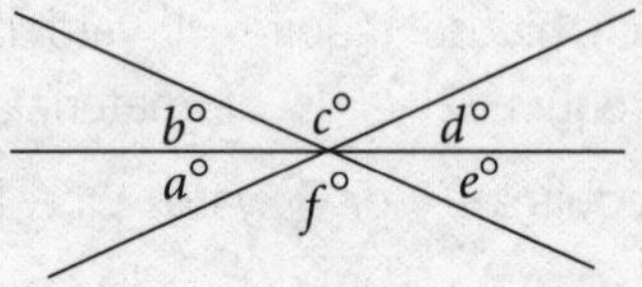

28. C

We have three pairs of vertical angles around the point of intersection: *a* and *d*, *b* and *e*, and *c* and *f*. Therefore, $a = d$, $b = e$, and $c = f$. Let's look at the three statements one at a time.

I: $a + b = d + e$. Since $a = d$ and $b = e$, this is true. Eliminate choice (D).

II: $b + e = c + f$. We know that $b = e$ and $c = f$, but we don't how the pairs relate to each other. Statement II does not have to be true. Eliminate choices (B) and (E).

III: $a + c + e = b + d + f$. This is true, since $a = d$, $c = f$, and $b = e$. That is, we can match each angle on one side of the equation with a different angle on the other side. Statement III must be true.

29. B

You are given two right triangles, so off the bat you already know the measure of one of the angles in each triangle. You're also given the measure of an additional angle in each triangle. Armed with the knowledge that the sum of all the angles in any triangle will always be 180 degrees, all you have to do is subtract the sum of the given angles in each separate triangle from 180 to get *a* and *b*, and then add *a* and *b*. It should look like this:

$$180 - (65 + 90) = 25$$
$$180 - (45 + 90) = 45$$
$$45 + 25 = 70$$

or

$$65 + (a + 45) + b = 180$$
$$110 + a + b = 180$$
$$a + b = 70.$$

30. D

Because the angles in a triangle sum to 180 degrees, $x + (x - 4) + 2x = 180$. So $4x - 4 = 180$ and $4x = 184$, so $x = 46$. The 3 angles are $x = 46$ degrees, $x - 4 = 46 - 4 = 42$ degrees, and $2x = 2(46) = 92$ degrees. The greatest angle in the triangle is 92 degrees, so I is false and (A) can be eliminated. $3x - 5 = 3(46) - 5 = 138 - 5 = 133$, so II is true, and we can eliminate (C) and (E). $42 + 48 = 90$, so III is true.

31. C

This question pulls together two topics that don't often cross paths: probability and the Triangle Inequality Theorem. The latter requires that in any triangle, the measure of any side be less than the sum of, but greater than the difference between, the 2 other sides. So x must be less than 20 and greater than 4. Given that x is an integer, you're left with these possibilities: 5, 6, 7, 8, 9, 10, 11, 12, 13, 14, 15, 16, 17, 18, 19. Probability is the number of desired outcomes over the number of possible outcomes. The possible outcomes in this situation are those 15 numbers just identified; the desired outcomes are the 7 integers in that set. So the probability that x is even is $\frac{7}{15}$.

32. A

A regular hexagon is composed of 6 equilateral triangles. In this case, each triangle has a side measure of 1, because the hexagon contains 6 equal sides—it's a regular hexagon—whose perimeter is 6. So if you figure out the area of one equilateral triangle with sides measuring 1, and then multiply that area by 6, you'll have your answer. Begin with a picture, including an altitude—that is, the height of the triangle.

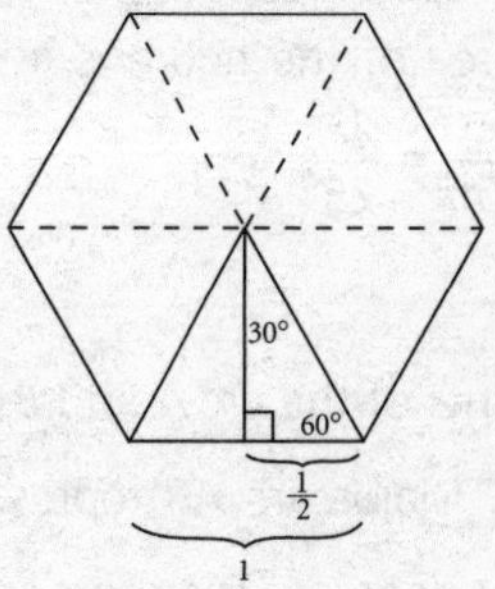

Notice the introduction of the altitude creates 2 congruent 30-60-90 triangles. Look at either one. If the side opposite 30° is $\frac{1}{2}$, the side opposite 60° is $\frac{\sqrt{3}}{2}$. So the area of the entire triangle above is $\left(\frac{1}{2}\right)(b)(h) = \left(\frac{1}{2}\right)(1)\left(\frac{\sqrt{3}}{2}\right) = \frac{\sqrt{3}}{4}$. The area of a hexagon containing six such triangles is $6\left(\frac{\sqrt{3}}{4}\right) = \frac{3\sqrt{3}}{2}$.

33. B

The sum of all 4 sides is $6w$. The 2 short sides add up to $\frac{w}{2} + \frac{w}{2}$, or w. This leaves $6w - w$, or $5w$, for the *sum* of the other 2 sides. *Each* long side is $\frac{1}{2}(5w)$, or $\frac{5}{2}w$.

So, Area $= \left(\frac{w}{2}\right)\left(\frac{5w}{2}\right) = \frac{5w^2}{4}$.

34. A

The probability that a randomly selected point will fall within the shaded area is equal to the ratio of the area that is shaded to the area of the entire figure. The area of the entire figure is equal to the area of the largest circle, and the area of the shaded area is equal to the area of the second circle minus the area of the smallest circle. To make the calculations easier, you can assume that the radius of the smallest circle equals 1, so its diameter is 2. Then the radius of the second circle is 3 and the radius of the largest circle is 5. Then the shaded area is $\pi(3^2) - \pi(1^2) = 9\pi - \pi = 8\pi$. The total area of the figure is $\pi(5^2) = 25\pi$. The probability is $\frac{8\pi}{25\pi} = \frac{8}{25}$.

35. D

Call the endpoints of the arc *A* and *B* and the center of the circle *C*. Major arc *AB* represents $\frac{3}{4}$ of 360 degrees, or 270 degrees. Therefore, minor arc *AB* is 360° – 270°, or 90°. Since *AC* and *CB* are both radii of the circle, ΔABC must be an isosceles right triangle:

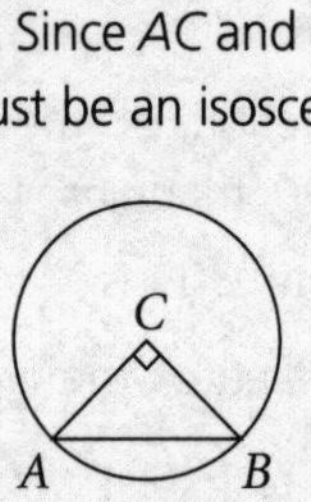

You can find the distance between *A* and *B* if you know the radius of the circle. Major arc *AB*, which takes up $\frac{3}{4}$ of the circumference, has a length of 12π, so the entire circumference is 16π. The circumference of any circle is 2π times the radius, so a circle with circumference 16π must have radius 8. The ratio of a leg to the hypotenuse in an isosceles right triangle is $1:\sqrt{2}$. The length of *AB* is $\sqrt{2}$ times the length of a leg, or $8\sqrt{2}$.

36. E

The 3 right angles define 3 sectors of the circle, each with a central angle of 90°. Together, the 3 sectors account for $\frac{270°}{360°}$, or $\frac{3}{4}$ of the area of the circle, leaving $\frac{1}{4}$ of the circle for the shaded regions. So the total area of the shaded regions $= \frac{1}{4} \times \pi(8)^2$, or 16π.

37. B

The total area of the shaded regions equals the area of the quarter circle minus the area of the rectangle. Since the length of arc *AB* (a quarter of the circumference of circle *O*) is 5π, the whole circumference equals $4 \times 5\pi$, or 20π. Thus, the radius *OE* has length 10. (We've added point *E* in the diagram for clarity.) Since *OB* also equals 10, *OC* = 10 – 4, or 6. This tells us that ΔOEC is a 6-8-10 right triangle and *EC* = 8.

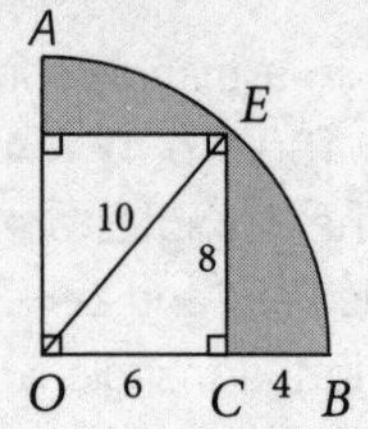

Now we know the dimensions of the rectangle, so we can find its area: area = $l \times w = 8 \times 6 = 48$. And the area of the quarter circle equals $\frac{1}{4}\pi(10)^2$ or 25π. Finally, we can get the total area of the shaded regions:

$$\text{Area of shaded regions} = \frac{1}{4} \times \pi \times (10)^2 - 48$$
$$= 25\pi - 48$$

38. B

Since the slope remains the same between any two points on a given line, the slope between the correct answer and *P* or *Q* will be the same as the slope between *P* and *Q*. First find the slope of the line:

$$\text{Slope} = \frac{\text{change in } y}{\text{change in } x}$$
$$= \frac{8 - 3}{5 - 1}$$
$$= \frac{5}{4}$$

Now see which answer choice also gives a slope of $\frac{5}{4}$:

Choice (A): $\frac{8-(-5)}{5-(-4)} = \frac{13}{9}$. Eliminate.

Choice (B): $\frac{8-(-2)}{5-(-3)} = \frac{10}{8} = \frac{5}{4}$.

So choice (B) is correct because the line between it and point Q has a slope of $\frac{5}{4}$. At this point on the actual test you would move on to the next question. However, we'll go through the remaining choices to prove that they're false.

Choice (C): $\frac{8-(-3)}{5-(-2)} = \frac{11}{7}$. Eliminate.

Choice (D): $\frac{8-(-4)}{5-(-1)} = \frac{12}{6}$. Eliminate.

Choice (E): $\frac{8-(-1)}{5-(-0)} = \frac{9}{5}$. Eliminate.

39. C

See what information you can glean from the graph. What should the slope of the line be? Where would the y-intercept be? Because the position of the dots on the graph increases along the y-axis slightly faster than it increases along the x-axis, the slope of the graph must be slightly greater than 1. Although it is difficult to locate the y-intercept precisely, it must certainly be negative. Each of these pieces of information allows you to rule out some of the possible answers, leaving only one, $y = 1.3x - 3$.

Choice (A) has a slope that is too small (too flat). Choice (B) has a y-intercept too large. Choice (C) is a good fit. Choice (D) has a y-intercept too large. Choice (E) has a slope that is too large (too steep).

40. C

To find the volume of the new cylinder, you have to find the area of its circular base. The volume of a cylinder is the area of the base × height, or $\pi r^2 \times h$. You're given the original height of the cylinder and its volume. So you can plug these values into the formula and solve for the area of the base:

$$\text{volume} = \pi r^2 h$$
$$72\pi = \pi r^2 \times 8$$
$$9\pi = \pi r^2$$

The area of the base equals 9π. Since the height of the new cylinder is 4 inches more, its height is 8 + 4, or 12. The volume of the new cylinder equals $9\pi r^2 \times 12$, or 108π, and choice (C) is correct.

You could also use logic to solve this problem. If the height were increased by 8 inches, you'd double the volume of the cylinder—an increase of 72π cubic inches. Increasing the height by 4 inches will increase the volume by 50 percent of the original 72π, or 36π. So $36\pi + 72\pi = 108\pi$, and again, choice (C) is correct.

Step Nine

Math Traps

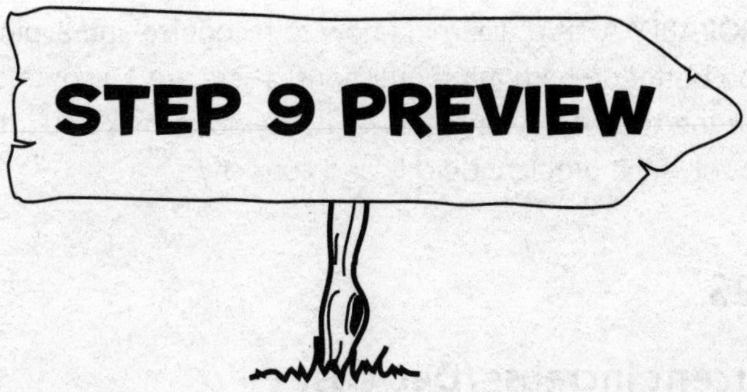

The Gist of it

The Traps

- Trap 1: Percent Increase/Decrease
- Trap 2: Weighted Averages
- Trap 3: Ratio:Ratio:Ratio
- Trap 4: "Least" and "Greatest"
- Trap 5: Percent "of" Versus Percent "Less" or "Greater"
- Trap 6: Hidden Instructions
- Trap 7: Average Rates
- Trap 8: Counting Numbers
- Trap 9: Ratio Versus Quantity
- Trap 10: Not all Numbers are Positive Integers

Summary

Practice

Remember

Answers: Did You Fall for the Traps

As we've mentioned at least 23 times, SAT problem sets are arranged in order of difficulty with the easiest problems coming first and the hardest problems coming last. Knowing this means you need to treat question #3 differently than question #14. This is where SAT Math traps come into play.

THE GIST OF IT

If you arrive at an answer choice to a late (hard) Math problem without too much effort, THAT ANSWER IS PROBABLY A TRAP. Learning how to recognize and avoid common SAT Math traps will help you do better on hard math questions. There are 10 common Math traps on the SAT. We'll show you the trap, the wrong answer it's trying to trick you into choosing, how to avoid it, and how to solve the problem quickly and correctly.

THE TRAPS

Trap 1: Percent Increase/Decrease

S. Ford Copeland purchased a new car in 1990. Three years later, he sold it to a dealer for 40 percent less than he paid for it in 1990. The dealer then added 20 percent onto the price she paid and resold it to another customer. The price the final customer paid for the car was what percent of the original price S. Ford Copeland paid in 1990?

(A) 40%
(B) 60%
(C) 72%
(D) 80%
(E) 88%

The Wrong Answer

The increase/decrease percentage problem usually appears at the end of a section and invariably contains a trap. Most students will figure that taking away 40 percent and then adding 20 percent will give them an overall loss of 20 percent, and they'll pick choice (D), 80%, as the correct answer. Most students will be wrong.

The Trap

When a quantity is increased or decreased by a percentage more than once, you can't simply add and subtract the percents to get the answer. In this kind of percent problem, the first percent change is a percent of the starting amount, but the second change is a percent of the new amount.

Avoiding the Trap

Don't blindly add and subtract percents. Percents can be added and subtracted only when they are percents of the same amount.

Finding the Right Answer

We know:

- The "40 percent less" that Mr. Copeland got for the car is 40 percent of his original price.
- The 20 percent the dealer adds on is 20 percent of what the dealer paid, a much smaller amount.
- Adding on 20 percent of that smaller amount is not the same thing as adding back 20 percent of the original price.

Solving the Problem Fast

Use 100 for a starting quantity, whether or not it's plausible in the real situation. The problem asks for the relative amount of change. So you can take any starting number and compare it with the final result. Because you're dealing with percents, 100 is the easiest number to work with.

- If Mr. Copeland paid \$100 for the car, what is 40 percent less?
- In the case of \$100, each percent equals \$1, so 100 – 40 = 60. S. Ford Copeland sold the car for \$60.
- If the dealer charges 20 percent more than his purchase price, she's raising the price by 20 percent of \$60, which is \$60 × 0.20 = \$12 (not 20 percent of \$100, which would be \$20!).
- Therefore, the dealer sold the car again for \$60 + \$12, or \$72.
- Finally, what percent of the starting price (\$100) is \$72? It's 72%. So the correct answer here is choice (C).

Trap 2: Weighted Averages

In a class of 27 plumbers, the average (arithmetic mean) score of the male plumbers on the final exam was 83. If the average score of the 15 female plumbers in the class was 92, what was the average of the whole class?

(A) 86.2
(B) 87.0
(C) 87.5
(D) 88.0
(E) 88.2

The Wrong Answer

Some students will rush in and simply average 83 and 92 to come up with 87.5 as the class average. They'll be as disappointed as an American Idol wannabe.

The Trap

You cannot combine averages of different quantities by taking the average of those averages. In an averages problem, if one value occurs more frequently than others, it is "weighted" more. Remember that the average formula calls for the *sum* of all the terms divided by the total number of terms.

Avoiding the Trap

Don't just take the average of the averages. Work with the sums, not the averages.

Finding the Right Answer

If 15 of the 27 plumbers are girls, the remaining 12 must be boys. We can't just add 83 to 92 and divide by two. In this class, there are more girls than boys, and therefore, the girls' test scores are "weighted" more—they contribute more to the class average. So the answer must be either (D) or (E).

To find each sum, multiply each average by the number of terms it represents. After you have found the sums of the different terms, find the combined average by plugging them into the average formula.

$$\text{Total class average} = \frac{\text{Sum of girls's scores + Sum of boy's scores}}{\text{Total number of students}}$$

$$= \frac{(\text{\# of girls} \times \text{girls' average score}) + (\text{\# of boys} \times \text{boys' average score})}{\text{Total \# of students}}$$

$$= \frac{15(92) + 12(83)}{27} = \frac{1{,}380 + 996}{27} = 88$$

So the class average is 88, answer choice (D).

Important

Notice how using a calculator helps in this problem.

Trap 3: Ratio:Ratio:Ratio

Dale's coin collection consists of quarters, dimes, and nickels. If the ratio of the number of quarters to the number of dimes is 5 to 2, and the ratio of the number of dimes to the number of nickels is 3 to 4, what is the ratio of the number of quarters to the number of nickels?

(A) 5 to 4
(B) 7 to 5
(C) 10 to 6
(D) 12 to 7
(E) 15 to 8

The Wrong Answer

If you chose 5 to 4 as the correct answer, you fell for the classic ratio trap.

The Trap

Parts of different ratios don't always refer to the same whole. In the classic ratio trap, two different ratios each share a common part that is represented by two different numbers. The two ratios do not refer to the same whole however, so they are not in proportion to each other.

To solve this type of problem, restate both ratios so that the numbers representing the common part (in this case "dimes") are the same. Then all the parts will be in proportion and can be compared to each other.

Avoiding the Trap

Restate ratios so that the same number refers to the same quantity. Make sure the common quantity in both ratios has the same number in both.

Finding the Right Answer

To find the ratio of quarters to nickels, restate both ratios so that the number of dimes is the same in both. You are given two ratios:

Quarters to Dimes = 5 to 2   Dimes to Nickels = 3 to 4

- The number corresponding to dimes in the first ratio is 2.
- The number corresponding to dimes in the second ratio is 3.
- To restate the ratios, find the least common multiple of 2 and 3.
- The least common multiple of 2 and 3 is 2 × 3, or 6.

Restate the ratios with the number of dimes as 6:

Quarters to Dimes = 15 to 6 (which is the same as 5 to 2)
Dimes to Nickels = 6 to 8 (which is the same as 3 to 4)

The ratios are still in their original proportions, but now they can be compared easily since dimes are represented by the same number in both. The ratio of quarters to dimes to nickels is 15 to 6 to 8, so the ratio of quarters to nickels is 15 to 8, which is answer choice (E).

Trap 4: "Least" and "Greatest"

What is the least positive integer that is divisible by both 2 and 5 and leaves a remainder of 3 when divided by 11?

(A) 30
(B) 32
(C) 33
(D) 70
(E) 80

The Wrong Answer

(A) is the choice *not* to go for here.

The Trap

In questions that ask for the *least*, *minimum*, *or smallest* something, the choice offering the smallest number is rarely right. In questions that ask for the greatest, *maximum*, *or largest* something, the choice offering the largest number is very rarely right.

Avoiding the Trap

Consider the constraints and requirements that the nature of the question has placed upon the possible answer. Don't leap to conclusions. In fact, if you ever need to guess on questions asking about the least number, the one place *not* to go is to the smallest choice and *vice versa* for questions asking about the largest number.

Finding the Right Answer

If the integer is divisible by both 2 and 5, it is a multiple of 2, 5, or 10, so eliminate (B) and (C). If it leaves a remainder of 3 when divided by 11, it is 3 more than a multiple of 11. In (A), 30 – 3 = 27, which isn't a multiple of 11. In (D), 70 – 3 = 67, which isn't a multiple of 11. In (E), 80 – 3 = 77, which is a multiple of 11, and the correct answer.

Trap 5: Percent "of" Versus Percent "Less" or "Greater"

What number is $33\frac{1}{3}\%$ less than 9?

The Wrong Answer

3

The Trap

Reading too quickly or with insufficient care, you could mistake $33\frac{1}{3}\%$ less than 9 for $33\frac{1}{3}\%$ of 9, which is $\frac{1}{3} \times 9 = 3$.

Avoiding the Trap

Be on the lookout for subtleties of wording, especially in questions appearing in the middle or end of a section. Consciously and actively distinguish these three things whenever percent questions arise:

a percent *of b;*

a percent *less than b;*

a percent *greater than b.*

For example:

25 percent *of* 8 means .25(8);

25 percent *less than* 8 means 8 – (.25)(8);

25 percent *greater than* 8 means 8 + (.25)(8).

Finding the Right Answer

$33\frac{1}{3}\%$ less than 9 means $9 - \left(\frac{1}{3}\right)(9) = 9 - 3 = 6$.

Trap 6: Hidden Instructions

At a certain dance club, the hourly wage for a DJ is 20 percent greater than the hourly wage for an usher, and the hourly wage for an usher is half as much as the hourly wage for a bouncer. If a bouncer earns $8.50 an hour, how much less than a bouncer does a DJ earn each hour?

(A) $2.55
(B) $3.40
(C) $4.25
(D) $5.10
(E) $5.95

The Wrong Answer

To solve this problem, you must find the hourly wage of the usher.

- The bouncer earns $8.50 an hour.
- The usher earns half that, or $4.25 an hour.
- The DJ earns 20 percent more than this: $4.25 × 1.2 = $5.10.

So the DJ earns $5.10 an hour, and you might reach automatically to fill in answer choice (D). But (D) is the wrong answer.

The Trap

A small step, easily overlooked, can mean the difference between a right and wrong answer. In this case the word is *less*. After spending all this time finding the DJ's hourly wage, many students skip right over the vital last step. They overlook the fact that the question asks not what the DJ earns, but how much less than the bouncer the DJ earns.

Avoiding the Trap

Watch for hidden instructions. MAKE SURE you answer the question that's being asked.

Finding the Right Answer

You have figured out that the DJ earns $5.10 an hour and the bouncer earns $8.50 an hour. To find out how much less than the bouncer the usher earns, subtract the DJ's hourly wage from the bouncer's hourly wage. The correct answer is (B), $3.40.

Trap 7: Average Rates

An unusually fast camel traveled from A to B at an average rate of 40 miles per hour and then immediately traveled back from B to A at an average speed of 60 miles per hour. What was the camel's average speed for the round trip, in miles per hour?

(A) 45
(B) 48
(C) 50
(D) 52
(E) 54

The Wrong Answer

Do you see which answer choice looks too good to be true? The temptation is simply to average 40 and 60. The answer is "obviously" (C), 50. But 50 is wrong.

The Trap

To get an average rate, you can't just average the rates. Why is the average speed not 50 mph? Because the camel spent more time traveling at 40 mph than at 60 mph. Each leg of the round trip was the same distance, but the first leg, at the slower speed, took more time.

Avoiding the Trap

You can solve almost any Average Rate problem if you apply this general formula:

$$\text{Average Rate} = \frac{\text{Total Distance}}{\text{Total Time}}$$

Use the given information to figure out the total distance and the total time. But how can you do that when many problems don't specify the distances?

Finding the Right Answer

In our sample above, we are told that a fast camel went "from A to B at 40 miles per hour and back from B to A at 60 miles per hour." In other words, it went half the total distance at 40 mph and half the total distance at 60 mph.

How do you use the formula $\text{Average Rate} = \frac{\text{Total Time}}{\text{Total Distance}}$ if you don't know the total distance? Why, by picking any number you want for the total distance.

Pick a number. Divide that total distance into half-distances. Calculate the time needed to travel each half-distance at the different rates.

Important

When plugging numbers into the Average Rate formula, pick numbers that are easy to work with.

A good number to pick here would be 240 miles for the total distance because you can easily figure in your head the times for two 120-mile legs at 40 mph and 60 mph:

$$A \text{ to } B\text{: } \frac{120 \text{ miles}}{40 \text{ miles per hour}} = 3 \text{ hours}$$

$$B \text{ to } A\text{: } \frac{120 \text{ miles}}{60 \text{ miles per hour}} = 2 \text{ hours}$$

Total Time = 5 hours

"Total Distance = 240 miles," so "Total Time = 5 hours" can be plugged into the general formula:

$$\text{Average Rate} = \frac{\text{Total Time}}{\text{Total Distance}}$$
$$= \frac{\text{240 miles}}{\text{5 hour}}$$
$$= \text{48 miles per hour}$$

Correct answer choice: (B).

Trap 8: Counting Numbers

The tickets for a helmet raffle are consecutively numbered. If Louis sold the tickets numbered from 75 to 148 inclusive, how many helmet raffle tickets did he sell?

(Note: This is a Grid-in, so there are no answer choices.)

The Wrong Answer

Many people would subtract 75 from 148 to get 73 as their answer. But that is not correct, and so these people DO NOT deserve a shiny new helmet.

The Trap

Subtracting the first and last integers in a range will give you the difference between the two numbers. It won't give you the number of integers in that range.

Avoiding the Trap

To count the number of integers in a range, subtract the endpoints and then add 1. If this doesn't seem logical to you, test the rule by picking two small numbers that are close together, such as 1 and 4. Obviously, there are four integers from 1 to 4, inclusive. But if you had subtracted 1 from 4, you would have gotten 3. In the diagram below, you can see that 3 is actually the distance between the integers, if the integers were on a number line or a ruler.

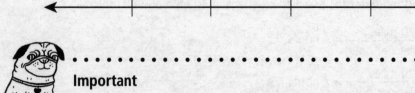

Important

To count the number of integers in an inclusive range, subtract the endpoints, and then add 1.

Finding the Right Answer

In the problem above, subtract 75 from 148. The result is 73. Add 1 to this difference to get the number of integers.

That gives you 74. This is the number you would grid in on your answer sheet.

The word "inclusive" tells you to include the first and last numbers given. So "the integers from 5 to 15 inclusive" include 5 and 15. Questions always make it clear whether you should include the outer numbers or not, since the correct answer hinges on this point.

Trap 9: Ratio Versus Quantity

The ratio of two quantities is 3:4. If each of the quantities is increased by 1, what is the ratio of these two new quantities?

(A) $\frac{9}{16}$

(B) $\frac{2}{3}$

(C) $\frac{3}{4}$

(D) $\frac{4}{5}$

(E) It cannot be determined from the information given.

The Wrong Answer

(D) is a trap.

The Trap

If all you have is a ratio, you cannot simply add to or subtract from the parts at will. Test takers unfamiliar with this rule would probably add 1 to 3 and to 4, coming up incorrectly with the ratio of 4:5.

Avoiding the Trap

Remember the rule that you can multiply or divide a ratio or part of a ratio, but you cannot add to or subtract from a ratio or part of a ratio. Imagine that at a meeting, the ratio of women to men is 6:5. If the number of women doubles, the new ratio of women to men is 12:5. In other words, you can multiply a ratio or part of a ratio. Or, if the number of women at the meeting were cut in half, the new ratio of women to men at the meeting would be 3:5.

However, you cannot add to or subtract from a ratio or part of a ratio because knowing the ratio doesn't tell you the actual quantities associated with it. Consider the meeting at which the ratio of women to men is 6:5. In situation I, the actual quantities of women and men are

12 and 10, respectively. In situation II, the actual quantities of women and men are 18 and 15, respectively. Now assume that one woman and one man enter the meeting. In situation I, the new ratio of women to men is 13:11. In situation II, the new ratio of women to men is 19:16. It is obvious that $\frac{13}{11} \neq \frac{19}{16}$; thus, this inequality demonstrates how it is possible to have the same ratio and get different results depending on the quantities with which you begin.

Finding the Right Answer

For students on the lookout for violations of the rule we've been discussing, this question means quick points. Once you realize that the ratio of the new quantities depends on the actual original quantities—not simply their ratio—you'll quickly recognize that the answer cannot be determined from the information provided. The correct answer is (E).

Trap 10: Not all Numbers are Positive Integers

If $n \neq 0$, then which of the following must be true?

I. $n^2 > n$

II. $2n > n$

III. $n + 1 > n$

(A) I only
(B) II only
(C) III only
(D) I and III only
(E) I, II, and III

The Wrong Answer

In the example above, if you considered only positive integers greater than 1 for the value of *n*, you would assume that all three statements are true. However, that is not the case.

The Trap

Not all numbers are positive integers. Don't forget there are negative numbers and fractions as well. This is important because negative numbers and fractions between 0 and 1 behave very differently from positive integers.

Avoiding the Trap

When Picking Numbers for variables, consider fractions and negative numbers.

Finding the Right Answer

Looking at statement I, you may assume that when you square a number, you end up with a larger number as a result. For example, $4^2 = 16$, or $10^2 = 100$. However, when you square a fraction between 0 and 1, the result is quite different: $\left(\frac{1}{2}\right)^2 = \frac{1}{4} \cdot \left(\frac{1}{10}\right)^2 = \frac{1}{100}$, so you get a smaller number.

In statement II, what happens when you multiply a number by 2? $7 \times 2 = 14$; $25 \times 2 = 50$. Multiplying any positive number by 2 doubles that number, so you get a larger result. However, if you multiply a negative number by 2, your result is smaller than the original number. For example, $-3 \times 2 = -6$.

Finally, look at statement III. What happens when you add 1 to any number? Adding 1 to any number gives you a larger number as a result. For example, $5 + 1 = 6$; $\frac{1}{2} + 1 = 1\frac{1}{2}$; and $-7 + 1 = -6$.

Therefore, only statement III must be true, so choice (C) is correct. If you didn't consider fractions or negative numbers, you would have fallen into the trap and answered the question incorrectly.

SUMMARY

- **The Traps:**
  - — Trap 1: Percent increase/decrease
    - Percents can only be added and subtracted when they are percents of the same amount
  - — Trap 2: Weighted averages
    - You cannot combine averages of different quantities by taking the average of those averages
    - Remember that the average formula calls for the sum of all the terms divided by the total number of terms
  - — Trap 3: Ratio:Ratio:Ratio
    - Parts of different ratios don't always refer to the same whole and are thus not in proportion to each other
    - Restate ratios so that the same number refers to the same quantity. Make sure the common quantity in both ratios has the same number in both
  - — Trap 4: "Least" and "Greatest"
    - In questions that ask for the least, minimum, or smallest something, the choice offering the smallest number is rarely right and vice versa
  - — Trap 5: Percent "of" versus percent "less" or "greater"

    - Be on the lookout for subtleties of wording, especially in questions appearing in the middle or end of a section
- Trap 6: Hidden instructions
    - Make sure you answer the question that is being asked
- Trap 7: Average rates
    - To get an average rate, you cannot just average the rates
    - You can solve almost any average rate problem if you apply the general formula: $\text{Average Rate} = \dfrac{\text{Total Distance}}{\text{Total Time}}$
- Trap 8: Counting numbers
    - Subtracting the first and last integers in a range will give you the difference between the two numbers, not the number of integers in the range
    - To count the number of integers in a range, subtract the endpoints and then add 1
- Trap 9: Ratio versus quantity
    - If you only have a ratio, you cannot add to or subtract from the parts at will
    - Remember the following rule: you can multiply or divide a ratio or part of a ratio, but you cannot add to or subtract from a ratio or part of a ratio
- Trap 10: Not all numbers are positive integers
    - When picking numbers for variables, consider fractions and negative numbers

PRACTICE

Directions: Identify the trap in each problem (and solve the problem correctly). Answers are found on page 206. There's no time limit.

1. If x is 300 percent of 25 and y is 25 percent more than 40, then x is what percent of y? (Disregard the % sign when you grid your answer.)

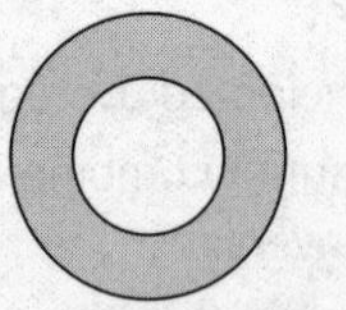

2. In the figure above, what is the maximum number of nonoverlapping regions into which the shaded area can be divided using exactly two straight lines?

    (A) 3
    (B) 4
    (C) 5
    (D) 6
    (E) 7

3. A certain school event was open only to juniors and seniors. Half the number of juniors who had planned to attend actually attended. Double the number of seniors who had planned to attend actually attended. If the ratio of the number of juniors who had planned to attend to the number of seniors who had planned to attend was 4 to 5, then juniors were what fraction of attendees?

(A) $\frac{1}{6}$

(B) $\frac{1}{5}$

(C) $\frac{4}{19}$

(D) $\frac{4}{15}$

(E) It cannot be determined from the information given.

4. If $p - q = 4$ and r is the number of integers less than p and greater than q, then which of the following could be true?

I. $r = 3$

II. $r = 4$

III. $r = 5$

(A) I only
(B) II only
(C) III only
(D) I and II
(E) I, II, and III

5. Pump #1 can drain a 400-gallon water tank in 1.2 hours. Pump #2 can drain the same tank in 1.8 hours. How many minutes longer than pump #1 would it take pump #2 to drain a 100-gallon tank?

(A) 0.15
(B) 1.2
(C) 6
(D) 9
(E) 18

6. Volumes 12 through 30 of a certain encyclopedia are located on the bottom shelf of a bookcase. If the volumes of the encyclopedia are numbered consecutively, how many volumes of the encyclopedia are on the bottom shelf?

(A) 17
(B) 18
(C) 19
(D) 29
(E) 30

7. A reservoir is at full capacity at the beginning of summer. By the first day of fall, the level in the reservoir is 30 percent below full capacity. Then during the fall, a period of heavy rains increases the level by 30 percent. After the rains, the reservoir is at what percent of its full capacity?

(A) 60%
(B) 85%
(C) 91%
(D) 95%
(E) 100%

8. Two classes, one with 50 students and the other with 30, take the same exam. The combined average of both classes is 84.5. If the larger class averages 80, what is the average of the smaller class?

(A) 87.2
(B) 89.0
(C) 92.0
(D) 93.3
(E) 94.5

9. In a pet shop, the ratio of puppies to kittens is 7:6, and the ratio of kittens to guinea pigs is 5:3. What is the ratio of puppies to guinea pigs?

   (A) 7:3
   (B) 6:5
   (C) 13:8
   (D) 21:11
   (E) 35:18

10. A typist typed the first n pages of a book, where $n > 0$, at an average rate of 12 pages per hour and typed the remaining n pages at an average rate of 20 pages per hour. What was the typist's average rate in pages per hour for the entire book?

    (A) 14
    (B) 15
    (C) 16
    (D) 17
    (E) 18

REMEMBER...

The SAT loves to use traps on harder math problems. Their favorite 10 traps are:

Trap 1: Percent Increase/Decrease

Trap 2: Weighted Averages

Trap 3: Ratio:Ratio:Ratio

Trap 4: "Least" and "Greatest"

Trap 5: Percent "Of" Versus Percent "Less" or "Greater"

Trap 6: Hidden Instructions

Trap 7: Average Rates

Trap 8: Counting Numbers

Trap 9: Ratio Versus Quantity

Trap 10: Not All Numbers Are Positive Integers

ANSWERS: DID YOU FALL FOR THE TRAPS?

Each wrong answer represents one trap you need to work on. Go back and reread the section on that trap. Then look at the practice set's problem again. Do you see the trap now?

1. **150** (Trap 5)
2. **C** (Trap 4)
3. **A** (Trap 9)
4. **D** (Trap 10)
5. **D** (Trap 6)
6. **C** (Trap 8)
7. **C** (Trap 1)
8. **C** (Trap 2)
9. **E** (Trap 3)
10. **B** (Trap 7)

Part 5

Final Preparations

Step Ten

Dealing with Test Stress

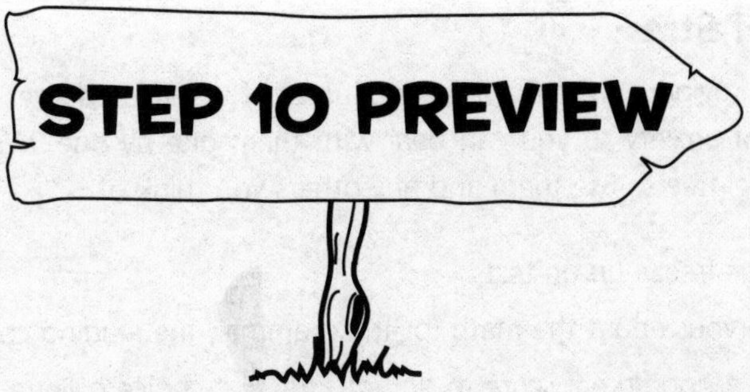

The Gist of It

- Sources of Stress
- Strengths and Weaknesses

How to Deal

- Visualize
- Exercise
- Stay Drug Free
- Isometrics

The Days Before the Test

- Three Days Before the Test
- Two Days Before the Test
- The Night Before the Test: Don't Study
- The Morning of the Test
- During the Test
- After the Test

Summary

You can beat anxiety the same way you can beat the SAT—by knowing what to expect beforehand and developing strategies to deal with it. You have completed nine steps specifically designed to help you with every nook and cranny of the SAT. This step helps you with every nook and cranny of YOUR BRAIN.

THE GIST OF IT

Sources of Stress

In the space provided, write down your sources of test-related stress. The idea is to pin down any sources of anxiety so you can deal with them one by one. We have provided common examples—feel free to use them and any others you think of.

- I always freeze up on tests.
- I'm nervous about the math (or the grammar, the reading comp, etc.).
- I need a good/great score to get into my first-choice college.
- My older brother/sister/best friend/girlfriend/boyfriend did really well. I must match their scores or do better.
- My parents, who are paying for school, will be quite disappointed if I don't do well.
- I'm afraid of losing my focus and concentration.
- I'm afraid I'm not spending enough time preparing.
- I study like crazy but nothing seems to stick in my mind.
- I always run out of time and get panicky.
- The simple act of thinking, for me, is like wading through refrigerated honey.

My Sources of Stress

____

____

____

____

____

____

Read through the list. Cross out things or add things. Now rewrite the list in order of most disturbing to least disturbing.

My Sources of Stress, In Order

Chances are, the top of the list is a fairly accurate description of exactly how you react to test anxiety, both physically and mentally. The later items usually describe your fears (disappointing mom and dad, looking bad, etc.). Taking care of the major items from the top of the list should go a long way towards relieving overall test anxiety. That's what we'll do next.

Strengths and Weaknesses

Take 60 seconds to list the areas of the SAT or any other test that you are good at. They can be general (math) or specific (addition of even numbers). Put down as many as you can think of, and, if possible, time yourself. Write for the entire time; don't stop writing until you've reached the one-minute stopping point. Go.

Strong Test Subjects

Now take one minute to list areas of the test you're not so good at, just plain bad at, have failed at, or keep failing at. Again, keep it to one minute, and continue writing until you reach the cutoff. Go.

Weak Test Subjects

Taking stock of your assets and liabilities lets you know the areas you don't have to worry about and the ones that will demand extra attention and effort. It helps a lot to find out where you need to spend extra effort. We mostly fear what we don't know and are probably afraid to face. You can't help feeling more confident when you know you're actively strengthening your chances of earning a higher overall score.

Now, go back to the "good" list, and expand on it for two minutes. Take the general items on that first list and make them more specific; take the specific items and expand them into more general conclusions. Naturally, if anything new comes to mind, jot it down. Focus all of your attention and effort on your strengths. Don't underestimate yourself or your abilities. Give yourself full credit. At the same time, don't list strengths you don't really have; you'll only be fooling yourself.

Expanding from general to specific might go as follows. If you listed "world history" as a broad topic you feel strong in, you would then narrow your focus to include areas of this subject about which you are particularly knowledgeable. Your areas of strength might include modern European history, the events leading up to World War I, the Bolshevik revolution, etc. Whatever you know well goes on your "good" list. OK. Check your starting time. Go.

Strong Test Subjects: An Expanded List

After you've stopped, check your time. Did you find yourself going beyond the two minutes allotted? Did you write down more things than you thought you knew? Is it possible you know more than you've given yourself credit for? Could that mean you've found a number of areas in which you feel strong?

You just took an active step towards helping yourself. Enjoy your increased feelings of confidence, and use them when you take the SAT.

HOW TO DEAL

Visualize

This next little group of activities is a follow-up to the "good at" and "bad at" lists. Sit in a comfortable chair in a quiet setting. If you wear glasses, take them off. Close your eyes, and breathe in a deep, satisfying breath of air. Really fill your lungs until your rib cage is fully expanded and you can't take in any more. Then, exhale the air completely. Imagine you're blowing out a candle with your last little puff of air. Do this two or three more times, filling your lungs to their maximum and emptying them totally. Keep your eyes closed, comfortably but not tightly. Let your body sink deeper into the chair as you become even more comfortable.

With your eyes shut you can notice something very interesting. You're no longer dealing with the worrisome stuff going on in the world outside of you. Now you can concentrate on what happens inside you. The more you recognize your own physical reactions to stress and anxiety, the more you can do about them. You may not realize it, but you've begun to regain a sense of being in control.

Let images begin to form on TV screens on the back of your eyelids. Allow the images to come easily and naturally; don't force them. Visualize a relaxing situation. It might be in a special place you've visited before or one you've read about. It can be a fictional location that you create in your imagination, but a real-life memory of a place or situation you know is usually better. Make it as detailed as possible and notice as much as you can.

Stay focused on the images as you sink farther into your chair. Breathe easily and naturally. You might have the sensations of any stress or tension draining from your muscles and flowing downward, out your feet, and away from you.

Take a moment to check how you're feeling. Notice how comfortable you've become. Imagine how much easier it would be if you could take the test feeling this relaxed and in this state of ease. You've coupled the images of your special place with sensations of comfort and relaxation. You've also found a way to become relaxed simply by visualizing your own safe, special place.

Close your eyes and start remembering a real-life situation in which you did well on a test. If you can't come up with one, remember a situation in which you did something that you were really proud of—a genuine accomplishment. Make the memory as detailed as possible. Think about the sights, the sounds, the smells, even the tastes associated with this remembered experience. Remember how confident you felt as you accomplished your goal. Now start thinking about the SAT. Keep your thoughts and feelings in line with that prior, successful experience. Don't make comparisons between them. Just imagine taking the upcoming test with the same feelings of confidence and relaxed control.

This exercise is a great way to bring the test down to earth. You should practice this exercise often, especially when you feel burned out on SAT preparation. The more you practice it, the more effective the exercise will be for you.

Exercise

Whether it's jogging, walking, biking, mild aerobics, pushups, or a pickup basketball game, physical exercise is a very effective way to stimulate both your mind and body and to improve your ability to think and concentrate. Lots of students get out of the habit of regular exercise when they're prepping for the exam. Also, sedentary people get less oxygen to the blood, and hence to the brain, than active people. You can watch TV fine with a little less oxygen; you just can't think as well.

Any big test is a bit like a race. Finishing the race strong is just as important as being quick early on. If you can't sustain your energy level in the last sections of the exam, you could blow it. Along with a good diet and adequate sleep, exercise is an important part of keeping yourself in fighting shape and thinking clearly for the long haul.

There's another thing that happens when students don't make exercise an integral part of their test preparation. Like any organism in nature, you operate best if all your "energy systems" are in balance. Studying uses a lot of energy, but it's all mental. When you take a study break, do something active. Take a five- to ten-minute exercise break for every 50 or 60 minutes that you study. The physical exertion helps keep your mind and body in sync. This way, when you finish studying for the night and go to bed, you won't lie there unable to sleep because your head is wasted while your body wants to run a marathon.

One warning about exercise: It's not a good idea to exercise vigorously right before you go to bed. This could easily cause sleep-onset problems. For the same reason, it's also not a good idea to study right up to bedtime. Make time for a "buffer period" before you go to bed. Take 30 to 60 minutes to take a long hot shower, to meditate, or to watch any show on television.

Stay Drug Free

Using drugs to prepare for or take a big test is not a good idea. Don't take uppers to stay alert. Amphetamines make it hard to retain information. Mild stimulants, such as coffee, cola, or over-the-counter caffeine pills can help you study longer since they keep you awake, but they can also lead to agitation, restlessness, and insomnia. Some people can drink a pot of coffee sludge and sleep like a baby. Others have one cup and start to vibrate. It all depends on your tolerance for caffeine. Remember, a little anxiety is a good thing. The adrenaline that gets pumped into your bloodstream helps you stay alert and think more clearly.

You can also rely on your brain's own endorphins. Endorphins have no side effects and they're free. It just takes some exercise to release them. Running, bicycling, swimming, aerobics, and power walking all cause endorphins to occupy the happy spots in your brain's neural synapses. In addition, exercise develops your mental stamina and increases the oxygen transfer to your brain.

To reduce stress you should eat fruits and vegetables (raw is best or just lightly steamed or nuked), low-fat protein such as fish, skinless poultry, beans, and legumes (like lentils), or whole grains such as brown rice, whole wheat bread, and pastas (no bleached flour). Don't eat sweet, high-fat snacks. Simple carbohydrates like sugar make stress worse, and fatty foods lower your immunity. Don't eat salty foods either. They can deplete potassium, which you need for nerve functions. You can go back to your Combos-and-Dew diet after the SAT.

Isometrics

Here's another natural route to relaxation and invigoration. You can do it whenever you get stressed out, including during the test. Close your eyes. Starting with your eyes and—without holding your breath—gradually tighten every muscle in your body (but not to the point of pain) in the following sequence:

- Close your eyes tightly.
- Squeeze your nose and mouth together so that your whole face is scrunched up. (If it makes you self-conscious to do this in the test room, skip the face-scrunching part.)
- Pull your chin into your chest, and pull your shoulders together.
- Tighten your arms to your body, then clench your fists.
- Pull in your stomach.
- Squeeze your thighs and buttocks together, and tighten your calves.
- Stretch your feet, then curl your toes (watch out for cramping in this part).

At this point, every muscle should be tightened. Now, relax your body, one part at a time, in reverse order, starting with your toes. Let the tension drop out of each muscle. The entire process might take five minutes from start to finish (maybe a couple of minutes during the test). This clenching and unclenching exercise will feel silly at first, especially the buttocks part, but if you get good at it, you will feel very relaxed.

THE DAYS BEFORE THE TEST

As the test gets closer, you may find your anxiety is on the rise. To calm any pretest jitters you may have, let's go over a few strategies for the couple of days before and after the test.

Three Days Before the Test

Take a full-length practice test under timed conditions. Try to use all of the techniques and tips you've learned in this book. Approach the test strategically, actively, and confidently.

WARNING: DO NOT take a full practice SAT if you have fewer than 48 hours left before the test. Doing so will probably exhaust you, hurting your score on the actual test. You wouldn't run a marathon the day before the real thing.

Two Days Before the Test

Go over the results of your practice test. Don't worry too much about your score or whether you got a specific question right or wrong. The practice test doesn't count, remember. But do examine your performance on specific questions with an eye to how you might get through each one faster and with greater accuracy on the actual test to come.

The Night Before the Test: Don't Study

Get together an "SAT survival kit" containing the following items:

- A calculator with fresh batteries
- A watch
- A few No. 2 pencils (pencils with slightly dull points fill the ovals better)
- Erasers
- Photo ID card
- Your admission ticket from ETS
- A snack—there are two breaks, and you'll probably get hungry

Know exactly where you're going, exactly how you're getting there, and exactly how long it takes to get there. It's probably a good idea to visit your test center sometime before the day of the test, so that you know what to expect—what the rooms are like, how the desks are set up, and so on.

Relax the night before the test. Read a good book, take a long hot shower, or watch TV. Get a good night's sleep. Go to bed early, and leave yourself extra time in the morning.

The Morning of the Test

First, wake up. After that:

- Eat breakfast. Make it something substantial, but not anything too heavy or greasy.
- Don't drink a lot of coffee if you're not used to it; bathroom breaks cut into your time, and too much caffeine is a bad idea.
- Dress in layers so that you can adjust to the temperature of the test room.
- Read something. Warm up your brain with a newspaper or a magazine. You shouldn't let the SAT be the first thing you read that day.
- Be sure to get there early. Allow yourself extra time for traffic, mass transit delays, and/or detours around people who might only add to your stress level if you stopped to talk to them.

During the Test

Don't be shaken. If you find your confidence slipping, remind yourself how well you've prepared. You know the structure of the test; you know the instructions; you've had practice with—and have learned strategies for—every question type.

Even if something goes really wrong, don't panic. If the test booklet is defective—two pages are stuck together or the ink has run—try to stay calm. Raise your hand and tell the proctor you need a new book. If you accidentally misgrid your answer page or put the answers in the wrong section, again, don't panic. Raise your hand and tell the proctor. He or she might be able to arrange for you to regrid your test after it's over, when it won't cost you any time.

Don't think about which section is experimental. Remember, you never know for sure which section won't count. Besides, you can't work on any other section during that section's designated time slot.

Remember to pace yourself, and rack up points on the questions you definitely know. And remember—taking time out to relax, breathe, and plan your essay before you write it will really pay off in the final product.

After the Test

You might walk out of the SAT thinking that you blew it. This is a normal reaction. Lots of people—even the highest scorers—feel that way. You tend to remember the questions that stumped you, not the ones that you knew. You can always call ETS within 24 hours to find out about canceling your score, but there's usually no good reason to do so. Remember, colleges typically accept your highest SAT score. And no test experience is going to be perfect.

We're positive that you will have performed well and scored your best on the exam because you followed the Kaplan strategies outlined in this section. Be confident in your preparation, and celebrate the fact that the SAT is soon to be a distant memory.

SUMMARY

- **How to Deal:**
  - Visualize
  - Exercise
  - Stay Drug Free
  - Isometrics
- **The Days Before the Test:**
  - Three days before the test
    - Take a full length practice test under timed conditions
  - Two days before the test
    - Go over the results of your practice tests
  - The night before the test
    - Don't study
    - Get together an SAT survival kit
      - A calculator with fresh batteries
      - A watch
      - A few No. 2 pencils
      - Erasers
      - Photo ID card
      - Your admission ticket from ETS
      - A snack
  - The morning of the test
    - Eat breakfast
    - Don't drink a lot of coffee
    - Dress in layers
    - Read something
    - Get to the test early
  - During the test
    - Don't panic
    - Don't think about which section is experimental
    - Pace yourself
  - After the Test
    - Be confident in your preparation

Part 6

Take the Practice Test

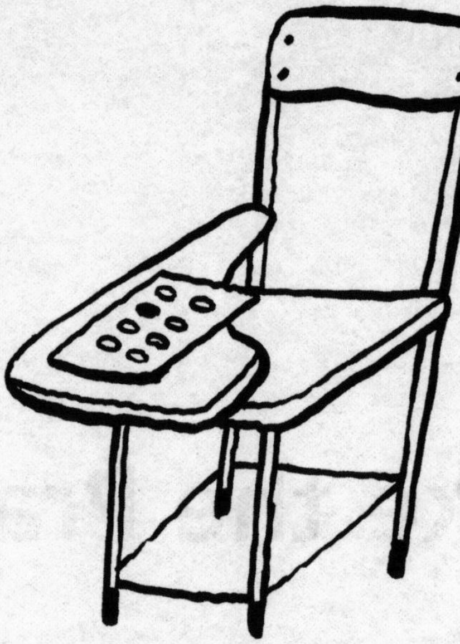

Practice Test

HOW TO TAKE THIS PRACTICE TEST

Before taking this practice test, find a quiet room where you can work uninterrupted for about four hours. Make sure you have a comfortable workspace and several No. 2 pencils. Use the answer sheet on the following page to record your answers. (You can tear it out or photocopy it.)

Once you start this practice test, do not stop until you have finished. Remember, you may review any questions within a section, but you may not go back and forth between sections.

When you have finished taking your practice test, you can go on to the section that follows to calculate your score.

Good luck.

SAT Practice Test
Answer Sheet

Remove (or photocopy) the answer sheet and use it to complete the practice test. See the answer key following the test when finished. The "Compute Your Score" section at the end of Section Six will show you how to find your score.

Start with number 1 for each section. If a section has fewer questions than answer spaces, leave the extra spaces blank.

SECTION 1

Section One is the writing section's essay component.
Lined pages on which you will write your essay can be found in that section.

SECTION 2

1. Ⓐ Ⓑ Ⓒ Ⓓ Ⓔ 11. Ⓐ Ⓑ Ⓒ Ⓓ Ⓔ 21. Ⓐ Ⓑ Ⓒ Ⓓ Ⓔ 31. Ⓐ Ⓑ Ⓒ Ⓓ Ⓔ
2. Ⓐ Ⓑ Ⓒ Ⓓ Ⓔ 12. Ⓐ Ⓑ Ⓒ Ⓓ Ⓔ 22. Ⓐ Ⓑ Ⓒ Ⓓ Ⓔ 32. Ⓐ Ⓑ Ⓒ Ⓓ Ⓔ
3. Ⓐ Ⓑ Ⓒ Ⓓ Ⓔ 13. Ⓐ Ⓑ Ⓒ Ⓓ Ⓔ 23. Ⓐ Ⓑ Ⓒ Ⓓ Ⓔ 33. Ⓐ Ⓑ Ⓒ Ⓓ Ⓔ
4. Ⓐ Ⓑ Ⓒ Ⓓ Ⓔ 14. Ⓐ Ⓑ Ⓒ Ⓓ Ⓔ 24. Ⓐ Ⓑ Ⓒ Ⓓ Ⓔ 34. Ⓐ Ⓑ Ⓒ Ⓓ Ⓔ # right in Section 2
5. Ⓐ Ⓑ Ⓒ Ⓓ Ⓔ 15. Ⓐ Ⓑ Ⓒ Ⓓ Ⓔ 25. Ⓐ Ⓑ Ⓒ Ⓓ Ⓔ 35. Ⓐ Ⓑ Ⓒ Ⓓ Ⓔ
6. Ⓐ Ⓑ Ⓒ Ⓓ Ⓔ 16. Ⓐ Ⓑ Ⓒ Ⓓ Ⓔ 26. Ⓐ Ⓑ Ⓒ Ⓓ Ⓔ 36. Ⓐ Ⓑ Ⓒ Ⓓ Ⓔ
7. Ⓐ Ⓑ Ⓒ Ⓓ Ⓔ 17. Ⓐ Ⓑ Ⓒ Ⓓ Ⓔ 27. Ⓐ Ⓑ Ⓒ Ⓓ Ⓔ 37. Ⓐ Ⓑ Ⓒ Ⓓ Ⓔ
8. Ⓐ Ⓑ Ⓒ Ⓓ Ⓔ 18. Ⓐ Ⓑ Ⓒ Ⓓ Ⓔ 28. Ⓐ Ⓑ Ⓒ Ⓓ Ⓔ 38. Ⓐ Ⓑ Ⓒ Ⓓ Ⓔ # wrong in Section 2
9. Ⓐ Ⓑ Ⓒ Ⓓ Ⓔ 19. Ⓐ Ⓑ Ⓒ Ⓓ Ⓔ 29. Ⓐ Ⓑ Ⓒ Ⓓ Ⓔ 39. Ⓐ Ⓑ Ⓒ Ⓓ Ⓔ
10. Ⓐ Ⓑ Ⓒ Ⓓ Ⓔ 20. Ⓐ Ⓑ Ⓒ Ⓓ Ⓔ 30. Ⓐ Ⓑ Ⓒ Ⓓ Ⓔ 40. Ⓐ Ⓑ Ⓒ Ⓓ Ⓔ

SECTION 3

1. Ⓐ Ⓑ Ⓒ Ⓓ Ⓔ 11. Ⓐ Ⓑ Ⓒ Ⓓ Ⓔ 21. Ⓐ Ⓑ Ⓒ Ⓓ Ⓔ 31. Ⓐ Ⓑ Ⓒ Ⓓ Ⓔ
2. Ⓐ Ⓑ Ⓒ Ⓓ Ⓔ 12. Ⓐ Ⓑ Ⓒ Ⓓ Ⓔ 22. Ⓐ Ⓑ Ⓒ Ⓓ Ⓔ 32. Ⓐ Ⓑ Ⓒ Ⓓ Ⓔ
3. Ⓐ Ⓑ Ⓒ Ⓓ Ⓔ 13. Ⓐ Ⓑ Ⓒ Ⓓ Ⓔ 23. Ⓐ Ⓑ Ⓒ Ⓓ Ⓔ 33. Ⓐ Ⓑ Ⓒ Ⓓ Ⓔ
4. Ⓐ Ⓑ Ⓒ Ⓓ Ⓔ 14. Ⓐ Ⓑ Ⓒ Ⓓ Ⓔ 24. Ⓐ Ⓑ Ⓒ Ⓓ Ⓔ 34. Ⓐ Ⓑ Ⓒ Ⓓ Ⓔ # right in Section 3
5. Ⓐ Ⓑ Ⓒ Ⓓ Ⓔ 15. Ⓐ Ⓑ Ⓒ Ⓓ Ⓔ 25. Ⓐ Ⓑ Ⓒ Ⓓ Ⓔ 35. Ⓐ Ⓑ Ⓒ Ⓓ Ⓔ
6. Ⓐ Ⓑ Ⓒ Ⓓ Ⓔ 16. Ⓐ Ⓑ Ⓒ Ⓓ Ⓔ 26. Ⓐ Ⓑ Ⓒ Ⓓ Ⓔ 36. Ⓐ Ⓑ Ⓒ Ⓓ Ⓔ
7. Ⓐ Ⓑ Ⓒ Ⓓ Ⓔ 17. Ⓐ Ⓑ Ⓒ Ⓓ Ⓔ 27. Ⓐ Ⓑ Ⓒ Ⓓ Ⓔ 37. Ⓐ Ⓑ Ⓒ Ⓓ Ⓔ
8. Ⓐ Ⓑ Ⓒ Ⓓ Ⓔ 18. Ⓐ Ⓑ Ⓒ Ⓓ Ⓔ 28. Ⓐ Ⓑ Ⓒ Ⓓ Ⓔ 38. Ⓐ Ⓑ Ⓒ Ⓓ Ⓔ # wrong in Section 3
9. Ⓐ Ⓑ Ⓒ Ⓓ Ⓔ 19. Ⓐ Ⓑ Ⓒ Ⓓ Ⓔ 29. Ⓐ Ⓑ Ⓒ Ⓓ Ⓔ 39. Ⓐ Ⓑ Ⓒ Ⓓ Ⓔ
10. Ⓐ Ⓑ Ⓒ Ⓓ Ⓔ 20. Ⓐ Ⓑ Ⓒ Ⓓ Ⓔ 30. Ⓐ Ⓑ Ⓒ Ⓓ Ⓔ 40. Ⓐ Ⓑ Ⓒ Ⓓ Ⓔ

Remove (or photocopy) this answer sheet and use it to complete the practice test.

Start with number 1 for each section. If a section has fewer questions than answer spaces, leave the extra spaces blank.

SECTION 4

1. Ⓐ Ⓑ Ⓒ Ⓓ Ⓔ	11. Ⓐ Ⓑ Ⓒ Ⓓ Ⓔ	21. Ⓐ Ⓑ Ⓒ Ⓓ Ⓔ	31. Ⓐ Ⓑ Ⓒ Ⓓ Ⓔ
2. Ⓐ Ⓑ Ⓒ Ⓓ Ⓔ	12. Ⓐ Ⓑ Ⓒ Ⓓ Ⓔ	22. Ⓐ Ⓑ Ⓒ Ⓓ Ⓔ	32. Ⓐ Ⓑ Ⓒ Ⓓ Ⓔ
3. Ⓐ Ⓑ Ⓒ Ⓓ Ⓔ	13. Ⓐ Ⓑ Ⓒ Ⓓ Ⓔ	23. Ⓐ Ⓑ Ⓒ Ⓓ Ⓔ	33. Ⓐ Ⓑ Ⓒ Ⓓ Ⓔ
4. Ⓐ Ⓑ Ⓒ Ⓓ Ⓔ	14. Ⓐ Ⓑ Ⓒ Ⓓ Ⓔ	24. Ⓐ Ⓑ Ⓒ Ⓓ Ⓔ	34. Ⓐ Ⓑ Ⓒ Ⓓ Ⓔ
5. Ⓐ Ⓑ Ⓒ Ⓓ Ⓔ	15. Ⓐ Ⓑ Ⓒ Ⓓ Ⓔ	25. Ⓐ Ⓑ Ⓒ Ⓓ Ⓔ	35. Ⓐ Ⓑ Ⓒ Ⓓ Ⓔ
6. Ⓐ Ⓑ Ⓒ Ⓓ Ⓔ	16. Ⓐ Ⓑ Ⓒ Ⓓ Ⓔ	26. Ⓐ Ⓑ Ⓒ Ⓓ Ⓔ	36. Ⓐ Ⓑ Ⓒ Ⓓ Ⓔ
7. Ⓐ Ⓑ Ⓒ Ⓓ Ⓔ	17. Ⓐ Ⓑ Ⓒ Ⓓ Ⓔ	27. Ⓐ Ⓑ Ⓒ Ⓓ Ⓔ	37. Ⓐ Ⓑ Ⓒ Ⓓ Ⓔ
8. Ⓐ Ⓑ Ⓒ Ⓓ Ⓔ	18. Ⓐ Ⓑ Ⓒ Ⓓ Ⓔ	28. Ⓐ Ⓑ Ⓒ Ⓓ Ⓔ	38. Ⓐ Ⓑ Ⓒ Ⓓ Ⓔ
9. Ⓐ Ⓑ Ⓒ Ⓓ Ⓔ	19. Ⓐ Ⓑ Ⓒ Ⓓ Ⓔ	29. Ⓐ Ⓑ Ⓒ Ⓓ Ⓔ	39. Ⓐ Ⓑ Ⓒ Ⓓ Ⓔ
10. Ⓐ Ⓑ Ⓒ Ⓓ Ⓔ	20. Ⓐ Ⓑ Ⓒ Ⓓ Ⓔ	30. Ⓐ Ⓑ Ⓒ Ⓓ Ⓔ	40. Ⓐ Ⓑ Ⓒ Ⓓ Ⓔ

right in Section 4

wrong in Section 4

SECTION 5

1. Ⓐ Ⓑ Ⓒ Ⓓ Ⓔ	11. Ⓐ Ⓑ Ⓒ Ⓓ Ⓔ	21. Ⓐ Ⓑ Ⓒ Ⓓ Ⓔ	31. Ⓐ Ⓑ Ⓒ Ⓓ Ⓔ
2. Ⓐ Ⓑ Ⓒ Ⓓ Ⓔ	12. Ⓐ Ⓑ Ⓒ Ⓓ Ⓔ	22. Ⓐ Ⓑ Ⓒ Ⓓ Ⓔ	32. Ⓐ Ⓑ Ⓒ Ⓓ Ⓔ
3. Ⓐ Ⓑ Ⓒ Ⓓ Ⓔ	13. Ⓐ Ⓑ Ⓒ Ⓓ Ⓔ	23. Ⓐ Ⓑ Ⓒ Ⓓ Ⓔ	33. Ⓐ Ⓑ Ⓒ Ⓓ Ⓔ
4. Ⓐ Ⓑ Ⓒ Ⓓ Ⓔ	14. Ⓐ Ⓑ Ⓒ Ⓓ Ⓔ	24. Ⓐ Ⓑ Ⓒ Ⓓ Ⓔ	34. Ⓐ Ⓑ Ⓒ Ⓓ Ⓔ
5. Ⓐ Ⓑ Ⓒ Ⓓ Ⓔ	15. Ⓐ Ⓑ Ⓒ Ⓓ Ⓔ	25. Ⓐ Ⓑ Ⓒ Ⓓ Ⓔ	35. Ⓐ Ⓑ Ⓒ Ⓓ Ⓔ
6. Ⓐ Ⓑ Ⓒ Ⓓ Ⓔ	16. Ⓐ Ⓑ Ⓒ Ⓓ Ⓔ	26. Ⓐ Ⓑ Ⓒ Ⓓ Ⓔ	36. Ⓐ Ⓑ Ⓒ Ⓓ Ⓔ
7. Ⓐ Ⓑ Ⓒ Ⓓ Ⓔ	17. Ⓐ Ⓑ Ⓒ Ⓓ Ⓔ	27. Ⓐ Ⓑ Ⓒ Ⓓ Ⓔ	37. Ⓐ Ⓑ Ⓒ Ⓓ Ⓔ
8. Ⓐ Ⓑ Ⓒ Ⓓ Ⓔ	18. Ⓐ Ⓑ Ⓒ Ⓓ Ⓔ	28. Ⓐ Ⓑ Ⓒ Ⓓ Ⓔ	38. Ⓐ Ⓑ Ⓒ Ⓓ Ⓔ
9. Ⓐ Ⓑ Ⓒ Ⓓ Ⓔ	19. Ⓐ Ⓑ Ⓒ Ⓓ Ⓔ	29. Ⓐ Ⓑ Ⓒ Ⓓ Ⓔ	39. Ⓐ Ⓑ Ⓒ Ⓓ Ⓔ
10. Ⓐ Ⓑ Ⓒ Ⓓ Ⓔ	20. Ⓐ Ⓑ Ⓒ Ⓓ Ⓔ	30. Ⓐ Ⓑ Ⓒ Ⓓ Ⓔ	40. Ⓐ Ⓑ Ⓒ Ⓓ Ⓔ

right in Section 5

wrong in Section 5

If section 5 of your test book contains math questions that are not multiple choice, continue to item 9 below. Otherwise, continue to item 9 above.

Grid-in answer boxes for items 9, 10, 11, 12, 13, 14, 15, 16, 17, 18 (each grid):

	/	/	
.	.	.	.
	0	0	0
1	1	1	1
2	2	2	2
3	3	3	3
4	4	4	4
5	5	5	5
6	6	6	6
7	7	7	7
8	8	8	8
9	9	9	9

Remove (or photocopy) this answer sheet and use it to complete the practice test.

Start with number 1 for each section. If a section has fewer questions than answer spaces, leave the extra spaces blank.

SECTION 6

1. A B C D E	11. A B C D E	21. A B C D E	31. A B C D E
2. A B C D E	12. A B C D E	22. A B C D E	32. A B C D E
3. A B C D E	13. A B C D E	23. A B C D E	33. A B C D E
4. A B C D E	14. A B C D E	24. A B C D E	34. A B C D E
5. A B C D E	15. A B C D E	25. A B C D E	35. A B C D E
6. A B C D E	16. A B C D E	26. A B C D E	36. A B C D E
7. A B C D E	17. A B C D E	27. A B C D E	37. A B C D E
8. A B C D E	18. A B C D E	28. A B C D E	38. A B C D E
9. A B C D E	19. A B C D E	29. A B C D E	39. A B C D E
10. A B C D E	20. A B C D E	30. A B C D E	40. A B C D E

\# right in Section 6

\# wrong in Section 6

SECTION 7

1. A B C D E	11. A B C D E	21. A B C D E	31. A B C D E
2. A B C D E	12. A B C D E	22. A B C D E	32. A B C D E
3. A B C D E	13. A B C D E	23. A B C D E	33. A B C D E
4. A B C D E	14. A B C D E	24. A B C D E	34. A B C D E
5. A B C D E	15. A B C D E	25. A B C D E	35. A B C D E
6. A B C D E	16. A B C D E	26. A B C D E	36. A B C D E
7. A B C D E	17. A B C D E	27. A B C D E	37. A B C D E
8. A B C D E	18. A B C D E	28. A B C D E	38. A B C D E
9. A B C D E	19. A B C D E	29. A B C D E	39. A B C D E
10. A B C D E	20. A B C D E	30. A B C D E	40. A B C D E

\# right in Section 7

\# wrong in Section 7

SECTION 8

1. A B C D E	11. A B C D E	21. A B C D E	31. A B C D E
2. A B C D E	12. A B C D E	22. A B C D E	32. A B C D E
3. A B C D E	13. A B C D E	23. A B C D E	33. A B C D E
4. A B C D E	14. A B C D E	24. A B C D E	34. A B C D E
5. A B C D E	15. A B C D E	25. A B C D E	35. A B C D E
6. A B C D E	16. A B C D E	26. A B C D E	36. A B C D E
7. A B C D E	17. A B C D E	27. A B C D E	37. A B C D E
8. A B C D E	18. A B C D E	28. A B C D E	38. A B C D E
9. A B C D E	19. A B C D E	29. A B C D E	39. A B C D E
10. A B C D E	20. A B C D E	30. A B C D E	40. A B C D E

\# right in Section 8

\# wrong in Section 8

Remove (or photocopy) this answer sheet and use it to complete the practice test.

Start with number 1 for each section. If a section has fewer questions than answer spaces, leave the extra spaces blank.

SECTION

9

1. Ⓐ Ⓑ Ⓒ Ⓓ Ⓔ	11. Ⓐ Ⓑ Ⓒ Ⓓ Ⓔ	21. Ⓐ Ⓑ Ⓒ Ⓓ Ⓔ	31. Ⓐ Ⓑ Ⓒ Ⓓ Ⓔ
2. Ⓐ Ⓑ Ⓒ Ⓓ Ⓔ	12. Ⓐ Ⓑ Ⓒ Ⓓ Ⓔ	22. Ⓐ Ⓑ Ⓒ Ⓓ Ⓔ	32. Ⓐ Ⓑ Ⓒ Ⓓ Ⓔ
3. Ⓐ Ⓑ Ⓒ Ⓓ Ⓔ	13. Ⓐ Ⓑ Ⓒ Ⓓ Ⓔ	23. Ⓐ Ⓑ Ⓒ Ⓓ Ⓔ	33. Ⓐ Ⓑ Ⓒ Ⓓ Ⓔ
4. Ⓐ Ⓑ Ⓒ Ⓓ Ⓔ	14. Ⓐ Ⓑ Ⓒ Ⓓ Ⓔ	24. Ⓐ Ⓑ Ⓒ Ⓓ Ⓔ	34. Ⓐ Ⓑ Ⓒ Ⓓ Ⓔ
5. Ⓐ Ⓑ Ⓒ Ⓓ Ⓔ	15. Ⓐ Ⓑ Ⓒ Ⓓ Ⓔ	25. Ⓐ Ⓑ Ⓒ Ⓓ Ⓔ	35. Ⓐ Ⓑ Ⓒ Ⓓ Ⓔ
6. Ⓐ Ⓑ Ⓒ Ⓓ Ⓔ	16. Ⓐ Ⓑ Ⓒ Ⓓ Ⓔ	26. Ⓐ Ⓑ Ⓒ Ⓓ Ⓔ	36. Ⓐ Ⓑ Ⓒ Ⓓ Ⓔ
7. Ⓐ Ⓑ Ⓒ Ⓓ Ⓔ	17. Ⓐ Ⓑ Ⓒ Ⓓ Ⓔ	27. Ⓐ Ⓑ Ⓒ Ⓓ Ⓔ	37. Ⓐ Ⓑ Ⓒ Ⓓ Ⓔ
8. Ⓐ Ⓑ Ⓒ Ⓓ Ⓔ	18. Ⓐ Ⓑ Ⓒ Ⓓ Ⓔ	28. Ⓐ Ⓑ Ⓒ Ⓓ Ⓔ	38. Ⓐ Ⓑ Ⓒ Ⓓ Ⓔ
9. Ⓐ Ⓑ Ⓒ Ⓓ Ⓔ	19. Ⓐ Ⓑ Ⓒ Ⓓ Ⓔ	29. Ⓐ Ⓑ Ⓒ Ⓓ Ⓔ	39. Ⓐ Ⓑ Ⓒ Ⓓ Ⓔ
10. Ⓐ Ⓑ Ⓒ Ⓓ Ⓔ	20. Ⓐ Ⓑ Ⓒ Ⓓ Ⓔ	30. Ⓐ Ⓑ Ⓒ Ⓓ Ⓔ	40. Ⓐ Ⓑ Ⓒ Ⓓ Ⓔ

right in Section 9

wrong in Section 9

SECTION 1

Time—25 Minutes

The essay gives you an opportunity to show how effectively you can develop and express ideas. You should, therefore, take care to develop your point of view, present your ideas logically and clearly, and use language precisely.

Your essay must be written in your Answer Grid Booklet—you will receive no other paper on which to write. You will have enough space if you write on every line, avoid wide margins, and keep your handwriting to a reasonable size. Remember that people who are not familiar with your handwriting will read what you write. Try to write or print so that what you are writing is legible to those readers.

You have twenty-five minutes to write an essay on the topic assigned below.

DO NOT WRITE ON ANOTHER TOPIC. AN OFF-TOPIC ESSAY WILL RECEIVE A SCORE OF ZERO.

Think carefully about the issue presented in the following excerpt and the assignment below.

> "Nothing in the world can take the place of persistence. Talent will not; nothing is more common than unsuccessful men with talent. Genius will not; unrewarded genius is almost a proverb. Education will not; the world is full of educated derelicts. Persistence and determination are omnipotent. The slogan, "Press on!" has solved and always will solve the problems of the human race."
>
> — Calvin Coolidge, *Autobiography*

Assignment: Do you agree that persistence is the major factor in success, and that talent, genius, and education play, at best, secondary roles? In an essay, support your position by discussing an example (or examples) from literature, science and technology, the arts, current events, or your own experience or observations.

DO NOT WRITE YOUR ESSAY IN YOUR TEST BOOK.
You will receive credit only for what you write in your Answer Grid Booklet.

GO ON TO THE NEXT PAGE

If you finish before time is called, you may check your work on this section only. Do not turn to any other section in the test.

STOP

SECTION 2

Time—25 Minutes

20 Questions

Directions: For this section, solve each problem and decide which is the best of the choices given. Fill in the corresponding oval on the answer sheet. You may use any available space for scratchwork.

Notes:

(1) Calculator use is permitted.

(2) All numbers used are real numbers.

(3) Figures are provided for some problems. All figures are drawn to scale and lie in a plane UNLESS otherwise indicated.

(4) Unless otherwise specified, the domain of any function f is assumed to be the set of all real numbers x for which $f(x)$ is a real number.

Information

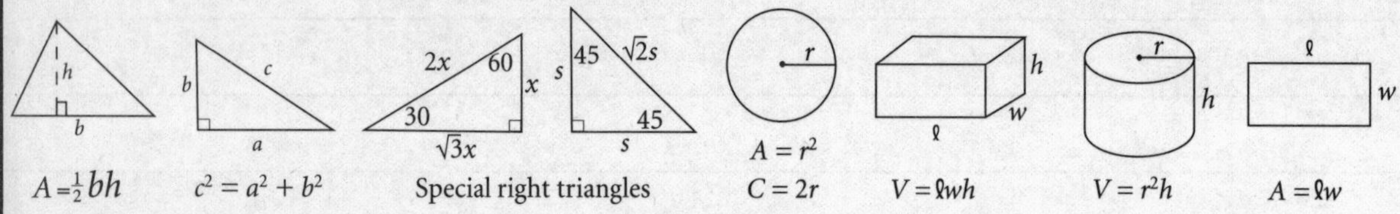

The sum of the degree measures of the angles of a triangle is 180.
The number of degrees of arc in a circle is 360.
A straight angle has a degree measure of 180.

1. $\left(\frac{1}{5}+\frac{1}{3}\right) \div \frac{1}{2} =$

(A) $\frac{1}{8}$

(B) $\frac{1}{4}$

(C) $\frac{4}{15}$

(D) $\frac{1}{2}$

(E) $\frac{16}{15}$

2. What is the value of $x^2 - 2x$ when $x = -2$?

(A) –8

(B) –4

(C) 0

(D) 4

(E) 8

3. Vito read 96 pages in 2 hours and 40 minutes. What was Vito's average rate of pages per hour?

(A) 24

(B) 30

(C) 36

(D) 42

(E) 48

4. For how many integer values of x will $\frac{7}{x}$ be greater than $\frac{1}{4}$ and less than $\frac{1}{3}$?

(A) 6

(B) 7

(C) 12

(D) 28

(E) Infinitely many

GO ON TO THE NEXT PAGE

5. What is the average (arithmetic mean) of $2x + 5$, $5x - 6$, and $-4x + 2$?

(A) $x + \frac{1}{3}$
(B) $x + 1$
(C) $3x + \frac{1}{3}$
(D) $3x + 3$
(E) $3x + 3\frac{1}{3}$

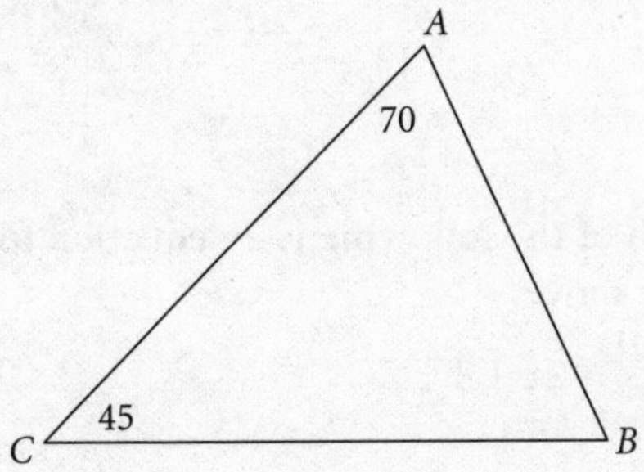

6. In the triangle above, what is the degree measure of angle B?

(A) 45
(B) 60
(C) 65
(D) 75
(E) 80

7. For all $x \neq 0$, $\frac{x^2 + x^2 + x^2}{x^2} =$

(A) 3
(B) $3x$
(C) x^2
(D) x^3
(E) x^4

8. The equation $x^2 = 5x - 4$ has how many distinct real solutions?

(A) 0
(B) 1
(C) 2
(D) 3
(E) Infinitely many

9. Which of the following sets of numbers has the property that the sum of any two numbers in the set is also a number in the set?

I. The set of even integers
II. The set of odd integers
III. The set of prime numbers

(A) I only
(B) III only
(C) I and II only
(D) I and III only
(E) I, II, and III

10. Martin's average (arithmetic mean) score after 4 tests is 89. What score on the 5th test would bring Martin's average up to exactly 90?

(A) 90
(B) 91
(C) 92
(D) 93
(E) 94

11. The price s of a sweater is reduced by 25% for a sale. After the sale, the reduced price is increased by 20%. Which of the following represents the final price of the sweater?

(A) $1.05s$
(B) $.95s$
(C) $.90s$
(D) $.85s$
(E) $.80s$

12. How many distinct prime factors does the number 36 have?

(A) 2
(B) 3
(C) 4
(D) 5
(E) 6

GO ON TO THE NEXT PAGE

13. If the area of a triangle is 36 and its base is 9, what is the length of the altitude to that base?

(A) 2
(B) 4
(C) 6
(D) 8
(E) 12

14. Let $a♣$ be defined for all positive integers a by the equation $a♣ = \frac{a}{4} - \frac{a}{6}$. If $x♣ = 3$, what is the value of x?

(A) 18
(B) 28
(C) 36
(D) 40
(E) 54

15. Joan has q quarters, d dimes, n nickels, and no other coins in her pocket. Which of the following represents the total number of coins in Joan's pocket?

(A) $q + d + n$
(B) $5q + 2d + n$
(C) $.25q + .10d + .05n$
(D) $(25 + 10 + 5)(q + d + n)$
(E) $25q + 10d + 5n$

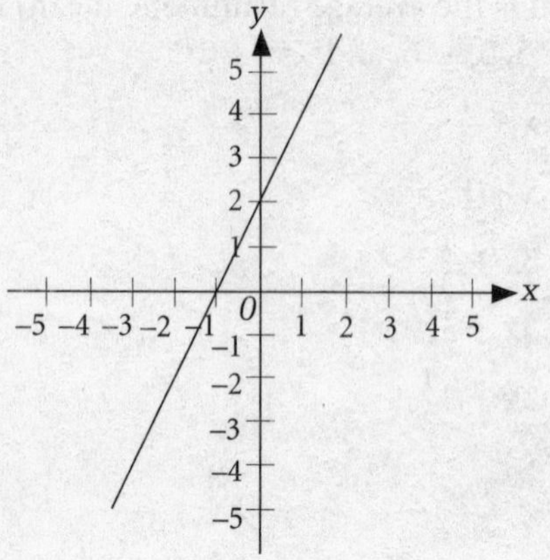

16. Which of the following is an equation for the graph above?

(A) $y = -2x + 1$
(B) $y = x + 1$
(C) $y = x + 2$
(D) $y = 2x + 1$
(E) $y = 2x + 2$

17. If an integer is divisible by 6 and by 9, then the integer must be divisible by which of the following?

I. 12
II. 18
III. 36

(A) I only
(B) II only
(C) I and II only
(D) II and III only
(E) I, II, and III

GO ON TO THE NEXT PAGE

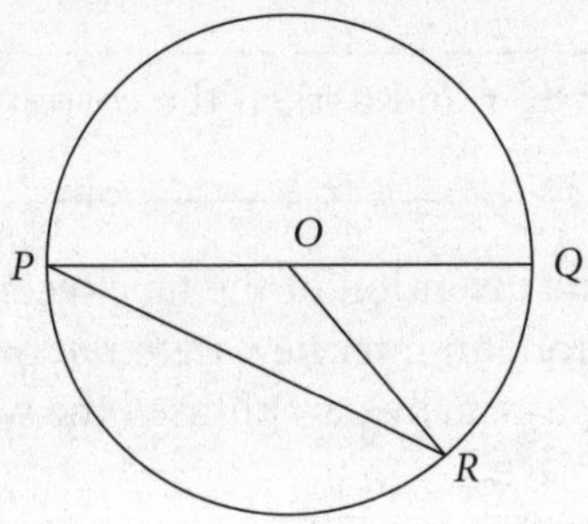

18. In the figure above, O is the center of the circle, and P, O, and Q are collinear. If $\angle ROQ$ measures 50°, what is the degree measure of $\angle RPQ$?

(A) 20
(B) 25
(C) 30
(D) 35
(E) 40

19. A wooden cube with volume 64 is sliced in half horizontally. The two halves are then glued together to form a rectangular solid which is not a cube. What is the surface area of this new solid?

(A) 128
(B) 112
(C) 96
(D) 56
(E) 48

20. A drawer contains 6 blue socks, 12 black socks, and 14 white socks. If one sock is chosen at random, what is the probability that it will be black?

(A) $\frac{1}{4}$
(B) $\frac{1}{3}$
(C) $\frac{3}{8}$
(D) $\frac{1}{2}$
(E) $\frac{5}{8}$

If you finish before time is called, you may check your work on this section only. Do not turn to any other section in the test. **STOP**

SECTION 3

Time—25 Minutes

24 Questions

Directions: For each of the following questions, choose the best answer and darken the corresponding oval on the answer sheet.

Each sentence below has one or two blanks, each blank indicating that something has been omitted. Beneath the sentence are five words or sets of words labeled (A) through (E). Choose the word or set of words that, when inserted in the sentence, best fits the meaning of the sentence as a whole.

EXAMPLE:

Today's small, portable computers contrast markedly with the earliest electronic computers, which were ----.

(A) effective
(B) invented
(C) useful
(D) destructive
(E) enormous

Ⓐ Ⓑ Ⓒ Ⓓ ●

1. Finding an old movie poster that is still ---- usually proves difficult because such posters were meant to be used and then ----.

(A) recognizable . . returned
(B) relevant . . discarded
(C) intact . . destroyed
(D) immaculate . . restored
(E) displayed . . maintained

2. The Kemp's Ridley turtle, long considered one of the most ---- creatures of the sea, finally appears to be making some headway in its battle against extinction.

(A) elusive
(B) prevalent
(C) combative
(D) voracious
(E) imperiled

3. Before the invention of the tape recorder, quotes from an interview were rarely ---- ; journalists usually paraphrased the words of their subject.

(A) verbatim
(B) misconstrued
(C) pragmatic
(D) extensive
(E) plagiarized

4. Batchelor's reputation as ---- novelist encouraged hopes that his political thriller would offer more ---- characterizations than are usually found in the genre.

(A) a serious . . subtle
(B) a maturing . . sweeping
(C) a prolific . . accurate
(D) an accomplished . . fictional
(E) a reclusive . . authentic

5. The governor commented on the disadvantages of political ----, saying that after his extended tenure in office the voters had grown used to blaming him for everything.

(A) acumen
(B) savvy
(C) longevity
(D) decorum
(E) celebrity

GO ON TO THE NEXT PAGE

6. Although normally ---- , the researcher was ---- by the news that her work had not been accepted for publication.

(A) introverted . . devastated
(B) imperious . . incensed
(C) melodramatic . . electrified
(D) buoyant . . subdued
(E) reserved . . bewildered

7. The agency's failure to ---- policies that it has acknowledged are flawed is a potent demonstration of its ---- approach to correcting its problems.

(A) support . . ambiguous
(B) institute . . earnest
(C) rescind . . lackadaisical
(D) amend . . devoted
(E) chasten . . meticulous

8. The inconsistency of the educational policies adopted by various schools across the state has been greatly ---- by the rapid turnover of school superintendents.

(A) counteracted
(B) stabilized
(C) criticized
(D) exacerbated
(E) understated

Questions 9–11 are based on the following passages.

Passage 1

Captive breeding programs now demand a sizable portion of the annual budget and research efforts at many major zoological gardens. Originally, these programs were designed to keep zoos stocked while causing as little disruption to nature as possible; every animal bred in a zoo represented an animal that needn't be taken from the wild. Now, however, zoos often consider captive breeding programs an insurance policy for severely endangered species. If a species is on the brink of extinction, the thinking goes, animals bred in captivity may, with careful research and planning, be introduced into the wild.

Passage 2

Zoos have oversold captive breeding programs as a method of reversing the tide of extinctions that threatens to engulf the much of the planet, but such action ignore the true cause of species extinction. Advocates of these programs often single out the recent examples of the reintroduction of the golden lion tamarin, a small primate native to the tropical forests of Brazil, and the Arabian oryx, an antelope in the deserts of Oman. These programs were remarkably expensive, however, and produced mixed results at best. Instead, we should concentrate our efforts on conserving the habitats that host a diversity of life forms. Only thus can we guarantee lasting safety for endangered species.

GO ON TO THE NEXT PAGE

9. According to Passage 1, zoos now regard captive breeding programs as

(A) primarily a means to provide animals for zoo exhibits
(B) a method to assure the survival of endangered species
(C) a distraction from the true mission of wildlife preservation
(D) a means to expand their collections of animals
(E) an important effort largely without drawbacks

10. In line 12 of Passage 1, the phrase *the thinking goes* serves primarily to convey that

(A) the viewpoint may not be shared by the author
(B) considerable research goes into such an effort
(C) the author disagrees strongly with the policy
(D) such a policy is now only theoretical and has not been put into practice
(E) this course of action is unlikely to actually succeed

11. In Passage 2, the writer's outlook on captive breeding programs may best be described as

(A) enthusiastic
(B) critical
(C) cautiously positive
(D) impartial
(E) unique

Questions 12–13 are based on the following passage.

Surprisingly, recent studies have demonstrated that sufferers from gum disease are actually at increased risk for atherosclerosis, the narrowing of the arteries that may lead to heart attack and stroke. Though scientists are not yet sure about the reasons, some researchers have hypothesized that bacteria in the gums may enter the bloodstream and establish themselves in the arteries, contributing to the formation of plaque, the material that helps create blockages. Three specific types of bacteria, in fact, have been identified in an analysis of plaque. It now seems that regular brushing and flossing may result in health benefits extending far beyond the teeth and gums.

12. Which of the following is introduced by the author to help confirm the hypothesis cited in lines 6–10?

(A) Regular brushing and flossing promote good dental hygiene.
(B) Plaque helps create the blockages associated with atherosclerosis.
(C) Sufferers from gum disease are at an increased risk of heart attack and stroke.
(D) Three types of bacteria have been identified in an analysis of plaque.
(E) Atherosclerosis is characterized by a narrowing of the arteries

13. The author's purpose in writing this passage was most likely to

(A) entertain
(B) persuade
(C) inform
(D) amuse
(E) argue

GO ON TO THE NEXT PAGE

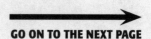

Questions 14–15 are based on the following passage.

I am a shameless word maniac. You can imagine, then, my excitement when a friend told me about the "Word a Day" website in the Internet. This wonderful site presents an unusual word every day, along with a definition and a word history. The researchers who write the material often feature a weekly theme. Last week, for example, the site featured such choice items as octothorpe (the eight-pointed pound sign on your telephone keyboard), ennead (a group of nine), and doyenne (the senior woman of a group, derived from the Latin word for "ten").

14. The word *shameless* (line 1) serves to

(A) emphasize the writer's interest in a humorous way

(B) show that the author defies those who disapprove of such interests

(C) illustrate the author's delight at discovering the "Word a Day" website

(D) provide an example of a word featured on the website

(E) reveal a regrettable characteristic of the author's personality

15. The author cites the words *octothorpe*, *ennead*, and *doyenne* (lines 10–12) to serve as examples primarily because they

(A) have similar origins

(B) are highly unusual words

(C) are favorite entries of the author

(D) were featured on the "Word a Day" website

(E) are related to a single theme

Questions 16–20 are based on the following passage.

The following passage is an excerpt from a book about wolves, written by a self-taught naturalist who studied them in the wild.

My precautions against disturbing the wolves were superfluous. It had required me a week to get their measure, but they must have taken mine at our first meeting; and while there was nothing disdainful in their evident assessment of me, they managed to ignore my presence, and indeed my very existence, with a thoroughness which was somehow disconcerting.

Quite by accident I had pitched my tent within ten yards of one of the major paths used by the wolves when they were going to, or coming from, their hunting paths to the westward; and only a few hours after I had taken up my residence one of the wolves came back from a trip and discovered me and my tent.

He was at the end of a hard night's work and was clearly tired and anxious to go home to bed. He came over a small rise fifty yards from me with his head down, his eyes half-closed, and a preoccupied air about him. Far from being the preternaturally alert and suspicious beast of fiction, this wolf was so self-engrossed that he came straight on to within fifteen yards of me, and might have gone right past the tent without seeing it at all, had I not banged an elbow against the teakettle, making a resounding clank. The wolf's head came up and his eyes opened wide, but he did not stop or falter in his pace. One brief, sidelong glance was all he vouchsafed to me as he continued on his way.

By the time this happened, I had learned a great deal about my wolfish neighbors, and

GO ON TO THE NEXT PAGE

one of the facts which had emerged was that they were not nomadic roamers, as is almost universally believed, but were settled beasts and the possessors of a large permanent estate with very definite boundaries. The territory owned by my wolf family comprised more than a hundred square miles, bounded on one side by a river but otherwise not delimited by geographical features. Nevertheless there were boundaries, clearly indicated in wolfish fashion.

Once a week, more or less, the clan made the rounds of the family lands and freshened up the boundary markers—a sort of lupine* beating of the bounds. This careful attention to property rights was perhaps made necessary by the presence of two other wolf families whose lands abutted on ours, although I never discovered any evidence of bickering or disagreements between the owners of the various adjoining estates. I suspect, therefore, that it was more of a ritual activity.

In any event, once I had become aware of this strong feeling of property among the wolves, I decided to use this knowledge to make them at least recognize my existence. One evening, after they had gone off for their regular nightly hunt, I staked out a property claim of my own, embracing perhaps three acres, with the tent at the middle, and including a hundred yard long section of the wolves' path. This took most of the night and required frequent returns to the tent to consume copious quantities of tea; but before dawn brought the hunters home the task was done and I retired, somewhat exhausted, to observe the results.

I had not long to wait. At 0814 hours, according to my wolf log, the leading male of the clan appeared over the ridge behind me, padding homeward with his usual air of preoccupation. As usual, he did not deign to look at the tent; but when he reached the point where my property line intersected the trail, he stopped as abruptly as if he had run into an invisible wall. His attitude of fatigue vanished and was replaced by one of bewilderment. Cautiously he extended his nose and sniffed at one of my marked bushes. After a minute of complete indecision he backed away a few yards and sat down. And then, finally, he looked directly at the tent and me. It was a long, considering sort of look.

Having achieved my object—that of forcing at least one of the wolves to take cognizance of my existence—I now began to wonder if, in my ignorance, I had transgressed some unknown wolf law of major importance and would have to pay for my temerity. I found myself regretting the absence of a weapon as the look I was getting became longer, more thoughtful, and still more intent. In an effort to break the impasse I loudly cleared my throat and turned my back on the wolf to indicate as clearly as possible that I found his continued scrutiny impolite, if not actually offensive.

He appeared to take the hint. Briskly, and with an air of decision, he turned his attention away from me and began a systematic tour of the area, sniffing each boundary marker once or twice, and carefully placing his mark on the outside of each clump of grass or stone. In fifteen minutes he rejoined the path at the point where it left my property and trotted off towards his home, leaving me with a good deal to occupy my thoughts.

**lupine*: relating to wolves

GO ON TO THE NEXT PAGE

16. According to the author, why were his precautions against disturbing the wolves "superfluous" (line 2)?

(A) It was several weeks before he encountered his first wolf.
(B) Other wild animals posed a greater threat to his safety.
(C) The wolves noticed him, but were not interested in harming him.
(D) He was not bothered by the wolves until he started interfering with them.
(E) The wolves were unable to detect him due to their poor eyesight.

17. The author mentions the wolves' "assessment" of him (line 6) in order to

(A) account for their strange behavior towards him
(B) convey his initial fear of being attacked
(C) emphasize his ignorance on first encountering them
(D) indicate the need for precautions against disturbing them
(E) suggest his courage in an unfamiliar situation

18. In the third paragraph, the author is primarily surprised to find that the wolf

(A) is traveling alone
(B) lacks the energy to respond
(C) is hunting at night
(D) is not more on its guard
(E) does not attack him

19. The author suggests that boundary marking was a "ritual activity" (lines 58–59) because

(A) the wolves marked their boundaries at regular intervals
(B) no disputes over territory ever seemed to occur
(C) the boundaries were marked by geographical features
(D) the boundaries were marked at the same time each week
(E) the whole family of wolves participated in the activity

20. Which of the following discoveries would most weaken the author's thesis concerning the wolves' "strong feeling of property" (line 61)?

(A) Disputes over boundaries are a frequent occurrence.
(B) Wolf territories are typically around one hundred square miles in area.
(C) Wolf families often wander from place to place to find food.
(D) Territorial conflicts between wolves and human beings are rare.
(E) Wolves are generally alert when encountering other animals.

GO ON TO THE NEXT PAGE

Questions 21–24 are based on the following passage.

In this excerpt from a short story, the narrator describes an afternoon visit to the farm of Mrs. Hight and her daughter, Esther. The narrator is accompanied on her visit by William, a fisherman.

Mrs. Hight, like myself, was tired and thirsty. I brought a drink of water, and remembered some fruit that was left from my lunch. She revived vigorously, and told me the history of her later years since she had been been struck in the prime of her life by a paralyzing stroke, and her husband had died and left her with Esther and a mortgage on their farm. There was only one field of good land, but they owned a large area of pasture and some woodland. Esther had always been laughed at for her belief in sheep-raising when one by one their neighbors were giving up their flocks. When everything had come to the point of despair she had raised some money and bought all the sheep she could, insisting that Maine lambs were as good as any, and that there was a straight path by sea to the Boston market. By tending her flock herself she had managed to succeed; she had paid off the mortgage five years ago, and now what they did not spend was in the bank. "It has been stubborn work, day and night, summer and winter, and now she's beginning to get along in years," said the old mother. "She's tended me along with the sheep, and she's been good right along, but she should have been a teacher."

We heard voices, and William and Esther entered; they did not know that it was so late in the afternoon. William looked almost bold, like a young man rather than an ancient boy. As for Esther, she might have been Joan of Arc returned to her sheep*, touched with age and gray. My heart was moved by the sight of her face, weather-worn and gentle, her thin figure in its close dress, and the strong hand that clasped a shepherd's staff, and I could only hold William in new awe; this silent fisherman who alone knew the heart that beat within her. I am not sure that they acknowledged even to themselves that they had always been lovers. Esther was untouched by the fret and fury of life; she had lived in sunshine and rain among her sheep and been refined instead of coarsened, while her patience with an angry old mother, stung by defeat and mourning her lost activities, had given back a self-possession and habit of sweet temper. I had seen enough of Mrs. Hight to know that nothing a sheep might do could vex a person who was used to the severities of her companionship.

*Joan of Arc (1412–31): a young shepherdess who led the French army against the English during the Hundred Years' War

21. The main purpose of the passage is to

(A) suggest some of the essential attributes of a character

(B) speculate about a romantic link between two people

(C) show that people's lives are determined by events beyond their control

(D) identify the major causes of Mrs. Hight's unhappiness

(E) recount an incident that changed the narrator's life

GO ON TO THE NEXT PAGE

22. Mrs. Hight's description of Esther's sheep-raising efforts (lines 9–19) reveals her daughter's

(A) desire to succeed no matter what the cost
(B) humility and grace in accepting defeat
(C) considerable regard for her neighbors' opinions
(D) calm determination in meeting difficulties
(E) dogged refusal to admit a mistake

23. In lines 43–45, the narrator speculates that Esther and William may be

(A) resigned to being permanently separated from one another
(B) apprehensive about each other's true feelings
(C) impatient to make a formal commitment to one another
(D) ambivalent in their regard for one another
(E) unaware of the extent of their attachment

24. The narrator is most impressed with Esther's

(A) aloofness and reserve
(B) serenity and devotion
(C) lively sense of humor
(D) stubborn pride
(E) material success

If you finish before time is called, you may check your work on this section only. Do not turn to any other section in the test.

STOP

SECTION 4

Time—25 Minutes

35 Questions

Directions: For each question in this section, select the best answer from among the choices given and fill in the corresponding oval on the answer sheet.

The following sentences test correctness and effectiveness of expression. Part of each sentence or the entire sentence is underlined; beneath each sentence are five ways of phrasing the underlined material. Choice (A) repeats the original phrasing; the other four choices are different. If you think the original phrasing produces a better sentence than any of the alternatives, select choice (A); if not, select one of the other choices.

In making your selection, follow the requirements of standard written English; that is, pay attention to grammar, choice of words, sentence construction, and punctuation. Your selection should result in the most effective sentence—clear and precise, without awkwardness or ambiguity.

EXAMPLE: ANSWER:

Every apple in the baskets are ripe and labeled according to the date it was picke(D) Ⓐ ● Ⓒ Ⓓ Ⓔ

(A) are ripe and labeled according to the date it was picked
(B) is ripe and labeled according to the date it was picked
(C) are ripe and labeled according to the date they were picked
(D) is ripe and labeled according to the date they were picked
(E) are ripe and labeled as to the date it was picked

1. By the time I graduate from college three years from now, my brother has practiced law for five years.

(A) has practiced
(B) has been practicing
(C) will have been practicing
(D) would have practiced
(E) is practicing

2. The historians at the university who are researching the Napoleonic Wars from the Russian perspective includes more than two professors who emigrated from Russia to the United States.

(A) perspective includes more than two professors who emigrated from Russia
(B) perspective included more than two professors who emigrated from Russia
(C) perspective include more than two professors who emigrated from Russia
(D) perspective include more than two professors whom emigrated from Russia
(E) perspective includes at least two professors who emigrated from Russia

3. In her Comparative Literature class, Nancy enjoyed reading Marcel Proust's groundbreaking novel, which she considered to be more brilliant than the other writers we read.

(A) which she considered to be more brilliant than the other writers we read
(B) whom she considered to have been more brilliant than the other writers we read
(C) which she considered to be more brilliant than the other novels we read
(D) which she considered to be brilliant opposed to the other novels we read
(E) whom she considered to be more brilliant than the other novels we read

GO ON TO THE NEXT PAGE

4. Many people watching the baseball series seen the hometown hero arriving at the stadium before the game.

(A) watching the baseball series seen the hometown hero arriving
(B) watching the baseball series saw the hometown hero arriving
(C) who watch the baseball series seen the hometown hero arriving
(D) watching the baseball series saw the hometown hero have arrived
(E) who watch the baseball series seen the hometown hero arrived

5. The oxygen tank's increased capacity allows divers to discover new species that congregate and feed close to the bottom of the ocean.

(A) to discover new species that congregate and feed close to
(B) to have discovered new species that congregate and feed close to
(C) to discover new species that congregate in and feed close to
(D) to discover new species that congregate in and feed from close to
(E) to discover new species who congregate and feed close to

6. The referee halted play in an effort at avoiding serious altercations in the stadium between fans of the opposing teams.

(A) at avoiding serious altercations in the stadium between fans of
(B) at avoiding a serious altercation in the stadium between fans of
(C) to avoid serious altercations in the stadium between fans of
(D) to avoid serious altercations in the stadium between fans on
(E) to avoid serious altercations between fans in the stadium of

7. Primarily a strategy to attract the votes of the elderly, the social security adjustment carried great weight among the entire voting public of the day.

(A) Primarily a strategy to attract the votes of the elderly
(B) Primarily a strategy of attracting the votes of the elderly
(C) Primarily the strategy to attract the votes of the elders
(D) Primarily strategic to attracting the votes of the elderly
(E) Primarily elderly voters' votes were attracted

8. A group of experts researching the bizarre occurrences theorized that the configuration of bright lights were rather unusual but probably due to optical illusion.

(A) were rather unusual but probably due to optical illusion
(B) were hardly unusual but probably due to optical illusion
(C) were rather unusual and probably due to optical illusion
(D) was rather unusual but probably due to optical illusion
(E) was rather unusual probably due to optical illusion

GO ON TO THE NEXT PAGE

9. The school's new retro rock-and-roll band has drawn such huge crowds that an entirely new team has been hired to determine new methods of providing security for their concerts.

(A) to determine new methods of providing security for their concerts
(B) to determine new methods of providing security for its concerts
(C) to determine new methods for providing security for its concerts
(D) to determining new methods for providing security for their concerts
(E) to be determining new methods of providing security for their concerts

10. If the concert had begun later, the conductor might have succeeded in giving the difficult last-minute corrections for the symphony to the orchestra.

(A) If the concert had begun later, the conductor might have succeeded in giving the difficult last-minute corrections for the symphony to the orchestra.
(B) If the concert had began later, the conductor might have succeeded in giving the difficult last-minute corrections for the symphony to the orchestra.
(C) If the concert had begun later, the conductor will succeed in giving last-minute corrections to the difficult orchestra for the symphony.
(D) If the concert had begun afterwards, the conductor might have succeeded in having given last-minute corrections for the difficult symphony to the orchestra.
(E) If the concert had begun later, the orchestra would have succeeded in having difficulty last-minute corrections for the symphony from the conductor.

11. Supporters of the Eighteenth Amendment thought that banning alcohol would improve citizens' morals and enhance their quality of life by removing the temptation to drink; national prohibition ushered in thirteen years of bootlegging, speakeasies, and violent gangster crime.

(A) national prohibition
(B) in fact, national prohibition
(C) furthermore, national prohibition
(D) but national prohibition
(E) consequently, national prohibition

GO ON TO THE NEXT PAGE

Directions: The following sentences test your ability to recognize grammar and usage errors. Each sentence contains either a single error or no error at all. No sentence contains more than one error. The error, if there is one, is underlined and lettered. If the sentence contains an error, select the one underlined part that must be changed to make the sentence correct. If the sentence is correct, select choice (E). In choosing answers, follow the requirements of standard written English.

EXAMPLE:

Whenever (A) one is driving late at night, you (B) must take extra precautions against (C) falling asleep at the wheel (D). No error (E)

Ⓐ ● Ⓒ Ⓓ Ⓔ

12. The great blue heron, perhaps the most elegant species among birds, live (A) in most (B) parts of the United States, at home (C) in wetland habitats in both (D) inland and coastal regions. No error (E)

13. At the football stadium, Susan liked watching (A) the home team's pre-game warm-ups, which she (B) considered more interesting (C) than the visiting team (D). No error (E)

14. By tracing (A) the source of artifacts found in Europe, researchers determined (B) that the pattern of Viking settlements were (C) generally (D) similar, but varied in response to different climates. No error (E)

15. The cake recipe actually called (A) for a generous amount of sugar, and (B) Chad used a sugar substitute instead since (C) he wanted to lower (D) the cake's calorie count. No error (E)

GO ON TO THE NEXT PAGE

16. Although Luther Burbank conducted
A B
experiments that led to many new or
improved plants, such as the blight-resistant
C
potato, his attempt to develop a spineless
D
cactus was not a success. No error
E

17. They were relieved when monsoons carried
A B C
rain from the southern seas and replenished
D
India's drought-stricken water supply.

No error
E

18. All of the children waiting for the school bus
A
seen the crossing guard walking out into the
B C
street to stop traffic. No error
D E

19. Arthur Miller's moral viewpoint allows
him to produce plays that uniquely and
A B
dramatically expresses the damaging effect
C
modern life has had on Americans. No error
D E

20. While many small children claim hearing
A B
Santa and his reindeer on the roof, few
teenagers believe that such a person truly
C D
exists. No error
E

21. This week, the company initiated Hawaiian
A
Shirt Day in an attempt at creating a higher
B
degree of team spirit in the office. No error
C D E

22. As Shirin Abadi was awarded the Nobel Peace
A B
Prize, many of her colleagues praised her
C
exceptional efforts about democracy and
D
human rights in Iran. No error
E

23. Although the San Francisco Earthquake
in the spring of 1906 was leveling many
A B
buildings, the subsequent series of fires
C
actually destroyed most of the city. No error
D E

24. The quarterback, after his startling failure to
A
throw a complete pass, went about
B
absolute shamefaced and was available to
C
only a few of his teammates. No error
D E

25. In the mid-twentieth century, much of the
scientific writing about intellect and language
A
were extensively influenced by the novels of
B C D
James Joyce. No error
E

GO ON TO THE NEXT PAGE

26. While the effect of disease-causing agents on
A
cigarette smokers has been known for years,
B
only recently has the damaging effects of
C
cigarette smoke on second-hand smokers
become widely recognized. No error
D E

27. The FBI maintains strict requirements for
A B
citizens when they are interested in joining
C D
the Bureau. No error
E

28. Although James Joyce, Samuel Beckett, and
A
Seamus Deane drew on similar aspects of
B
Irish culture in their novels, Beckett was
C
more abstract in his interpretations. No error
D E

29. José Limón, assuredly one of the today's
A
most inventive modern dance choreographers,
B
brought to the stage a startling approach to
C D
movement and musicality. No error
E

GO ON TO THE NEXT PAGE

Directions: The following passage is an early draft of an essay. Some parts of the passage need to be rewritten.

Read the passage and select the best answer for each question that follows. Some questions are about particular sentences or parts of sentences and ask you to improve sentence structure or word choice. Other questions ask you to consider organization and development. In choosing answers, follow the conventions of standard written English.

Questions 30–35 are based on the following passage.

(1) Last year, the members of the English department at my high school debated whether or not to continue lessons on Shakespeare. **(2)** They thought that Shakespeare's language and content took too long to teach and therefore took away from class time that could be spent on other books. **(3)** If, in fact, a student read Romeo and Juliet for class. **(4)** This would take the student more than twice as long as reading The Great Gatsby, a novel by F. Scott Fitzgerald.

(5) I disagree with this argument. **(6)** And it does take longer to read Shakespeare, the benefits are great. **(7)** So much of literature has developed from Shakespeare's ideas, language and characters that to study Shakespeare is really to study all of literature. **(8)** This is not the case with F. Scott Fitzgerald. **(9)** He was an important author, but not as influential as Shakespeare. **(10)** Consider, for example, one of Shakespeare's most famous plays, Hamlet. **(11)** Shakespeare's character, Hamlet, is a basis of many characters in today's books. **(12)** Many books today also base their characters on Shakespeare's Ophelia. **(13)** Hamlet can be seen, for instance, in James Joyce's work. **(14)** Shakespeare is an important literary and historical source. **(15)** English departments have the right to choose the curriculum. **(16)** They should consider the effects of eliminating Shakespeare from English class.

30. Which sentence would be most appropriate to follow sentence 1?

(A) Many teachers did not want to continue lessons on him.

(B) Some teachers wanted to continue lessons on him.

(C) We high school students should have a say.

(D) Therefore, Shakespeare will no longer be taught.

(E) I believe they were wrong.

31. Which of the following best describes the relationship between sentences 1 and 2?

(A) Sentence 2 offers a rebuttal to the pont made in sentence 1.

(B) Sentence 2 provides an example to illustrate an idea presented in sentence 1.

(C) Sentence 2 adds to information reported in sentence 1.

(D) Sentence 2 concludes that the theory mentioned in sentence 1 is wrong.

(E) Sentence 2 introduces a new source that confirms the claim made in sentence 1.

GO ON TO THE NEXT PAGE

32. Which of the following is the best way to revise the underlined portions of sentences 3 and 4 (reproduced below) in order to combine the sentences?

If, in fact, a student read Romeo and Juliet *for class. This would take the student more than twice as long as reading* The Great Gatsby, *a novel by F. Scott Fitzgerald.*

(A) class, this would take the student more than twice as long
(B) class, taking more than twice as long
(C) class, it would take more than twice as long
(D) class; this would take more than twice as long
(E) class; therefore taking more than twice as long

33. Which is the best way to deal with sentence 6?

(A) Leave it as it is.
(B) Change "to read" to "reading".
(C) Change "And" to "Although".
(D) Switch its position with that of sentence 7.
(E) Replace the comma with a semicolon.

34. Which of the following is the best way to combine sentences 11, 12, and 13 (reproduced below) in order to convey clearly the relationship of the ideas?

Shakespeare's character, Hamlet, is a basis of many characters in today's books. Many books today also base their characters on Shakespeare's Ophelia. Hamlet can be seen, for instance, in James Joyce's work.

(A) Many books today base their heroines on Shakespeare's Ophelia, as they do on Hamlet, and Hamlet can be seen, for instance, in James Joyce's work.
(B) Shakespeare's character Hamlet and his heroine Ophelia are the basis of many characters in today's books, being used for example by James Joyce.
(C) Shakespeare's characters Hamlet and Ophelia are the basis of many characters in today's books, but James Joyce used Hamlet, for instance, in his work.
(D) Being used for many characters in today's books is Hamlet, the same as Ophelia, for instance in James Joyce's work.
(E) Shakespeare's characters, such as Hamlet, who can be seen in James Joyce's work, and Ophelia, are the basis for many characters in today's books.

GO ON TO THE NEXT PAGE

35. In context, which is the best version of the underlined portions of sentences 15 and 16 (reproduced below)?

English departments have the right to choose the curriculum. They should consider the effects of eliminating Shakespeare from English class.

(A) (As it is now)

(B) English departments have the right to choose the curriculum, regardless of the effects of

(C) Therefore, while English departments have the right to choose the curriculum they should consider the effects of

(D) Although English departments choose the curriculum, they also consider the effects of

(E) Apparently, English departments have the right to choose the curriculum. They should consider the effects of

If you finish before time is called, you may check your work on this section only. Do not turn to any other section in the test. **STOP**

SECTION 5

Time—25 Minutes

18 Questions

Directions: For this section, solve each problem and decide which is the best of the choices given. Fill in the corresponding oval on the answer sheet. You may use any available space for scratchwork.

Notes:

(1) Calculator use is permitted.
(2) All numbers used are real numbers.
(3) Figures are provided for some problems. All figures are drawn to scale and lie in a plane UNLESS otherwise indicated.
(4) Unless otherwise specified, the domain of any function f is assumed to be the set of all real numbers x for which $f(x)$ is a real number.

Information

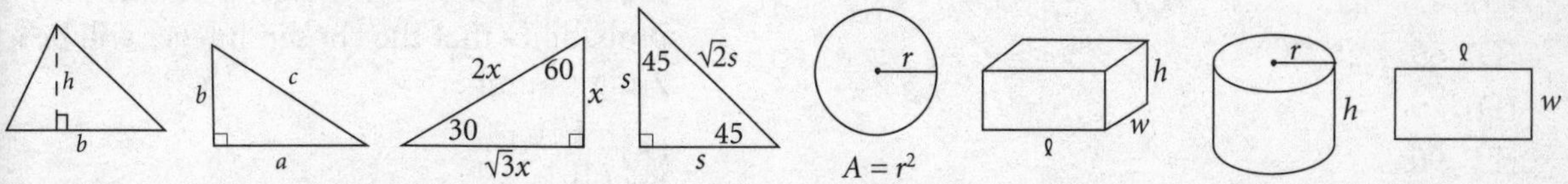

$A = \frac{1}{2}bh$ $c^2 = a^2 + b^2$ Special right triangles $A = r^2$ $C = 2r$ $V = \ell wh$ $V = r^2h$ $A = \ell w$

The sum of the degree measures of the angles of a triangle is 180.
The number of degrees of arc in a circle is 360.
A straight angle has a degree measure of 180.

1. If $3(x + y) = 6 + 3x$, then $y =$

(A) -1
(B) 0
(C) 1
(D) 2
(E) 3

2. A machine places caps on 7 bottles every 3 seconds. At this rate, how many bottles will the machine place a cap on in one minute?

(A) 14
(B) 21
(C) 140
(D) 210
(E) 420

3. If $a^3 + 2b - 5c = -3$, what is a when $b = 2$ and $c = 3$?

(A) -3
(B) -2
(C) 0
(D) 2
(E) 3

GO ON TO THE NEXT PAGE

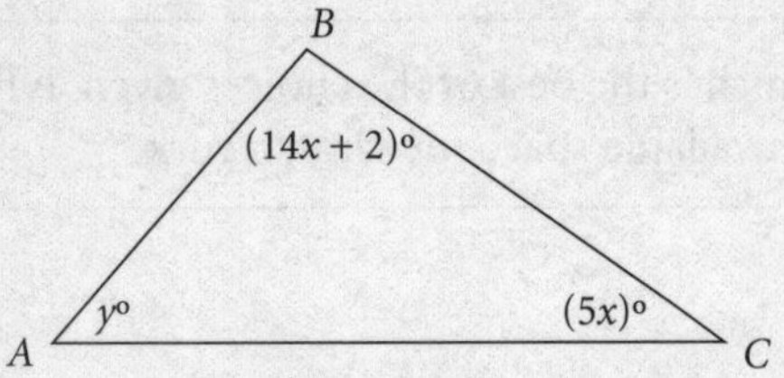

Note: Figure not drawn to scale.

4. In the triangle above, if $\angle ABC$ is 100°, what is the value of y?

(A) 30
(B) 45
(C) 60
(D) 75
(E) 90

5. A certain school has F floors. Each floor has R classrooms. If each classroom has 20 chairs, which of the following equations describes the total number of chairs in the school?

(A) $F + R + 20$
(B) $F(R + 20)$
(C) $RF \div 20$
(D) $20R \div F$
(E) $20RF$

6. Set J is the set of all positive even integers and set K is the set of all numbers between –2 and 2, inclusive. Which of the following represents the intersection of J and K?

(A) all integers
(B) all positive integers
(C) all positive even integers
(D) {2}
(E) {0,2}

7. If $|-3x - 7| = 5$, $x =$

(A) $-\frac{2}{3}$
(B) –4
(C) $-\frac{2}{3}$ or –4
(D) $\frac{2}{3}$ or –4
(E) 4

8. If an integer is randomly chosen from the first 100 positive integers, what is the probability that the chosen integer will be a 2-digit number?

(A) $\frac{1}{10}$
(B) $\frac{1}{9}$
(C) $\frac{2}{9}$
(D) $\frac{1}{2}$
(E) $\frac{9}{10}$

GO ON TO THE NEXT PAGE

Directions for Student-Produced Response Questions

For each of the questions below (9–18), solve the problem and indicate your answer by darkening the ovals in the special grid. For example:

Answer: 1.25 or $\frac{5}{4}$ or 5/4

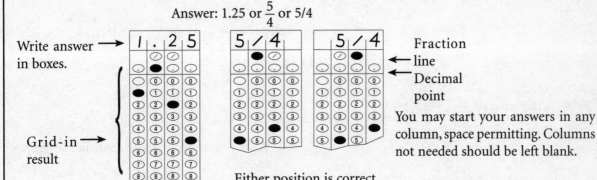

Write answer in boxes.

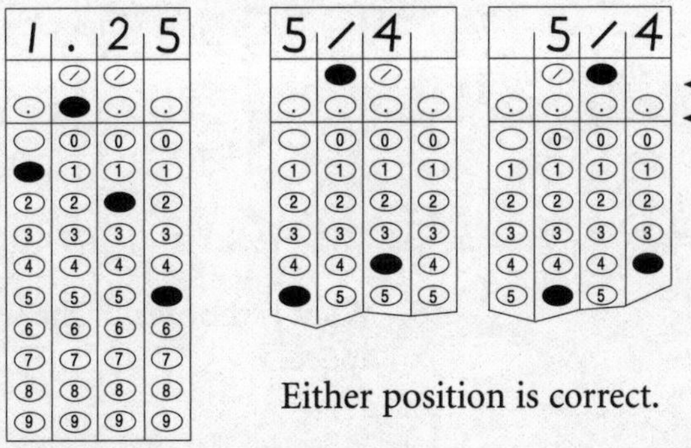

Grid-in result

Fraction line

Decimal point

You may start your answers in any column, space permitting. Columns not needed should be left blank.

Either position is correct.

- It is recommended, though not required, that you write your answer in the boxes at the top of the columns. However, you will receive credit only for darkening the ovals correctly.
- Grid only one answer to a question, even though some problems have more than one correct answer.
- Darken no more than one oval in a column.
- No answers are negative.
- Mixed numbers cannot be gridded. For example: the number $1\frac{1}{4}$ must be gridded as 1.25 or 5/4.

  (If | 1 | 1 | / | 4 | is gridded, it will be interpreted as $\frac{11}{4}$, not $1\frac{1}{4}$.)

- Decimal Accuracy: Decimal answers must be entered as accurately as possible. For example, if you obtain an answer such as 0.1666..., you should record the result as .166 or .167. **Less accurate values such as .16 or .17 are not acceptable.**

  Acceptable ways to grid $\frac{1}{6}$ = .1666...

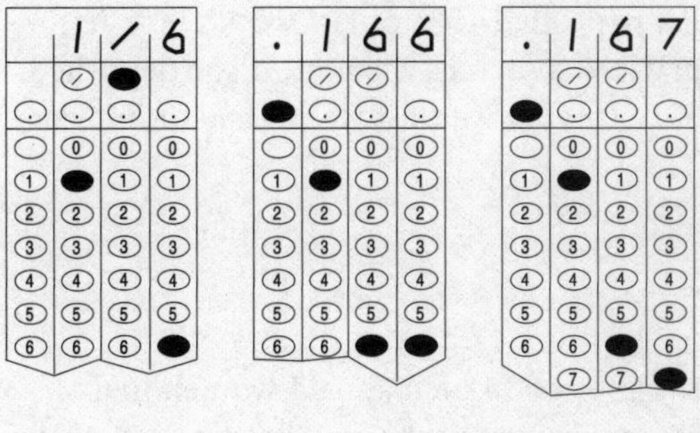

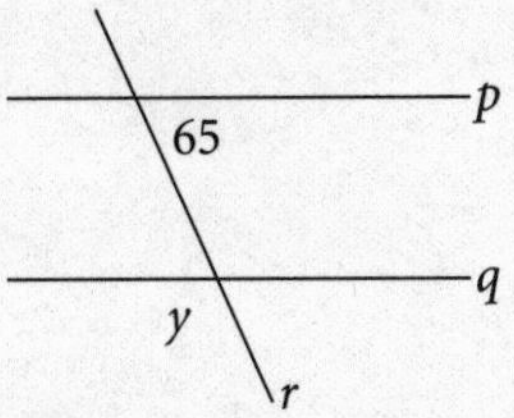

9. In the figure above, if line p is parellel to line q, what is the value of y ?

10. What is $\frac{1}{4}$ percent of 16?

GO ON TO THE NEXT PAGE

$$\frac{3}{a}, \frac{5}{a}, \frac{14}{a}$$

11. Each of the fractions above is in its simplest reduced form and a is an integer greater than 1 and less than 50. Grid in one possible value of a.

12. What is the value of $\frac{3s+5}{4}$ when $s = 9$?

13. If the positive integer x leaves a remainder of 2 when divided by 6, what will the remainder be when $x + 8$ is divided by 6?

14. Pat deposited 15% of last week's take-home pay into a savings account. If she deposited $37.50, what was last week's take-home pay?

15. If there are 36 men and 24 women in a group, women make up what fraction of the entire group?

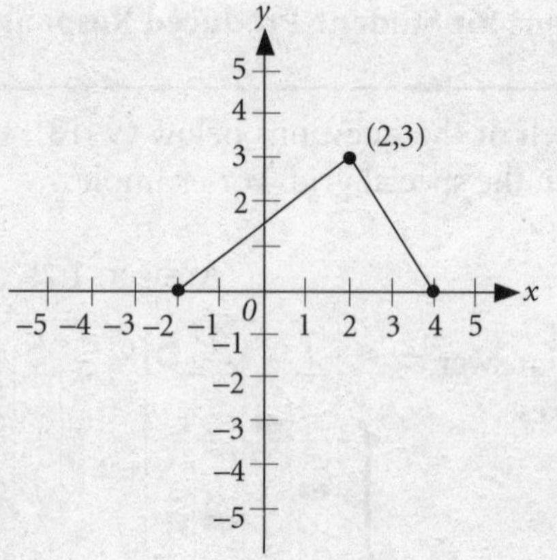

16. What is the area of the triangle in the figure above?

17. A square is divided in half to form two congruent rectangles, each with perimeter 24. What is the area of the original square?

18. The formula for converting a Fahrenheit temperature reading to a Celsius temperature reading is $C = \frac{5}{9}(F - 32)$, where C is the reading in degrees Celsius and F is the reading in degrees Fahrenheit. What is the Fahrenheit equivalent to a reading of 95° Celsius?

If you finish before time is called, you may check your work on this section only. Do not turn to any other section in the test. **STOP**

SECTION 6

Time—25 Minutes

24 Questions

<u>Directions:</u> For each of the following questions, choose the best answer and darken the corresponding oval on the answer sheet.

Each sentence below has one or two blanks, each blank indicating that something has been omitted. Beneath the sentence are five words or sets of words labeled (A) through (E). Choose the word or set of words that, when inserted in the sentence, <u>best</u> fits the meaning of the sentence as a whole.

EXAMPLE:

Today's small, portable computers contrast markedly with the earliest electronic computers, which were ----.

(A) effective
(B) invented
(C) useful
(D) destructive
(E) enormous

Ⓐ Ⓑ Ⓒ Ⓓ ●

1. The band has courted controversy before in order to get attention, and the ---- lyrics on their new album demonstrate that they found the strategy ---- .

(A) sedate . . plausible
(B) vacuous . . rewarding
(C) belligerent . . counterproductive
(D) scandalous . . effective
(E) provocative . . comparable

2. James Joyce regarded ---- as central to the creative process, which is evident in the numerous scribbled edits that cover even his supposedly final drafts.

(A) contrivance
(B) revision
(C) inspiration
(D) obsession
(E) disavowal

3. Fans who believe that the players' motivations are not ---- would be ---- to learn that they now charge for their signatures.

(A) self-serving . . vindicated
(B) venal . . chagrined
(C) altruistic . . unsurprised
(D) atypical . . disillusioned
(E) tainted . . gratified

4. Though the film ostensibly deals with the theme of ---- , the director seems to have been more interested in its absence—in isolation and the longing for connection.

(A) reliance
(B) fraternity
(C) socialism
(D) privation
(E) levity

5. Everything the candidate said publicly was ---- ; he manipulated the media in order to present the image he wanted.

(A) incendiary
(B) calculated
(C) facetious
(D) scrupulous
(E) impromptu

GO ON TO THE NEXT PAGE

Answer the questions below based on the information in the accompanying passages.

Questions 6–7 are based on the following passage.

One of the hazards of swimming in the ocean is an unexpected encounter with a jellyfish. Contact with the poison in a jellyfish's tentacles can result in sharp, lingering pain, or even death if the person stung is highly allergic. While everyone, including the jellyfish, would like to avoid these encounters, they are not uncommon. This is hardly surprising considering that jellyfish live in every ocean in the world and have done so for more than 650 million years. The animals are likely so widespread because of their extreme adaptability—they are quite hardy and can withstand a wide range of temperatures and conditions in their environment.

6. The author uses the phrase *including the jellyfish* (line 7) in order to

(A) introduce a small note of humor to an otherwise serious discussion

(B) encourage the reader's sympathy for the jellyfish

(C) ridicule humans' fear of jellyfish

(D) emphasize the danger that jellyfish pose for swimmers

(E) contrast the jellyfish's reaction to the encounter to that of humans

7. According to the passage, encounters between humans and jellyfish in the ocean are relatively common because jellyfish

(A) are more than 650 million years old

(B) live in all the world's oceans

(C) are extremely robust

(D) have poisonous tentacles

(E) can endure a range of temperatures

Questions 8–9 are based on the following passage.

Connecting the northern frontier of Pakistan with Afghanistan, the Khyber Pass is one of the most noteworthy mountain passes in the world. At its narrowest point in the north, the pass is walled on either side by precipitous cliffs up to 300 meters in height, though the pass itself is only 3 meters wide. Because it is only 53 kilometers long, the Pass offers the best land route between India and Pakistan. This has led to a long and often violent history—conquering armies have used the Khyber as an entry point for their invasions of India, Pakistan, and Afghanistan. Today there are two highways that snake their way through the Khyber Pass, one for motor traffic and another for traditional caravans.

8. Which of the following topics is NOT addressed by the passage?

(A) the origin of the pass

(B) the countries that border the pass

(C) the length of the pass

(D) the role of the pass in history

(E) the uses of the pass today

9. In line 15, the word *snake* most directly emphasizes the

(A) function of the Khyber Pass as a means to connect two points

(B) danger of crossing the Khyber Pass

(C) Khyber Pass as a direct route through the Hindu Kush mountains

(D) relatively short length of the Khyber Pass

(E) winding quality of the Khyber Pass

GO ON TO THE NEXT PAGE

Questions 10–22 are based on the following passage.

Revisionist historians maintain that it was within the power of the United States, in the years during and immediately after the Second World War, to prevent the Cold War with the Soviet Union. Revisionists suggest that the prospect of impending conflict with the Soviets could have been avoided in several ways. The U.S. could have officially recognized the new Soviet sphere of influence in Eastern Europe instead of continuing to call for self-determination in those countries. A much-needed reconstruction loan could have helped the Soviets recover from the war. The Americans could have sought to assuage Soviet fears by giving up the U.S. monopoly of the atomic bomb and turning the weapons over to an international agency (with the stipulation that future nuclear powers do the same).

This criticism of the post-war American course of action fails to take into account the political realities in America at the time, and unfairly condemns the American policy-makers who did consider each of these alternatives and found them to be unworkable. Recognition of a Soviet Eastern Europe was out of the question. Roosevelt had promised self-determination to the Eastern European countries, and the American people, having come to expect this, were furious when Stalin began to shape his spheres of influence in the region. The President was in particular acutely conscious of the millions of Polish-Americans who would be voting in the upcoming election.

Negotiations had indeed been conducted by the administration with the Soviets about a reconstruction loan, but the Congress refused to approve it unless the Soviets made enormous concessions tantamount to restructuring their system and withdrawing from Eastern Europe. This, of course, made Soviet rejection of the loan a foregone conclusion. As for giving up the bomb—the elected officials in Washington would have been in deep trouble with their constituents had that plan been carried out. Polls showed that 82 percent of the American people understood that other nations would develop bombs eventually, but that 85 percent thought that the U.S. should retain exclusive possession of the weapon. Policy-makers have to abide by certain constraints in deciding what is acceptable and what is not. They, and not historians, are in the best position to perceive those constraints and make the decisions.

Revisionist historians tend to eschew this type of political explanation of America's supposed failure to reach a peaceful settlement with the Soviets in favor of an economic reading of events. They point to the fact that in the early post-war years American businessmen and government officials cooperated to expand American foreign trade vigorously and to exploit investment opportunities in many foreign countries. In order to sustain the lucrative expansion, revisionists assert, American policy-makers were obliged to maintain an "Open Door" foreign policy, the object of which was to keep all potential trade opportunities open. Since the Soviets could jeopardize such opportunities in Eastern Europe and elsewhere, they had to be opposed. Hence, the Cold War. But if American policy-makers were simply pawns in an economic game of expansionist

GO ON TO THE NEXT PAGE

capitalism, as the revisionists seem to think, why do the revisionists hold them responsible for not attempting to reach an accord with the Soviets? The policy-makers, swept up by a tidal wave of capitalism, clearly had little control and little choice in the matter.

Even if American officials had been free and willing to make conciliatory gestures toward the Soviets, the Cold War would not have been prevented. Overtures of friendship would not have been reciprocated (as far as we can judge; information on the inner workings of the Kremlin during that time is scanty). Soviet expert George F. Kennan concluded that Russian hostility could not be dampened by any effort on the part of the United States. The political and ideological differences were too great, and the Soviets had too long a history of distrust of foreigners—exacerbated at the time by Stalin's rampant paranoia, which infected his government—to embark on a process of establishing trust and peace with the United States, though it was in their interest to do so.

10. The primary purpose of the passage is to

(A) explode a popular myth
(B) criticize historical figures
(C) refute an argument
(D) analyze an era
(E) reconcile opposing views

11. In line 9, the word *recognized* most nearly means

(A) identified
(B) noticed
(C) acknowledged
(D) distinguished
(E) remembered

12. A fundamental assumption underlying the author's argument in the second and third paragraphs is that

(A) the Soviets were largely to blame for the failure of conciliatory U.S. initiatives
(B) the American public was very well-informed about the incipient Cold War situation
(C) none of the proposed alternatives would have had its intended effect
(D) the American public was overwhelmingly opposed to seeking peace with the Soviets
(E) the government could not have been expected to ignore public opinion

13. Which statement best summarizes the revisionist argument concerning the origin of the Cold War (lines 58–76)?

(A) The United States started the Cold War in order to have a military cover for illegal trading activities.
(B) The Soviets were oblivious to the negative impact they had on the American economy.
(C) The economic advantage of recognizing Soviet Europe outweighed the disadvantage of an angry public.
(D) America could trade and invest with foreign countries only if it agreed to oppose the Soviet Union.
(E) American economic interests abroad would have been threatened by any Soviet expansion.

GO ON TO THE NEXT PAGE

14. The question at the end of the fourth paragraph (lines 76–82) serves to

(A) point out an inconsistency in a position
(B) outline an area that requires further research
(C) contrast two different historical interpretations
(D) sum up a cynical view of post-war economic activity
(E) restate the central issue of the passage

Questions 15–16 refer to the following passage.

The struggle to balance a family life and a career is significant in many women's lives. This tension is a theme in *The Yellow Wallpaper*, written by Charlotte Perkins Gilman in 1892. In this short story, the narrator struggles to fulfill her role as mother and wife at the expense of her work, a sublimation that ultimately makes her depressed. Though women today certainly have more options and freedom than those of Gillman's time, they still often face the conflict between being caretakers and having careers—a conflict that Charlotte Perkins Gilman chronicled over 100 years ago.

15. In line 7, the word *expense* most nearly means

(A) burden
(B) taxation
(C) expenditure
(D) sacrifice
(E) income

16. In the last sentence, the author suggests that

(A) modern women rarely use their new freedom to its fullest potential
(B) there has been little progress in the women's rights movement in more than 100 years
(C) if women do not balance their family lives and careers they will become depressed
(D) women will never be able to hold meaningful careers
(E) the issues in Gilman's short story have relevance today

GO ON TO THE NEXT PAGE

Questions 17–24 are based on the following passage.

James Weldon Johnson was a poet, diplomat, composer and historian of black culture who wrote around the turn of the century. In this narrative passage Johnson recalls his first experience of hearing rag-time jazz.

When I had somewhat collected my senses, I realized that in a large back room into which the main room opened, there was a young fellow singing a song, accompanied on the piano by a short, thickset black man. After each verse he did some dance steps, which brought forth great applause and a shower of small coins at his feet. After the singer had responded to a rousing encore, the stout man at the piano began to run his fingers up and down the keyboard. This he did in a manner which indicated that he was a master of a good deal of technique. Then he began to play; and such playing! I stopped talking to listen. It was music of a kind I had never heard before. It was music that demanded physical response, patting of the feet, drumming of the fingers, or nodding of the head in time with the beat. The dissonant harmonies, the audacious resolutions, often consisting of an abrupt jump from one key to another, the intricate rhythms in which the accents fell in the most unexpected places, but in which the beat was never lost, produced a most curious effect . . .

This was rag-time music, then a novelty in New York, and just growing to be a rage, which has not yet subsided. It was originated in the questionable resorts about Memphis and St. Louis by Negro piano-players who knew no more of the theory of music than they did of the theory of the universe, but were guided by natural musical instinct and talent. It made its way to Chicago, where it was popular some time before it reached New York. These players often improvised simple and, at times, vulgar words to fit the melodies. This was the beginning of the rag-time song . . .

American musicians, instead of investigating rag-time, attempt to ignore it, or dismiss it with a contemptuous word. But that has always been the course of scholasticism in every branch of art. Whatever new thing the people like is pooh-poohed; whatever is popular is spoken of as not worth the while. The fact is, nothing great or enduring, especially in music, has ever sprung full-fledged and unprecedented from the brain of any master; the best that he gives to the world he gathers from the hearts of the people, and runs it through the alembic* of his genius. In spite of the bans which musicians and music teachers have placed upon it, the people still demand and enjoy rag-time. One thing cannot be denied; it is music which possesses at least one strong element of greatness: it appeals universally; not only the American, but the English, the French, and even the German people find delight in it. In fact, there is not a corner of the civilized world in which it is not known, and this proves its originality; for if it were an imitation, the people of Europe, anyhow, would not have found it a novelty . . .

I became so interested in both the music and the player that I left the table where I was sitting, and made my way through the hall into the back room, where I could see as well as hear. I talked to the piano player between the musical numbers and found out that he was just a natural musician, never having taken a lesson in his life. Not only could he play almost anything he heard, but he could accompany singers in songs he had never heard. He had, by ear alone, composed some pieces, several of which he played over for me; each of them was properly proportioned and balanced. I began to wonder what this man with such a lavish natural endowment would have done had he been trained. Perhaps he wouldn't have done anything at

GO ON TO THE NEXT PAGE

all; he might have become, at best, a mediocre imitator of the great masters in what they have already done to a finish, or one of the modern innovators who strive after originality by seeing how cleverly they can dodge about through the rules of harmony and at the same time avoid melody. It is certain that he would not have been so delightful as he was in rag-time.

**alembic*: scientific apparatus used in the process of distillation

17. In relating his initial impression of rag-time music to the reader, the narrator makes use of

(A) comparison with the improvisations of classical music
(B) reference to the audience's appreciative applause
(C) description of the music's compelling rhythmic effect
(D) evocation of poignant visual images
(E) allusion to several popular contemporary tunes

18. In line 29, *questionable* most nearly means

(A) disreputable
(B) ambiguous
(C) doubtful
(D) approachable
(E) unconfirmed

19. The narrator's perspective during the second and third paragraphs is that of

(A) an impartial historian of events in the recent past
(B) a mesmerized spectator of a musical spectacle
(C) a knowledgeable critic of the contemporary musical scene
(D) a commentator reflecting on a unique experience
(E) an adult reminiscing fondly about his youth

20. In line 32, the reference to "the theory of the universe" serves to

(A) emphasize that rag-time at its inception was an unconventional musical form
(B) show that the originators of rag-time were wholly engrossed in their own music
(C) imply that the attainment of musical proficiency should take priority over academic pursuits
(D) suggest that those who founded rag-time could not have imagined the extent of its future influence
(E) demonstrate that level of education is not commensurate with artistic success

GO ON TO THE NEXT PAGE

21. The discussion in the third paragraph of the refusal of American musicians to investigate rag-time suggests that they

(A) have little or no interest in pleasing people with their music
(B) need to be made aware of the popularity of rag-time in Europe
(C) are misguided in their conservative and condescending attitude
(D) attack rag-time for being merely an imitation of an existing style
(E) know that it would be difficult to refine rag-time as a musical form

22. Which statement best summarizes the author's argument in the third paragraph?

(A) Any type of music that is extremely popular should be considered great.
(B) The two criteria for musical greatness are popularity and originality.
(C) Music that has become popular overseas cannot be ignored by American musicians.
(D) Rag-time must be taken up by a musical master and purified to earn critical acclaim.
(E) Mass appeal in music can be a sign of greatness rather than a stigma.

23. The statement in lines 82–83 ("Perhaps he wouldn't have done anything at all") is best interpreted as conveying

(A) doubt about the depth of the piano player's skill
(B) understanding that no amount of talent can compensate for a lack of discipline
(C) cynicism about the likelihood that a man can live up to his potential
(D) a recognition that the piano player might have wasted his talent
(E) frustration at the impossibility of knowing what might have been

24. The author's view (lines 79–92) about the rag-time piano player's lack of formal training can best be summarized as which of the following?

(A) The piano player's natural talent had allowed him to develop technically to the point where formal training would have been superfluous.
(B) Formal lessons would have impaired the piano player's native ability to play and compose by ear alone.
(C) More would have been lost than gained if the piano player had been given formal lessons.
(D) The piano player's potential to be a truly innovative rag-time artist had been squandered because he had not been formally trained.
(E) Although dazzling when improvising rag-time, the piano player could never have been more than mediocre as a classical pianist.

If you finish before time is called, you may check your work on this section only. Do not turn to any other section in the test.

STOP

SECTION 7

Time—20 Minutes

16 Questions

Directions: For this section, solve each problem and decide which is the best of the choices given. Fill in the corresponding oval on the answer sheet. You may use any available space for scratchwork.

Notes:

(1) Calculator use is permitted.

(2) All numbers used are real numbers.

(3) Figures are provided for some problems. All figures are drawn to scale and lie in a plane UNLESS otherwise indicated.

(4) Unless otherwise specified, the domain of any function f is assumed to be the set of all real numbers x for which $f(x)$ is a real number.

Information

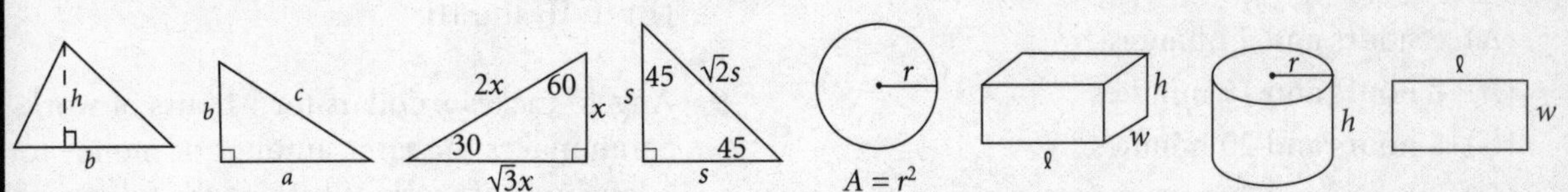

$A = \frac{1}{2}bh$ $c^2 = a^2 + b^2$ Special right triangles $A = r^2$ $C = 2r$ $V = \ell wh$ $V = r^2h$ $A = \ell w$

The sum of the degree measures of the angles of a triangle is 180.
The number of degrees of arc in a circle is 360.
A straight angle has a degree measure of 180.

1. For all x, $(3x + 4)(4x - 3) =$

(A) $7x + 1$
(B) $7x - 12$
(C) $12x^2 - 12$
(D) $12x^2 - 25x - 12$
(E) $12x^2 + 7x - 12$

2. In a certain set of numbers, the ratio of integers to nonintegers is 2:3. What percent of the numbers in the set are integers?

(A) 20%
(B) $33\frac{1}{3}$%
(C) 40%
(D) 60%
(E) $66\frac{2}{3}$%

3. If $xyz \neq 0$, which of the following is equivalent to $\frac{x^2y^3z^4}{(xyz^2)^2}$?

(A) $\frac{1}{y}$
(B) $\frac{1}{z}$
(C) y
(D) $\frac{x}{yz}$
(E) xyz

4. When the positive integer p is divided by 7, the remainder is 5. What is the remainder when $5p$ is divided by 7?

(A) 0
(B) 1
(C) 2
(D) 3
(E) 4

GO ON TO THE NEXT PAGE

5. What is the y-intercept of the line with the equation $2x - 3y = 18$?

(A) –9
(B) –6
(C) –3
(D) 6
(E) 9

6. Jan types at an average rate of 12 pages per hour. At that rate, how long will it take Jan to type 100 pages?

(A) 8 hours and 3 minutes
(B) 8 hours and 15 minutes
(C) 8 hours and 20 minutes
(D) 8 hours and 30 minutes
(E) 8 hours and $33\frac{1}{3}$ minutes

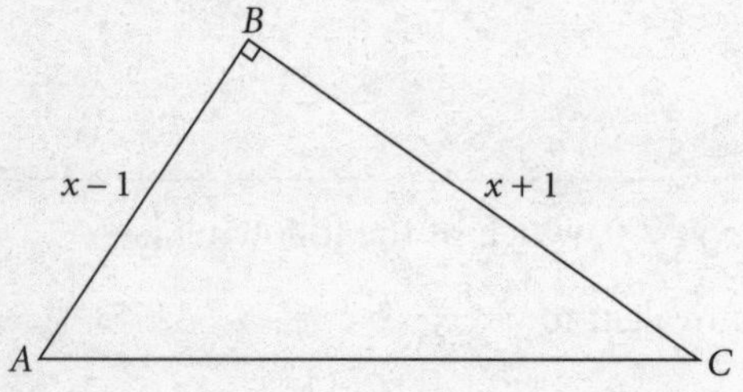

7. In the figure above, AB is perpendicular to BC. The lengths of AB and BC are given in terms of x. Which of the following represents the area of ΔABC for all $x > 1$?

(A) x
(B) $2x$
(C) x^2
(D) $x^2 - 1$
(E) $\frac{x^2 - 1}{2}$

8. If Jim and Bill have less than \$15 between them, and Bill has \$4, which of the following could be the number of dollars that Jim has?

I. 10
II. 11
III. 15

(A) I only
(B) II only
(C) I and II only
(D) II and III only
(E) I, II, and III

9. Angelo makes x dollars for y hours of work. Sarah makes the same amount of money for 1 less hour of work. Which of the following expressions represents the positive difference between the two people's hourly wage?

(A) $\frac{x}{y-1} - \frac{x}{y}$
(B) $\frac{x}{y} - \frac{x}{y-1}$
(C) $\frac{x}{y-1} + \frac{x}{y}$
(D) $\frac{y-1}{x} - \frac{y}{x}$
(E) $\frac{y}{x} - \frac{y-1}{x}$

10. Erica has 8 squares of felt, each with area 16. For a certain craft project she cuts the largest circle possible from each square of felt. What is the combined area of the excess felt left over after cutting out all the circles?

(A) $4(4 - \pi)$
(B) $8(4 - \pi)$
(C) $8(\pi - 2)$
(D) $32(4 - \pi)$
(E) $16(16 - \pi)$

GO ON TO THE NEXT PAGE

11. If $q \neq 0$ and $q = q{-}2$, what is the value of q?

(A) -1
(B) 1
(C) $\frac{0}{2}$
(D) 1
(E) 2

Price of One Can	Projected Number of Cans Sold
\$0.75	10,000
\$0.80	9,000
\$0.85	8,000
\$0.90	7,000
\$0.95	6,000
\$1.00	5,000

12. The chart above describes how many cans of a new soft drink a company expects to sell at a number of possible prices per can. Which of the following equations best describes the relationship shown in the chart, where n indicates the number of cans sold and p represents the price in dollars of one can?

(A) $n = -20{,}000p - 25{,}000$
(B) $n = -20{,}000p + 25{,}000$
(C) $n = -200p - 250$
(D) $n = 200p + 250$
(E) $n = 20{,}000p - 25{,}000$

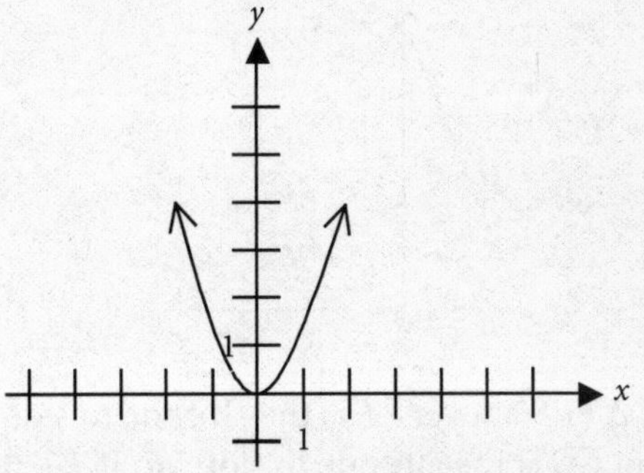

13. Which of the following equations best describes the curve shown in the graph?

(A) $y = x$
(B) $y = x^2$
(C) $y = x^3$
(D) $y = \overline{x}$
(E) $y = \frac{1}{2}x$

14. What is the area of a right triangle if the length of one leg is a and the length of the hypotenuse is c?

(A) $\frac{ac}{2}$
(B) $\frac{ac - a^2}{2}$
(C) $\frac{ac + c^2}{2}$
(D) $\frac{\overline{ac^2 - a^2}}{2}$
(E) $\overline{a^2 + c^2}$

GO ON TO THE NEXT PAGE

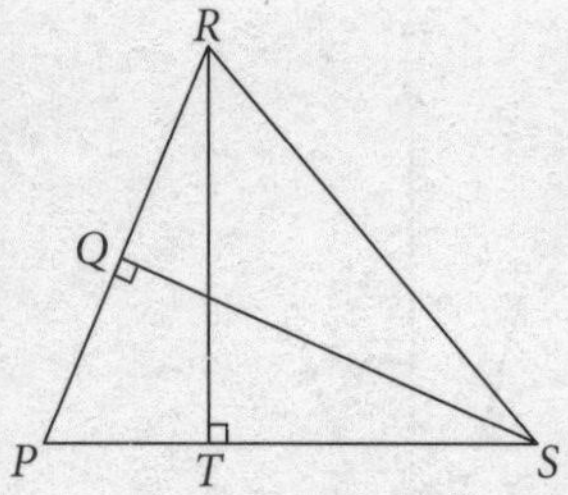

15. In ΔPRS above, RT is the altitude to side PS and QS is the altitude to side PR. If $RT = 7$, $PR = 8$, and $QS = 9$, what is the length of PS ?

(A) $5\frac{1}{7}$

(B) $6\frac{2}{9}$

(C) $7\frac{7}{8}$

(D) $10\frac{2}{7}$

(E) $13\frac{4}{9}$

16. There are 3 routes from Bay City to Riverville. There are 4 routes from Riverville to Straitstown. There are 3 routes from Straitstown to Frog Pond. If a driver must pass through Riverville and Straitstown exactly once, how many possible ways are there to go from Bay City to Frog Pond?

(A) 6

(B) 10

(C) 12

(D) 24

(E) 36

If you finish before time is called, you may check your work on this section only. Do not turn to any other section in the test. **STOP**

SECTION 8

Time—20 Minutes

19 Questions

Directions: For each of the following questions, choose the best answer and darken the corresponding oval on the answer sheet.

Each sentence below has one or two blanks, each blank indicating that something has been omitted. Beneath the sentence are five words or sets of words labeled (A) through (E). Choose the word or set of words that, when inserted in the sentence, best fits the meaning of the sentence as a whole.

EXAMPLE:

Today's small, portable computers contrast markedly with the earliest electronic computers, which were ----.

(A) effective
(B) invented
(C) useful
(D) destructive
(E) enormous   (A) (B) (C) (D) ●

1. The journalist's claim of ---- is belied by her record of contributing to the campaign funds of only one party's candidates.

(A) innocence
(B) corruption
(C) impartiality
(D) affluence
(E) loyalty

2. The repeated breakdown of negotiations only ---- the view that the two sides were not truly committed to the goal of ---- a military confrontation.

(A) established . . escalating
(B) undermined . . avoiding
(C) distorted . . financing
(D) strengthened . . initiating
(E) reinforced . . averting

3. These are times of national budgetary ---- now that a long era of sustained growth has been succeeded by a period of painful ---- .

(A) turmoil . . acquisition
(B) stringency . . decline
(C) expansion . . stagnation
(D) indecision . . renewal
(E) prudence . . development

4. To the ---- of those who in bygone years tiptoed their way past poinsettia displays for fear of causing leaves to fall, breeders have developed more ---- versions of the flower.

(A) consternation . . amorphous
(B) dismay . . fragrant
(C) surprise . . alluring
(D) disappointment . . diversified
(E) relief . . durable

5. Aristotle espoused a ---- biological model in which all extant species are unchanging and eternal and no new species ever come into existence.

(A) paradoxical
(B) morbid
(C) static
(D) holistic
(E) homogeneous

6. Most young artists struggle, producing works that have but ---- of future greatness, but Walt Whitman's transformation into a genius was ----.

(A) glimmers . . effortless
(B) shadows . . noteworthy
(C) features . . protracted
(D) critiques . . immediate
(E) aspirations . . unforeseeable

GO ON TO THE NEXT PAGE

Answer the questions below based on the information in the accompanying passages.

Questions 7–14 are based on the following passages.

These passages present two critics' perspectives on the topic of design museums.

Passage 1

City museums are places where people can learn about various cultures by studying objects of particular historical or artistic value. The increasingly popular "design museums" that are opening today perform quite a different function. Unlike most city museums, the design museum displays and assesses objects that are readily available to the general public. These museums place ignored household appliances under spotlights, breaking down the barriers between commerce and creative invention.

Critics have argued that design museums are often manipulated to serve as advertisements for new industrial technology. But their role is not simply a matter of merchandising—it is the honoring of impressive, innovative products. The difference between the window of a department store and the showcase in a design museum is that the first tries to sell you something, while the second informs you of the success of the attempt.

One advantage that the design museum has over other civic museums is that design museums are places where people feel familiar with the exhibits. Unlike the average art gallery patron, design museum visitors rarely feel intimidated or disoriented. Partly this is because design museums clearly illustrate how and why mass-produced consumer objects work and look as they do, and show how design contributes to the quality of our lives. For example, an exhibit involving a particular design of chair would not simply explain how it functions as a chair. It would also demonstrate how its various features combine to produce an artistic effect or redefine our manner of performing the basic act of being seated. The purpose of such an exhibit would be to present these concepts in ways that challenge, stimulate and inform the viewer. An art gallery exhibit, on the other hand, would provide very little information about the chair and charge the visitor with understanding the exhibit on some abstract level.

Within the past decade, several new design museums have opened their doors. Each of these museums has responded in totally original ways to the public's growing interest in the field. London's Design Museum, for instance, displays a collection of mass-produced objects ranging from Zippo lighters to electric typewriters to a show of Norwegian sardine-tin labels. The options open to curators of design museums seem far less rigorous, conventionalized and pre-programmed than those applying to curators in charge of public galleries of paintings and sculpture. The humorous aspects of our society are better represented in the display of postmodern playthings or quirky Japanese vacuum cleaners in pastel colors than in an exhibition of Impressionist landscapes.

Passage 2

The short histories of some of the leading technical and design museums make clear an underlying difficulty in this area. The tendency everywhere today is to begin with present machines and technological processes and to show how they operate and the scientific principles on which they are based without paying much attention to

GO ON TO THE NEXT PAGE

their historical development, to say nothing of the society that produced them. Only a few of the oldest, largest and best-supported museums collect historical industrial objects. Most science centers put more emphasis on mock-ups, graphs and multimedia devices. This approach of "presentism" often leads the museum to drop all attempts at study and research; if industry is called upon to design and build the exhibits, curators may be entirely dispensed with, so that impartial and scientific study disappears, and emphasis is placed on the idea that progress automatically follows technology.

Industrialization and the machine have, of course, brought much progress; a large portion of humankind no longer works from sunup to sundown to obtain the bare necessities of life. But industrialization also creates problems—harm to the environment and ecology, neglect of social, cultural and humanistic values, depletion of resources, and even threats of human extinction. Thus progress needs to be considered critically—from a wider social and humanitarian point of view. Unfortunately, most museums of science and technology glorify machines. Displayed in pristine condition, elegantly painted or polished, they can make the observer forget the noise, dirt, danger and frustration of machine-tending. Mines, whether coal, iron or salt, are a favorite museum display but only infrequently is there even a hint of the dirt, the damp, the smell, the low headroom, or the crippling and destructive accidents that sometimes occur in industry.

Machinery also ought to be operated to be meaningful. Consequently, it should not be shown in sculptured repose but in full, often clattering, action. This kind of operation is difficult to obtain, and few museums can command the imagination, ingenuity, and manual dexterity it requires. Problems also arise in providing adequate safety devices for both the public and the machine operators. These, then, are some of the underlying problems of the technical museum—problems not solved by the usual push buttons, cranks or multimedia gimmicks. Yet attendance figures show that technical museums outdraw all the others; the public possesses lively curiosity and a real desire to understand science and technology.

7. In lines 18–23, the author of Passage 1 suggests that design museums are different from store windows in that

(A) design museums display more technologically advanced products

(B) store window displays are not created with as much concern to the visual quality of the display

(C) design museums are not concerned with the commercial aspects of a successful product

(D) design museums focus on highlighting the artistic qualities that help sell products

(E) the objects in store displays are more commercially successful than those in design museums

GO ON TO THE NEXT PAGE

8. From lines 24–34, it can be inferred that the author believes that most museum visitors

(A) are hostile towards the concept of abstract art
(B) prefer to have a context in which to understand museum exhibits
(C) are confused when faced with complex technological exhibits
(D) are unfamiliar with the exhibits in design museums
(E) undervalue the artistic worth of household items

9. The third paragraph of Passage 1 suggests that one important difference between design museums and the art galleries is

(A) the low price of admission at design museums
(B) the amount of information presented with design museum exhibits
(C) the intelligence of the average museum visitor
(D) that art galleries feature exhibits that have artistic merit
(E) the contribution that design museums make to our quality of life

10. In line 58, the word *options* most likely refers to the ability of curators of design museums to

(A) afford large collections of exhibits
(B) attract a wide range of visitors
(C) put together unconventional collections
(D) feature rare objects that interest the public
(E) satisfy their own personal whims in planning exhibitions

11. Which of the following best describes the *underlying difficulty* mentioned in line 70 of Passage 2?

(A) Design museums rarely mention the historical origin of objects they display.
(B) Industrial involvement often forces curators out of their jobs.
(C) Design museums appropriate technology that is essential for study and research.
(D) Technology almost never leads to progress.
(E) Industry places too much emphasis on impartial research.

12. The author uses the phrase *sculptured repose* (line 116) in order to

(A) condemn the curators of design museums for poor planning
(B) illustrate the greatest problem inherent in design museums
(C) present an idealized vision of a type of exhibit
(D) describe the unrealistic way in which machinery is generally displayed
(E) compare the shape of a machine to a work of art

GO ON TO THE NEXT PAGE

13. The author of Passage 2 would probably object to the statement that design "contributes to the quality of our lives" (lines 33–34) on the grounds that

(A) technical innovation has historically posed threats to our physical and social well-being
(B) the general public would benefit more from visiting art galleries
(C) machinery that is not shown in action is meaningless to the viewer
(D) industry has made a negligible contribution to human progress
(E) few people have a genuine interest in the impact of science and technology

14. The authors of both passages would probably agree that

(A) machinery is only enjoyable to watch when it is moving
(B) most people are curious about the factors behind the design of everyday objects
(C) the public places a higher value on packaging than it does on quality
(D) the very technology that is displayed in the museums is likely to cost curators their jobs
(E) design museums are flawed because they fail to accurately portray the environmental problems that technology sometimes causes

Questions 15–16 are based on the following passage.

Folklorists have found that holidays and holiday customs often bear interesting traces of their origins. For example, the beginning of the European April Fools' Day is linked to the replacement of the Julian calendar by the Gregorian calendar in the year 1582. The new calendar changed New Year's Day from March 25 to January 1. However, people who refused to accept the change continued to celebrate New Year's as an eight-day festival that concluded with the exchange of gifts on April 1. According to folklore, these laggards were derided by their more progressive contemporaries, who called them "April Fools."

15. As used in the passage, *bear* (line 2) most nearly means

(A) carry
(B) endure
(C) tolerate
(D) abide
(E) generate

16. The *laggards* cited in line 12 were

(A) people who mocked those who failed to adopt the new Gregorian Calendar
(B) the holidays that marked the beginning of the year under the Julian calendar
(C) those who continued to observe the Julian calendar
(D) folklorists who described the origins of April Fools Day
(E) people who advocated the adoption of the Gregorian Calendar

GO ON TO THE NEXT PAGE

Questions 17–19 are based on the following passages.

Passage 1

Musicologists and linguists argue about the relationship between music and language. Prominent ethnomusicologist Bruno Nettl has concluded that like language, music is a "series of symbols." However, music has traditionally been used purely to express emotions, while language has also been used for more functional, prosaic tasks. This distinction was especially evident in the Romantic era of Western music, when many composers and critics felt that music could stand by itself to connote emotions without any extra-musical references.

Passage 2

The fundamental building blocks of both language and music are quite similar, as are the manners in which these components are combined to form a cohesive whole. In the same way that an entire piece of music can be divided into phrases, and further subdivided into specific notes, language can be subdivided into paragraphs, sentences, and words. A single note can have different meanings depending on the piece; a lone word can have different meanings depending on the context in the sentence. Words and notes are also similar in that they have little intrinsic meaning, but instead act as symbols to convey larger ideas.

17. Author 1 most likely cites the Romantic era of Western music (line 10) in order to establish that

(A) our modern perception of Romantic music is different from the one held during the Romantic era

(B) unlike language, Romantic music is not used functionally

(C) composers of Romantic music always used music to express emotion

(D) during the Romantic era it was a commonly held opinion that music was itself sufficient to carry emotion

(E) the music of the Romantic era is compromised because it does not contain extra-musical references

18. In both passages, the authors state that music and language are

(A) symbols

(B) subdivided sections

(C) functional parts

(D) clues

(E) conveyers of emotion

19. Which of the following statements would Authors 1 and 2 most likely disagree about?

(A) Music and language can both be subdivided into several parts.

(B) Although significantly similar, music and language have several fundamentally distinct aspects.

(C) A group of notes used in a musical composition has the same meaning in a piece by a different composer.

(D) Language is not an effective means to express emotions.

(E) The meaning of a particular word is solely dependent on context.

If you finish before time is called, you may check your work on this section only. Do not turn to any other section in the test.

STOP

SECTION 9

Time—10 Minutes

14 Questions

Directions: For each question in this section, select the best answer from among the choices given and fill in the corresponding oval on the answer sheet.

The following sentences test correctness and effectiveness of expression. Part of each sentence or the entire sentence is underlined; beneath each sentence are five ways of phrasing the underlined material. Choice (A) repeats the original phrasing; the other four choices are different. If you think the original phrasing produces a better sentence than any of the alternatives, select choice (A); if not, select one of the other choices.

In making your selection, follow the requirements of standard written English; that is, pay attention to grammar, choice of words, sentence construction, and punctuation. Your selection should result in the most effective sentence—clear and precise, without awkwardness or ambiguity.

EXAMPLE: ANSWER:

Every apple in the baskets are ripe and labeled according to the date it was picke(D) Ⓐ ● Ⓒ Ⓓ Ⓔ

(A) are ripe and labeled according to the date it was picked
(B) is ripe and labeled according to the date it was picked
(C) are ripe and labeled according to the date they were picked
(D) is ripe and labeled according to the date they were picked
(E) are ripe and labeled as to the date it was picked

1. Arranged as an event for funding a new wing for the art museum, the museum's Board of Directors organized a fundraiser for the construction of one.

(A) Arranged as an event to for funding a new wing for the art museum
(B) Having been arranged as an event to fund a new wing for the art museum
(C) A new wing for the art museum needed an event for funding
(D) Although an event for funding a new wing for the art museum
(E) Realizing that the art museum needed funding for a new wing

2. Developed by a scientific team at his university, the president informed the reporters that the new process would facilitate the diagnosis of certain congenital diseases.

(A) Developed by a scientific team at his university
(B) Having been developed by a scientific team at his university
(C) Speaking of the discovery made by a scientific team at his university
(D) Describing the development of a scientific team at his university
(E) As it had been developed by a scientific team at his university

GO ON TO THE NEXT PAGE

3. One ecological rule of thumb states that there is opportunity for the accumulation of underground water reservoirs but in regions where vegetation remains undisturbed.

(A) but in regions where vegetation remains undisturbed
(B) unless vegetation being left undisturbed in some regions
(C) only where undisturbed vegetation is in regions
(D) only in regions where vegetation remains undisturbed
(E) except for vegetation remaining undisturbed in some regions

4. The traffic rules were ignored by each of us, failing to appreciate their role in ensuring safety.

(A) The traffic rules were ignored by each of us, failing to appreciate their role in ensuring safety.
(B) Each of us ignored traffic rules, because we failed to appreciate their role in ensuring safety.
(C) Traffic rules, ignored by each of us, fail to appreciate their role in ensuring safety.
(D) Failing to appreciate their role in ensuring safety, traffic rules were ignored by each of us.
(E) Traffic rules ignored by each of us, failing to appreciate their role in ensuring safety.

5. Developing a suitable environment for house plants is in many ways like when you are managing soil fertilization for city parks.

(A) is in many ways like when you are managing
(B) is in many ways similar to when you are managing
(C) in many ways is on a par with managing your
(D) is in many ways similar to the managing of
(E) is in many ways like managing

6. If they do not go into bankruptcy, the company will probably survive its recent setbacks.

(A) If they do not go into bankruptcy
(B) Unless bankruptcy cannot be avoided
(C) If they can avoid bankruptcy
(D) If bankruptcy will be avoided
(E) Unless it goes bankrupt

7. Now that I have read the works of both Henry and William James, I am convinced that Henry is the best psychologist and William the best writer.

(A) the best psychologist and William the best writer
(B) a better psychologist, William is the best writer
(C) the best as a psychologist, William the best as a writer
(D) the best psychologist, William the better writer
(E) the better psychologist and William the better writer

GO ON TO THE NEXT PAGE

8. When he arrived at the hospital, the doctor found that several emergency cases had been admitted before he went on duty.

(A) several emergency cases had been admitted before

(B) there were several emergency cases admitted prior to

(C) two emergency cases were being admitted before

(D) a couple of emergency cases were admitted before

(E) several emergency cases was admitted before

9. The variety of Scandinavian health care services offered to residents at reduced cost far exceeds low-cost health programs available in the United States.

(A) far exceeds low-cost health programs

(B) far exceeds the number of low-cost health programs

(C) tends to be greater than low-cost programs

(D) far exceed the number of low-cost health programs

(E) are greater than comparable low-cost health programs

10. The poet Oscar Wilde was known for his aphoristic wit and brilliant conversation, he wrote a number of memorable literary essays including "The Critic as Artist."

(A) The poet Oscar Wilde was known for his aphoristic wit and brilliant conversation, he

(B) The poet Oscar Wilde, known for his aphoristic wit and brilliant conversation; he

(C) Known for his aphoristic wit and brilliant conversation, the poet Oscar Wilde

(D) The poet Oscar Wilde was known for his aphoristic wit and brilliant conversation, however he

(E) Oscar Wilde, the poet, known for his aphoristic wit and brilliant conversation, and he

GO ON TO THE NEXT PAGE

11. According to Westin's book, the typical Victorian family was more interested in maintaining the appearance of propriety than in securing happiness for its individual members.

(A) the typical Victorian family was more interested in maintaining the appearance of propriety than in

(B) the appearance of propriety was more interesting to the typical Victorian family than

(C) the typical Victorian family, more interested in maintaining the appearance of propriety than it was in

(D) for a Victorian family it was typical that they would be more interested in maintaining the appearance of propriety than in

(E) the typical Victorian family was more interested in the appearance of propriety than in

12. During the Renaissance, artists such as Michelangelo and Fra Angelico, who have worked for the Church, did not have to search far for subject matter.

(A) who have worked

(B) which worked

(C) who worked

(D) who worked mostly

(E) who have always worked

GO ON TO THE NEXT PAGE

13. Though multimedia presentations have their place in the school curriculum, it is ridiculous to claim, as some do, that children learn as much from watching a one-hour video as a book.

(A) that children learn as much from watching a one-hour video as a book
(B) that children will learn as much from watching a one-hour video as they did from a book
(C) that children learn as much from watching a one-hour video as they do from reading a book
(D) that a one-hour video teaches more to children than book-reading
(E) that children watching a one-hour video learn as much as reading a book

14. Three women in the booth of the Swan Diner were angrily discussing the terms of the lease, and arguing about the level of commitment expected from each of them.

(A) were angrily discussing the terms of the lease, and arguing about
(B) were angrily discussing the terms of the lease, but they argued about
(C) were discussing angrily the terms of the lease, and arguing for
(D) was angrily discussing the terms of the lease, and arguing with
(E) had been angrily in discussion about the terms of the lease, and arguing about

If you finish before time is called, you may check your work on this section only. Do not turn to any other section in the test.

STOP

ANSWER KEY

Section 1

Essay

Section 2

1. E
2. E
3. C
4. A
5. A
6. C
7. A
8. C
9. A
10. E
11. C
12. A
13. D
14. C
15. A
16. E
17. B
18. B
19. B
20. C

Section 3

1. C
2. E
3. A
4. A
5. C
6. D
7. C
8. D
9. B
10. A
11. B
12. D
13. C
14. A
15. E
16. C
17. A
18. D
19. B
20. C
21. A
22. D
23. E
24. B

Section 4

1. C
2. C
3. C
4. B
5. A
6. C
7. A
8. D
9. B
10. A
11. B
12. A
13. D
14. C
15. B
16. E
17. A
18. B
19. C
20. B
21. B
22. D
23. B
24. C
25. B
26. C
27. E
28. D
29. E
30. A
31. B
32. C
33. C
34. E
35. C

Section 5

1. D
2. C
3. D
4. B
5. E
6. D
7. C
8. E
9. 115
10. .04
11. 11, 13, 17, 19, 23, 29, 31, 37, 41, 43, or 47
12. 8
13. 4
14. 250
15. 2/5 or.4
16. 9
17. 64
18. 203

Section 6

1. D
2. B
3. B
4. B
5. B
6. A
7. B
8. A
9. E
10. C
11. C
12. E
13. E
14. A
15. D
16. E
17. C
18. A
19. C
20. A
21. C
22. E
23. D
24. C

Section 7

1. E
2. C
3. C
4. E
5. B
6. C
7. E
8. A
9. A
10. D
11. D
12. B
13. B
14. D
15. D
16. E

Section 8

1. C
2. E
3. B
4. E
5. C
6. A
7. D
8. B
9. B
10. C
11. A
12. D
13. A
14. B
15. A
16. C
17. D
18. A
19. B

Section9

1. E
2. C
3. D
4. B
5. E
6. E
7. E
8. A
9. B
10. C
11. A
12. C
13. C
14. A

Answers and Explanations

SECTION 1

6 Essay

The first time I encountered a thought similar to the one expressed above by Calvin Coolidge was when I read a quote by Benjamin Franklin: "Energy and persistence conquer all things." The truth that Franklin expressed continues to affect me. I agree, therefore, that persistence is the major factor in someone's success. In fact, I know it's true because I've witnessed it first hand.

When I was 10 years old, my mother was in a car accident that left her a paraplegic; she is paralyzed from the waist down. I have watched her struggle from that day to this to reclaim a normal life and to be a mother to me and a wife to my father. She has come so far because she never gives up. She is a model of persistence. After the initial trauma she suffered from the accident faded she had to begin a long period of training to strengthen her upper body and to gain whatever strength she could in her legs. It was hard work. I used to go with her to the training room in the hospital and watch her sweat through the routines the therapist gave her.

Even today, almost 7 years since the accident, she trains three times a week. She also had to learn to use a wheelchair and how to drive a car using hand controls. She had to re-learn things she knew how to do before the accident like cooking and gardening. In fact, she had to learn how to do almost everything all over again, and she did.

I once asked her how she did all this and she said she did it because she was grateful that she survived the accident and could still be part of my father's and my life. So, Coolidge was right, and so was Franklin; persistence pays off. My mother is persistent and I'm so proud of her and so happy that her persistence means that she is still part of my life.

Grader's Comments: All essays are evaluated on 4 basic criteria: Topic, Support, Organization, and Language. This is a strongly written essay in which the writer sticks to the assigned topic and develops it in a creative way. She has a stirring story to tell, and she tells it very well. She never strays from her main idea, which is that persistence pays off and her mother is living proof of that. The author's clear recounting of her mother's heroic actions since the accident offers much support for her thesis.

The essay has an interesting and strong organization. The first paragraph offers another quote that is similar to the statement given. The author whets the reader's appetite by not jumping immediately into her main point. The last sentence keeps the reader's interest going. The remaining 3 paragraphs support her thesis.

The essay exhibits a high degree of skill with language. Both the sentence structure and the vocabulary indicate that the essay is written by an adept writer. The sentence structure is varied, and even long, complex sentences are correctly punctuated.

4 Essay

I think that Pres. Coolidge is right. It seems to me that if your persistent you do well in life. An example I can think of is Albert Einstein who said something like 99% of genius was hard work and the remaining 1% was because you are a genius.

This shows that Einstein agreed that you need more persistence than genius to succeed. Of course, Albert Einstein was a genius, too, but as the quote above says a lot of geniuses don't get rewarded. Einstein is famous because he was a persistent genius.

When Einstein was young he failed some math tests and he didn't always get great grades. He didn't let this stop him, though. He knew he wanted to be a mathematician and a physics professor and he worked hard to get to these goals. His persistence paid off. He became a teacher and later he won the Nobel Prize.

Later on Einstein came to America where he taught at Princeton University. In this way he fulfilled his dream of being a teacher of physics and mathematics. This was what he said he wanted to do when he was young and he did it because he persisted until he reached his goal. I believe that his persistence more than his genius is what brought Einstein the things he wanted.

In conclusion, Einstein is a great example of why I agree with Calvin Coolidge that persistence is the most important quality a person can have to be successful.

Grader's Comments: This writer sticks to the topic, agreeing with the quote. The writer's use of Einstein's life is great support for his agreement. Note, however: the writer misattributes the quote about genius. Thomas Edison actually said that, not Einstein. But the essay is not testing for content; a mistake like this won't hurt the score.

The essay is well organized with an introduction, body, and conclusion. The writer's use of *In conclusion* in the last paragraph helps the sense of organization. (Using words and phrases that indicate to the reader what your intentions are is a good technique for SAT essays.)

The writer's language is generally good, though not very challenging. He makes a common error in the second sentence of the first paragraph—using *your* when he meant *you're*. He also should not have abbreviated *President*.

2 Essay

It's good to be persistent as the statement above says. I seen this many times. For example, my brother was not very good at basketball but he kept on shooting hoops in our backyard and after a while he got better he made the team. He not good enough to be on the varsity but he plays intrmurels.

I think persistent is importent but I also think being a genius is pretty cool. I'd like to be a genius but I guess its not gonna happen. I guess I will have to just be persistent and see if that works. I think it will because as I said above I agree with the statement of Calvin Coolidge.

Grader's Comments: The author starts out pretty strongly by agreeing with the statement and using her brother as an example. However, she strays in the first part of the second paragraph and then returns to the topic at the end. The development of the topic is rudimentary. The writer's example is good support for her opinion. She doesn't, however, develop her support enough. The essay meanders on and off topic, making the organization too loose.

The writer's language is generally below standard. There are grammatical and spelling errors. The grammar is particularly poor. There are numerous verb tense errors, run-on sentences, and slang words. Here's a sampling: *I seen* instead of *I've seen*; *He not good enough* instead of *He's not good enough*; *persistent* for *persistence*; *gonna* instead of *going to*. The second sentence of the first paragraph is a long run-on. *Intramurals* and *important* are misspelled.

SECTION 2

1. E

Do what's in parentheses first:

$$\left(\frac{1}{5}+\frac{1}{3}\right)\div\frac{1}{2}=\frac{3}{15}+\frac{5}{15}\div\frac{1}{2}$$

$$=\frac{8}{15}\div\frac{1}{2}$$

Then, to divide fractions, invert the one after the division sign and multiply:

$$\frac{8}{15}\div\frac{1}{2}=\frac{8}{15}\times\frac{2}{1}=\frac{16}{15}$$

2. E

Plug in $x = -2$ and see what you get:

$$\begin{aligned} x^2 - 2x &= (-2)^2 - 2(-2) \\ &= 4 - (-4) \\ &= 4 + 4 \\ &= 8 \end{aligned}$$

3. C

To get Vito's rate in pages per hour, take the 96 pages and divide by the time *in hours*. The time is given as "2-hours and 40 minutes." Forty minutes is $\frac{2}{3}$ of an hour, so you can express Vito's time as $2\frac{2}{3}$ hours, or $\frac{8}{3}$ hours:

$$\text{Pages per hour} = \frac{96 \text{ pages}}{\frac{8}{3}\text{ hours}}$$

$$= 96\times\frac{3}{8} = 36$$

4. A

For $\frac{7}{x}$ to be greater than $\frac{1}{4}$, the denominator x has to be less than 4 times the numerator, or 28. And for $\frac{7}{x}$ to be less than $\frac{1}{3}$, the denominator x has to be greater than 3 times the numerator, or 21. Thus, x could be any of the integers 22 through 27, of which there are 6.

5. A

To find the average of three numbers—even if they're algebraic expressions—add them up and divide by 3:

$$\text{Average} = \frac{(2x+5)+(5x-6)+(-4x+2)}{3}$$

$$= \frac{3x+1}{3}$$

$$= x + \frac{1}{3}$$

6. C

The measures of the interior angles of a triangle add up to 180, so add the two given measures and subtract the sum from 180. The difference will be the measure of the third angle:

$$45 + 70 = 115$$

$$180 - 115 = 65$$

7. A

$$\frac{x^2+x^2+x^2}{x^2}=\frac{3x^2}{x^2}=3$$

8. C

To solve a quadratic equation, put it in the "$ax^2 + bx + c = 0$" form, factor the left side (if you can), and set each factor equal to 0 separately to get the two solutions. To solve $x^2 = 5x - 4$, first rewrite it as $x^2 - 5x + 4 = 0$. Then factor the left side:

$$x^2 - 5x + 4 = 0$$

$$(x-1)(x-4) = 0$$

$$x = 1 \text{ or } 4$$

9. A

Picking numbers is the easiest, fastest way to do this problem. Choose a pair of numbers from each set, and add them together. If you are unable to prove immediately that a set does not have the property described in the question stem, you may want to choose another pair. In set I, if we add 2 and 4, we get 6. Adding 12 and 8 gives us 20. Adding –2 and 8 gives us 6. Since each sum is a member of the set of even integers, set I seems to be true. For set II, adding 3 and 5 yields 8, which is not an odd integer. Therefore, II is not true. Finally, if we add two primes, say 2 and 3, we get 5. That example is true. If we add 3 and 5, however, we get 8, and 8 is not a prime number. Therefore, only set I has the property and the answer is (A).

10. E

The best way to deal with changing averages is to use the sum. Use the old average to figure out the total of the first 4 scores:

$$\text{Sum of first 4 scores} = (4)(89) = 356$$

Use the new average to figure out the total he needs after the 5th score:

$$\text{Sum of 5 scores} = (5)(90) = 450$$

To get his sum from 356 to 450, Martin needs to score 450 – 356 = 94.

11. C

Don't fall for the trap choice (B): You can't add or subtract percents of different wholes. Let the original price $s = 100$. Reducing s by 25% gives you a sale price of 75. This price is then increased by 20%, so the final price is 90. Since $s = 100$, it's easy to see that this is equal to choice (C), .90s.

12. A

The prime factorization of 36 is $2 \times 2 \times 3 \times 3$. That factorization includes 2 distinct prime factors, 2 and 3.

13. D

The area of a triangle is equal to one-half the base times the height:

$$\text{Area} = \frac{1}{2}(\text{base})(\text{height})$$

$$36 = \frac{1}{2}(9)(\text{height})$$

$$36 = \frac{9}{2}h$$

$$h = \frac{2}{9} \times 36 = 8$$

14. C

According to the definition, $x♣ = \frac{x}{4} - \frac{x}{6}$. Set that equal to 3 and solve for x:

$$\frac{x}{4} - \frac{x}{6} = 3$$

$$12\left(\frac{x}{4} - \frac{x}{6}\right) = 12(3)$$

$$3x - 2x = 36$$

$$x = 36$$

15. A

Read carefully. This question's a lot easier than you might think at first. It's asking for the total number of coins, not the total value. q quarters, d dimes, and n nickels add up to a total of $q + d + n$ coins.

16. E

Use the points where the line crosses the axes—(–1, 0) and (0, 2)—to find the slope:

$$\text{Slope} = \frac{y_2 - y_1}{x_2 - x_1} = \frac{2-0}{0-(-1)} = 2$$

The y-intercept is 2. Now plug $m = 2$ and $b = 2$ into the slope-intercept equation form:

$$y = mx + b$$

$$y = 2x + 2$$

17. B

An integer that's divisible by 6 has at least one 2 and one 3 in its prime factorization. An integer that's divisible by 9 has at least two 3's in its prime factorization. Therefore, an integer that's divisible by both 6 and 9 has at least one 2 and two 3's in its prime factorization. That means it's divisible by 2, 3, $2 \times 3 = 6$, $3 \times 3 = 9$, and $2 \times 3 \times 3 = 18$. It's *not* necessarily divisible by 12 or 36, each of which includes *two* 2's in its prime factorization.

You could also do this one by picking numbers. Think of a common multiple of 6 and 9 and use it to eliminate some options. $6 \times 9 = 54$ is an obvious common multiple—and it's not divisible by 12 or 36, but it is divisible by 18. The *least* common multiple of 6 and 9 is 18, which is also divisible by 18. It looks like every common multiple of 6 and 9 is also a multiple of 18.

18. B

Angles *POR* and *ROQ* are adjacent and supplementary, so the measure of $\angle ROP$ is 180° – 50° = 130°. Now look at ΔPOR:

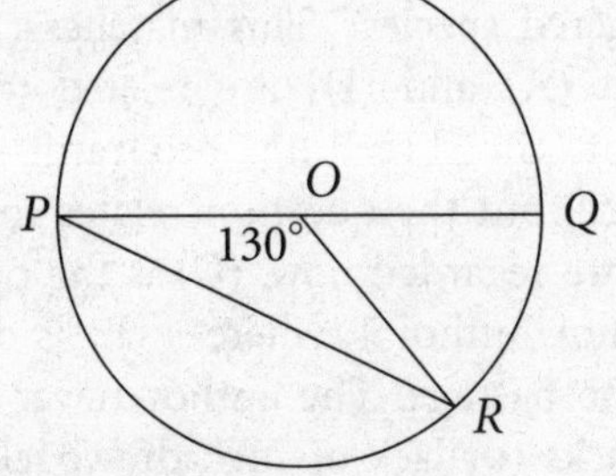

OP and *OR* are radii of the same circle, so they are equal, and ΔPOR is isosceles. That means $\angle P$ and $\angle R$ are equal. The two of them need to add up to 50° so that the triangle's 3 interior angles will add up to 180°. If $\angle P$ and $\angle R$ are equal and add up to 50°, then they each measure 25°.

19. B

The volume of a cube is equal to an edge cubed, so $e^3 = 64$, and each edge of the cube has length 4. If the cube is sliced horizontally in two, each of the resulting solids will have two sides of length 4 and one of length 2. So when they are glued together, the resulting figure will have one edge of length 2, one of length 4, and one of length 4 + 4 or 8.

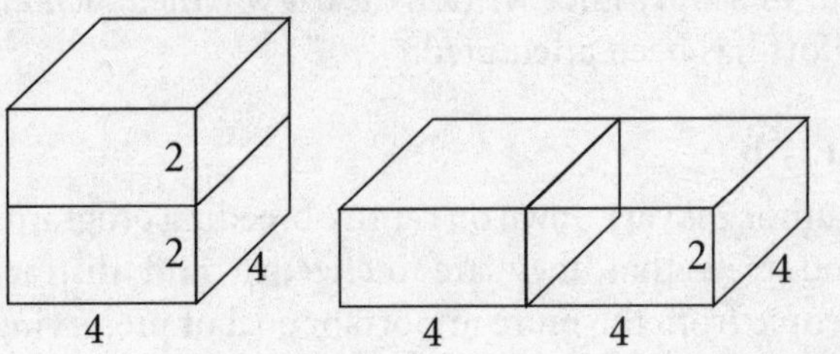

The surface area is the sum of the areas of the solid's six faces. The top and bottom each have area 8 × 4 = 32, the front and back each have area 8 × 2 = 16, and each side has area 4 × 2 = 8. So the surface area of the new solid is 2(32) + 2(16) + 2(8) = 64 + 32 + 16 = 112.

20. C

Probability equals the number of favorable outcomes over the number of total outcomes. In this case, the favorable outcome is that the chosen sock will be black. Since there are 12 black socks, there are 12 favorable outcomes. The number of total outcomes is the total number of socks. 6 + 12 + 14 = 32, so there are 32 total outcomes. The probability is $\frac{12}{32}$, which can be reduced to $\frac{3}{8}$.

SECTION 3

1. C

The phrase *proves difficult* is a clue: the two missing words have to be opposite in meaning. Choice (C) is correct because few posters would be *intact* if they were meant to be *destroyed.* None of the other choices makes sense: being (A) *returned* would not stop something from being *recognizable*, being (B) *discarded* would not necessarily stop something from being *relevant*, and so on.

2. E

The phrases *long considered* and *finally* suggest contrast. The missing word is probably the opposite of "making some headway in its battle against extinction." (E) *imperiled*, "in danger," is the best answer. (A) *elusive* means "hard to find"; (B) *prevalent* means "common"; (C) *combative* means "eager to fight"; (D) *voracious* means "having a huge appetite."

3. A

The sentence sets up a contrast between the situation before the invention of the tape recorder and the situation after. We need a word that's the opposite of *paraphrased*, which means "expressed in different words." The answer is *verbatim*, "word-for-word."

4. A

The phrase *encouraged hopes* suggests that the two missing words will be somewhat related in meaning. Choice (A) is the best answer, because we expect *a serious* novelist to use *subtle* characterizations. The other choices make less sense; in fact, it's not clear what (C) *accurate*, (D) *fictional*, or (E) *authentic* characterizations would be. (C) *prolific* means "highly productive"; (D) *accomplished* means "skillful, experienced"; (E) *reclusive* means "unsociable."

5. C

The missing word has to be related in meaning to *extended tenure.* (C) *longevity* is the best choice. (A) *acumen* and (B) *savvy* both mean "skill" or "knowledge." (D) *decorum* means "proper behavior"; (E) *celebrity* means "fame."

6. D

The word *although* indicates contrast: the two missing words have to be opposite in meaning. This is the case with *buoyant*, "light-hearted, cheerful," and *subdued*, "quiet." In (A), *introverted* means "reserved, not outgoing." In (B), *imperious* means "commanding," and *incensed* means "angry."

7. C

The phrase *failure to* establishes the negative tone of the sentence. An agency ought to *fix* or "get rid of" flawed policies. Possible answers for the first blank are (C) *rescind* or "remove, cancel," and (D) *amend* or "fix." Failure to do this is a bad thing, so we need a negative word for the second blank. The best choice is *lackadaisical*, "careless, sloppy."

8. D

Rapid turnover would tend to increase *inconsistency*, so we need a word that means "increased" or "worsened." *Exacerbated* means "made worse."

Captive Breeding Passages

9. B

In Passage 1, the author writes that the programs were used simply to provide animals for the zoos but are now often considered "an insurance policy for endangered species." This matches (B) nicely. Notice that (A) and (D) are related to the old purpose of the breeding programs—keeping zoos stocked, but the question relates to how the programs are regarded now. (C) is the opinion of Author 2, not Author 1, whereas (E) is out of the scope of the passage. The author never discusses the drawbacks (or lack of such drawbacks) of the breeding programs.

10. A

The author of Passage 1 is quite objective and never actually says whether she considers captive breeding programs a good idea. So the phrase *so the thinking goes* shows that the thoughts are not her own. She doesn't necessarily believe that a captive breeding program can introduce endangered species back into the wild, (A). (B) is a distortion of the word *thinking.* Here the word is used to refer to the thought that such an effort would be successful, not the thought and research involved in implementing such an effort. (C) and (E) are too negative, since the author never indicates whether she believes the reintroduction could work. (D) is out of scope, since we don't learn whether such an effort has been attempted.

11. B

Author 2 is very down on captive breeding programs and feels that they are ineffective and distract people from the more important goal of preserving environments. In other words, he is highly critical, (B). (A) and (C) are the opposite of what we're looking for. (D) doesn't fit because the author does take a stand and so can't be described as *impartial.* There's no support that the outlook is *unique*, (E), since we don't know if other people believe the same thing.

Gum and Heart Disease Passage

12. D

The hypothesis in question is that gum bacteria enters the bloodstream and helps to form plaque, which blocks arteries. After explaining the hypothesis, the author states that three types of bacteria have been identified in this plaque. This acts as evidence in support of the hypothesis, since it makes it quite feasible that bacteria contributes to plaque formation.

(A) relates to good dental hygiene, but it does nothing to confirm the hypothesis about plaque. (B) is tempting, but it actually describes the hypothesis itself, not the *evidence* of the hypothesis, which is what you're being asked. Similarly, (C) is an effect of the hypothesis, not evidence for the hypothesis. (E) is a definition of the term atherosclerosis, not evidence for the hypothesis in question.

13. C

The passage is quite scientific and factual and describes recent findings in medicine. So, the author's purpose was probably to *inform* (C) the reader. (A) and (D) are closely related and don't fit with the fairly dry presentation of factual information in the passage. The author doesn't recommend any particular course of action or argue against another point of view, so it doesn't make sense that the author attempted to *persuade* (B) or *argue* (E). (C) is correct: The passage is quite scientific and factual and describes recent findings in medicine. So, the author's purpose was probably to *inform* the reader.

Word a Day Passage

14. A

The word *shameless* usually means someone who *should* be ashamed but isn't. That's not the case here. In this passage, the author certainly doesn't believe that loving words is something to be ashamed of. Instead, the word *shameless* serves to show that the person is really into this hobby. It's also supposed to be mildly humorous, since it's silly to consider an interest in words a shameful hobby. All of this is nicely summed up by (A).

(B) and (E) are too literal because it seems unlikely anyone would actually disapprove of an interest in words or consider it regrettable. Although the author seems delighted about the website (C), the term *shameless* doesn't emphasize this. There's no reason to think that the word *shameless* was featured on the website (D).

15. E

Before mentioning the words in question, the passage states that the website often features a weekly theme. He then lists three words, all of which relate to numbers in some way. So, these three words are examples of choices that center on a weekly theme—a great match for (E).

The words in question are all unusual words (B) featured on the website (D) and all have origins related to numbers (A). However, these answer choices miss the point of this example—that the website often features words that relate to a theme. (After all, the author could have picked many different words as examples, but he chose these because they have a similar theme.) (C) is out of scope, since the author never implies that these three words are his favorites from the website.

The Wolves Passage

This Science passage is written by a naturalist who recounts how he went into the wilderness and, through trial and error experimentation and observation, learned some new and surprising things about the way wolves live. For example, wolves are a lot less suspicious and aggressive than people think they are, and contrary to popular belief, wolf families are not nomadic—they live and stay in territories with very definite boundaries.

16. C

In the first paragraph, the author explains how the wolves were aware of his presence but ignored him. That's why the author's precautions were superfluous.

(C) basically paraphrases that idea: the author's precautions were unnecessary because the wolves weren't interested in him. (A) doesn't work because the author never really says how long it was before he encountered the wolves. (B) is out because the author never mentions any wild animals other than wolves. Contrary to (D), even after the author interfered with the wolves' boundaries, they never bothered him. (E) is out because it's never suggested that the wolves have poor eyesight.

17. A

The author's basic point in paragraph 1 is that he was surprised at the way the wolves behaved towards him: they sized him up quickly right at the beginning and, from then on, ignored him. He found this behavior disconcerting, or *strange*, as (A) puts it. (B) sounds exaggerated—the author never really suggests that he was fearful of attack. With (C), the author says that he took longer to assess the wolves than they took to assess him, but his basic point is not to emphasize his own ignorance. (D) doesn't work because the wolves left the author alone—precautions weren't necessary. (E), like (B), isn't suggested—that the author thinks he has a lot of courage.

18. D

In paragraph 3, the author describes how the wolf was so preoccupied that he came within 15 yards of the tent without seeing it. It wasn't until the author made noise that the wolf suddenly became aware of its surroundings. (D) paraphrases this idea: that the wolf was not *on its guard*—it was self-absorbed. The author expresses no surprise about the wolf traveling alone (A) or hunting at night (C). As for (B), the point is not that the wolf lacks energy—it does respond when the author startles it. (E) is out because the author doesn't really mention any fear of attack.

19. B

In the middle of paragraph 5 the author describes how the wolf family regularly made the rounds of their lands and *freshened up the boundary markers*. He guessed that this was done because there were other wolves living in adjacent areas, although he never saw any sign of trouble between the neighboring wolf families. Then you get the quoted idea: since he never witnessed any disputes, he figured that it was all basically a ritual activity. (B) catches the idea. The idea that the activity was a ritual isn't related to the fact that it was repeated (A), that the boundaries were marked by geographic features (C), that they were marked at the same time each week (D)—that's never suggested—or that the whole family participated (E). The wrong choices miss the point.

20. C

One of the author's discoveries is that the wolves live in territories with clearly marked boundaries. So, contrary to what most people think, they aren't nomadic—they don't travel endlessly from place to place looking for food and sleeping in new areas. The idea in (C), if it were true, would contradict or weaken that idea. The idea in (A) would strengthen the thesis—if there were disputes over boundaries, that would suggest that the wolves are protective of their territory. The idea in (B)—the particular size of the wolves' territory—is irrelevant—it doesn't really relate to the question. (D) is tricky, but it doesn't work: the author finds that the wolves are territorial even though they actually don't have conflicts with their neighbors. The idea in (E) is irrelevant: the passage never discusses whether or not wolves are alert when encountering other animals.

Mrs. Hight Passage

This fiction passage is about Mrs. Hight and her daughter Esther, who live together on a farm. Through a conversation with Mrs. Hight, paragraph 1 gives us some background detail on how Esther saved the family farm by raising sheep singlehandedly. Paragraph 2 centers on the narrator's admiration for Esther, for her achievement on the farm, and her steadfast loyalty to her mother.

21. A

From line 10 onward, the story of the passage is really about Esther—her success with sheep farming, and her patience in looking after her mother. The purpose of the passage is to (A) *suggest some of the essential attributes* of her character—determination, good nature, and so on.

Both (B), the *romance* between William and Esther, and (D), *the causes of Mrs. Hight's unhappiness*, are topics only briefly touched on. (C) is not supported by the story at all—Esther's success in sheep raising seems to show that people's lives are very much under *their own control.* And (E) is too extreme—there's no indication that the visit to the farm has *changed the narrator's life* in any major way.

22. D

In *Mrs. Hight's* words, we're told that even though raising the sheep had been "stubborn work," Esther had been "good right along" (line 28). Choice (D) captures Esther's approach here—not only did she overcome *difficulties* with *determination*—she kept *calm* throughout.

(A) is too extreme; Esther didn't put *success* before all other considerations. She wasn't *defeated* (B), and she didn't bow to her *neighbors' opinions* (C). And her success suggests that her efforts were not a *mistake* (E).

23. E

The author speculates that William and Esther had "always been lovers" but had not acknowledged it "even to themselves." In other words, she thinks that William and Esther have a strong attachment that they're not fully aware of. (E) captures this situation.

(B) is wrong because it's their *own* feelings that William and Esther haven't acknowledged, which also makes (C) *a formal commitment* unlikely as yet. (D) *ambivalence* is wrong because there's no suggestion of uncertainty or contradictory feelings. Finally, there's no evidence of a *permanent separation* (A).

24. B

This question touches again on the qualities Esther showed in managing to raise sheep *and* look after her mother at the same time. We're told that she had been "refined instead of coarsened" by her work and had shown "patience," "self-possession," and "sweet temper" in caring for her mother. (B) *serenity and devotion* fits the bill here.

(B) *aloofness and reserve* sounds like the opposite of "sweet temper." Esther's (C) *sense of humor* is never mentioned, and the author doesn't seem particularly impressed by her (E) *material success.* Finally, (D) *stubborn pride* exaggerates Esther's determination in overcoming adversity, without acknowledging her good points.

SECTION 4

1. C

This sentence tests your knowledge of the sequence of tenses. By the time the speaker graduates from college in the future, her brother *will have been* practicing law—you need the future perfect tense. (C) expresses the sequence correctly. All the remaining choices have incorrect tenses. (B) places this action in the past. (D) makes it inappropriately conditional. (E) places it in the present.

2. C

The intervening phrase and clause make it difficult to see that the subject and verb don't agree. The plural subject *historians* needs a plural verb, so *includes* should be *include.* (B) incorrectly changes *includes* to the past tense. (C) and (D) both correct this problem, but only (C) keeps the correct relative pronoun. (D) incorrectly changes the subjective *who* to the objective *whom.* (E) doesn't correct the subject-verb problem and changes the idiomatically correct *more than* to *at least,* which changes the meaning.

3. C

Nancy illogically compares Marcel Proust's novel with other writers. Nancy should compare Proust's novel with other novels, as in (C), (D), and (E). Only (C) makes that change without introducing new errors. (D) illogically changes the comparison *more brilliant* (which is correct because two things are compared) to *brilliant opposed to*. (E) changes the correct relative pronoun *which* to *whom*—perhaps thinking that the authors, not the books, are compared. (B) also introduces that mistake and incorrectly changes the second clause to the past tense.

4. B

The past tense of the irregular verb *to see* is *saw*. (B) and (D) correct this problem, but (D) introduces another error by changing *arriving* to *have arrived*. (C) and (E) illogically change the correct *watching* to *who watch*. (C) also doesn't correct the original problem, and (E) incorrectly changes *arriving* to *arrived*.

5. A

This sentence is correct as written. (B) illogically changes *to discover* to the past tense *to have discovered*. (C) incorrectly adds the preposition *in* (the species don't congregate in the floor). (D) needlessly adds the preposition *from*. (E) incorrectly changes *that* to *who*.

6. C

In this sentence we must sort through all the prepositions to see that *in an effort at avoiding* is not good, idiomatic English. The correct phrase is *in an effort to avoid*. (C), (D), and (E) all make this change. However, (D) and (E) distort the meaning. (D) is incorrect because fans are not on the team. (E) switches the phrases *in the stadium* and *between fans* which would mean that the altercations happen in more than one stadium.

7. A

Look through the answer choices: all except (E) focus on the phrase *a means to attract*. Is that idiomatically correct? Yes, *a strategy to attract* is correct. (B), (C), and (D) alter the phrase. (C) also changes the adjective *elderly* to *elder*. (E) rearranges the introductory phrase so that the votes incorrectly modify the social security adjustment.

8. D

The words *bright lights* interrupt the subject and verb, making the agreement problem difficult to see. The singular subject *configuration* agrees with the singular verb *was*. (D) and (E) make this change, but (E) omits the transition word *but*. (B) and (C) don't address the agreement problem, and (C) changes the contrasting transition word *but* to *and*.

9. B

The plural pronoun *their* actually refers to the singular subject *band*. (B) and (C) correctly change *their* to *its*. (C) incorrectly changes the preposition *of* to *for*. The expression *methods of providing* is idiomatically correct. Neither (D) nor (E) address the pronoun problem. They both also change the infinitive *to determine* to *to determining*, which is not standard English.

10. A

This is a complex sentence, so break it down to see if it is correct. (B) changes *had begun* (which is correctly in the past perfect tense) to the incorrect form *had began*. (C) illogically puts the second clause in the future tense. (D) incorrectly changes *later* (which is good standard written English) to the illogical *afterwards*. (E) changes the subject of the sentence from the conductor to the orchestra, altering the meaning.

11. B

What actually occurred when alcohol was banned turned out to be the opposite of what the prohibitionists had envisioned. Drinking continued (illegally) and crime actually increased. Therefore, you're looking for words that will express this ironic contrast between the idea and the reality. *In fact* is the best choice. (D) is wrong because although *but* expresses a contrast, it also creates a fragment (but must follow a comma, not a semicolon). (A), (C), and (E) fail to express the logical contrast between the two halves of the sentence.

12. A

It's especially important to check subject-verb agreement when a verb is separated from its subject. The subject is the singular *heron*, but the verb is the plural *live*. To correct this, you would change *live* to *lives*. *Most* (B) is correctly in the superlative form, since all parts of the United States are compared. (C) is idiomatically correct. (D) uses *both* correctly with *and*.

13. D

Susan compares the home team's warm-ups to the visiting team. She should compare the warm-ups of both teams. (D) is your answer. The phrase *liked watching* in (A) is correctly in the past tense. (B) uses the correct relative pronoun. In (C), the phrase *more interesting* works because two things are compared.

14. C

The intervening phrase *of Viking settlements* interrupts the subject and verb. The singular subject *pattern* doesn't agree with the plural verb *were*. The phrase *by tracing* (A) is idiomatically correct. The verb *determined* (B) is correctly in the past tense. The adverb *generally* (D) correctly modifies the adjective *similar*.

15. B

This sentence sets up a contrast between what the recipe required and what Chad did. However, the conjunction *and* indicates an addition rather than a contrast and should be replaced with a word like *but*. In (A), *actually* is an adverb correctly used to modify the verb, and *called for* is an idiomatic expression meaning *needed in the circumstances*. (C) sets up the right causal relationship required by the meaning of the sentence. (D) is idiomatically correct.

16. E

Read all sentences carefully looking for common errors, but remember that about 20% will be error-free. (A) is the correct word to express the contrast that the sentence sets up. (B) is correctly the past tense. (C) is a phrase that indicates an example is being given. (D) is idiomatically correct after the verb *attempt*. (E) is the correct choice since this sentence is correct as written.

17. A

When there are underlined pronouns in a Usage question, check to see that they have clear antecedents. The pronoun *they* doesn't. You can guess that *they* are the people of India, but that would be only a guess since the sentence doesn't provide that information. (B) is correctly used here. In (C), the past tense verb is correct. In (D), the conjunction *and* correctly expresses a continuation of the idea that precedes it.

18. B

The action took place in the past and should use the simple past tense *saw* instead of the past participle of the verb *to see* (*seen*). The verbs *waiting* (A) and *walking* (C) are in the correct form, and the phrase *to stop traffic* (D) is idiomatically correct.

19. C

The plural subject *plays* doesn't agree with the singular verb *expresses*. (C) should read *express*. The infinitive verb *to produce* (A) is correct. (B) and (D) are in the correct tense and idiomatically correct.

20. B

The phrase *claim hearing* is not idiomatically correct. (B) should read *claim to have heard*. The contrasting transition word *while* (A) is used appropriately as is the adverb *truly* (D). The phrase *such a person* is idiomatically correct.

21. B

The preposition *to* should follow the phrase *in an attempt*. The phrase *at creating* (B) should read *to create*. The verb *initiated* (A) is correctly in the present tense. The phrases *of team spirit* (C) and *in the office* (D) use the correct prepositions.

22. D

Did efforts *about* democracy sound correct when you read this sentence? Probably not. What you would need is something like *efforts on behalf of*. In (A), the adverb *as* is correctly used to modify the verb. In (B), the verb tense is correct—past perfect, which indicates that something happened before something else happened. Abadi got the Nobel Prize before her colleagues praised her. (C) correctly uses the simple past.

23. B

Be sure that the verbs in the sentence correctly express the time of the action. This sentence contains a clear indication of time—1906, which is in the past. Anything that happened in 1906 is done. The verb tenses should express this completeness. (B) should be in the simple past tense—*leveled*. (A) is idiomatically correct. (C) uses the right words and the correct preposition. (D) uses the correct tense—the simple past.

24. C

The phrase *absolute shamefaced* has an adjective modifying an adjective (*shamefaced*). The phrase should read *absolutely shamefaced*. The phrases *failure to* (A), *went about* (B), and *only a few* (D) are all idiomatically correct.

25. B

The phrase *about intellect and language* masks the fact that the singular subject *scientific writing* doesn't agree with the plural verb *were*. (B) should read *was*. The prepositions *about* (A), *by* (C), and *of* (D) are all idiomatically correct.

26. C

Reversing the sentence order can help you find the error. Does it make sense to say *The damaging effects of cigarette smoking has become recognized*? No. The plural subject *effects* takes the plural verb *have*, rather than *has* (C). The transition word *while* (A) correctly sets up a contrast. The verb *has been known* (B) is in the correct tense because it takes place before the second part of the sentence. Therefore, the past participle *become* (D) is also in the correct tense (you can also reverse the order to say *the damaging effects have become known*).

27. E

The sentence is correct as written. The verb *maintains* (A) agrees with the singular subject *FBI* and is correctly in the present tense. The prepositions *for* (B) and in (D) correctly follow *maintains* and *interested*, respectively. The pronoun *they* (C) clearly refers to *citizens*.

28. D

When three people are being compared, the superlative phrase *most* should be used. (D) should read *most abstract*, rather than *more abstract*. The phrase *although* (A) is idiomatically correct. (B) is an idiomatically correct phrase, and *similar* is correctly used to modify *aspects*. The verb *was* (C) is correctly in the past tense.

29. E

The sentence is correct as written. (A) correctly uses the adverb. (B) correctly uses the superlative, since all choreographers are compared, and *inventive* correctly modifies the noun *choreographers*. (C) is correctly in the past tense and is the correct form of the irregular verb, and the noun *approach* takes the preposition *to* (D).

Shakespeare Passage

30. A

To determine which sentence should be inserted, consider how sentence 1 relates to sentence 2.

Sentence 1 states that there was a debate. Sentence 2 offers one side of the debate. (A) gives a clear transition between the two and inserts the plural noun *teachers* which defines *they* in sentence 2. (B) would only be a clear transition if the paragraph discussed teachers who wanted to continue teaching Shakespeare. (C) is out of scope. The author never argues for this. (D) draws a conclusion that is not apparent in the passage. (E) incorrectly states that the author thinks the debate itself is wrong.

31. B

This is a Reading Comp question: what is the role of sentence 2? Sentence 1 introduces a debate among English teachers, and sentence 2 offers the consensus opinion in that debate, so (B) is the best choice. The other choices all misinterpret the relationship between these sentences.

32. C

These two sentences contain an *if...then* scenario. (C) correctly states that *if* a student read *Romeo and Juliet, it would take* more time. (C) also combines the two into a complete sentence (sentence 4 is a fragment). (A) needlessly repeats *the student*, making it too wordy. (B) changes the verb in sentence 4 into a modifier, making a fragment of the combined *sentences.* (D) and (E) combine the two *sentences* with a semicolon, which doesn't fix the fragment problem of the original.

33. C

The problem with sentence 6 is that the first word *And* suggests that this sentence simply continues the ideas in sentence 5. This isn't the case. Moreover, there is clearly a contrast set up within sentence 6: it takes longer to read, but the benefits are great. (C) fixes both problems. (B) would not address the problems and would make the sentence nonidiomatic. (D) would break the close flow of ideas between sentences 7 and 8. (E) doesn't address the problem; it even makes the relationship between the two parts of this sentence less clear.

34. E

To combine the sentences you need to understand their relationships. Shakespeare's characters, for example Hamlet and Ophelia, are the basis of many characters in today's books, and Hamlet can be seen in James Joyce's work. (E) ties these ideas together well without redundancies. (A) simply adds on the James Joyce example with *and*, without showing the relationship. (B) inserts the modifying phrase *being used for example by James Joyce*, which is in the passive voice and misplaced (Hamlet, not today's books, is used by James Joyce). (C) incorrectly uses the contrasting transition word *but.* (E) states that both Ophelia and Hamlet *can be seen* in Joyce's work.

35. C

These two short sentences are related and can be combined. (C) establishes the relationship between the sentences with the transition word *while* and also uses the transition word *therefore* to relate the sentence to the previous idea. (D) begins well with the contrasting transition word *although* but alters the meaning by eliminating *have the right to* and changing *they should* to *they also.* (B) incorrectly uses the phrase *regardless of*, which is opposite of the author's meaning. (E) doesn't establish a relationship between the sentences.

SECTION 5

1. D

Note that you're looking for the value of y, not the value of x. Distribute the 3: $3x + 3y = 6 + 3x$. Subtract $3x$ from both sides of the equation to get $3y = 6$. Then $y = 2$.

2. C

You know that the machine can cap 7 bottles in 3 seconds. Since there are 20 three-second periods in 1 minute, the number of bottles capped in 1 minute is $7(20) = 140$.

3. D

First, plug in the numbers given. This gives you $a^3 + 2(2) - 5(3) = -3$, which can be simplified to $a^3 + 4 - 15 = -3$ and then to $a^3 = 8$. The cube root of 8 is 2.

4. B

If $\angle ABC$ is 100 degrees, then $14x + 2 = 100$. Therefore, $14x = 98$, and $x = 7$. Since $x = 7$, $\angle BCA$ must be 35 degrees. Since the angles of any triangle add up to 180, $100 + 35 + y = 180$, and $y = 45$.

5. E

There are at least two ways to approach this problem. You can think of the school as having *F* floors times *R* rooms per floor times 20 chairs per room and note that the units cancel out neatly, leaving you with 20*FR* chairs, or you can try picking numbers for *F* and *R*. Let's say the school has 3 floors, each with 4 rooms. In this case, the school would have $3 \times 4 \times 20 = 240$ chairs in it. Plug these numbers into the answer choices. The only answer choice that gives you 240 chairs is (E).

6. D

Set *J* is {2, 4, 6, ...} and Set *K* is all values from –2 to 2, including the endpoints themselves. The only number that is both a positive even integer and in the range is 2.

7. C

If $|-3x - 7| = 5$, then $-3x - 7 = 5$ or $-3x - 7 = -5$. Solve for *x*:

$$-3x = 12 \text{ or } -3x = 2$$
$$x = -4 \text{ or } x = -\frac{2}{3}$$

8. E

Of the first 100 positive integers, 9 are 1-digit numbers (1, 2, 3, 4, 5, 6, 7, 8, and 9), 1 is a 3-digit number (100), and the other 90 are 2-digit numbers (10 to 99). If you select one integer at random from this group, the probability of selecting a 2-digit number is 90 out of 100 possible numbers, or $\frac{9}{10}$.

9. 115

Since lines *p* and *q* are parallel, we can use the rule about alternate interior angles to fill in the following:

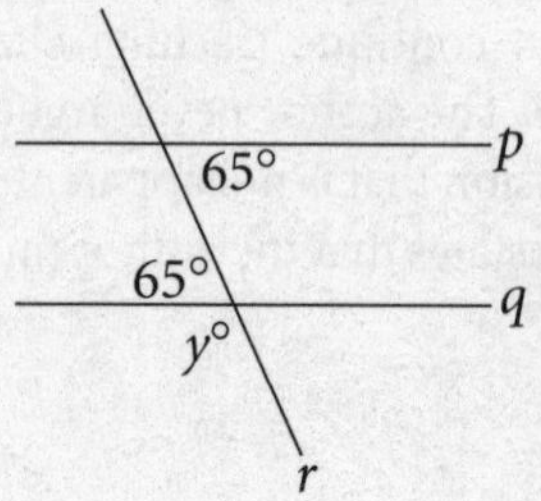

Since the angle marked $y°$ is adjacent and supplementary to a 65° angle, $y = 180 - 65 = 115$.

10. .04

Be careful. The question is not asking: "What is $\frac{1}{4}$ of 16?" It's asking: "What is $\frac{1}{4}$ percent of 16?" One-fourth of 1 percent is 0.25%, or 0.0025: $\frac{1}{4}$ % of $16 = 0.0025 \times 16 = 0.04$

11. 11, 13, 17, 19, 23, 29, 31, 37, 41, 43, or 47

In order for each of these fractions to be in its simplest form, *a* would have to be a number that has no prime factors in common with 3, 5, or 14. So just find a value between 2 and 50 that fits that description. Your best bet is to use a prime number, such as 11. That's one of 11 acceptable answers.

12. 8

To evaluate this expression when $s = 9$, simply plug 9 in for *s*. Substituting 9 into the expression yields:

$$\frac{3(9) + 5}{4} = \frac{27 + 5}{4} = \frac{32}{4} = 8$$

13. 4

The easiest way to get the answer here is to pick numbers. Pick a number for *x* that has a remainder of 2 when divided by 6, such as 8. Increase the number you picked by 8. In this case, $8 + 8 = 16$. Now divide 16 by 6, which gives you 2 remainder 4. Therefore, the answer is 4.

14. 250

Percent times Whole equals Part:

$$(15\%) \times (\text{take-home pay}) = \$37.50$$
$$(0.15) \times (\text{take-home pay}) = \$37.50$$
$$\text{take-home pay} = \frac{\$37.50}{0.15} = \$250.00$$

15. 2/5 or .4

If there are 36 men and 24 women in the group, then the total number of group members is 60. The women make up $\frac{26}{40}$ of the group. Since this fraction cannot be gridded, reduce it or turn it into a decimal. To reduce it, divide both the numerator and denominator by 12, and you end up with $\frac{2}{5}$. To turn it into a decimal, divide 60 into 24, and you end up with .4.

16. 9

The area of a triangle is equal to one-half the base times the height. Here the base (along the x-axis) is 6 and the height (perpendicular to the base—i.e., parallel to the y-axis) is 3, so the area is $\frac{1}{2}bh = \frac{1}{2}(6)(3) = 9$.

17. 64

You cannot find the area of the square without finding the length of a side, so use the information you are given about the rectangles to find the length of the square's sides. Since the rectangles have the same dimensions, we know that the side of the square must be twice the length of the shorter side of either rectangle. The side of the square must also be the longer side of either rectangle.

Call the length of a side of the square, which is also the length of a longer side of either rectangle, x. Then the shorter side of either rectangle is $\frac{x}{2}$. Now use the formula for the perimeter:

$$P = 2l + 2w$$

For either rectangle, you have

$$24 = 2x + 2\left(\frac{x}{2}\right)$$
$$24 = 2x + x$$
$$24 = 3x$$
$$8 = x$$

To find the area of the square, simply multiply 8 by 8. The answer is 64.

18. 203

This looks like a physics question, but, in fact, it's just a "plug-in-the-number-and-see-what-you-get" question. Be sure you plug 95 in for C (not F):

$$C = \frac{5}{9}(F - 32)$$
$$95 = \frac{5}{9}(F - 32)$$
$$\frac{9}{5} \times 95 = F - 32$$
$$F - 32 = 171$$
$$F = 171 + 32 = 203$$

SECTION 6

1. D

The word in the first blank has to be similar in meaning to "controversy": (C) *belligerent*, (D) *scandalous*, and (E) *provocative* would fit. The band wouldn't do this if they didn't find that the strategy worked, so (B) *rewarding* and (D) *effective* fit for the second blank. Only (D) fits for both blanks.

2. B

The correct answer is implied by *numerous scribbled edits that cover even his supposed final drafts*. In other words, Joyce attached great importance to (B) *revision*.

3. B

The key is that the players *now charge for their signatures*. Either the fans who believe that the players are not *greedy* would be *surprised* or *disappointed*, or the fans who believe that the players are not *ungreedy* would be *confirmed*. Choice (B) fits the former prediction.

4. B

The words *though* and *absence* indicate contrast, so the missing word has to be nearly opposite in meaning to "isolation and the longing for connection." *Fraternity*—brotherhood or fellowship—is the best choice. Choice (D) may be tempting, but the term *socialism* refers to a specific set of political and economic doctrines, not just to any sort of society.

5. B

The part of the sentence after the semicolon pretty basically defines the missing word. The word is *calculated*, consciously planned. (A) *Incendiary* means "inflaming"; (C) *facetious* means "joking"; (D) *scrupulous* means "honest"; (E) *impromptu* means "unplanned."

Jellyfish Passage

6. A

Since it's clear that a jellyfish couldn't have any feelings about its encounter with humans, the author is apparently using this image to make the reader smile (A). (Even if you don't think it's funny, you should note that this is the author's intent.)

The author doesn't ask us to feel *sympathy* for either the jellyfish or humans (B) and doesn't discuss whether or not humans are *afraid* of jellyfish (C). Though the author does discuss the danger of jellyfish (D), the quote in question doesn't accomplish that purpose. The passage never discusses how humans or jellyfish *react* to these encounters (E).

7. B

The third and fourth sentences contain the key here. You learn there that the relatively common encounters are not surprising because jellyfish *live in every ocean in the world* (B).

(A), (C), (D), and (E) are all details from the passage, but none of them helps to explain why encounters are so common.

Khyber Pass Passage

8. A

For this question, eliminate everything that *does* appear, and you'll be left with the answer. The passage answers (B) (Pakistan and Afghanistan), (C) (53 kilometers), (D) (was used in several wars), and (E) (two roads pass through today). The *origin* of the pass (A) is never mentioned.

9. E

Function questions ask you to consider what a statement adds to the author's reasoning. What claim or argument does it relate to and what does it add to the author's argument? Here, the word *snakes* implies a *twisting, turning* path, like a snake (E).

Although the Khyber Pass *connects* two points, the use of the word *snake* is not referring to that, so (A) is out. And while crossing the Khyber Pass may be *dangerous* (B), that doesn't follow from the word *snake*, either. (C) is the opposite of what you're looking for; the word implies that the pass is anything but direct. (D) comes from the wrong part of the passage. The short length of the Khyber Pass is mentioned earlier in the passage, but this is not why the author stated that the path *snakes.*

The Cold War Passage

The author of this passage has one overarching strategy: Set up the arguments of the revisionist historians and then knock 'em down. Paragraph 1 explains the things that, according to the revisionists, could have been done to avoid the Cold War, which are 1) the U.S. could have just accepted Soviet domination in Eastern Europe, 2) the U.S. could have given them money for reconstruction, and 3) the U.S. could have given up its monopoly of the bomb. Paragraphs 2 and 3 outline the author's refutation of these arguments; he concentrates on the American political atmosphere as the main reason that the revisionists' ideas were not really workable at the time. Revisionists, he then asserts in paragraph 4, would reject this politics-based argument and claim instead that it was the economic situation that forced American policy makers to oppose the Soviets. The author of course then knocks down this new argument; it is contradictory, he says, to say that American officials were caught in an economic tide and then to blame them for not doing things differently. The author concludes in the final paragraph by stating that there was essentially no way, given the climate in the Soviet Union, that the Cold War could have been avoided.

10. C

As we noted above, the author of this passage is primarily engaged in setting up and knocking down the arguments of the revisionist historians of the Cold War. This makes (C) correct and (E) wrong (the author is definitely not interested in reconciling his view with that of the revisionists). (A) is wrong because the ideas of the revisionists are not, as far as we know, a popular myth. (B) is out because the author is defending historical figures—the policy makers—for what they did, not criticizing them. (D) is too neutral a choice for this passage; the author does engage in analysis of the era of the beginning of the Cold War, but his purpose is to do far more than just analyze events. He wants to poke holes in revisionist theories.

11. C

When revisionists say that the U.S. could have *recognized* the Soviet influence in Eastern Europe, they mean that the U.S. could have formally *acknowledged* this Soviet presence. (C) is correct.

12. E

In the second and third paragraphs, the author refutes the suggestions of the revisionists primarily by saying that the policy-makers couldn't do what was necessary to avoid the Cold War because the American people were against it. The assumption the author makes is that the policy makers *could not have been expected to ignore public opinion* (E). The author never says in the second and third paragraphs that the Soviets were to blame for failed U.S. peace initiatives (A) or that none of the alternatives would work (C)—what he does say, in a later paragraph, is that if peace initiatives had not run aground due to American politics, then they would have run aground due to the Soviet climate. The author also does not say in the second and third paragraphs that the American public was *well-informed* (B) or *overwhelmingly opposed to seeking peace* (D); all we know is that they opposed Soviet influence in Eastern Europe as well as the idea of giving up the atom bomb monopoly.

13. E

This question centers on the fourth paragraph, which is where the author explains the revisionists' view that American policy makers decided to oppose the Soviet Union because Soviet expansion could jeopardize U.S. trade and investment opportunities in Eastern Europe and elsewhere. (E) captures this idea. The author says nothing about illegal trading activities (A), nor does he indicate whether or not the Soviets knew about the negative impact they could have on the American economy (B). (C) is out because the Soviet Union was not recognized by the United States, so this could not possibly have had anything to do with the origin of the Cold War. (D) is wrong because there is no evidence in the paragraph to support it.

14. A

The author poses the question in order to show that there is a problem with the revisionists' economic interpretation of the Cold War: you can't blame the policy-makers if they didn't have any control. Thus, the question serves to *point out an inconsistency* (A) in the revisionists' position. (D) might be tempting since the revisionists' view is pretty cynical, but the author is questioning that view here, not summing it up.

Yellow Wallpaper Passage

15. D

The word *expense* is used to mean that the narrator has given up something. In particular, she's given up her work in favor of her domestic role. (D) *sacrifice* matches that prediction.

Although the word *burden* (A) might be tempting, it doesn't necessarily indicate that something is given up in order to obtain something else. So, it doesn't capture the full meaning of what you're looking for here. (B), (C), and (E) have to do with money; a common meaning of *expense*, but not in this context.

16. E

The last phrase, *a conflict which Charlotte Perkins Gilman chronicled over 100 years ago*, implies that issues in Gilman's short story are as relevant now as they were in 1892 (E).

The author's tone is generally balanced throughout the passage, so the extremely negative tones of (A), (B), (C), and (D) are all out of place. Also, (C) and (D) make pronouncements about the future, whereas the text simply describes the present situation.

The James Weldon Johnson Passage

Johnson, the author of this autobiographical piece, does not just describe the experience he had watching the piano player playing rag-time; he also uses the scene as a jumping-off point from which to comment on the origin of rag-time (second paragraph), to disparage American musicians for refusing to accept rag-time (third paragraph), and to speculate on what the piano player could have amounted to under different circumstances (fourth paragraph).

17. C

The author's initial impression of rag-time can be found in the first paragraph. He emphasizes how the beat demanded a physical response and meshed with the *dissonant harmonies*, etc., to produce a *curious effect*. (C) is the correct answer. The only other choice that has anything to do with the first paragraph is (B). (B) is wrong because the audience is said to have applauded the singer's dance steps, not the rag-time music.

18. A

In the context of the phrase *questionable resorts about Memphis and St. Louis*, the word *questionable* means *disreputable* (A).

19. C

Choice (B) might have jumped right out at you since the narrator's perspective in paragraph 1 is that of a mesmerized spectator, but his perspective in paragraphs 2 and 3 changes. He steps back from the description of his first encounter with rag-time and begins to discuss rag-time's history, appeal, and impact on the contemporary musical scene. Therefore, (C) is the correct answer. (A) is wrong because the author is not impartial; he thinks highly of rag-time. Watching rag-time playing is not a *unique experience*, which eliminates (D). As for (E), the narrator says nothing about his youth in the second and third paragraphs.

20. A

Put the reference to the *theory of the universe* in the context of the second paragraph. The author says that the players who first developed rag-time knew *no more of the theory of music than they did of the theory of the universe*—in other words, they had no formal music education—but their natural talent guided them. Since they had no conventional schooling in music, you can infer that their invention, rag-time, was *an unconventional musical form* (A).

(B) and (E) are the close wrong answers. (B) is out because the originators of rag-time could have been interested in other people's music, even though they had no formal music education. (E) is wrong since it misunderstands the overall point of the paragraph; the author is not interested in making general statements about the relationship between education and artistic success. (C) is the sort of choice you can rule out by common sense; no SAT question is going to have a correct answer that downplays the importance of academics. Finally, there is no evidence that indicates (D) could be true.

21. C

The narrator argues in the third paragraph that rag-time should not be ignored or dismissed by American musicians just because it is popular. All great music, he states, comes from the hearts of the people. In other words, he is saying that the *conservative and condescending attitude* of American musicians is misguided (C). There is no evidence in the third paragraph to support any of the other choices. (B) is perhaps the most tempting, since the author talks in the third paragraph about rag-time's popularity in Europe, but it seems as though American musicians do know about rag-time's popularity and find it distasteful.

22. E

This question is a follow-up on the previous one. As we've said, the author's argument in the third paragraph is that music should not be dismissed by serious musicians just because it happens to be popular. (E) paraphrases this idea. (A) stretches the author's argument way too far. (B) is wrong because the author does not try to establish criteria for musical greatness. (C) focuses too narrowly on the author's mention of the fact that rag-time was popular abroad. (D) is clearly wrong since rag-time gained popularity even though it had not been *taken up by a musical master.*

23. D

The narrator poses to himself the question about what might have become of the piano player had he been properly trained and then answers himself by saying *perhaps he wouldn't have done anything at all.* The narrator goes on to say that even if the piano player achieved some success as an imitator of the greats or as an innovator, he still would not have been as *delightful* as he was playing rag-time. Thus, the statement that *perhaps he wouldn't have done anything at all* can best be interpreted as a *recognition that the piano player might have wasted his talent* (D) had he been formally trained. (A) and (B) are wrong because the narrator thinks highly of the piano player's skill, even if that skill is not genius-level or particularly disciplined. (C) and (E) are both far too broad and too negative to be the correct answer.

24. C

The correct answer here is going to be a paraphrase of the idea that no matter how far the piano player would have gone if trained, he would not have been as delightful as he was as a rag-time player. (C) is the choice you're looking for. (E) is the most tempting wrong answer since the author's statements at the end of the passage can easily be misconstrued to mean that the piano player could never have been more than mediocre as a classical artist. However, *never* is too strong a word here—the narrator is not, and cannot be, as sure as that—so this choice is wrong.

SECTION 7

1. E

Use FOIL:

$$(3x + 4)(4x - 3)$$
$$= (3x \times 4x) + [3x \times (-3)] + (4 \times 4x) + [4 \times (-3)]$$
$$= 12x^2 - 9x + 16x - 12$$
$$= 12x^2 + 7x - 12$$

2. C

When you know that the given parts add up to the whole, then you can turn a part-to-part ratio into 2 part-to-whole ratios—put each term of the ratio over the sum of the terms. In this case, since all the numbers in the set must be either integers or nonintegers, the parts do add up to the whole. The sum of the terms in the ratio 2:3 is 5, so the two part-to-whole ratios are 2:5 and 3:5.

$$\frac{\text{integers}}{\text{numbers}} = \frac{2}{5} = \frac{2}{5}(100\%) = \frac{200\%}{5} = 40\%$$

3. C

Get rid of the parentheses in the denominator, and then cancel factors the numerator and denominator have in common:

$$\frac{x^2y^3z^4}{(xyz^2)^2} = \frac{x^2y^3z^4}{x^2y^2z^4}$$

$$= \frac{x^2}{x^2}\times\frac{y^3}{y^2}\times\frac{z^4}{z^4}$$

$$= y$$

4. E

If p divided by 7 leaves a remainder of 5, you can say that $p = 7n + 5$, where n represents some integer. Multiply both sides by 5 to get $5p = 35n + 25$. The remainder when you divide 7 into $35n$ is 0. The reminder when you divide 7 into 25 is 4, so the remainder when you divide $5p$ by 7 is $0 + 4 = 4$.

For most people this one's a lot easier to do by picking numbers. Think of an example for p and try it out. p could be 12, for example, because when you divide 12 by 7, the remainder is 5. (p could also be 19, 26, 33, or any of infinitely many more possibilities.) Now multiply your chosen p by 5: $12 \times 5 = 60$. Divide 60 by 7 and see what the remainder is: $60 \div 7 = 8$, remainder 4.

5. B

To find the y-intercept of a line from its equation, put the equation in slope-intercept form:

$$2x - 3y = 18$$

$$-3y = -2x + 18$$

$$y = \frac{2}{3}x - 6$$

In this form, the y-intercept is what comes after the x—in this case it's –6.

6. C

Set up a proportion:

$$\frac{12 \text{ pages}}{1\text{hour}} = \frac{100 \text{ pages}}{x \text{ hours}}$$

$$12x = 100$$

$$x = \frac{100}{12} = 8\frac{1}{3}$$

One-third of an hour is $\frac{1}{3}$ of 60 minutes, or 20 minutes. So $8\frac{1}{3}$ hours is 8 hours and 20 minutes.

7. E

With a right triangle you can use the 2 legs as the base and the height to figure out the area. Here the leg lengths are expressed algebraically. Just plug the 2 expressions in for b and h in the triangle area formula:

$$\text{Area} = \frac{1}{2}(x-1)(x+1)$$

$$= \frac{1}{2}(x^2-1) = \frac{x^2-1}{2}$$

8. A

The easiest way to do this problem is to subtract Bill's money from the total of the money that Jim and Bill have. Doing this gives you 15 – 4 = 11. However, the problem states that they have LESS THAN 15 dollars. Therefore, Jim must have less than 11 dollars. Of I, II, and III, the only value that is less than 11 is I, so the answer must be (A).

To solve this problem algebraically, set up an inequality where J is Jim's money and B is Bill's money:

$$J + B < 15 \text{ where } B = 4$$

$$J + 4 < 15$$

$$J < 11$$

Again, be wary of the fact that this is an inequality, NOT an equation.

9. A

Pick numbers for x and y. For instance, say that Angelo makes 20 dollars for working 5 hours and Sarah makes 20 dollars for working 4 hours. In this case, Angelo makes \$4 per hour and Sarah makes \$5. The difference between their wages is \$1 per hour. Now plug 20 in for x and 5 in for y in each of the answer choices. Which ones give you a result of 1? Only (A), which is the answer.

10. D

A square with area 16 has sides of length 4. Therefore, the largest circle that could possibly be cut from such a square would have a diameter of 4.

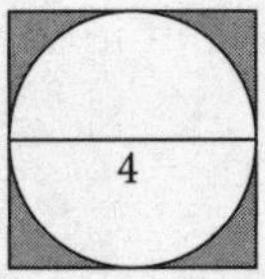

Such a circle would have a radius of 2, making its area 4π. So the amount of felt left after cutting such a circle from one of the squares of felt would be $16 - 4\pi$, or $4(4 - \pi)$. There are 8 such squares, so the total area of the left over felt is $8 \times 4(4 - \pi) = 32(4 - \pi)$.

11. D

$$q = q^{-2} = \frac{1}{q^2}$$

If $q = \frac{1}{q^2}$, then $q^3 = 1$ and $q = 1$

12. B

Backsolving is a great way to answer this question. Pick a set of p and n from the chart; then, plug them in to each given equation to see whether the pair works. If you would rather see how the equation was derived, you can follow the steps below. On test day, follow whichever approach gets you to the answer faster. The relationship between n and p can be expressed in the form $n = -kp + b$, where k and b are constants. There is a negative sign before k to indicate that as the price increases, the number of expected sales decreases. Pick two points from the chart and insert those values of p and n into this equation, then solve for k and b:

First point:

$$10{,}000 = -k(.75) + b$$

Second point:

$$5{,}000 = -k(1.00) + b$$
$$5{,}000 = -k + b$$
$$5{,}000 + k = b$$

Substitute:

$$10{,}000 = -k(.75) + 5{,}000 + k$$
$$5{,}000 = k - .75k$$
$$5{,}000 = .25k$$
$$20{,}000 = k$$
$$25{,}000 = b$$

$n = -20{,}000p + 25{,}000$

13. B

It's a good idea to know what the graphs of common equations such as $y = x^2$ look like, but if you forget or would like to double-check your answer, you can plug the x and y values of a few points on the graph into the given equations to see which one works. Be careful of using points like (0, 0), as they may work for several (or in this case, all) of the answer choices. In this case, some useful points to check are (–2, 4) and (2, 4): $4 = (-2)^2$ and $4 = 2^2$.

14. D

You can use the 2 legs of a right triangle to get the area. Here one leg is a and you can use the Pythagorean theorem to get the other leg:

$$(\text{leg}_1)^2 + (\text{leg}_2)^2 = (\text{hypotenuse})^2$$
$$a^2 + b^2 = c^2$$
$$b^2 = c^2 - a^2$$
$$b = \sqrt{c^2 - a^2}$$

Now plug the legs a and $\sqrt{c^2 - a^2}$ into the triangle area formula:

$$\text{Area} = \frac{1}{2}(\text{base})(\text{height})$$

$$= \frac{1}{2}(\text{leg}_1)(\text{leg}_2)$$

$$= \frac{1}{2}\, a\sqrt{c^2 - a^2}$$

$$= \frac{a\sqrt{c^2 - a^2}}{2}$$

15. D

The area of a triangle is equal to one-half the base times the height. You can use any of the 3 sides of a triangle for the base—each side has a height to go along with it. It doesn't make any difference which base-height pair you use—a triangle has the same area no matter how you figure it. Thus one-half times *PR* times *QS* will be the same as one-half times *PS* times *RT*:

$$\frac{1}{2}(PR)(QS) = \frac{1}{2}(PS)(RT)$$

$$\frac{1}{2}(8)(9) = \frac{1}{2}(PS)(7)$$

$$(8)(9) = (PS)(7)$$

$$(PS) = \frac{72}{7} = 10\frac{2}{7}$$

16. E

In order to find the number of possibilities, multiply the number of possibilities in each step. In other words, there are 3 routes from Bay City to Riverville and 4 routes from Riverville to Straitstown. There are 3 more routes from Straitstown to Frogs Pond, so there are 12 × 3 = 36 total routes from Bay City to Frog Pond.

SECTION 8

1. C

What claim would be *belied* or contradicted by a record of contributing to only one party? A claim of *impartiality*, of not favoring one side over the other.

2. E

Repeated breakdown of negotiations would tend to *support* or *reinforce* the view that the sides were not truly committed to *preventing* or *averting* a military confrontation. In (A) and (D), *established* and *strengthened* fit the first blank, but *escalating* and *initiating* are wrong for the second. In (B), *avoiding* fits the second blank, but *undermined* is wrong for the first.

3. B

The phrase *now that* suggests a similarity of tone between the two missing words, and the word *painful* tells us that the words will be negative. Only (B) provides a negative word for both blanks. A painful *decline* would indeed tend to cause budgetary *stringency* or tightness.

4. E

The word in the second blank has to relate in some logical way to *fear of causing leaves to fall*, and the only word that does so is *durable*, "tough, not fragile." If the plant has become more *durable*, that should be a *relief* to those who were afraid of damaging it. In (A), *consternation* is "concern or worry," and *amorphous* means "shapeless."

5. C

Words like *unchanging* and *eternal* provide a definition of the missing word, (C) *static*. (D) *Holistic* means "functioning as a whole," and (E) *homogeneous* means "all of one kind"; neither word implies species being unchanging and no new species coming into existence.

6. A

The word *but* after the comma indicates that the word in the second blank contrasts with *struggle*. (A) *Effortless* and (D) *immediate* are possibilities. The word *but* before the first blank means something like *merely*, so the word in the first blank has to suggest something small, like a faint prediction. *Glimmers* fits the meaning.

The Design Museums Passages

Passage 1

The position of the author of this passage starts to become clear in the second paragraph: she likes design museums and is willing to defend them against critics. She thinks design museums are not just advertisements for new technology but places where new products can be honored. Design museums, she asserts, are comfortable for visitors because the exhibits provide a lot of information about the objects displayed—information you wouldn't get in an art gallery. Another advantage of design museums, she says, is that their curators have more freedom than do the curators of public art galleries.

Passage 2

Author 2 does not hold technical and design museums in the same high regard as Author 1 does, you soon find out in this passage. Author 2 complains about several things: 1) technical museums concentrate on present technology and ignore historical study and research; 2) they glorify machines and industrialization when these things do harm as well as good; and 3) they do not (and cannot safely and imaginatively) show machinery in action. Author 2 does admit at the very end, however, that the public has shown a healthy curiosity about science and technology.

7. D

Author 1 says that department store windows try to sell you something, whereas design exhibits try to give you an appreciation of the aesthetic value of something. (D) paraphrases this idea. (A), (B), and (E) can be readily eliminated. Be careful with (C), though. Even though design museums focus on the artistic qualities of products, it does not automatically follow from this that design museums are not concerned at all with the commercial aspects of a successful product. (C) is wrong.

8. B

In the third paragraph of Passage 1, the author argues that design museums make visitors feel comfortable because the exhibits illustrate the purpose behind the look and function of the displayed object; art gallery exhibits, by contrast, provide no such information. From this argument you can infer that Author 1 thinks that visitors want to be informed about the object they are viewing. This makes (B) correct. There is no evidence to support any of the other choices, all of which are misreadings of paragraph 3. (A) can be eliminated as soon as you see *hostile towards . . . abstract art*. (C) and (D) contradict the author, who says that visitors are not confused by technological exhibits since they are familiar and informative. (E) is an unwarranted inference based on the author's statement that design exhibits point out the artistic qualities of the displayed items; you cannot conclude from this that most museum visitors undervalue the artistic worth of household items.

9. B

Since you just reviewed paragraph 3 for the last question, the answer to this one should jump right out at you. The difference between a design museum exhibit and an art gallery exhibit is that a design museum exhibit provides you with information about the object being displayed, whereas the art gallery exhibit does not. (B) is correct. None of the other choices has any basis in the passage.

10. C

After mentioning the collection of Zippo lighters, etc., in London's Design Museum, Author 1 says that curators of design museums have options that are far less rigorous, conventionalized, and pre-programmed than those open to curators of art galleries. This is a fancy way of saying that the curators of design museums have more freedom to put together unconventional collections (C). (E) is the tempting wrong answer to this question. It's wrong because it goes too far: the design curators have freedom, but not, as far as we know, the freedom to satisfy *their own personal whims.*

11. A

The answer to this question will be the choice that summarizes paragraph 1. Since the author spends paragraph 1 complaining that design museums ignore the historical aspect of technology, choice (A) is the best answer. (B) focuses too narrowly on the last part of the paragraph, where the author says that since industry builds the exhibits, curators may be dispensed with. This is not the underlying difficulty referred to at the beginning of the paragraph. The other choices have nothing to do with the first paragraph.

12. D

Put the phrase in context. Author 2 says that displayed machinery should be in action, not in "sculptured repose," as is the case with the machinery in technology museums. To Author 2, you can infer, the *sculptured repose* is meaningless and *unrealistic* (D). (A) is out because the author is not condemning the curators for poor planning; in fact, the author admits that displaying operating machinery would be extremely difficult. (B) can be eliminated because it's too extreme. The author never says which—if any—of the problems he discusses is the *greatest problem.* (C) and (E) miss the author's point and the context in which the phrase *sculptured repose* is found.

13. A

Predict the answer to the question before you go looking through the choices. You know that Author 2 thinks that technology has had a lot of negative consequences, so you can assume that he would point this out in response to Author 1's optimistic statement. This makes (A) the best answer. We don't know what Author 2's position on art galleries is, so (B) is out. (C) comes from Passage 2 but is irrelevant to the question asked in the stem. (D) and (E) contradict specific things Author 2 says in the course of his passage.

14. B

In questions like this one, wrong answer choices are often statements that one author, but not both, would agree with. For example, Author 2 would probably agree with choice (A) and would definitely agree with (D) and (E), but Author 1 would most likely not agree with any of these three. That narrows the field to (B) and (C). (C) is a very general statement that really has no basis in either passage. (B), on the other hand, is an idea that can be found in both passages, so it is the correct answer.

Origin of April Fool's Passage

15. A

Start by paraphrasing the sentence: "The author is stating that holidays often keep or retain traces of their origins." (A) is a close match—the holidays carry traces of their origins. (B) might be tempting, but notice it is the *traces* that endure, while the sentence is about what the holidays themselves do. (C) and (D) are common meanings of *bear*, as in "I just can't bear it," but they don't make sense here. Likewise, (E) refers to another common meaning, as in "to bear fruit," that doesn't fit either.

16. C

Laggards are people who move slowly, or lag behind. You don't need to know that to answer this question however. The passage states that the *progressive* adopters of the new calendar made fun of the laggards by calling them April Fools. So, the laggards are the people who *didn't* adopt the new calendar, (C).

(A) and (E) describe the people who invented the term April Fool's, while the question is asking about the laggards to whom the term referred. (B) misses the point that laggards are people, not holidays, and (D) refers to modern folklorists, while the laggards lived in the sixteenth century.

Music and Language Passages

17. D

The author includes lines 5–12 as evidence that in the Romantic era, folks believed that music by itself could signify *emotion* (D).

There is no evidence in the passage to support (A). While you know what the perception was during the Romantic era, there's no mention of the current perception. As for (B), though the author states that language is used functionally as opposed to music, this claim is not made specifically for Romantic Music. (C) is too extreme—the author isn't saying that Romantic music composers *always* used music to connote emotions. And (E) expresses a negativity absent from the passage.

18. A

Both authors mention the *symbolic* nature of music and language (A). Passage 1 says "Nettl has concluded that, like language, music is a 'series of symbols.'" Passage 2 says something similar in the last line.

Only the author of Passage 2 compares both to *subdivided sections* (B). Only the author of Passage 1 compares both to *functional parts* (C). As for (D), clues are never mentioned. (E) fits Passage 2 pretty well, but Passage 1 never links emotions and language. (A) is the answer.

19. B

The wrong answer here will be something that the authors agree on or something that is not mentioned at all in one of the passages. Author 1 would agree with (B), while Author 2 would disagree.

Author 2 would agree with (A) and (E), but you don't know how Author 1 would feel; she might agree, or she might disagree. Author 2 would probably disagree with (C), since context is so important, but there's no telling what Author 1 would think about the statement. (D) is too extreme—you don't know that Author 1 would agree with this.

SECTION 9

1. E

The introductory phrase doesn't modify the correct noun. The fundraiser is *arranged as an event*, not the Board of Directors. Also, the words *for funding* repeat information provided in the main clause. You need an introductory phrase that modifies the correct noun—the museum's Board of Directors. Only (E) does that. (B) and (D) don't correct the modification problem. (C) creates a run-on with a comma splice.

2. C

Ask yourself: what was developed? As it stands, the sentence tells us that the president himself was developed by a scientific team (a scary thought!). Only choice (C) corrects the problem by providing a phrase that logically modifies *the president*.

3. D

The second part of the sentence describes regions that have certain characteristics. *Only* is the correct linking word to set those regions apart. Choice (C) doesn't make sense, so (D) is correct.

4. B

Be sure you understand the logic of the sentence: the traffic rules are the *they*, and their role was not appreciated. (B) puts all these ideas into clear order by introducing the transition word *because* instead of relying on a modifier. (C) distorts the meaning of the sentence. (D) creates a misplaced modifier problem—the traffic rules fail to appreciate their role. (E) is a fragment, with no verb in an independent clause.

5. E

Choice (E) is the most clear and concise, omitting the unnecessary *when you are* from the original sentence.

6. E

The company is singular, so the use of the pronoun *they* in choices (A) and (C) is incorrect. Choices (B) and (D) awkwardly use the passive voice. (E) is the most clear and concise choice.

7. E

When comparing two people, *better* should be used instead of *best*. Only choice (E) does this correctly.

8. A

The original sentence is best.

9. B

The original sentence compares *the variety . . . of services* with *low-cost programs*, which doesn't make much sense. Choices (B) and (D) clarify the sentence by inserting *the number of*, and making a more appropriate comparison. However, choice (D) uses the wrong verb form, making choice (B) the best choice.

10. C

(C) is the only choice that corrects this run-on sentence in a logical way: *Known for his aphoristic wit and brilliant conversation* introduces Oscar Wilde; the rest of the sentence provides additional information about him. (B) contains a fragment, (D) is a run-on that presents an illogical contrast between Wilde's wit and his writing, and (E) is extremely garbled.

11. A

The sentence is correct: *maintaining* and *securing* are in the proper parallel form (both gerunds). (B) is convoluted and slightly alters the meaning of the sentence. (C) is a fragment. (D) is verbose and tangled. (E) has sacrificed correct parallel structure for the sake of brevity, comparing the *appearance* (a noun) to *securing* (a gerund).

12. C

Be sure that each verb tense is the appropriate choice in the context of the sentence. Because this sentence talks about the Renaissance, which is long over, it requires simple past tenses. Look for a choice that provides it. (B) uses the incorrect pronoun to refer to people. You need the correct form of *who.* (C) This choice provides the simple past tense that you were looking for. (D) changes the meaning of the sentence. (E) has a similar problem to (D).

13. C

What is being compared here? You can't compare an action (*watching* a video) to an object (*a book*)—it's not logical, and it violates the rules of parallelism. (C) corrects the sentence by putting the two activities in parallel form. (B) fails to fix the parallelism problem, and it introduces strange and unnecessary changes in verb tense. (D) is awkwardly phrased (would you say *book-reading*?), and (E) also fails to fix the parallelism problem, creating a somewhat confusing comparison.

14. A

If you think there are no errors in a sentence, there's at least a 20% chance that you're right. Check the sentence for common errors if you're not sure—subject-verb, pronoun agreement, parallelism, logical comparisons. If this all checks out, choose (A). (B) substitutes the incorrect conjunction, *but*, for the correct one. It also incorrectly changes the past progressive tense to the simple past. (C) changes the correct preposition *about* to *for*. (D) The subject, *three women*, is plural, so you need the plural verb *were* not was. (E) uses the wrong verb tense and changes the meaning of the sentence by changing discussing to in discussion.

Compute Your Score

The official score range for each section of the SAT will be 200–800. Taken together, the perfect total score becomes 2400. Your performance on this practice test is a good indicator of your abilities and skills.

These scores are intended to give you an approximate idea of your performance. There is no way to determine your exact score for the following reasons.

- Various statistical factors and formulas are taken into account on the real test.
- For each grade, the scaled score range changes from year to year.
- There is no way to accurately grade your essay on these practice tests. Additionally, there will be two graders reading your essay on the real test.

STEP 1: SCORE YOUR ESSAY

Your essay will account for one-third of your writing grade, and the multiple-choice questions will account for two-thirds. Your essay is scored on a scale from 1–6, and that score is later calculated with the multiple-choice score into the 200–800 range.

Naturally, it will be difficult for you to score your own essay here. Ask someone whose opinion you respect to read it and assign it a value from 1 to 6, based on the following criteria:

6. **Outstanding essay**—Though it may have a few small errors, is well organized and fully developed with supporting examples. Displays consistent language facility, varied sentence structure, and range of vocabulary.

5. **Solid essay**—Though it has occasional errors or lapses in quality, it is generally organized and well-developed with appropriate examples. Displays language facility, with syntactic variety and a range of vocabulary.

4. **Adequate essay**—Though it has some flaws, it is organized and developed adequately with some examples. Displays adequate but inconsistent language facility.

3. **Limited essay**—Does not adequately fulfill the writing assignment and has many flaws. Has inadequate organization and development, along with many errors in grammar and/or diction. Has little variety.

2. **Flawed essay**—Demonstrates some incompetence with one or more weaknesses. Ideas are vague and thinly developed. Has frequent errors in grammar and diction and has no variety.

1. **Deficient essay**—Demonstrates incompetence, with serious flaws. Has no organization, no development, and severe grammar and diction errors. Is so seriously flawed that basic meaning is obscured.

STEP 2: COMPUTE YOUR RAW SCORE

First, check your answers to the multiple-choice questions against the answer key. Count up the number of answers you got right and the number you got wrong for each section. Remember, do not count questions left blank as wrong. Round up to the nearest whole number. Now, plug them in below.

Note: Grid-in questions do not have a wrong-answer penalty. So, do not deduct anything for wrong answers.

Critical Reading

	Number Right		Number Wrong		Raw Score
Section 3:	☐	–	(.25 × ☐)	=	☐
Section 6:	☐	–	(.25 × ☐)	=	☐
Section 8:	☐	–	(.25 × ☐)	=	☐
Critical Reading Raw Score				=	☐ (rounded up)

Writing

	Number Right		Number Wrong		Raw Score
Section 1:	Use the table on pages 308–309 to match your essay score and your writing raw score to find your overall scaled score.				
Section 4:	☐	–	(.25 × ☐)	=	☐
Section 9:	☐	–	(.25 × ☐)	=	☐
Writing Raw Score				=	☐ (rounded up)

Math

	Number Right		Number Wrong		Raw Score
Section 2:	☐	×	(.25 × ☐)	=	☐
Section 5: (QUESTIONS 1–8)	☐	–	(.25 × ☐)	=	☐
Section 5: (QUESTIONS 9–18)	☐	–	(no wrong answer penalty)	=	☐
Section 7:	☐	–	(.25 × ☐)	=	☐
Math Raw Score				=	☐ (rounded up)

STEP 3: CONVERT YOUR RAW SCORE TO A SCALED SCORE

For each subject area in the practice test, convert your raw score to your scaled score using the table below.

	SCALED*								
RAW	Critical Reading	Math	Writing 0	Writing 1	Writing 2	Writing 3	Writing 4	Writing 5	Writing 6
67	800								
66	800								
65	790								
64	770								
63	750								
62	740								
61	730								
60	720								
59	700								
58	690								
57	690								
56	680								
55	670								
54	660	800							
53	650	790							
52	650	760							
51	640	740							
50	630	720							
49	620	710	670	700	720	740	780	790	800
48	620	700	660	680	700	730	760	780	790
47	610	680	650	670	690	720	750	770	780
46	600	670	640	660	680	710	740	750	770
45	600	660	630	650	670	700	740	750	770
44	590	650	620	640	660	690	730	750	760
43	590	640	600	630	650	680	710	740	750
42	580	630	600	620	640	670	700	730	750
41	570	620	590	610	630	660	690	730	740
40	570	620	580	600	620	650	690	720	740
39	560	610	570	590	610	640	680	710	740
38	550	600	560	590	610	630	670	700	730
37	550	590	550	580	600	630	660	690	720
36	540	580	540	570	590	620	650	680	710
35	540	580	540	560	580	610	640	680	710
34	530	570	530	550	570	600	640	670	700
33	520	560	520	540	560	590	630	660	690
32	520	550	510	540	560	580	620	650	680
31	520	550	500	530	550	580	610	640	670
30	510	550	490	520	540	570	600	630	660
29	510	540	490	510	530	560	590	630	650

*These are not official College Board scores. They are rough estimates to help you get an idea of your performance.

RAW	Critical Reading	Math	Writing 0	Writing 1	Writing 2	Writing 3	Writing 4	Writing 5	Writing 6
28	500	540	480	500	520	550	590	620	640
27	490	530	470	490	510	540	580	610	640
26	480	520	460	490	500	530	570	600	630
25	470	510	450	480	500	520	560	590	620
24	460	500	440	470	490	510	550	580	610
23	460	500	430	460	480	510	540	570	600
22	450	490	430	450	470	500	530	570	590
21	450	490	430	450	470	500	530	570	590
20	440	480	420	440	460	490	520	560	580
19	430	470	410	430	450	480	520	550	570
18	420	460	400	420	440	470	510	540	570
17	410	460	390	420	430	460	500	530	560
16	400	450	380	410	430	450	490	520	550
15	390	440	370	400	420	450	480	510	540
14	380	430	360	390	410	440	470	500	530
13	360	420	360	380	400	430	460	500	520
12	340	400	340	370	390	420	450	490	510
11	330	390	340	360	380	410	450	480	510
10	320	380	330	350	370	400	440	470	500
9	310	370	320	350	360	390	430	460	490
8	300	360	310	340	360	390	420	450	480
7	290	350	300	330	350	380	410	440	470
6	270	340	290	320	340	370	400	430	460
5	270	330	290	310	330	360	390	430	450
4	260	300	280	300	320	350	390	420	450
3	240	280	270	290	310	340	380	410	440
2	230	260	260	280	300	330	370	400	430
1	210	240	250	270	290	320	340	380	410
0	200	220	250	260	280	310	340	370	400
neg 1	200	200	240	260	270	290	320	360	380
neg 2	200	200	230	250	260	270	310	340	370
neg 3	200	200	220	240	250	260	300	330	360
neg 4	200	200	220	230	240	250	290	320	350
neg 5	200	200	200	220	230	240	280	310	340
neg 6	200	200	200	210	220	240	280	310	340
neg 7	200	200	200	210	220	230	270	300	330
neg 8	200	200	200	210	220	230	270	300	330
neg 9	200	200	200	210	220	230	270	300	330
neg 10	200	200	200	210	220	230	270	300	330

Part 7

Super Busy Resources

Resource A

100 Essential Math Concepts

The math on the SAT covers a lot of ground—from arithmetic to algebra to geometry.

Don't let yourself be intimidated. We've highlighted the 100 most important concepts that you'll need for SAT Math and listed them in this chapter.

Use this list to remind yourself of the key areas you'll need to know. Do four concepts a day, and you'll be ready within a month. If a concept continually causes you trouble, circle it, and refer back to it as you try to do the questions.

You've probably been taught most of these concepts in school already, so this list is a great way to refresh your memory.

NUMBER PROPERTIES

1. Number Categories

Integers are **whole numbers**; they include negative whole numbers and zero.

A **rational number** is a number that can be expressed as a **ratio of two integers**. Irrational numbers are real numbers—they have locations on the number line—but they can't be expressed precisely as a fraction or decimal. For the purposes of the SAT, the most important irrational numbers are $\sqrt{2}$, $\sqrt{3}$, and π.

2. Adding/Subtracting Signed Numbers

To **add a positive and a negative**, first ignore the signs and find the positive difference between the number parts. Then attach the sign of the original number with the larger number part. For example, to add 23 and –34, first ignore the minus sign and find the positive difference between 23 and 34—that's 11. Then attach the sign of the number with the larger number part—in this case it's the minus sign from the –34. So, $23 + (-34) = -11$.

Make **subtraction** situations simpler by turning them into addition. For example, you can think of $-17 - (-21)$ as $-17 + (+21)$.

To **add or subtract a string of positives and negatives**, first turn everything into addition. Then combine the positives and negatives so that the string is reduced to the sum of a single positive number and a single negative number.

3. Multiplying/Dividing Signed Numbers

To multiply and/or divide positives and negatives, treat the number parts as usual and **attach a minus sign if there were originally an odd number of negatives**. For example, to multiply –2, –3, and –5, first multiply the number parts: $2 \times 3 \times 5 = 30$. Then go back and note that there were *three*—an *odd* number—negatives, so the product is negative: $(-2) \times (-3) \times (-5) = -30$.

4. PEMDAS

When performing multiple operations, remember to perform them in the right order: **PEMDAS**, which means **Parentheses** first, then **Exponents**, then **Multiplication** and **Division** (left to right), and lastly **Addition** and **Subtraction** (left to right). In the expression $9 - 2 \times (5 - 3)^2 + 6 \div 3$, begin with the parentheses: $(5 - 3) = 2$. Then do the exponent: $2^2 = 4$. Now the expression is: $9 - 2 \times 4 + 6 \div 3$. Next do the multiplication and division to get: $9 - 8 + 2$, which equals 3. If you have difficulty remembering PEMDAS, use this sentence to recall it: Please Excuse My Dear Aunt Sally.

5. Counting Consecutive Integers

To count consecutive integers, **subtract the smallest from the largest and add 1**. To count the integers from 13 through 31, subtract: 31 – 13 = 18. Then add 1: 18 + 1 = 19.

NUMBER OPERATIONS AND CONCEPTS

6. Exponential Growth

If r is the ratio between consecutive terms, a_1 is the first term, a_n is the nth term, and S_n is the sum of the first n terms, then $a_n = a_1r^{n-1}$ and $S_n = \frac{a_1 - a_1r^n}{1 - r}$.

7. Union and Intersection of Sets

The things in a set are called elements or members. The union of Set A and Set B, sometimes expressed as $A \cup B$, is the set of elements that are in either or both of Set A and Set B. If Set $A = \{1, 2\}$ and Set $B = \{3, 4\}$, then $A \cup B = \{1, 2, 3, 4\}$. The intersection of Set A and Set B, sometimes expressed as $A \cap B$, is the set of elements common to both Set A and Set B. If Set $A = \{1, 2, 3\}$ and Set $B = \{3, 4, 5\}$, then $A \cap B = \{3\}$.

DIVISIBILITY

8. Factor/Multiple

The **factors** of integer n are the positive integers that divide into n with no remainder. The **multiples** of n are the integers that n divides into with no remainder. For example, 6 is a factor of 12, and 24 is a multiple of 12. 12 is both a factor and a multiple of itself, since 12 × 1 = 12 and 12 ÷ 1 = 12.

9. Prime Factorization

To find the prime factorization of an integer, just keep breaking it up into factors until **all the factors are prime**. To find the prime factorization of 36, for example, you could begin by breaking it into 4 × 9: 36 = 4 × 9 = 2 × 2 × 3 × 3.

10. Relative Primes

Relative primes are integers that have no common factor other than 1. To determine whether two integers are relative primes, break them both down to their prime factorizations. For example: 35 = 5 × 7, and 54 = 2 × 3 × 3 × 3. They have **no prime factors in common**, so 35 and 54 are relative primes.

11. Common Multiple

A common multiple is a number that is a multiple of two or more integers. You can always get a common multiple of two integers by **multiplying** them, but, unless the two numbers are relative primes, the product will not be the *least* common multiple. For example, to find a common multiple for 12 and 15, you could just multiply: $12 \times 15 = 180$.

To find the **least common multiple**, check out the **multiples of the larger integer** until you find one that's **also a multiple of the smaller**. To find the LCM of 12 and 15, begin by taking the multiples of 15: 15 is not divisible by 12; 30 is not; nor is 45. But the next multiple of 15, 60, *is* divisible by 12, so it's the LCM.

12. Greatest Common Factor (GCF)

To find the greatest common factor, break down both integers into their prime factorizations and multiply **all the prime factors they have in common**. $36 = 2 \times 2 \times 3 \times 3$, and $48 = 2 \times 2 \times 2 \times 2 \times 3$. What they have in common is two 2s and one 3, so the GCF is $2 \times 2 \times 3 = 12$.

13. Even/Odd

To predict whether a sum, difference, or product will be even or odd, just **take simple numbers like 1 and 2 and see what happens**. There are rules—"odd times even is even," for example—but there's no need to memorize them. What happens with one set of numbers generally happens with all similar sets.

14. Multiples of 2 and 4

An integer is divisible by 2 (even) if the **last digit** is even. An integer is divisible by 4 if the **last two digits form a multiple of 4**. The last digit of 562 is 2, which is even, so 562 is a multiple of 2. The last two digits form 62, which is *not* divisible by 4, so 562 is not a multiple of 4. The integer 512, however is divisible by four because the last two digits form 12, which is a multiple of 4.

15. Multiples of 3 and 9

An integer is divisible by 3 if the **sum of its digits is divisible by 3**. An integer is divisible by 9 if the **sum of its digits is divisible by 9**. The sum of the digits in 957 is 21, which is divisible by 3 but not by 9, so 957 is divisible by 3 but not by 9.

16. Multiples of 5 and 10

An integer is divisible by 5 if the **last digit is 5 or 0**. An integer is divisible by 10 if the **last digit is 0**. The last digit of 665 is 5, so 665 is a multiple of 5 but *not* a multiple of 10.

17. Remainders

The remainder is the **whole number left over after division**. 487 is 2 more than 485, which is a multiple of 5, so when 487 is divided by 5, the remainder will be 2.

FRACTIONS AND DECIMALS

18. Reducing Fractions

To reduce a fraction to lowest terms, **factor out and cancel** all factors the numerator and denominator have in common.

$$\frac{28}{36} = \frac{4 \times 7}{4 \times 9} = \frac{7}{9}$$

19. Adding/Subtracting Fractions

To add or subtract fractions, first find a **common denominator**, then add or subtract the numerators.

$$\frac{2}{15} + \frac{3}{10} = \frac{4}{30} + \frac{9}{30} = \frac{4+9}{30} = \frac{13}{30}$$

20. Multiplying Fractions

To multiply fractions, **multiply** the numerators and **multiply** the denominators.

$$\frac{5}{7} \times \frac{3}{4} = \frac{5 \times 3}{7 \times 4} = \frac{15}{28}$$

21. Dividing Fractions

To divide fractions, **invert** the second one and **multiply**.

$$\frac{1}{2} \div \frac{3}{5} = \frac{1}{2} \times \frac{5}{3} = \frac{1 \times 5}{2 \times 3} = \frac{5}{6}$$

22. Mixed Numbers and Improper Fractions

To convert a mixed number to an improper fraction, **multiply** the whole number part by the denominator, then **add** the numerator. The result is the new numerator (over the same denominator). To convert $7\frac{1}{3}$, first multiply 7 by 3, then add 1, to get the new numerator of 22. Put that over the same denominator, 3, to get $\frac{22}{3}$.

To convert an improper fraction to a mixed number, divide the denominator into the numerator to get a **whole number quotient with a remainder**. The quotient becomes the whole number part of the mixed number, and the remainder becomes the new numerator—with the same denominator. For example, to convert $\frac{108}{5}$, first divide 5 into 108, which yields 21 with a remainder of 3. Therefore, $\frac{108}{5} = 21\frac{3}{5}$.

23. Reciprocal

To find the reciprocal of a fraction, **switch the numerator and the denominator**. The reciprocal of $\frac{3}{7}$ is $\frac{7}{3}$. The reciprocal of 5 is $\frac{1}{5}$. The product of reciprocals is 1.

24. Comparing Fractions

One way to compare fractions is to **re-express them with a common denominator**. $\frac{3}{4} = \frac{21}{28}$ and $\frac{5}{7} = \frac{20}{28}$. $\frac{21}{28}$ is greater than $\frac{20}{28}$, so $\frac{3}{4}$ is greater than $\frac{5}{7}$. Another method is to **convert them both to decimals**. $\frac{3}{4}$ converts to .75, and $\frac{5}{7}$ converts to approximately .714.

25. Converting Fractions and Decimals

To convert a fraction to a decimal, **divide the bottom into the top**. To convert $\frac{5}{8}$, divide 8 into 5, yielding .625.

To convert a decimal to a fraction, set the decimal over 1 and **multiply the numerator and denominator by 10** raised to the number of digits to the right of the decimal point.

To convert .625 to a fraction, you would multiply $\frac{.625}{1}$ by $\frac{10^3}{10^3}$ or $\frac{1{,}000}{1{,}000}$.

Then simplify: $\frac{625}{1{,}000} = \frac{5 \times 125}{8 \times 125} = \frac{5}{8}$.

26. Repeating Decimal

To find a particular digit in a repeating decimal, note the **number of digits in the cluster that repeats**. If there are 2 digits in that cluster, then every second digit is the same. If there are 3 digits in that cluster, then every third digit is the same. And so on. For example, the decimal equivalent of $\frac{1}{27}$ is .037037037 . . . , which is best written $.\overline{037}$. There are 3 digits in the repeating cluster, so every third digit is the same: 7. To find the 50th digit, look for the multiple of 3 just less than 50—that's 48. The 48th digit is 7, and with the 49th digit the pattern repeats with 0. The 50th digit is 3.

27. Identifying the Parts and the Whole

The key to solving most fractions and percents story problems is to identify the **part** and the whole. Usually you'll find the part associated with the verb ***is/are*** and the **whole** associated with the word ***of***. In the sentence, "Half of the boys are blonds," the whole is the boys ("*of* the boys"), and the part is the blonds ("*are* blonds").

PERCENTS

28. Percent Formula

Whether you need to find the part, the whole, or the percent, use the same formula:

Part = Percent × Whole

Example: What is 12 percent of 25?
Setup: Part = .12 × 25

Example: 15 is 3 percent of what number?
Setup: 15 = .03 × Whole

Example: 45 is what percent of 9?
Setup: 45 = Percent × 9

29. Percent Increase and Decrease

To increase a number by a percent, **add the percent to 100 percent**, convert to a decimal, and multiply. To increase 40 by 25 percent, add 25 percent to 100 percent, convert 125 percent to 1.25, and multiply by 40. 1.25 × 40 = 50.

30. Finding the Original Whole

To find the **original whole before a percent increase or decrease**, set up an equation. Think of the result of a 15 percent increase over x as $1.15x$.

Example: After a 5 percent increase, the population was 59,346. What was the population before the increase?
Setup: $1.05x = 59{,}346$

31. Combined Percent Increase and Decrease

To determine the combined effect of multiple percent increases and/or decreases, **start with 100 and see what happens**.

Example: A price went up 10 percent one year, and the new price went up 20 percent the next year. What was the combined percent increase?

Setup: First year: 100 + (10 percent of 100) = 110. Second year: 110 + (20 percent of 110) = 132. That's a combined 32 percent increase.

RATIOS, PROPORTIONS, AND RATES

32. Setting up a Ratio

To find a ratio, put the number associated with the word ***of*** **on top** and the quantity associated with the word ***to*** **on the bottom** and reduce. The ratio of 20 oranges to 12 apples is $\frac{20}{12}$, which reduces to $\frac{5}{3}$.

33. Part-to-Part Ratios and Part-to-Whole Ratios

If the parts add up to the whole, a part-to-part ratio can be turned into two part-to-whole ratios by putting **each number in the original ratio over the sum of the numbers**. If the ratio of males to females is 1 to 2, then the males-to-people ratio is $\frac{1}{1+2} = \frac{1}{3}$ and the females-to-people ratio is $\frac{2}{1+2} = \frac{2}{3}$. In other words, $\frac{2}{3}$ of all the people are female.

34. Solving a Proportion

To solve a proportion, cross multiply:

$$\frac{x}{5} = \frac{3}{4}$$
$$4x = 3 \times 5$$
$$x = \frac{15}{3} = 3.75$$

35. Rate

To solve a rates problem, **use the units** to keep things straight.

Example: If snow is falling at the rate of one foot every four hours, how many inches of snow will fall in seven hours?

Setup:

$$\frac{1 \text{ foot}}{4 \text{ hours}} = \frac{x \text{ inches}}{7 \text{ hours}}$$
$$\frac{12 \text{ inches}}{4 \text{ hours}} = \frac{x \text{ inches}}{7 \text{ hours}}$$
$$4x = 12 \times 7$$
$$x = 21$$

36. Average Rate

Average rate is *not* simply the average of the rates.

$$\text{Average } A \text{ per } B = \frac{\text{Total } A}{\text{Total } B}$$

$$\text{Average Speed} = \frac{\text{Total distance}}{\text{Total time}}$$

To find the average speed for 120 miles at 40 mph and 120 miles at 60 mph, **don't just average the two speeds**. First, figure out the total distance and the total time. The total distance is 120 + 120 = 240 miles. The times are two hours for the first leg and three hours for the second leg, or five hours total. The average speed, then, is $\frac{240}{5} = 48$ miles per hour.

AVERAGES

37. Average Formula

To find the average of a set of numbers, **add them up and divide by the number of numbers**.

$$\textbf{Average} = \frac{\textbf{Sum of the terms}}{\textbf{Number of terms}}$$

To find the average of the 5 numbers 12, 15, 23, 40, and 40, first add them: 12 + 15 + 23 + 40 + 40 = 130. Then, divide the sum by 5: 130 ÷ 5 = 26.

38. Average of Evenly Spaced Numbers

To find the average of evenly spaced numbers, just **average the smallest and the largest**. The average of all the integers from 13 through 77 is the same as the average of 13 and 77:

$$\frac{13 + 77}{2} = \frac{90}{2} = 45$$

39. Using the Average to Find the Sum

Sum = (Average) × (Number of terms)

If the average of 10 numbers is 50, then they add up to 10 × 50, or 500.

40. Finding the Missing Number

To find a missing number when you're given the average, **use the sum**. If the average of 4 numbers is 7, then the sum of those 4 numbers is 4 × 7, or 28. Suppose that 3 of the numbers are 3, 5, and 8. These 3 numbers add up to 16 of that 28, which leaves 12 for the fourth number.

41. Median and Mode

The median of a set of numbers is the **value that falls in the middle of the set**. If you have 5 test scores, and they are 88, 86, 57, 94, and 73, you must first list the scores in increasing or decreasing order: 57, 73, 86, 88, 94.

The median is the middle number, or 86. If there is an even number of values in a set (6 test scores, for instance), simply take the average of the 2 middle numbers.

The mode of a set of numbers is the **value that appears most often**. If your test scores were 88, 57, 68, 85, 99, 93, 93, 84, and 81, the mode of the scores would be 93 because it appears more often than any other score. If there is a tie for the most common value in a set, the set has more than one mode.

POSSIBILITIES AND PROBABILITY

42. Counting the Possibilities

The fundamental counting principle: If there are ***m* ways** one event can happen and ***n* ways** a second event can happen, then there are ***m* × *n* ways** for the 2 events to happen. For example, with 5 shirts and 7 pairs of pants to choose from, you can have 5 × 7 = 35 different outfits.

43. Probability

$$\textbf{Probability} = \frac{\textbf{Favorable Outcomes}}{\textbf{Total Possible Outcomes}}$$

For example, if you have 12 shirts in a drawer and 9 of them are white, the probability of picking a white shirt at random is $\frac{9}{12} = \frac{3}{4}$. This probability can also be expressed as .75 or 75%.

POWERS AND ROOTS

44. Multiplying and Dividing Powers

To multiply powers with the same base, **add the exponents and keep the same base**:

$$x^3 \times x^4 = x^{3+4} = x^7$$

To divide powers with the same base, **subtract the exponents and keep the same base**:

$$y^{13} \div y^8 = y^{13-8} = y^5$$

45. Raising Powers to Powers

To raise a power to a power, **multiply the exponents**:

$$(x^3)^4 = x^{3 \times 4} = x^{12}$$

46. Simplifying Square Roots

To simplify a square root, **factor out the perfect squares** under the radical, unsquare them, and put the result in front.

$$\sqrt{12} = \sqrt{4 \times 3} = \sqrt{4} \times \sqrt{3} = 2\sqrt{3}$$

47. Adding and Subtracting Roots

You can add or subtract radical expressions **when the part under the radicals is the same**:

$$2\sqrt{3} + 3\sqrt{3} = 5\sqrt{3}$$

Don't try to add or subtract when the radical parts are different. There's not much you can do with an expression like:

$$3\sqrt{5} + 3\sqrt{7}$$

48. Multiplying and Dividing Roots

The product of square roots is equal to the **square root of the product**:

$$\sqrt{3} \times \sqrt{5} = \sqrt{3 \times 5} = \sqrt{15}$$

The quotient of square roots is equal to the **square root of the quotient**:

$$\frac{\sqrt{6}}{\sqrt{3}} = \sqrt{\frac{6}{3}} = \sqrt{2}$$

49. Negative Exponent and Rational Exponent

To find the value of a number raised to a negative exponent, simply rewrite the number, without the negative sign, as the bottom of a fraction with 1 as the numerator of the fraction: $3^{-2} = \frac{1}{3^2} = \frac{1}{9}$. If x is a positive number and a is a nonzero number, then $x^{\frac{1}{a}} = \sqrt[a]{x}$. So $4^{\frac{1}{2}} = \sqrt[2]{4} = 2$. If p and q are integers, then $x^{\frac{p}{q}} = \sqrt[q]{x^p}$. So $4^{\frac{3}{2}} = \sqrt[2]{4^3} = \sqrt{64} = 8$.

ABSOLUTE VALUE

50. Determining Absolute Value

The absolute value of a number is the distance of the number from zero on the number line. Because absolute value is a distance, it is always positive. The absolute value of 7 is 7; this is expressed $|7| = 7$. Similarly, the absolute value of –7 is 7: $|-7| = 7$. Every positive number is the absolute value of 2 numbers: itself and its negative.

ALGEBRAIC EXPRESSIONS

51. Evaluating an Expression

To evaluate an algebraic expression, **plug in** the given values for the unknowns and calculate according to **PEMDAS**. To find the value of $x^2 + 5x - 6$ when $x = -2$, plug in –2 for x: $(-2)^2 + 5(-2) - 6 = -12$.

52. Adding and Subtracting Monomials

To combine like terms, **keep the variable part unchanged while adding or subtracting the coefficients**:

$$2a + 3a = (2 + 3)a = 5a$$

53. Adding and Subtracting Polynomials

To add or subtract polynomials, **combine like terms**.

$$(3x^2 + 5x - 7) - (x^2 + 12) =$$
$$(3x^2 - x^2) + 5x + (-7 - 12) =$$
$$2x^2 + 5x - 19 =$$

54. Multiplying Monomials

To multiply monomials, **multiply the coefficients and the variables separately**:

$$2a \times 3a = (2 \times 3)(a \times a) = 6a^2$$

55. Multiplying Binomials—FOIL

To multiply binomials, use **FOIL**. To multiply $(x + 3)$ by $(x + 4)$, first multiply the **F**irst terms: $x \times x = x^2$. Next the **O**uter terms: $x \times 4 = 4x$. Then the **I**nner terms: $3 \times x = 3x$. And finally the **L**ast terms: $3 \times 4 = 12$. Then add and combine like terms:

$$x^2 + 4x + 3x + 12 = x^2 + 7x + 12$$

56. Multiplying Other Polynomials

FOIL works only when you want to multiply two binomials. If you want to multiply polynomials with more than two terms, make sure you **multiply each term in the first polynomial by each term in the second**.

$$(x^2 + 3x + 4)(x + 5) =$$
$$x^2(x + 5) + 3x(x + 5) + 4(x + 5) =$$
$$x^3 + 5x^2 + 3x^2 + 15x + 4x + 20 =$$
$$x^3 + 8x^2 + 19x + 20$$

After multiplying two polynomials together, the number of terms in your expression before simplifying should equal the number of terms in one polynomial multiplied by the number of terms in the second. In the example, you should have $3 \times 2 = 6$ terms in the product before you simplify like terms.

FACTORING ALGEBRAIC EXPRESSIONS

57. Factoring out a Common Divisor

A factor common to all terms of a polynomial can be **factored out**. All three terms in the polynomial $3x^3 + 12x^2 - 6x$ contain a factor of $3x$. Pulling out the common factor yields $3x(x^2 + 4x - 2)$.

58. Factoring the Difference of Squares

One of the test maker's favorite factorables is the **difference of squares**.

$$\mathbf{a^2 - b^2 = (a - b)(a + b)}$$

$x^2 - 9$, for example, factors to $(x - 3)(x + 3)$.

59. Factoring the Square of a Binomial

Recognize polynomials that are squares of binomials:

$$\mathbf{a^2 + 2ab + b^2 = (a + b)^2}$$
$$\mathbf{a^2 - 2ab + b^2 = (a - b)^2}$$

For example, $4x^2 + 12x + 9$ factors to $(2x + 3)^2$, and $n^2 - 10n + 25$ factors to $(n - 5)^2$.

60. Factoring Other Polynomials—FOIL in Reverse

To factor a quadratic expression, **think about what binomials you could use FOIL on to get that quadratic expression**. To factor $x^2 - 5x + 6$, think about what **F**irst terms will produce x^2, what **L**ast terms will produce +6, and what **O**uter and **I**nner terms will produce $-5x$. Some common sense—and a little trial and error—lead you to $(x - 2)(x - 3)$.

61. Simplifying an Algebraic Fraction

Simplifying an algebraic fraction is a lot like simplifying a numerical fraction. The general idea is to **find factors common to the numerator and denominator and cancel them**. Thus, simplifying an algebraic fraction begins with factoring.

For example, to simplify $\frac{x^2 - x - 12}{x^2 - 9}$, first factor the numerator and denominator:

$$\frac{x^2 - x - 12}{x^2 - 9} = \frac{(x - 4)(x + 3)}{(x - 3)(x + 3)}$$

Canceling $x + 3$ from the numerator and denominator leaves you with $\frac{(x - 4)}{(x - 3)}$.

SOLVING EQUATIONS

62. Solving a Linear Equation

To solve an equation, do whatever is necessary to both sides to **isolate the variable**. To solve the equation $5x - 12 = -2x + 9$, first get all the x's on one side by adding $2x$ to both sides: $7x - 12 = 9$. Then add 12 to both sides: $7x = 21$. Then divide both sides by 7: $x = 3$.

63. Solving "in Terms Of"

To solve an equation for one variable **in terms of** another means to **isolate the one variable on one side of the equation**, leaving an expression containing the other variable on the other side of the equation. To solve the equation $3x - 10y = -5x + 6y$ for x in terms of y, isolate x:

$$3x - 10y = -5x + 6y$$
$$3x + 5x = 6y + 10y$$
$$8x = 16y$$
$$x = 2y$$

64. Translating from English into Algebra

To translate from English into algebra, look for the key words and systematically turn phrases into algebraic expressions and sentences into equations. Be careful about order, especially when subtraction is called for.

Example: The charge for a phone call is r cents for the first 3 minutes and s cents for each minute thereafter. What is the cost, in cents, of a phone call lasting exactly t minutes? ($t > 3$)

Setup: The charge begins with r, and then something more is added, depending on the length of the call. The amount added is s times the number of minutes past 3 minutes. If the total number of minutes is t, then the number of minutes past 3 is $t - 3$. So the charge is $r + s(t - 3)$.

65. Solving a Quadratic Equation

To solve a quadratic equation, put it in the "$ax^2 + bx + c = 0$" form, **factor** the left side (if you can), and set each factor equal to 0 separately to get the two solutions. To solve $x^2 + 12 = 7x$, first rewrite it as $x^2 - 7x + 12 = 0$. Then factor the left side:

$$(x - 3)(x - 4) = 0$$

$$x - 3 = 0 \text{ or } x - 4 = 0$$

$$x = 3 \text{ or } 4$$

66. Solving a System of Equations

You can solve for 2 variables only if you have 2 distinct equations. 2 forms of the same equation will not be adequate. **Combine the equations** in such a way that **one of the variables cancels out**. To solve the 2 equations $4x + 3y = 8$ and $x + y = 3$, multiply both sides of the second equation by -3 to get: $-3x - 3y = -9$. Now add the 2 equations; the $3y$ and the $-3y$ cancel out, leaving: $x = -1$. Plug that back into either one of the original equations and you'll find that $y = 4$.

67. Solving an Inequality

To solve an inequality, do whatever is necessary to both sides to **isolate the variable**. Just remember that when you **multiply or divide both sides by a negative number**, you must **reverse the sign**. To solve $-5x + 7 < -3$, subtract 7 from both sides to get: $-5x < -10$. Now divide both sides by -5, remembering to reverse the sign: $x > 2$.

68. Radical Equations

A radical equation contains at least one radical expression. Solve radical equations by using standard rules of algebra. If $5\sqrt{x} - 2 = 13$, then $5\sqrt{x} = 15$ and $\sqrt{x} = 3$, so $x = 9$.

FUNCTIONS

69. Function Notation and Evaluation

Standard function notation is written $f(x)$ and read "f of x." To evaluate the function $f(x) = 2x + 3$ for $f(4)$, replace x with 4 and simplify: $f(4) = 2(4) + 3 = 11$.

70. Direct and Inverse Variation

In direct variation, $y = kx$, where k is a nonzero constant. In direct variation, the variable y changes directly as x does. If a unit of Currency A is worth 2 units of Currency B, then $A = 2B$. If the number of units of B were to double, the number of units of A would double, and so on for halving, tripling, etc. In inverse variation, $xy = k$, where x and y are variables and k is a constant. A famous inverse relationship is *rate* × *time* = *distance*, where distance is constant. Imagine having to cover a distance of 24 miles. If you were to travel at 12 miles per hour, you'd need 2 hours. But if you were to halve your rate, you would have to double your time. This is just another way of saying that rate and time vary inversely.

71. Domain and Range of a Function

The domain of a function is the set of values for which the function is defined. For example, the domain of $f(x) = \frac{1}{1 - x^2}$ is all values of x except 1 and −1, because for those values the denominator has a value of 0 and is therefore undefined. The range of a function is the set of outputs or results of the function. For example, the range of $f(x) = x^2$ is all numbers greater than all or equal to zero, because x^2 cannot be negative.

COORDINATE GEOMETRY

72. Finding the Distance Between Two Points

To find the distance between points, **use the Pythagorean theorem** or **special right triangles**. The difference between the x's is one leg and the difference between the y's is the other.

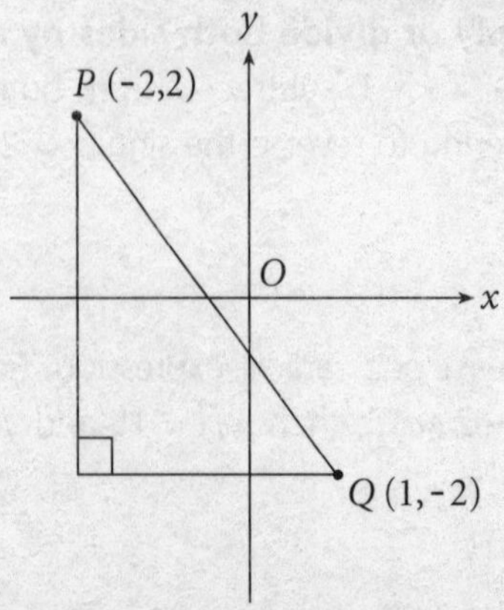

In the figure above, *PQ* is the hypotenuse of a 3-4-5 triangle, so *PQ* = 5.

You can also use the **distance formula**:

$$d = \sqrt{(x_1 - x_2)^2 + (y_1 - y_2)^2}$$

To find the distance between *R*(3, 6) and *S*(5, –2):

$$d = \sqrt{(3-5)^2 + [6-(-2)^2]}$$

$$= \sqrt{(-2)^2 + (8)^2}$$

$$= \sqrt{68} = 2\sqrt{17}$$

73. Using Two Points to Find the Slope

$$\textbf{Slope} = \frac{\textbf{Change in } y}{\textbf{Change in } x} = \frac{\textbf{Rise}}{\textbf{Run}}$$

The slope of the line that contains the points *A*(2, 3) and *B*(0, –1) is:

$$\frac{y_A - y_B}{x_A - x_B} = \frac{3-(-1)}{2-0} = \frac{4}{2} = 2$$

74. Using an Equation to Find the Slope

To find the slope of a line from an equation, put the equation into the **slope-intercept** form:

$$y = mx + b$$

The **slope is** m. To find the slope of the equation $3x + 2y = 4$, rearrange it:

$$3x + 2y = 4$$

$$2y = -3x + 4$$

$$y = -\frac{3}{2}x + 2$$

The slope is $-\frac{3}{2}$.

75. Using an Equation to Find an Intercept

To find the *y*-intercept, you can either put the equation into $y = mx + b$ **(slope-intercept)** form—in which case **b is the y-intercept**—or you can just **plug $x = 0$** into the equation and **solve for y**. To find the *x*-intercept, plug $y = 0$ into the equation and **solve for x**.

LINES AND ANGLES

76. Intersecting Lines

When two lines intersect, **adjacent angles are supplementary and vertical angles are equal**.

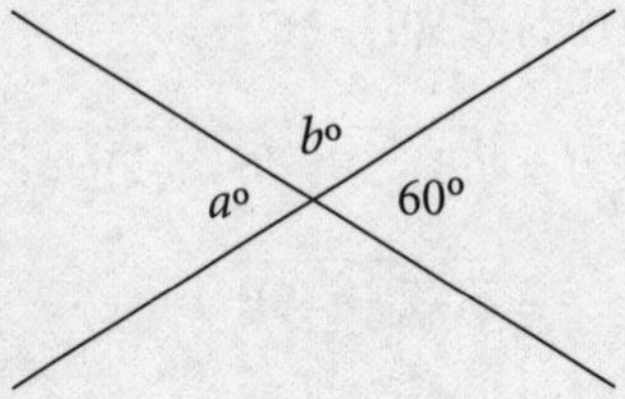

In the figure above, the angles marked $a°$ and $b°$ are adjacent and supplementary, so $a + b = 180$. Furthermore, the angles marked $a°$ and $60°$ are vertical and equal, so $a = 60$.

77. Parallel Lines and Transversals

A transversal across parallel lines forms **four equal acute angles and four equal obtuse angles**.

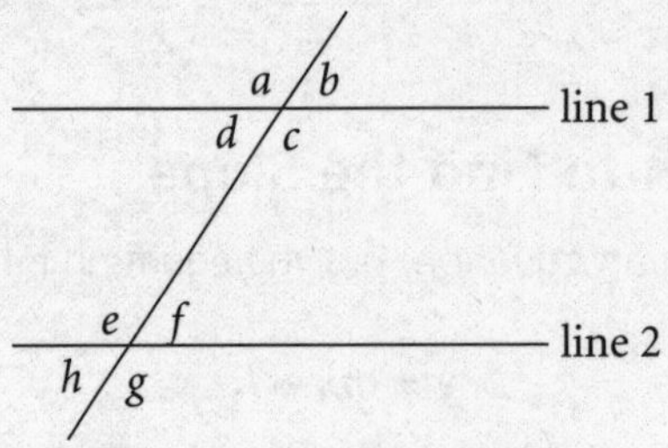

In the figure above, line 1 is parallel to line 2. Angles *a, c, e,* and *g* are obtuse, so they are all equal. Angles *b, d, f,* and *h* are acute, so they are all equal.

Furthermore, **any of the acute angles is supplementary to any of the obtuse angles**. Angles *a* and *h* are supplementary, as are *b* and *e, c* and *f,* and so on.

TRIANGLES—GENERAL

78. Interior and Exterior Angles of a Triangle

The 3 angles of any triangle **add up to 180 degrees**.

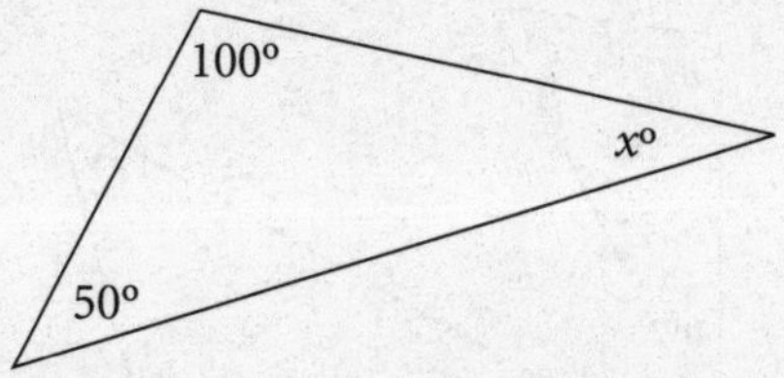

In the figure above, $x + 50 + 100 = 180$, so $x = 30$.

An exterior angle of a triangle is equal to the **sum of the remote interior angles**.

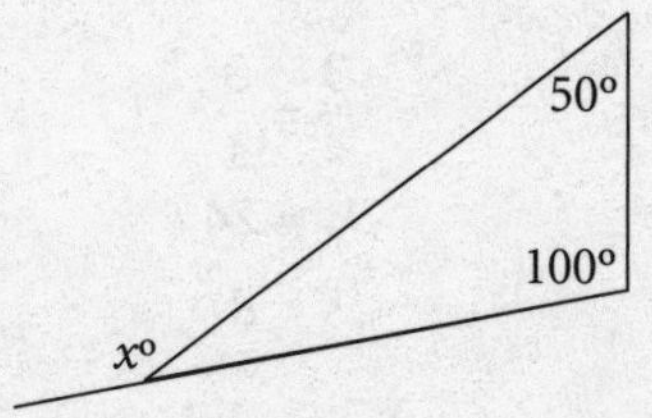

In the figure above, the exterior angle labeled $x°$ is equal to the sum of the remote angles: $x = 50 + 100 = 150$.

The 3 exterior angles of a triangle add up to 360 degrees.

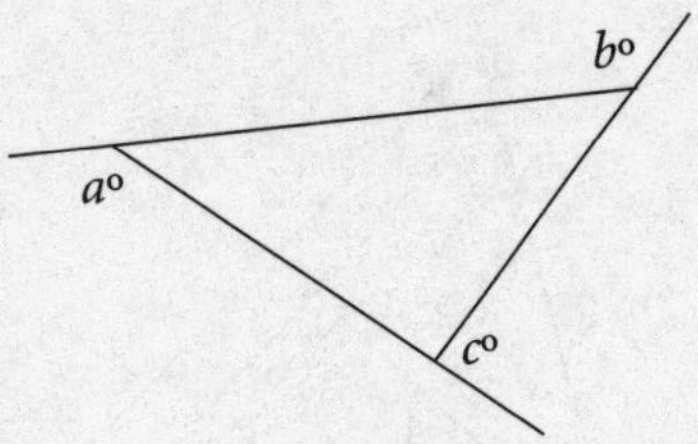

In the figure above, $a + b + c = 360$.

79. Similar Triangles

Similar triangles have the same shape: **corresponding angles are equal and corresponding sides are proportional**.

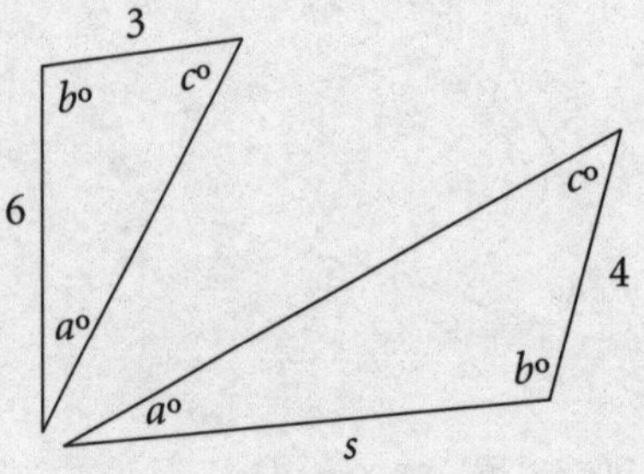

The triangles above are similar because they have the same angles. The 3 corresponds to the 4 and the 6 corresponds to the s.

$$\frac{3}{4} = \frac{6}{s}$$
$$3s = 24$$
$$s = 8$$

80. Area of a Triangle

$$\textbf{Area of Triangle} = \frac{1}{2}\textbf{(base)(height)}$$

The height is the perpendicular distance between the side that's chosen as the base and the opposite vertex.

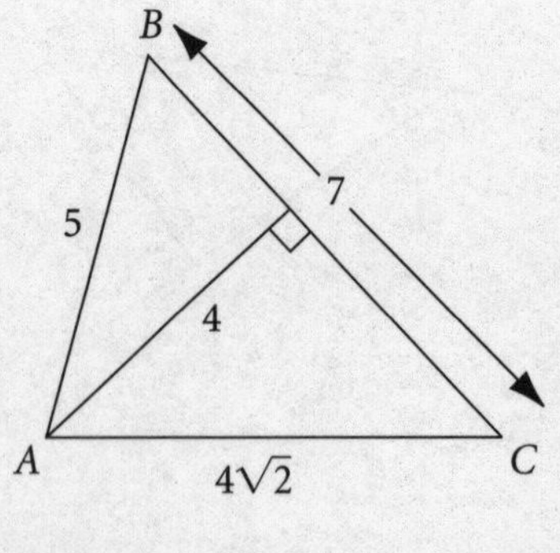

In the triangle above, 4 is the height when the 7 is chosen as the base.

$$\text{Area} = \frac{1}{2}bh = \frac{1}{2}(7)(4) = 14$$

81. Triangle Inequality Theorem

The length of one side of a triangle must be **greater than the difference and less than the sum** of the lengths of the other two sides. For example, if it is given that the length of one side is 3 and the length of another side is 7, then you know that the length of the third side must be greater than 7 – 3 = 4 and less than 7 + 3 = 10.

82. Isosceles and Equilateral Triangles

An isosceles triangle is a triangle that has **2 equal sides**. Not only are 2 sides equal, but the angles opposite the equal sides, called **base angles**, are also equal.

Equilateral triangles are triangles in which **all 3 sides are equal**. Since all the sides are equal, all the angles are also equal. All 3 angles in an equilateral triangle measure 60 degrees, regardless of the lengths of sides.

RIGHT TRIANGLES

83. Pythagorean Theorem

For all right triangles:

$$(\text{leg}_1)^2 + (\text{leg}_2)^2 = (\text{hypotenuse})^2$$

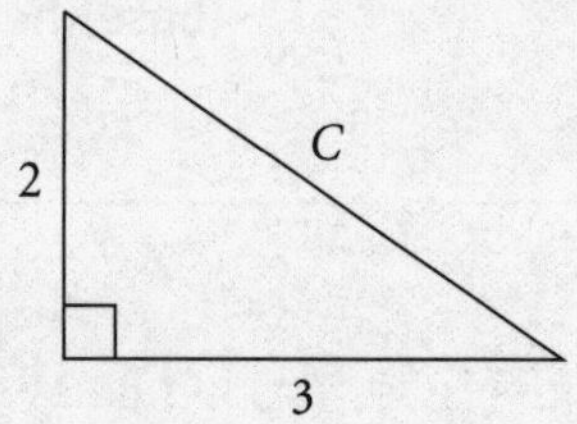

If one leg is 2 and the other leg is 3, then:

$$2^2 + 3^2 = c^2$$
$$c^2 = 4 + 9$$
$$c = \sqrt{13}$$

84. The 3-4-5 Triangle

If a right triangle's leg-to-leg ratio is 3:4, or if the leg-to-hypotenuse ratio is 3:5 or 4:5, it's a 3-4-5 triangle and you don't need to use the Pythagorean theorem to find the third side. Just figure out what multiple of 3-4-5 it is.

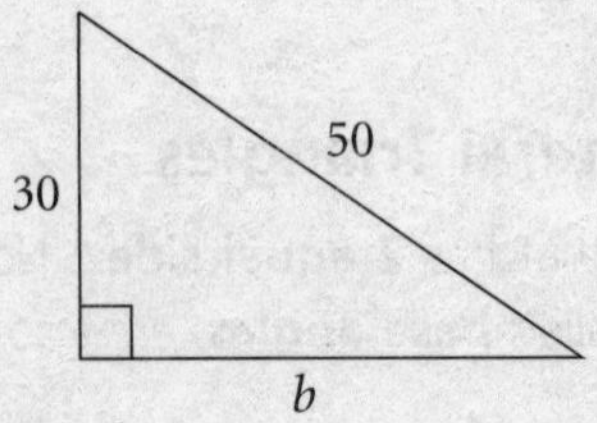

In the right triangle shown, one leg is 30 and the hypotenuse is 50. This is 10 times 3-4-5. The other leg is 40.

85. The 5-12-13 Triangle

If a right triangle's leg-to-leg ratio is 5:12, or if the leg-to-hypotenuse ratio is 5:13 or 12:13, then it's a 5-12-13 triangle and you don't need to use the Pythagorean theorem to find the third side. Just figure out what multiple of 5-12-13 it is.

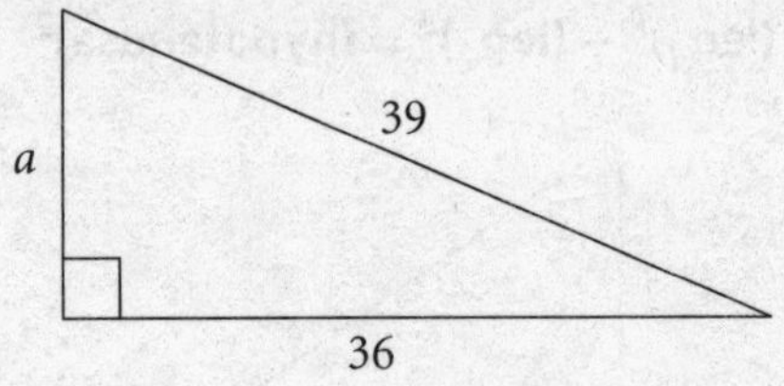

Here one leg is 36 and the hypotenuse is 39. This is 3 times 5-12-13. The other leg is 15.

86. The 30-60-90 Triangle

The sides of a 30-60-90 triangle are in a ratio of $\boldsymbol{x : x\sqrt{3} : 2x}$. You don't need the Pythagorean theorem.

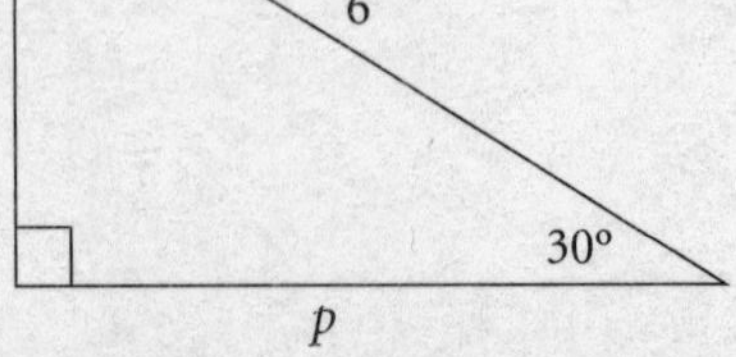

If the hypotenuse is 6, then the shorter leg is half that, or 3; and then the longer leg is equal to the short leg times $\sqrt{3}$, or $3\sqrt{3}$.

87. The 45-45-90 Triangle

The sides of a 45-45-90 triangle are in a ratio of $\boldsymbol{x : x : x\sqrt{2}}$.

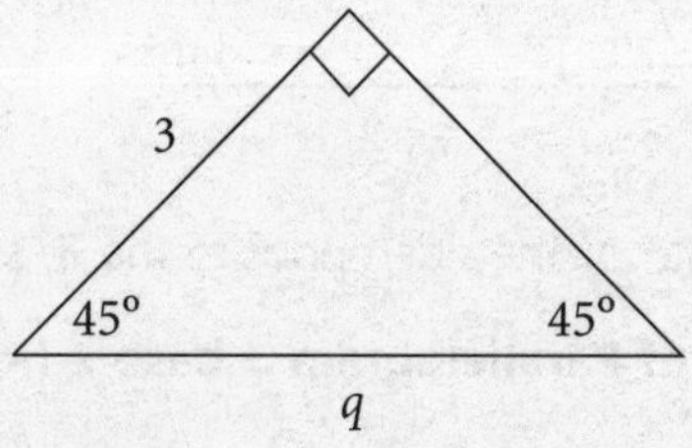

If one leg is 3, then the other leg is also 3, and the hypotenuse is equal to a leg times $\sqrt{2}$, or $3\sqrt{2}$.

OTHER POLYGONS

88. Characteristics of a Rectangle

A rectangle is a **four-sided figure with four right angles**. Opposite sides are equal. Diagonals are equal.

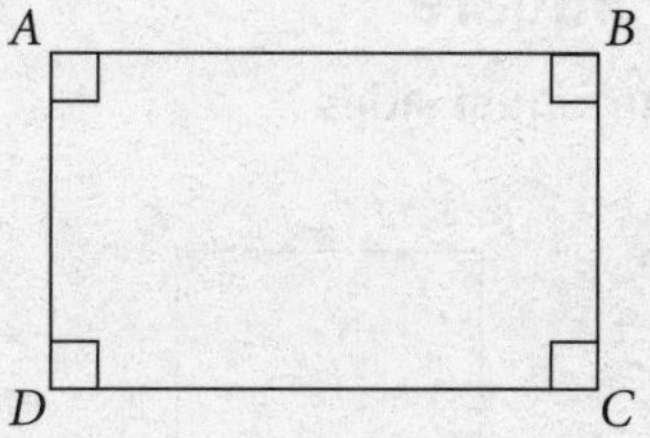

Quadrilateral *ABCD* above is shown to have three right angles. The fourth angle therefore also measures 90 degrees, and *ABCD* is a rectangle. The perimeter of a rectangle is equal to the sum of the lengths of the four sides, which is equivalent to 2(length + width).

Area of Rectangle = length × width

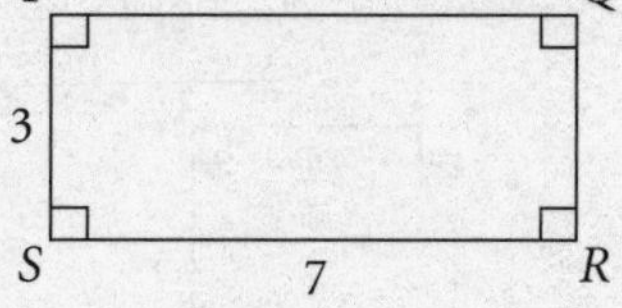

The area of a 7-by-3 rectangle is $7 \times 3 = 21$.

89. Characteristics of a Parallelogram

A parallelogram has **two pairs of parallel sides**. Opposite sides are equal. Opposite angles are equal. Consecutive angles add up to 180 degrees.

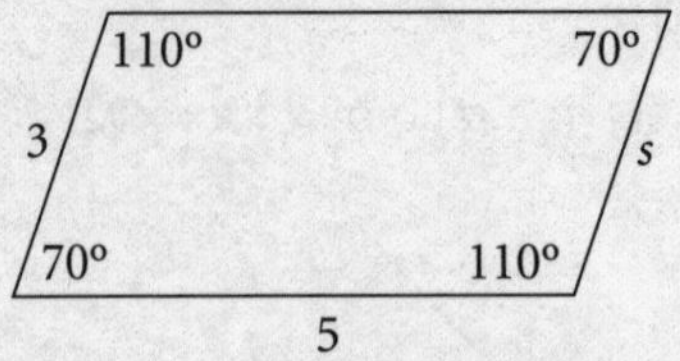

In the figure above, *s* is the length of the side opposite the 3, so *s* = 3.

Area of Parallelogram = base × height

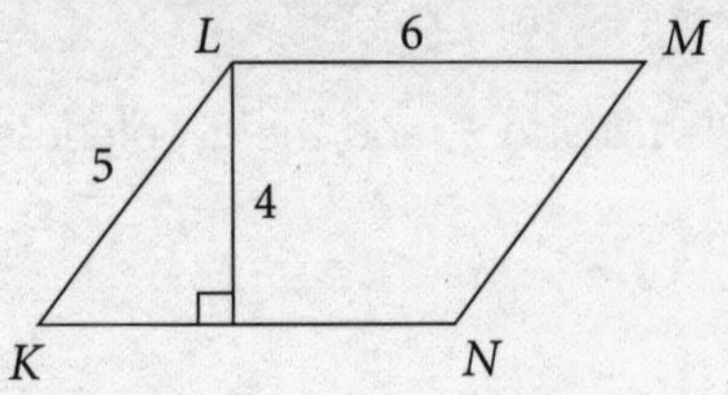

In parallelogram *KLMN* above, 4 is the height when *LM* or *KN* is used as the base.

Base × height = 6 × 4 = 24.

90. Characteristics of a Square

A square is a **rectangle with four equal sides**.

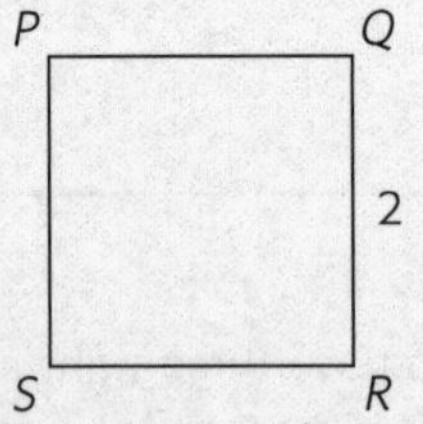

If *PQRS* is a square, all sides are the same length as *QR*. The perimeter of a square is equal to four times the length of one side.

Area of Square = (Side)^2

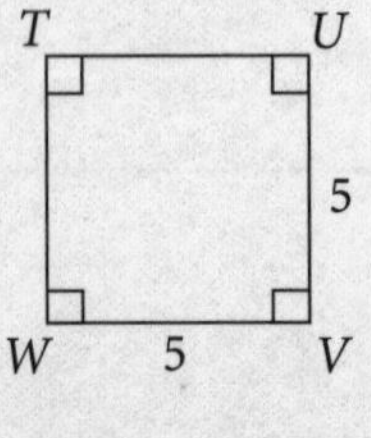

The square above, with sides of length 5, has an area of $5^2 = 25$.

91. Interior Angles of a Polygon

The **sum of the measures of the interior angles of a polygon = (*n* – 2) × 180**, where *n* is the number of sides.

Sum of the Angles = $(n - 2) \times 180$

The eight angles of an octagon, for example, add up to $(8 - 2) \times 180 = 1{,}080$.

CIRCLES

92. Circumference of a Circle

Circumference = $2\pi r$

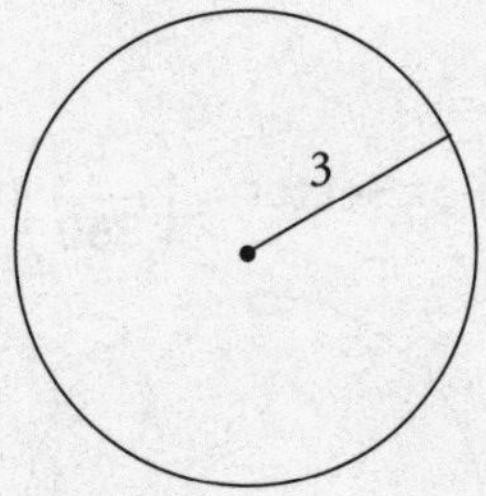

In the circle above, the radius is 3, and so the circumference is $2\pi(3) = 6\pi$.

93. Length of an Arc

An arc is a piece of the circumference. If *n* is the degree measure of the arc's central angle, then the formula is:

$$\text{Length of an Arc} = \left(\frac{n}{360}\right)(2\pi r)$$

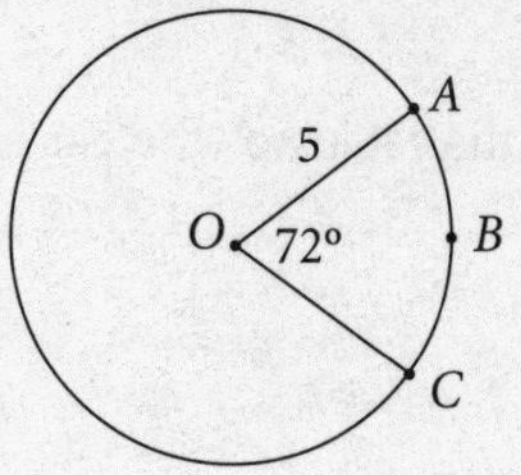

In the figure above, the radius is 5 and the measure of the central angle is 72 degrees. The arc length is $\frac{72}{360}$ or $\frac{1}{5}$ of the circumference:

$$\left(\frac{72}{360}\right)(2\pi)(5) = \left(\frac{1}{5}\right)(10\pi) = 2\pi$$

94. Area of a Circle

Area of a Circle = πr^2

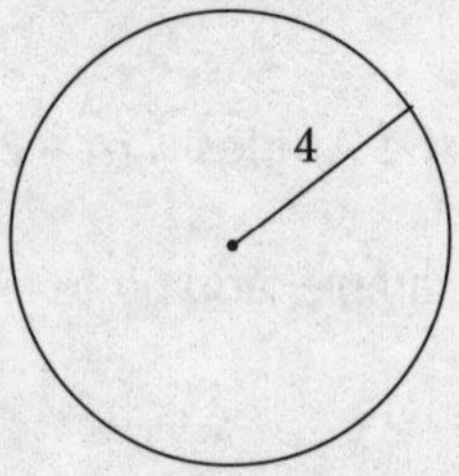

The area of the circle is $\pi(4)^2 = 16\pi$.

95. Area of a Sector

A sector is a piece of the area of a circle. If *n* is the degree measure of the sector's central angle, then the formula is:

$$\textbf{Area of Sector} = \left(\frac{n}{360}\right)(\pi r^2)$$

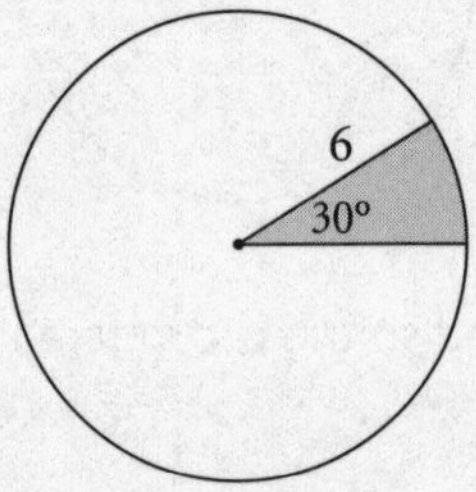

In the figure above, the radius is 6 and the measure of the sector's central angle is 30 degrees. The sector has $\frac{30}{360}$ or $\frac{1}{12}$ of the area of the circle:

$$\left(\frac{30}{360}\right)(\pi)(6^2) = \left(\frac{1}{12}\right)(36\pi) = 3\pi$$

96. Tangency

When a line is tangent to a circle, the radius of the circle is perpendicular to the line at the point of contact.

SOLIDS

97. Surface Area of a Rectangular Solid

The surface of a rectangular solid consists of three pairs of identical faces. To find the surface area, find the area of each face and add them up. If the length is *l*, the width is *w*, and the height is *h*, the formula is:

Surface Area = 2*lw* + 2*wh* + 2*lh*

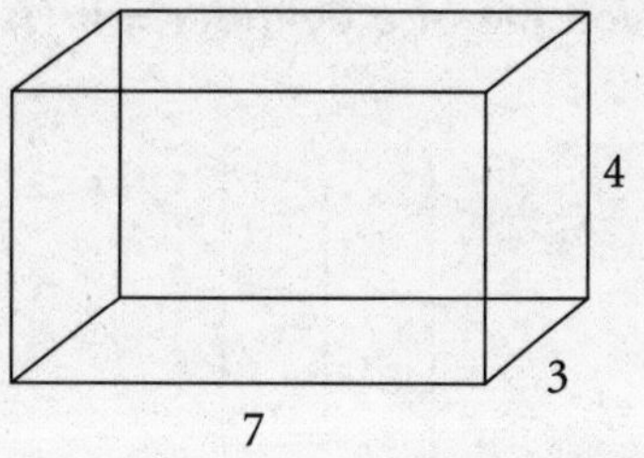

The surface area of the box above is: $2 \times 7 \times 3 + 2 \times 3 \times 4 + 2 \times 7 \times 4 = 42 + 24 + 56 = 122$

98. Volume of a Rectangular Solid

Volume of a Rectangular Solid = *lwh*

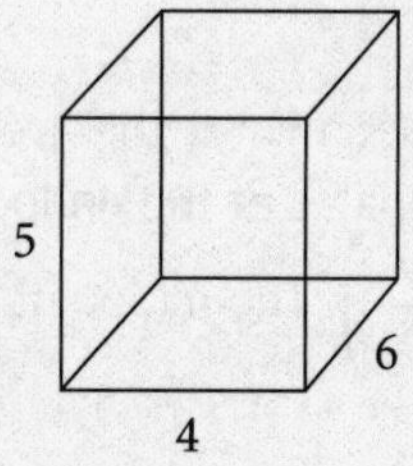

The volume of a 4-by-5-by-6 box is

$$4 \times 5 \times 6 = 120$$

A cube is a rectangular solid with length, width, and height all equal. If e is the length of an edge of a cube, the volume formula is:

Volume of a Cube = e^3

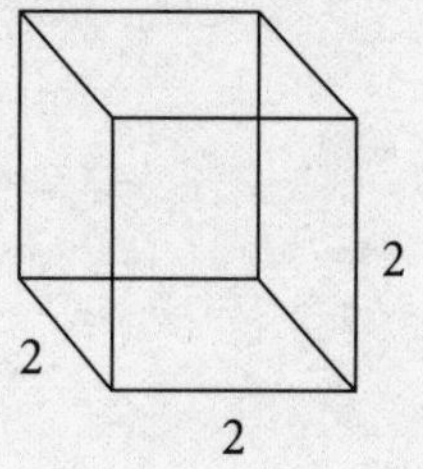

The volume of this cube is $2^3 = 8$.

99. Volume of a Cylinder

Volume of a Cylinder = $\pi r^2 h$

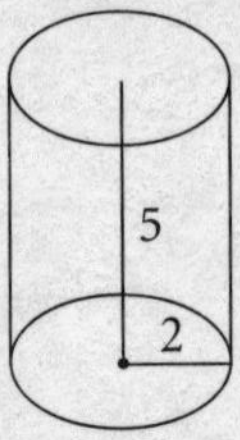

In the cylinder above, $r = 2$, $h = 5$, so:

$$\text{Volume} = \pi(2^2)(5) = 20\pi$$

100. Finding the Midpoint

The midpoint of two points on a line segment is the average of the *x*-coordinates of the endpoints and the average of the *y*-coordinates of the endpoints. If the endpoints are (x_1, y_1) and (x_2, y_2), the midpoint is $\left(\frac{x_1+x_2}{2}, \frac{y_1+y_2}{2}\right)$. The midpoint of (3, 5) and (9, 1) is $\left(\frac{3+9}{2}, \frac{5+1}{2}\right)$.

Resource B

Building Your Vocabulary

Both Critical Reading question types—Sentence Completion questions and Reading Comprehension questions—depend on your ability to work with unfamiliar words. You won't be asked to actually define any words on the SAT, but you will often need to have a sense of their meaning to answer both types of questions.

If you have only a week or two to prepare for the SAT, go straight to the "Decoding Strange Words on the Test" section of this chapter and master those skills. If you still have abundant time and energy, read on.

TOUGH SAT WORDS

There are two types of tough SAT words:

- Unfamiliar words
- Familiar words with secondary meanings

Some words are hard because you haven't seen them before. The words *scintilla* or *circumlocution*, for instance, are probably not part of your everyday vocabulary, but they might pop up on your SAT.

Easy words, such as *recognize* or *appreciation*, can also trip you up on the test because they have secondary meanings that you aren't used to. Reading Comprehension questions, in particular, will throw you familiar words with unfamiliar meanings.

KAPLAN'S THREE-STEP METHOD FOR VOCABULARY BUILDING

A great vocabulary can't be built overnight, but you can develop a better SAT vocabulary in a relatively short period of time with a minimum amount of pain. But you need to study wisely. Be strategic. How well you use your time between now and the day of the test is just as important as how much time you spend prepping.

Here's our three-step plan for building your vocabulary for the SAT:

Step 1. Learn words strategically.

Step 2. Learn word roots and prefixes.

Step 3. Personalize your study method.

Step 1. Learn Words Strategically

The best words to learn are words that have appeared often on the SAT. The test makers are not very creative in their choice of words for each test, so words that have appeared frequently are likely bets to show up again.

A good resource for SAT vocabulary is our online flashcards. Don't forget to log on to kaptest.com/booksonline to practice your SAT vocabulary skills.

Step 2. Learn Word Roots and Prefixes

Most SAT words are made up of prefixes and roots that can get you at least partway to a definition. Often, that's all you need to get a right answer. Use the Root Word list at the end of this chapter to learn the most valuable SAT word roots. Target these words in your vocabulary review. Learn a few new roots a day, then familiarize yourself with meanings and sample words.

Step 3. Personalize Your Study Method

There's not just one *right* way to study vocabulary. Figure out a study method that works best for you, and stick to it. Here are some proven strategies:

- Use flashcards. Write down new words or word groups and run through them whenever you have a few spare minutes. Put one new word or word group on one side of a 3 × 5 index card and a short definition on the back.
- Make a vocabulary notebook. List words in one column and their meaning in another. Test yourself. Cover up the meanings, and see what words you can define from memory. Make a sample sentence using each word in context.
- Make a vocabulary tape. Record unknown words and their definitions. Pause for a moment before you read the definition. This will give you time to define the word in your head when you play the tape back. Quiz yourself. Listen to your tape in your portable cassette player. Play it in the car, on the bus, or whenever you have a few spare moments.
- Think of hooks that lodge a new word in your mind: create visual images of words. For example, to remember the verb form of flag, you can picture a flag drooping or losing energy as the wind dies down.
- Use rhymes and other devices that help you remember the words. For example, you might remember that a *verbose* person uses a lot of verbs.

It doesn't matter which techniques you use, as long as you learn words steadily and methodically. Doing so over several months with regular reviews is ideal.

DECODING STRANGE WORDS ON THE TEST

Trying to learn every word that could possibly appear on the SAT is like trying to memorize the license plate number of every car on the freeway. There are just too many to commit to memory.

No matter how much time you spend with flashcards, vocabulary tapes, or word lists, you're bound to face some mystery words on your SAT. No big deal. Just as you can use your basic multiplication skills to find the product of even the largest numbers, you can use what you know about words to focus on likely meanings of tough vocabulary words.

Go With Your Hunches

When you look at an unfamiliar word, your first reaction may be to say, "Don't know it. Gotta skip it." Not so fast. Vocabulary knowledge on the SAT is not an all-or-nothing proposition.

- Some words you know so well you can rattle off a dictionary definition of them.
- Some words you "sort of" know. You understand them when you see them in context but don't feel confident using them yourself.
- Some words are vaguely familiar. You know you've heard them somewhere before.

If you think you recognize a word, go with your hunch!

Remember Where You've Heard the Word Before

If you can recall a phrase in which the word appears, that may be enough to eliminate some answer choices or even zero in on the right answer.

Between the two villages was a ---- through which passage was difficult and hazardous.

(A) precipice
(B) beachhead
(C) quagmire
(D) market
(E) prairie

To answer this question, you need to know whether or not to eliminate the word *quagmire*. You may remember *quagmire* from news reports referring to "a foreign policy *quagmire*" or "a *quagmire* of financial indebtedness." If you can remember how *quagmire* was used, you'll have a rough idea of what it means, and you'll see it fits. You may also be reminded of the word *mire*, as in "We got *mired* in the small details and never got to the larger issue." Sounds something like stuck, right? You don't need an exact definition. A *quagmire* is a situation that's difficult to get out of, so (C) is correct. Literally, a *quagmire* is a bog or swamp.

Decide Whether the Word Has a Positive or Negative Charge

Simply knowing that you're dealing with a positive or negative word can earn you points on the SAT. For example, look at the word *cantankerous*. Say it to yourself. Can you guess whether it's positive or negative? Often words that sound harsh (such as *irk*) have a negative meaning, whereas smooth-sounding words (such as *benevolent*) tend to have positive meanings. If *cantankerous* sounded negative to you, you're right. It means *ill-tempered, disagreeable*, or *difficult*.

You can also use prefixes and roots to help determine a word's charge. *Mal, de, dis, un, in, im, a*, and *mis* often indicate a negative, whereas *pro, ben*, and *magn* are often positives.

Not all SAT words sound positive or negative; some sound neutral. But if you can define the charge, you can probably eliminate some answer choices on that basis alone. Here's an example.

> He seemed at first to be honest and loyal, but before long it was necessary to ---- him for his ---- behavior.
>
> (A) admonish . . steadfast
> (B) extol . . conniving
> (C) reprimand . . scrupulous
> (D) exalt . . insidious
> (E) castigate . . perfidious

All you need to know to answer this question is that negative words are needed in both blanks. Then you can scan the answer choices for one that contains two clearly negative words. Even if you don't know what all the words mean, you can use your sense of positive or negative charge to eliminate answers. Choice (E) is right. *Castigate* means punish or *scold harshly*, and *perfidious* means *treacherous*.

Use Your Foreign Language Skills

Many of the roots you'll encounter in SAT words come from Latin. Spanish, French, and Italian also come from Latin and have retained much of it in their modern forms. English is also a cousin to German and Greek. That means that if you don't recognize a word, try to remember if you know a similar word in another language. Look at the word *carnal*. Unfamiliar? What about *carne*, as in *chili con carne*? *Carn* means *meat* or *flesh*, which leads you straight to the meaning of *carnal*—pertaining to the flesh.

You could decode *carnivorous* (meat eating) in the same way. You can almost always figure out something about strange words on the test because SAT words are never all that strange. Chances are that few words on the SAT will be totally new to you, even if your recollection is more subliminal than vivid.

When All Else Fails

If you feel totally at a loss, eliminate choices that are clearly wrong and make an educated guess from the remaining choices. A wrong answer won't hurt you much, but a right answer will help you a lot.

REMEMBER...

There are two types of hard SAT words:

- Unfamiliar words
- Familiar words with secondary meanings

A great vocabulary can't be built overnight, but you can develop a better SAT vocabulary with a minimum of pain.

The best words to learn are words that have appeared often on the SAT. Find them at kaptest.com/booksonline.

Word families are groups of words with common meanings.

Most SAT words are made up of prefixes and roots that can get you at least partway to a definition. Learning word roots will help you with these words.

There are more ways to decode hard words when you are taking the test:

- Go with your hunch.
- Remember where you've heard the word before.
- Determine whether the word has a positive or negative charge.
- Use your foreign language skills.

Use Word Roots

Most SAT words are made up of prefixes and roots that can get you at least partway to a definition. Often, that's all you need to get a right answer. Knowing roots can help you in others ways as well. First, instead of learning one word at a time, you can learn a whole group of words that contain a certain root. They'll be related in meaning, so if you remember one, it will be easier for you to remember others. Second, roots can often help you decode an unknown SAT word. If you recognize a familiar root, you could get a good enough idea of the word to answer the question.

Use the root list that follows to pick up the most valuable SAT roots. Target these words in your vocabulary preparation.

Word Roots

A, AN—not, without
amoral, atrophy, asymmetrical, anarchy, anesthetic, anonymity, anomaly, anarchist, anonymous

AB, A—from, away, apart
abnormal, abdicate, aberration, abject, abjure, ablution, abnegate, abortive, abrogate, abscond, abstemious, abstruse, annul, avert, aversion, abrasive, abridge, abrupt, atypical

AC, ACR—sharp, sour
acid, acerbic, acute, acuity, acumen, acrid

AD, A—to, towards
adhere, adjacent, adjunct, admonish, adroit, adumbrate, advent, abeyance, abet, accede, accretion, acquiesce, affluent, aggrandize, aggregate, alliteration, allude, allure, ascribe, aspersion, aspire, assail, assonance, attest, adulation, advantageous, affiliation

ALI, ALTR—another
alias, alienate, inalienable, altruism

AM, AMI—love
amorous, amicable, amity, amicable

AMBI, AMPHI—both
ambidextrous, amphibious

AMBL, AMBUL—walk
amble, ambulatory, perambulator, somnambulist

ANIM—mind, spirit, breath
animal, animosity, unanimous, magnanimous

ANN, ENN—year
annual, annuity, superannuated, biennial, perennial

ANTE, ANT—before
antecedent, antediluvian, antebellum, antepenultimate, anterior, antiquity, antiquated

ANTHROP—human
anthropology, anthropomorphic, misanthrope, philanthropy, anthropocentrism

ANTI, ANT—against, opposite
antipathy, antithesis, antacid, antonym

AUD—hear
audio, audience, audition, auditory, audible

AUTO—self
autobiography, autocrat

BELLI, BELL—war
bellicose, antebellum, rebellion

BENE, BEN—good
beneficent, beneficial

BI—two
bicycle, bisect, bilateral, bilingual, biped

BIBLIO—book
Bible, bibliography, bibliophile

BIO—life
biography, biology, amphibious, symbiotic, macrobiotics

BURS—money, purse
reimburse, disburse, bursar

CAD, CAS, CID—happen, fall
accident, cascade, deciduous

CAP, CIP—head
captain, decapitate, capitulate, precipitous, recapitulate

CAP, CAPT, CEPT, CIP—take, hold, seize
capable, capacious, captivate, deception, intercept, inception, anticipate, emancipation, incipient, percipient

CARN—flesh
carnal, carnage, carnival, incarnate

CED, CESS—yield, go
cease, cessation, incessant, cede, precede, accede, recede, antecedent, intercede, secede, cession, precedent

CHROM—color
chrome, chromatic, monochrome

CHRON—time
chronology, chronic, anachronism, anachronistic

CIDE—murder
suicide, homicide, regicide, patricide

CIRCUM—around
circumference, circumnavigate, circumspect, circumvent

CLIN, CLIV—slope
incline, declivity, proclivity

CLUD, CLUS, CLAUS, CLOIS—shut, close
conclude, reclusive, claustrophobia, cloister, occlude

CO, COM, CON—with, together
coeducation, coagulate, coalesce, coerce, cogent, cognate, collateral, colloquy, commensurate, commodious, compatriot, complacent, complicity, compunction, concerto, concord, concur, conflagration, congenial, congenital, conglomerate, conjugal, conjure, conscientious, consonant, constrained, contentious, contusion, convalescence, convene, convivial, convoke, congress, incongruous, coherent, cohesion, collusion, concordant, conceivable, conformity, consolation, contaminate, convergence, incompatible

COGN, GNO—know
recognize, cognition, cognizance, incognito, diagnosis, agnostic, prognosis, gnostic, ignorant, cognizant

CONTRA—against
controversy, incontrovertible, contravene, controversial

CORP—body
corpse, corporeal, corpulence

COSMO, COSM—world
cosmos, microcosm, macrocosm

CRAC, CRAT—rule, power
democracy, bureaucracy, theocracy, autocrat, aristocrat, technocrat

CRED—trust, believe
incredible, credulous, credence

CRESC, CRET—grow
crescent, accretion

CULP—blame, fault
culprit, inculpate

CURR, CURS—run
current, concur, cursory, precursor, incursion

DE—down, out, apart
depart, debilitate, declivity, decry, deface, defamatory, defunct, demarcation, demur, deplete, deplore, depravity, deprecate, desist, detest, devoid, debilitating, degradation, depose, detractor

DEC—ten, tenth
decade, decimal, decathlon, decimate, decibel

DEMO, DEM—people
democrat, demographics, epidemic, pandemic

DI, DIURN—day
diary, quotidian, diurnal

DIA—across
diagonal, diatribe, diaphanous

DIC, DICT—speak
abdicate, diction, interdict, predict, indict, verdict, predictable

DIS, DIF, DI—not, apart, away
indiscretion, indiscriminate, dispel, indistinct, devisive, distinctive, distortion, disdain, discrepancy, discredit, discourteous, discordance, disavow, discomfit, disconcert, discord, diffident, disaffected, disband, disbar, disburse, discordant, discursive, disheveled, dispassionate, dispirit, dissension, dissonant, dissuade, distend, differentiate, diffidence, digress, discourage, digression, discretion, discretionary, dismissal, disingenuous, disheveled, disputant

DOC, DOCT—teach
docile, doctrine, doctrinaire

DOL—pain
condolence, doleful, dolorous, indolent

DUC, DUCT—lead
seduce, induce, conduct, viaduct, induct, induce

EGO—self
ego, egocentric

EN, EM—in, into
enter, entice, encumber, ensconce, enthrall, entreat, embroil, ensemble, entangle, emend, emissary, emollient, encompass, emigrate, encroach

ERR—wander
aberration, errant, erroneous

EU—well, good
euphemism, euphony, eurhythmics, euthanasia

EX, E—out, out of
exit, excerpt, excommunicate, execrable, exhume, exonerate, extenuating, exorcise, expatriate, expedient, expunge, extenuate, extort, external, extremity, exult, evoke, evict, evince, elicit, egress, exultant, excursion, extroverted, exclude, exception, exasperation, exemplary, exemplify, exhaust, expedite, exploit, expropriate, expurgate, exterminate

FAC, FIC, FECT, FY, FEA—make, do
factory, facility, malefactor, fiction, fictive, beneficent, affect, confection, refectory, magnify, unify, rectify, vilify, feasible, beneficial, facile

FAL, FALS—deceive
infallible, false, falsify

FERV—boil
fervent, fervid, effervescent

FID—faith, trust
diffidence, diffident

FLU, FLUX—flow
fluent, affluent, confluence, effluvia, superfluous, flux

FORE—before
forecast, foreboding, forestall, foreshadow

FRAG, FRAC—break
fragment, fracture, diffract, fractious, refract, refracted, fragile

FUS—pour
profuse, effusive, profusion

GEN—birth, class, kin
generation, congenital, homogeneous, heterogeneous, ingenious, engender, progenitor, progeny, generalize

GRAD, GRESS—step
graduate, gradual, retrograde, centigrade, degrade, gradation, gradient, progress, congress, digress, transgress, ingress, egress, digression, degradation

GRAPH, GRAM—writing
biography, bibliography, epigraph, grammar, epigram

GRAT—pleasing
grateful, gratitude, gratis, ingrate, congratulate, gratuitous

GRAV, GRIEV—heavy
grave, aggravate, grieve, aggrieve, grievous

GREG—crowd, flock
segregate, gregarious, congregate, aggregate

HABIT, HIBIT—have, hold
habit, cohabit, habitat

HAP—by chance
happen, haphazard, hapless, mishap

HELIO, HELI—sun
heliocentric, heliotrope, aphelion, perihelion, helium

HETERO—other
heterosexual, heterogeneous, heterodox

HOL—whole
holocaust, catholic, holistic

HOMO—same
homosexual, homogenize, homogeneous, homonym

HOMO—man
homo sapiens, homicide, bonhomie

HYDR—water
hydrant, hydrate, dehydration

HYPER—too much, excess
hyperactive, hyperbole, hyperventilate

HYPO—too little, under
hypodermic, hypothermia, hypochondria, hypothetical

IN, IG, IL, IM, IR—not
incorrigible, indelible, indubitable, inert, insatiable, insentient, insolvent, insomnia, intractable, incessant, inextricable, infallible, infamy, inoperable, insipid, ignorant, ignominious, ignoble, illicit, illimitable, immaculate, impasse, impeccable, impecunious, impertinent, implacable, impregnable, improvident, impassioned, impervious, irregular, impassive

IN, IL, IM, IR—in, on, into
invade, inaugurate, incandescent, incarcerate, incense, indenture, induct, ingratiate, introvert, incarnate, inception, infer, ingress, innate, inquest, inscribe, inter, imbue, immerse, implicate, irrigate, irritate, incisive, induce, indebted, incumbent, impute, incriminate, illuminate, illusory, imaginative, imitate, immoderate, immunity, immutable, impassioned, impassive

INTER—between, among
intercede, intercept, interdiction, interject, interloper, intermediary, intermittent, interpolate, interpose, interregnum, interrogate, intersect, intervene, interminable, interlude

INTRA, INTR—within
intrastate, intravenous, intramural, intrinsic

IT, ITER—between, among
transit, itinerant, transitory

JECT, JET—throw
eject, interject, abject, trajectory, jettison

JOUR—day
journal, adjourn, sojourn

JUD—judge
judge, judicious, prejudice, adjudicate

JUNCT, JUG—join
junction, adjunct, injunction, conjugal, subjugate

JUR—swear, law
jury, abjure, adjure, conjure, jurisprudence

LAT—side
lateral, collateral, unilateral, bilateral, quadrilateral, latent

LAV, LAU, LU—wash
lavatory, laundry, ablution, antediluvian, lavish

LEG, LEC, LEX—read, speak
legible, lecture, lexicon

LEV—light
elevate, levitate, levity, alleviate, elevated

LIBER—free
liberty, liberal, libertarian, libertine, liberate

LIG, LECT—choose, gather
eligible, elect, select

LIG, LI, LY—bind
ligament, oblige, religion, liable, liaison, lien, ally, liability

LING, LANG—tongue
lingo, language, linguistics, bilingual

LITER—letter
literate, alliteration, literal

LITH—stone
monolith, lithograph, megalith

LOQU, LOC, LOG—speech, thought
loquacious, colloquy, soliloquy, monologue, dialogue, philology, neologism

LUC, LUM—light
lucid, elucidate, pellucid, translucent

LUD, LUS—play
ludicrous, allude, delusion, allusion

MACRO—great
macrocosm, macrobiotics

MAG, MAJ, MAS, MAX—great
magnanimous, magnate, magnitude, majesty, master, maximum

MAL—bad
malady, maladroit, malevolent, malodorous, malediction, malinger

MAN—hand
manuscript, emancipate, manumission, mandate

MAR—sea
submarine, marine, maritime

MATER, MATR—mother
maternal, matron, matrilineal, matriarch

MEDI—middle
intermediary, medieval

MEGA—great
megaphone, megalomania, megaton, megalith

MEM, MEN—remember
memory, memento, memorabilia, reminisce

METER, METR, MENS—measure
meter, thermometer, perimeter, metronome, commensurate

MICRO—small
microscope, microorganism, microcosm, microbe

MIS—wrong, bad, hate
misunderstand, misanthrope, misapprehension, misconstrue, misnomer, mishap, misconception

MIT, MISS—send
transmit, emit, missive, emissary

MOLL—soft
mollify, mollusk

MON, MONIT—warn
admonish, monitor, premonition

MONO—one
monologue, monotonous, monogamy, monolith, monochrome

MOR—custom, manner
moral, mores, morality

MOR, MORT—dead
morbid, moribund, mortal, amortize, morass, morose, remorseful

MORPH—shape
anthropomorphic, metamorphosis, morphology

MOV, MOT, MOB, MOM—move
remove, motion, mobile, momentum, momentary

MUT—change
mutate, mutability, commute

NAT, NASC—born
native, nativity, natal, neonate, innate, cognate, nascent, renascent, renaissance

NAU, NAV—ship, sailor
nautical, nauseous, navy, circumnavigate, navigable

NEG—not, deny
negative, abnegate, renege, negate, negligent, negligible

NEO—new
neoclassical, neophyte, neologism, neonate

NIHIL—none, nothing
annihilation, nihilism

NOM, NYM—name
nominate, nomenclature, nominal, cognomen, misnomer, ignominious, antonym, homonym, pseudonym, synonym, anonymity

NOX, NIC, NEC, NOC—harm
noxious, pernicious, internecine, innocuous

NOV—new
innovation, novitiate, novice

NUMER—number
numeral, numerous, enumerate

OB—against
obstruct, obfuscate, obsequious, objective, oblivious, obscure, obsolete, obstacle

OMNI—all
omnipresent, omnipotent, omniscient, omnivorous

ONER—burden
exonerate

OPER—work
operate, cooperate, inoperable

PAC—peace
pacify, pacifist, pacific

PALP—feel
palpable, palpitation

PAN—all
panorama, panacea, panegyric, pandemic, panoply, pantomime

PATER, PATR—father
paternal, paternity, patriot, compatriot, expatriate, patrimony, patricide, patrician

PATH, PASS—feel, suffer
sympathy, antipathy, apathy, apathetic

PEC—money
pecuniary, impecunious, peculation

PED, POD—foot
pedestrian, pediment, expedient, biped, quadruped, tripod, expedite

PEL, PULS—drive
compel, expel

PEN—almost
peninsula, penultimate, penumbra, penitent, penurious

PEND, PENS—hang
pendant, pendulous, compendium, suspense, propensity, compensate, suspend

PER—through, by, for, throughout
perambulator, percipient, permeable, pertinacious, perturbation, perusal, perennial, peregrinate, pertinent, perception, perceptive, persevere, persistence, pertinent, pervasive

PER—against, destruction
pernicious

PERI—around
perimeter, periphery, perihelion, peripatetic

PET—seek, go towards
petition, impetus, impetuous, petulant, centripetal

PHIL—love
philosopher, philanderer, philanthropy, bibliophile, philology

PHOB—fear
phobia, claustrophobia, xenophobia

PHON—sound
phonograph, megaphone, euphony, phonetics, phonics

PLAC—calm, please
implacable, placid, complacent, complacence, placebo

PON, POS—put, place
exponent, preposition, posit, interpose, prepossessing

PORT—carry
portable, deportment, rapport

POT—drink
potion, potable

POT—power
potential, potent, omnipotence

PRE—before
precede, precursor, predilection, predisposition, preponderance, presage, prescient, prejudice, predict, premonition, preposition, preamble, precedent, precept, predetermine, predictable, predominant

PRIM, PRI—first
prime, primal, primeval, primordial, pristine

PRO—ahead, forth
proceed, proclivity, procrastinator, profane, profuse, progenitor, progeny, prognosis, prologue, promontory, propose, proscribe, protestation, provoke, procrastinate, proliferate, prolific, promote, prominence, promulgate, proponent

PROTO—first
protocol

PROX, PROP—near
approximate, propinquity

PSEUDO—false
pseudoscientific, pseudonym

PYR—fire
pyre, pyrotechnics, pyromania

QUAD, QUAR, QUAT—four
quadrilateral, quadrant, quadruped, quarter, quarantine, quaternary

QUES, QUER, QUIS, QUIR—question
quest, inquest, inquisitive, inquiry, requisition

QUIE—quiet
disquiet, acquiesce, quiescent, requiem

QUINT, QUIN—five
quintuplets, quintessence

RADI, RAMI—branch
radius, radiate, ramification, radical

RECT, REG—straight, rule
rectangle, rectitude, rectify, regular

REG—king, rule
regal, regent, interregnum

RETRO—backward
retrospective, retrograde

RID, RIS—laugh
ridiculous, derision

ROG—ask
interrogate, derogatory, abrogate, arrogate, arrogant

RUD—rough, crude
erudite, rudimentary

RUPT—break
disrupt, interrupt, rupture

SACR, SANCT—holy
sacred, sacrilege, sanctify, sanction, sanctimonious

SCRIB, SCRIPT, SCRIV—write
scribe, ascribe, inscribe, proscribe, script, manuscript, scrivener, inscription, transcribe

SE—apart, away
separate, segregate, secede, sedition

SEC, SECT, SEG—cut
sector, dissect, bisect, intersect, segment, secant

SED, SID—sit
sedate, sedentary, supersede, reside, residence, sedative

SEM—seed, sow
seminar, seminal

SEN—old
senior, senile, senescent

SENT, SENS—feel, think
sentiment, nonsense, assent, sentient, sensual

SEQU, SECU—follow
sequence, subsequent, obsequious, obsequy, non sequitur, consecutive

SIM, SEM—similar, same
similar, semblance, dissemble

SIGN—mark, sign
signal, designation, assignation, signpost

SIN—curve
sine curve, sinuous

SOL—sun
solar, parasol, solarium, solstice, solitary, solace, solicitous

SOL—alone
solo, solitude, soliloquy, solipsism

SOMN—sleep
insomnia, somnolent, somnambulist

SON—sound
sonic, consonance, dissonance, assonance, sonorous, resonate

SOPH—wisdom
philosopher, sophistry, sophisticated, sophomoric, sophistication

SPEC, SPIC—see, look
spectator, circumspect, retrospective, perspective, perspicuous, specious

SPER—hope
prosper, prosperous, despair, desperate, prosperity

SPERS, SPAR—scatter
disperse, sparse, aspersion

SPIR—breathe
respire, spiritual, aspire, transpire

STRICT, STRING—bind
strict, stricture, constrict, stringent, astringent

STRUCT, STRU—build
structure, obstruct, construe

SUB—under
subconscious, subjugate, subliminal, subpoena, subsequent, subterranean, subterfuge, submissive

SUMM—highest
summit

SUPER, SUR—above
supervise, supercilious, supersede, superannuated, superfluous, insurmountable, superficial, surplus, superstitious

SURGE, SURRECT—rise
surge, resurgent, insurgent, insurrection

SYN, SYM—together
synthesis, sympathy, synonym, syncopation, synopsis, symposium, symbiosis, symmetry, synergy, synthesize

TACIT, TIC—silent
tacit, taciturn, reticent

TACT, TAG, TANG—touch
tactile, tangent

TEN, TIN, TAIN—hold, twist
detention, tenable, pertinacious, retinue, tentative, untenable

TEND, TENS, TENT—stretch
intend, distend, tension, tensile, contentious

TERM—end
terminal, terminus, terminate

TERR—earth, land
terrain, terrestrial, extraterrestrial, subterranean

TEST—witness
testify, attest, testimonial, testament, detest, protestation, testimony

THE—god
atheist, theology, apotheosis, theocracy

THERM—heat
thermometer, thermal, thermonuclear, hypothermia

TIM—fear, frightened
timid, intimidate

TOP—place
topic, topography

TORT—twist
distort, extort, tortuous, distortion

TORP—stiff, numb
torpedo, torpor

TOX—poison
toxic, toxin, intoxication

TRACT—draw
tractor, intractable, protract, tractable, retract

TRANS—across, over, through, beyond
transport, transgress, transitory, translucent, transmutation, transient, intransigent, transparent

TREM, TREP—shake
tremble, tremor, trepidation

TURB—shake
disturb, turbulent, perturbation

UMBR—shadow
umbrella, umbrage, adumbrate, penumbra

UNI, UN—one
unify, unilateral, unanimous, universal

URB—city
urban, suburban

VAC—empty
evacuate, vacuous, vacillate

VAL, VAIL—value, strength
valid, valor, convalescence, avail, prevail, countervail

VEN, VENT—come
convene, contravene, intervene, venue, convention, circumvent, advent, adventitious, venerability, venerable, venerate

VER—true
veracious, aver, verdict, verdant, verification

VERB—word
verbal, verbose, verbiage, verbatim

VERT, VERS—turn
avert, convert, pervert, revert, incontrovertible, versatile, aversion

VICT, VINC—conquer
victory, conviction, evict, evince, invincible, convict

VID, VIS—see
evident, vision, visage, supervise

VIL—base, mean
vilify, revile, villainous

VIV, VIT—life
convivial, vivacious, revive, vitiated

VOC, VOK, VOW—call, voice
vocal, equivocate, vociferous, convoke, evoke, invoke, avow

VOL—wish
voluntary, malevolent, volition

VOLV, VOLUT—turn, roll
revolve, evolve, convoluted

VOR—eat
devour, carnivore, omnivorous, voracious

Resource C

A Special Note for International Students

If you are an international student considering attending an American university, you are not alone. Nearly 600,000 international students pursued academic degrees at the undergraduate, graduate, or professional school level at U.S. universities during the 2004–2005 academic year, according to the Institute of International Education's Open Doors report. Almost 50 percent of these students were studying for a bachelor's or first university degree. This number of international students pursuing higher education in the United States is expected to continue to grow. Business, management, engineering, and the physical and life sciences are particularly popular majors for students coming to the United States from other countries.

If you are not a U.S. citizen and you are interested in attending college or university in the United States, here is what you'll need to get started.

- If English is not your first language, you'll probably need to take the TOEFL® (Test of English as a Foreign Language) or provide some other evidence that you are proficient in English. Colleges and universities in the United States will differ on what they consider to be an acceptable TOEFL score. A minimum TOEFL score of 213 (550 on the paper-based TOEFL) or better is often required by more prestigious and competitive institutions. Because American undergraduate programs require all students to take a certain number of general education courses, all students—even math and computer science students—need to be able to communicate well in spoken and written English.
- You may also need to take the SAT® or the ACT®. Many undergraduate institutions in the United States require both the SAT and TOEFL for international students.
- There are over 3,400 accredited colleges and universities in the United States, so selecting the correct undergraduate school can be a confusing task for anyone. You will need to get help from a good advisor or at least a good college guide that gives you detailed information on the different schools available. Since admission to many undergraduate programs is quite competitive, you may want to select three or four colleges and complete applications for each school.
- You should begin the application process at least a year in advance. An increasing number of schools accept applications year round. In any case, find out the application deadlines and plan accordingly. Although September (the fall semester) is the traditional time to begin university study in the United States, you can begin your studies at many schools in January (the spring semester).
- In addition, you will need to obtain an I-20 Certificate of Eligibility from the school you plan to attend if you intend to apply for an F-1 Student Visa to study in the United States.

KAPLAN ENGLISH PROGRAMS*

If you need more help with the complex process of university admissions, assistance preparing for the SAT, ACT, or TOEFL, or help building your English language skills in general, you may be interested in Kaplan's programs for international students.

Kaplan English Programs were designed to help students and professionals from outside the United States meet their educational and career goals. At locations throughout the United States, international students take advantage of Kaplan's programs to help them improve their academic and conversational English skills, raise their scores on the TOEFL, SAT, ACT, and other standardized exams, and gain admission to the schools of their choice. Our staff and instructors give international students the individualized attention they need to succeed. Here is a brief description of some of Kaplan's programs for international students:

General Intensive English

Kaplan's General Intensive English course is the fastest and most effective way for students to improve their English. This full-time program integrates the four key elements of language learning—listening, speaking, reading and writing. The challenging curriculum and intensive schedule are designed for both the general language learner and the academically bound student.

TOEFL and Academic English

Our world-famous TOEFL course prepares you for the TOEFL and also teaches you the academic language and skills needed to succeed in a university. Designed for high-intermediate to advanced-level English speakers, our course includes TOEFL-focused reading, writing, listening, speaking, vocabulary, and grammar instruction.

General English

Our General English course is a semi-intensive program designed for students who want to improve their listening and speaking skills without the time commitment of an intensive program. With morning class time and flexible computer lab hours throughout the week, our General English course is perfect for every schedule.

* Kaplan is authorized under federal law to enroll nonimmigrant alien students. Kaplan is accredited by ACCET (Accrediting Council for Continuing Education and Training).

KAPLAN PROGRAMS

Since 1938, more than 3 million students have come to Kaplan to advance their studies, prepare for entry to American universities, and further their careers. In addition to the above programs, Kaplan offers courses to prepare for the ACT, GMAT®, GRE®, MCAT®, DAT®, USMLE®, NCLEX®, and other standardized exams at locations throughout the United States.

Applying to Kaplan English Programs

To get more information, or to apply for admission to any of Kaplan's programs for international students and professionals, contact us at:

Kaplan English Programs

700 South Flower, Suite 2900
Los Angeles, CA 90017, USA
Phone (if calling from within the United States): 800-818-9128
Phone (if calling from outside the United States): 213-452-5800
Fax: 213-892-1364
Website: www.kaplanenglish.com
Email: world@kaplan.com

FREE Services for International Students

Kaplan now offers international students many services online—*free of charge*! Students may assess their TOEFL skills and gain valuable feedback on their English language proficiency in just a few hours with Kaplan's TOEFL Skills Assessment. Log onto www.kaplanenglish.com today.

KAPLAN
AP Psychology
2007 EDITION
POWERFUL, PRACTICAL TOOLS TO HELP YOU SCORE HIGHER
ISBN: 1-4195-5084-5
KAPLAN
AP Physics B & C
2007 EDITION
POWERFUL, PRACTICAL TOOLS TO HELP YOU SCORE HIGHER
ISBN: 1-4195-5083-7
KAPLAN
AP Environmental Science
2007 EDITION
POWERFUL, PRACTICAL TOOLS TO HELP YOU SCORE HIGHER
ISBN: 1-4195-9058-8
KAPLAN
AP Calculus AB & BC
2007 EDITION
POWERFUL, PRACTICAL TOOLS TO HELP YOU SCORE HIGHER
ISBN: 1-4195-5078-0
KAPLAN
AP English Language & Composition
2007 EDITION
POWERFUL, PRACTICAL TOOLS TO HELP YOU SCORE HIGHER
ISBN: 1-4195-5079-9
KAPLAN
AP Chemistry
2007 EDITION
POWERFUL, PRACTICAL TOOLS TO HELP YOU SCORE HIGHER
ISBN: 1-4195-5054-3
KAPLAN
AP English Literature & Composition
2007 EDITION
POWERFUL, PRACTICAL TOOLS TO HELP YOU SCORE HIGHER
HIGHER SCORE GUARANTEED
ISBN: 1-4195-5080-2
KAPLAN
AP U.S. Government & Politics
2007 EDITION
POWERFUL, PRACTICAL TOOLS TO HELP YOU SCORE HIGHER
HIGHER SCORE GUARANTEED
ISBN: 1-4195-5086-1
KAPLAN
AP U.S. History
2007 EDITION
POWERFUL, PRACTICAL TOOLS TO HELP YOU SCORE HIGHER
HIGHER SCORE GUARANTEED
ISBN: 1-4195-5087-X

NOTES

NOTES

NOTES

NOTES

NOTES

NOTES

NOTES

NOTES

NOTES

NOTES